Schools, Vouchers, *and* *the* American Public

Schools, Vouchers, and the American Public

and
the American Public

TERRY M. MOE

BROOKINGS INSTITUTION PRESS
Washington, D.C.

Copyright © 2001
THE BROOKINGS INSTITUTION
1775 Massachusetts Avenue, N.W., Washington, DC 20036
www.brookings.edu

Library of Congress Cataloging-in-Publication data

Moe, Terry M.
  Schools, vouchers, and the American public / Terry M. Moe.
    p. cm.
Includes bibliographical references and index.
  ISBN 0-8157-5808-1 (alk. paper)
    1. Educational vouchers—United States. 2. School choice—United
States. 3. Education—Political aspects—United States. I. Title.
  LB2828.8 .M64 2001   01-000444
  379.3´2´0973—dc21   CIP

                    9 8 7 6 5 4 3 2 1

The paper used in this publication meets minimum requirements of the
American National Standard for Information Sciences—Permanence of Paper
for Printed Library Materials: ANSI Z39.48-1992.

Typeset in Sabon

Composition by Cynthia Stock
Silver Spring, Maryland

Printed by R. R. Donnelley and Sons
Harrisonburg, Virginia

To Betsy

For her love and support
and for all that she has taught
me about what matters in life

Foreword

Iɴ 1990 Terry M. Moe and John E. Chubb stimulated
a national debate over school choice with their pathbreaking book, *Politics,
Markets, and America's Schools*. This highly controversial work, which promoted an approach to public education built around parent-student choice
and school competition, was hailed by the *Wall Street Journal* as "the
education book of the year . . . an icon-smashing book on school reform."

Now, as the nation moves into the twenty-first century—and with education reform still a pressing national concern—Terry Moe takes a pen-
etrating look at the school voucher movement and its growing challenge to
the traditional system of American education. *Schools, Vouchers, and the
American Public* examines the democratic foundations of the voucher issue,
what they mean for the political coalitions that are likely to form and the
policy proposals that are likely to win out—and what all this implies for the
role that vouchers will ultimately play in this nation's educational future.

Based on an extensive, nationally representative survey, this book is an
effort not only to comprehend where the American people stand on the
voucher issue, but to get beneath the surface to find out why people think
what they do, and how their underlying values, beliefs, and interests can
affect the course of political events.

The findings show (among other things) that while Americans like public
schools, they are also quite open to vouchers, which have special appeal to
those who are socially less advantaged, members of minority groups, and
residents from low-performing districts. The voucher movement gains its
greatest support, the analysis suggests, when it moves away from free

market ideals toward limited, regulated approaches that begin with the neediest children. As the movement follows this path in the years ahead, Moe argues, its successes are likely to grow, and vouchers will increasingly (if slowly) become a familiar, integral part of the American education system. The result will not be a radical shift toward privatization, as some voucher advocates might want, but the incremental development of a "mixed" system—one that relies much more heavily on choice and competition than today's system does, but that still affords a central and guiding role to government.

The author would like to thank the following organizations for the financial support that made this study possible. They are the Lynde and Harry Bradley Foundation, The Horace W. Goldsmith Foundation, The J. M. Foundation, the John M. Olin Foundation, Pacific Telesis Foundation, Quaker Oats Company, and The Walton Family Foundation.

During the course of this study, the author benefited from the advice and assistance of many people. He would like to thank Bruce Bueno de Mesquita, John E. Chubb, John E. Coons, Kenneth Godwin, James W. Guthrie, Eric A. Hanushek, Jeffrey R. Henig, Frederick M. Hess, Jennifer L. Hochschild, Shanto Iyengar, Michael W. Kirst, David E. Lewis, Tom Loveless, Barbara Morris, James D. Morrow, Paul E. Peterson, Douglas Rivers, Paul M. Sniderman, Paul Teske, Scott A. Wilson, and anonymous reviewers. He would like to extend a special thanks to William G. Howell, who served as his research assistant (and friend and adviser) for the last two years of the project, and whose energy, enthusiasm, intelligence, and hard work were absolutely crucial in bringing this study to fruition.

Finally, the author wishes to acknowledge the contributions of Paul C. Light, Thomas E. Mann, Sherra Merchant, and Elizabeth McAlpine of the Brookings Institution staff in preparing this book for publication.

At the Brookings Institution Press, Charles Dibble verified the manuscript for factual accuracy, edited it, and made many helpful suggestions on wording and style. Thanks are also extended to Janet Walker and Larry Converse, who managed the editorial and production processes, Susan Woollen, who oversaw development of the cover, and Inge Lockwood and Robert Elwood, respectively, who proofread and indexed the pages. The views expressed in this book are solely those of the author, and should not be ascribed to the persons or organizations acknowledged above, or to the trustees, officers, or other staff members of the Brookings Institution.

MICHAEL H. ARMACOST
President

May 2001
Washington, D.C.

Contents

Schools, Vouchers, and the American Public

Introduction

As the new century unfolds, the most controversial issue in American education is the issue of school vouchers. The idea seems simple enough: that the government should expand the choices of parents by providing them with publicly funded grants, or vouchers, that they can apply toward tuition at private schools. Its simplicity, however, is deceptive. The voucher idea, if widely and seriously applied, is capable of transforming the entire education system—perhaps in very good ways, perhaps in very bad ways, depending on which side you listen to. This is what all the fuss is about. The controversy over vouchers is a struggle over America's educational future.

Leaders of the voucher movement see the public school system as a stagnant bureaucracy that does not and cannot provide the nation's children with quality educations. Vouchers, they claim, would open up a range of new opportunities for these children, generate healthy competition for the public schools, promote higher student achievement, and bring about significant improvements in social equity for the disadvantaged, who are now trapped in the worst schools in the country and are most desperately in need of choice.[1]

Opponents see things very differently. The public schools are actually doing a reasonably good job given the burdens under which they operate, and they need more political support rather than less. The real effect of vouchers, they argue, would be to wreck the public schools by draining off resources and children. In the process, vouchers would undermine cherished values the public school system has long stood for—common schooling, equal opportunity, democratic control—and create a system driven by private interests.[2]

The combatants on both sides believe their own arguments and see themselves as fighting for noble causes. This in itself is enough to fuel political conflict. Ideas and values alone, however, cannot account for the explosive intensity of the voucher issue in American politics. There is another dimension to this fight that jacks the level of conflict and vitriol well beyond what it would otherwise be. Whatever the educational or social effects of vouchers, a genuine victory by the voucher movement would have far-reaching institutional consequences for the "system," affecting, possibly in big ways, the number of people it employs, the amount of money it controls, the distribution of power, the prospects for collective bargaining, and much more. As would be true in any area of public policy, these sorts of institutional changes are deeply threatening to the authorities and groups who run the system, because their careers, advantages, and powers are all rooted in current arrangements. In a very real sense, their institutional survival is at stake. And so they resist, with all the power they can muster. Which is considerable.

These insiders are at the forefront of the opposition to vouchers. The undisputed leaders are the teachers unions, which have vast resources, huge memberships, pervasive political clout, and by almost any estimate are among the most powerful interest groups in all of American politics. But while the unions provide most of the firepower against vouchers, they are hardly alone. They are joined by the overwhelming majority of Democratic officeholders, by most civil rights groups, by the American Civil Liberties Union, and by many other organizations usually associated with the broader liberal coalition. Together, these groups have mounted a formidable defense of the existing public school system.[3]

The voucher side is best thought of as a political movement. Like most movements, it is far less organized than the defenders of the system, has fewer resources, and has no institutional base. It is an aggregation of activists. The idea for vouchers was originally proposed in the 1950s by libertarian economist Milton Friedman, and since then the leading figures in the movement have tended to be conservatives and Republicans. Throughout, it has also attracted support on religious grounds from activists who object to the strictly secular moral climate of the public schools and who see vouchers as a means of enabling families to pursue a more religiously based education for their children in the private sector.[4]

These are the traditional pillars of the voucher movement: conservatism and religion. And had they remained the only pillars, it is questionable whether vouchers would now be a major force in American politics. The pivotal event came in 1990. In that year, the Wisconsin legislature adopted a pilot voucher program, the nation's first, for low-income children in Milwaukee. The movement was home grown, rooted in the realities of urban education and not in conservatism, the theory of markets, or religion. A contingent of poor, minority parents in inner-city Milwaukee, fed up with the sorry state of their schools and led by local activists, rose up and demanded vouchers. The groups that normally claim to represent the urban poor in education and politics—the teachers unions, the Democrats, the National Association for the Advancement of Colored People (NAACP), and other liberal organizations—came out in vigorous, full-force opposition. Abandoned by their usual allies, the leaders of Milwaukee's disaffected parents found support the only place they could—among conservatives and Republicans—and, after a hard-fought battle, this odd coalition ultimately won out.[5]

Milwaukee was a harbinger of things to come. The coalition between conservatives and the inner-city poor, when it has occurred, has proved very powerful. Normally, it is not as powerful as the liberal defenders of the current system. But when the conditions are right, it is capable of winning, as it did in gaining a voucher program for low-income children in Cleveland in 1995, a big expansion of the Milwaukee program in 1995, and a new statewide program in Florida in 1999 for children who attend "failing" public schools (almost all of whom are also low in income). Moreover, it has found a way of making progress without having to battle the liberal defenders at all: activists have set up some seventy-nine private voucher programs (at this writing) in inner-city areas around the country, involving more than 60,000 low-income children. These private programs, which the liberal coalition is powerless to stop, are at least as important to the voucher movement as its early political victories. They spread the word about vouchers, build a clientele, and provide a stronger political basis for pushing ahead with government reforms.[6]

The new coalition for vouchers has brought new power and progress to the movement. It has also changed the movement itself. For the most part, conservatives and Republicans continue to play the most active leading roles and to raise and control most of the money. Traditionalist ideas remain salient, and they are central to the movement's self-concept at the upper reaches. Yet increasingly the political action for vouchers focuses on disadvantaged children in inner-city schools, not on the kind of universal, free-market system that many traditionalists would vastly prefer, and the arguments for vouchers give heavy emphasis to social equity. These shifts in content and direction, in turn, have attracted new activists whose values and politics are fundamentally very different from those of traditional leaders. The movement is becoming more powerful and more successful. But it is also becoming a very different kind of movement than the one its leaders originally envisioned.

As is true for most political issues, this battle between the voucher movement and its liberal opponents is largely being fought out at the elite level. The key players on both sides are individuals and groups, many of them quite powerful, who are actively involved in politics on a continuing basis, knowledgeable about the relevant arguments and facts, and intent on using their influence to shape public policy. They are not ordinary citizens by any stretch of the imagination. But the outcome of their struggle will determine the kind of education system that everyone in the nation must live with.

The democratic roots of this elite-level struggle, however, cannot help but run deep. For in the American political system, there is a strong connection between what happens at the upper reaches of politics—the strategies and powers of elites, who wins and who loses, what policies are adopted—and the opinions of ordinary people in the population at large. Public opinion matters. Most Americans may not participate in the battle over vouchers, and they may not know much about the issue. But as the struggle plays itself out, and as advocates and opponents at the elite level compete aggressively to gain public support, the opinions of the American people will have a great deal to do with how much power each side can successfully wield in democratic politics—and whether, in the end, vouchers will prove to be a passing fancy, a revolution, or something in-between.

This is a book about public opinion on vouchers. The analysis I develop here, based upon a nationally representative survey of 4,700 adults, is an effort to shed light on what ordinary Americans think about the issue, why they take the positions they do, and what their views seem to mean for elite-level politics—and for the future of American education.[7]

As anyone who reads the newspapers knows, there have been plenty of surveys that ask Americans about vouchers. These surveys have generated useful information, and I will try to make the most of them. Almost all, however, are about a broad range of policy issues and ask people just one voucher question, designed to determine whether they would support or oppose a voucher system. These one-shot items are of course quite limited in what they can tell us and, for reasons I will discuss later in the book, are sometimes misleading. A few surveys explore the voucher issue in greater detail and are more helpful in giving us a sense of what is going on.[8] But these studies are brief reports that simply describe how people have responded to a variety of survey items on vouchers, and that offer educated judgments of what the responses seem to mean. They do not attempt to get beneath the surface and, through a sustained and systematic analysis—of considerations ranging from social class to school performance to religion to social equity—provide a coherent foundation for explaining why people think about the issue as they do, and how the underlying structure of public opinion (if there is one) connects to the structure of elite-level politics. That, in large measure, is what I will be trying to do here.

I want to emphasize, then, that this is an exercise in analysis and not simply an exercise in describing public opinion. Were description the goal, I would have written up a brief report of the more obvious findings very soon after the survey was conducted, which was in 1995, and that would have been the end of it. There would surely have been an audience for it in that form. Polls are an integral part of the American democratic culture, and whenever surveys are carried out on important issues, many people find them valuable for what they can say about the current, up-to-the-moment state of public opinion. That is why there are so many surveys and why virtually all of them are rushed into publication (or the newspapers) immediately after the data are collected. It is valuable to know what the public is thinking (assuming the "facts" are not misleading). But it is also important—more important, I would argue—to understand the deeper, more fundamental, and more enduring social influences that operate on public opinion, and that give meaning and political consequence to the descriptive layer we see on the surface.

There is an inherent risk in such a strategy. A serious effort to get at the fundamentals of the voucher issue is a complex undertaking that has required a lot of time; and with vouchers gaining in salience over the last several years, public opinion may have changed in some respects. Some of the conclusions I arrive at here, therefore, might be somewhat different were I working with a newly collected data set. This is a possibility that needs to be recognized and, for that matter, a risk quite common to most social science analysis. Yet I doubt it is actually of much consequence in this case. The basic descriptive findings from the 1995 data, as discussions throughout the book will show, are highly consistent with those from more recent surveys. Opinions don't seem to have changed much. There is good reason, moreover, to think that the fundamentals—the underlying influence of social class, for example, or of school performance—are more enduring than surface opinions and have changed even less. My best bet is that the basic findings of this book are essentially as valid today as they were several years ago.

I will not at this point provide a grand summary of all the findings, as is often done in introductory chapters. The analysis has a number of dimensions that, in my view, are interesting and important in their own right, and I don't think a quick overview can do justice to either the whole or its parts. Readers who can't stand the mystery are invited to take a look at the concluding chapter, the first half of which presents a detailed summary of the main results. Here, I will simply provide a road map of the terrain that will lead us there.

I begin in chapter 1 with an overview of the politics of vouchers, offering a historical perspective on the emergence of the issue, a discussion of the major players and arguments on both sides, and basic information about some of the key events and developments. I have covered a few of the highlights here in the introduction. Chapter 1 fills in the rest and provides important substantive background for the analysis to follow, background that will help clarify what the issues for analysis ought to be and why it is important to understand them.

Chapters 2, 3, and 4 are essentially transition chapters. They are the first data analysis chapters, and thus offer a first look at what the survey has to tell us about public opinion. But they do not deal with the voucher issue at all, at least not directly. What they provide is more—and essential—background, focusing on an issue that has always been right at the heart of the voucher debate: the issue of public school performance. Voucher leaders have long seen dissatisfaction with the schools as the key ingredient of their political success. But are Americans actually dissatisfied? And what happens to the movement if they aren't? We need to take a serious look at the way Americans evaluate their schools, and why, in order to figure these things out.

Chapter 5 takes a step closer to the voucher issue by exploring another, equally important component of the social background: the attractiveness of private schools among American parents. Like performance, this too is about as basic as it gets. The voucher movement cannot succeed unless enough public parents want to go private. But do they? And more important, what accounts for the desire to go private: does it arise from performance concerns, with less advantaged parents leading the way, as voucher advocates claim, or is it largely driven by social concerns—of class, race, religion—that prompt some parents (especially those who are advantaged) to favor private schools as a way of separating themselves off from others, as critics argue? Evidence on these scores clearly has something to tell us about the politics of vouchers and the constituencies we should expect on either side. At the same time, it also sheds light on a substantive controversy of enormous significance: whether the expansion of choice, due to the types of people inclined to go private, will help to break down the inequities of American society—or make them even worse.

Chapter 6 moves us into an analysis of public opinion on vouchers, beginning with the obvious first question: to what extent is the public even informed about the issue? Political scientists have long known that Americans tend to be poorly informed about government and public policy in general and, indeed, have long recognized that there are logical reasons why most would be "rationally ignorant" on such matters. There is little reason to think the voucher issue should be any different—and, as the data show, it isn't. Most Americans are very poorly informed. While this is unsurprising, it cannot help but have a big impact on the politics of the issue. Most immediately, it affects the movement's ability to attract supporters to the cause and raises a corollary matter that this chapter's analysis explores in some depth: whether the people who have a stake or interest in the voucher issue—for example, public school parents who want to go private—are better informed than other people are. If not, the movement faces a special challenge in overcoming the information barrier.

Whatever the answer, the public's low level of information also has a much more profound effect on politics and public opinion—and on our attempts to understand them—than these mobilization concerns can suggest. For if people are largely uninformed, they may not *have* what we would normally regard as opinions on the issue. When asked by an interviewer, of course, they may be quite willing to say that they support or oppose vouchers. But there is reason to wonder whether the positions they take actually mean much of anything, and whether, if we asked them days or months later, they wouldn't be just as comfortable expressing entirely opposite views. If so, public opinion may be essentially frivolous and may tell us little about what Americans are really thinking. They may not be thinking much of anything at all.

This dilemma sets the groundwork for chapter 7, which gets to the subject that, for many readers, is inherently the most interesting: the extent to which Americans support or oppose vouchers, and why. In light of the public's low level of information, there are really two dimensions to the analysis here. One has to do with whether the opinions people express are actually meaningful, and thus, most centrally, with whether they are able to connect the voucher issue in a systematic, sensible way to their underlying values, beliefs, and interests. The answer is surprisingly positive: despite their lack of information, people do a rather good job of making connections and expressing meaningful opinions. Because this is so, the second dimension of the analysis—concerning who supports vouchers, who opposes them, and why they take the positions they do—takes on added importance, and tells us something valuable about the democratic foundations of the issue: about the overall popularity of vouchers with the public, about the role of key concerns (school performance, say, or social equity) in influencing where people stand, and ultimately about the political constituencies that are most relevant to the elite-level struggle.

Chapter 8 provides greater detail by exploring what people think the consequences of a voucher system might be—for society as a whole and for them personally—if one were adopted. These sorts of considerations are essentially what the national voucher debate is all about. Would vouchers make the public schools better or weaken them? Would vouchers bring valuable new opportunities to the poor, or would they undermine social equity and encourage segregation? Purely on descriptive grounds, how people assess these issues tells us a good deal about what they like and don't like about vouchers, where their sympathies lie, and which side's arguments they find more compelling. But an analysis of their responses can tell us much more. It can tell us, for instance, which of these concerns really matter in shaping where Americans stand on vouchers, and which of them don't—for many concerns that are salient to elites, and that Americans are happy to express opinions on, may actually have little to do with public support and opposition. Analysis also makes possible a whole line of inquiry that is quite fundamental to the voucher issue and indeed to any political issue. The question is: when people take a stand on vouchers, are they mainly concerned with how vouchers will affect society as a whole, or are they mainly concerned with how vouchers will affect them personally? Are they motivated by the public interest or by self-interest? Nothing could be more relevant to the kinds of political appeals that elites on both sides must make if they are to attract public support.

Chapter 9 is the final step in the data analysis. It begins by noting that, while virtually all assessments of public opinion on this issue are based on how people respond to the generic concept of vouchers, the fact is that a voucher system is not a single thing, but a family of very different possibilities. One voucher system may include religious schools, another may not. One may involve government regulation of private schools, another may allow them to chart their own paths in the free market. One may limit vouchers to children from low-income families or from failing schools, another may make vouchers available to all children. These sorts of possibilities are not just arcane details. They are contentious, enormously consequential issues that are right at the heart of the elite-level voucher debate—and how the public comes down on them will clearly shape the kinds of elite proposals that can win support in the political arena. This chapter is an attempt to shed light on all this, presenting evidence to show where the American people seem to stand on these alternative approaches to vouchers, and why.

In the concluding chapter, I spend some time reviewing the main results of the analysis and pulling them together. But the real purpose in this final chapter is to use the data analysis as a springboard for assessing where the politics of vouchers is likely to lead. No one can predict the political future with total accuracy. But this book's analysis of public opinion, once joined with the basic features of American politics and institutions, ought to suggest that some political outcomes are more likely than others. And it does. Among other things, it has implications for the strategies that elites on both sides are likely to follow in their efforts to attract public support; it tells us about the internal problems and opportunities each is likely to experience in keeping its own coalition together; and it points to the kinds of choice proposals that are likely to win out over time—all of which says a great deal about the role that vouchers are destined to play in the future of American education. I cannot say that these predictions will hold with certainty. But based on the available evidence, I think they are very good bets.

I hope, of course, that this analysis will prove useful for readers who come to the book with an interest in vouchers, and who seek a better understanding of the issue and its politics. I should add, though, that I hope it will also prove useful for readers who are not interested in vouchers at all. For the fact is, the voucher issue is not unique. In basic respects, it is just an issue in public policy, much like any other, and some of the central questions that arise in exploring its political foundations—questions, for instance, about the relative roles of self-interest and the public interest, or about whether citizens have meaningful opinions—are questions that have been at the heart of political theory and research for decades. An analysis of the voucher issue, then, should be valuable for reasons that extend well beyond what it can say about this one issue. It should have something to tell us about politics more generally.

As these points begin to suggest, I am actually writing this book with two very different audiences in mind. One is a general audience whose main goal is to learn about the voucher issue and its politics. The second is an audience of social scientists, some with a special interest in vouchers, some with broader interests in public opinion, public policy, and government. Trying to reach these two audiences via the same book is something of a challenge. Most readers in the general audience would prefer an engaging treatment that doesn't force them to wade through a lot of theory, methodology, and statistics to get where they want to go. Social scientists are inclined to value precisely the kind of detailed, rigorously developed, steeped-in-the-literature analysis that the general audience considers deadly boring and is eager to avoid. Because I believe the subject matter holds inherent interest for both audiences, the approach I've adopted is a compromise of sorts. My aim is to create an analysis that is clear, straightforward, and readily accessible to a general audience—but at the same time rigorous enough and developed in sufficient detail to be the kind of research that social scientists can respect and put to use.

Inevitably, some readers will find that this compromise leaves them wanting more. Or less, as the case may be. These reactions are legitimate. To social scientists who want to see issues explored in greater depth or with different or more sophisticated methodologies, I can only say that I am happy to respond to any questions they might have—and that I invite their involvement. My hope is that they will carry out their own projects that put whatever concerns or special interests they might have into action, and that ultimately go well beyond what I try to do here.

My hope for readers in the general audience, on the other hand, is that they will understand the need for the more technical aspects of this analysis and won't allow the details to get in the way of the book's central themes. For those who find, nonetheless, that their eyes are glazing over at all the numbers and tables, I encourage a more selective approach to the book: these readers can simply skim over the more onerous sections of the analysis, or omit them altogether, and go right to the conclusions of each chapter—where, in each case, I summarize the results and discuss their implications. The advantage of including as many details as I do is that they are all available, should readers choose to explore them. Readers can gain information on what they care about most, while relying on the chapter summaries to fill in the rest.

One final point. Before we begin this analysis, readers should be aware that I am a supporter of vouchers. I can't really apologize for having a personal position. In fact, it would be a little odd if, after studying the subject for more than fifteen years, I had no views of my own. But I do think readers have a right to know where I stand. Anyone familiar with the school choice controversy is aware that some portion of what passes for scientific research is not scientific at all, but a thinly veiled extension of the political debate, with researchers on both sides of the issue allowing personal values and political agendas to infect their work and determine their findings. With social science so politicized on the subject, readers need to approach every study with skepticism.

I can honestly say, however, that my aim here is not to convince anyone that vouchers are a good thing. My aim is simply to understand what is going on, and this analysis is my best attempt to develop an account of politics and public opinion that is faithful to the evidence, makes good sense, and is capable of withstanding the expert scrutiny of others. Throughout the book, the topics addressed are politically controversial, and some of the findings, themes, and arguments are sure to rankle partisans on both sides. But this cannot be avoided. My job is to lay out the truth as best I know it. And that is what I do.

PART ONE

BACKGROUND

1 *The Politics*
of Vouchers

SCHOOL VOUCHERS MIGHT seem a natural for American society. Our culture has long been marked by widely shared beliefs in personal freedom, markets, and limited government, and someone who didn't know anything about the history of American education might expect to find these cultural values embodied in the nation's school system. A truly American system of education, it might seem, would give parents a maximum of choice. It would keep government control of the schools to a minimum. It would extend a prominent role to private schools. It would encourage competition among schools. And to make all these things possible, it would provide parents with vouchers.

But this is not the reality of American education, of course. Traditionally, the public school system has made little use of choice or markets, and virtually none of vouchers. Since the early years of Progressive reforms, it has always been a thoroughly governmental system. Elected and appointed officials make decisions about the structure and content of public education, and the government agencies under their control—the public schools—provide services directly to the public.[1]

In recent years, the choice movement has made progress. There are alternative and magnet schools for children to choose from in many of our cities. In some places, children can choose any public school in their district or even choose to attend school in another district. And three public voucher programs (at this writing) allow low-income children to attend private schools with governmental assistance.[2] Yet even with these recent expansions of market-based choice, the basic character of the American education system remains the same. It is a system of top-down governmental control. For most children, there is no choice. For most schools, there is no competition. Markets are minimally important. Vouchers are almost nonexistent.

Why is this the case? For starters, we need to recognize that libertarian values are just one segment of the larger American value system. Americans may well believe in individualism and limited government, at least at a conceptual level. But they have other beliefs too. They believe in equality. They believe in justice. They believe in democracy. They believe in having a government that can promote these basic values through its laws and procedures. And not least, they believe in positive government: meaning, they favor a government that provides them with services (including education) and takes action to address social problems of virtually every kind. So it is reasonable to suggest that, even if the public school system were a direct reflection of the underlying culture, it would probably *not* turn out to be a market-driven system that minimizes the role of government. If the people could have their way, the libertarians would be disappointed.[3]

There is another, even more important reason that vouchers have not traditionally been a part of American education. The reason is politics. Whatever the culture of a nation, whatever it is that people want or believe, these things are not automatically reflected in public policy. For ideas to find their way into policy, two conditions must be met. The ideas must be developed and promoted to the point that they gain the attention of well-positioned players in the political system. And raw political power then has to be mobilized behind them to see that they are enacted and implemented by the authorities.[4]

So it is with vouchers. For vouchers to become an integral part of American education, it is not enough that they be compatible with important aspects of the culture—especially if they are arguably incompatible with others. A broadly attractive intellectual case must be made for them, one that can persuade important political elites, and ultimately the public at large, that such reforms are desirable. And then the proponents of vouchers must be able to put together a political coalition that is powerful enough to overcome formidable opposition and gain victory through the democratic process.

For a long time, these conditions were not even close to being met. Few people even talked about vouchers, much less pushed for them, and there was no serious challenge to the familiar command-and-control model of public education. Although it has taken four decades to change all this, the groundwork for reform has clearly been laid. The voucher idea has been introduced and developed, the intellectual case for it has been vigorously made—and at the upper reaches of politics, people don't just talk about vouchers these days, they furiously debate the issue. Meantime, proponents have seen their movement grow from a small band of true believers to a far-flung, eclectic coalition that has genuine power in politics, has already achieved important victories, and stands a chance in the years ahead of transforming American education.

This was not inevitable or natural. It took generations to happen. And in the process, as I discuss in this chapter, both the ideas and the political coalition behind vouchers have emerged very different, if stronger for the experience.

The Voucher Idea and the Economic Argument for It

Vouchers were first proposed by Milton Friedman, a free-market economist and political conservative whose contributions to economic theory and social policy have made him one of the most influential scholars of the last century. His initial attempt to promote the idea, set out in a 1955 journal article, gained little attention.[5] But he went on to devote a separate chapter to the subject in his 1962 treatise *Capitalism and Freedom,* and it was this discussion that eventually provoked intellectual interest in the concept.

Friedman's argument for vouchers was founded on the economic theory of markets. The traditional public school system, he observed, is a government-run monopoly in which schools are guaranteed students and resources regardless of how well they perform. The inevitable result is that public schools have few incentives to produce high-quality education, to respond to parents, to allocate theirs funds efficiently, or to innovate in socially productive ways. The system, by its very logic, breeds mediocrity and stagnation.

Friedman didn't think that the government should get out of education altogether. For education, he noted, is at least partly a public good that has positive spillover effects: each citizen's education tends to have beneficial impacts (via a better economy, a better democracy, and the like) on the welfare of other citizens. And because of this public good feature, a totally free market can't be expected to work efficiently. Individuals, left to their own devices, will tend to ignore the benefits their own educations have for other people and thus will tend to underinvest in it, with results that are bad for society as a whole. The solution is for the government to step in and subsidize education, thereby lowering the cost to individuals and prompting them to invest in more of it.

The government has traditionally subsidized education, of course. But Friedman didn't think government should go the next step and actually supply education through its own monopolistic school system, which is destined to be horribly inefficient. How, then, to create an alternative system in which the government provides subsidies but does not operate as a monopoly supplier? His answer was a voucher system.

The government would give all parents vouchers—grants of public money—that can be used at any school of their choosing to offset the costs of education. The education system would then be based on choice and competition. Parents would no longer be a captive clientele forced to "support" the public schools regardless of their performance. They would be able to leave schools they consider undesirable and seek out schools they think are better. As a result, schools would have to compete with one another for parental support. And this competition would put all schools on notice that, if they do not perform, they stand to lose students and resources to other schools that can do a better job. Under a voucher system, therefore, schools would be energized by vastly stronger performance incentives: to educate, to be responsive, to be efficient, to innovate. Schools that respond to these incentives would tend to prosper, while those that don't would be weeded out, unable to attract support from parents, who are free to take their children elsewhere. Over the long haul, then, choice and competition would tend to produce better schools than a government monopoly could, and to keep them improving and innovating.

This, in simple terms, is the classic economic argument for vouchers. But another aspect of Friedman's argument is important too. Under the traditional public system, he noted, political authorities make detailed decisions about curricula and values, and these policies are imposed on everyone whether they like it or not. This is the nature of democracy. Inevitably, however, many parents lose out and are prevented from receiving the kind of education they want for their children. With vouchers, parents who dissent from one-size-fits-all policies and want other things from their schools—a more rigorous curriculum, for instance, or greater emphasis on moral values—are no longer forced to conform and can seek out schools that reflect their own preferences. In a competitive system of schools, they are likely to find something close to what they want, because schools will have incentives to diversify and appeal to specialized clienteles in order to attract support.

To put the argument in more normative terms, then, Friedman's economic logic is implicitly grounded in a respect for diversity and a tolerance of individual values. People are different. They want different things from the schools. And vouchers allow them to pursue those differences, and schools to cater to them, without the government stepping in to judge whether the values involved are right or wrong. The point is not just to give parents and students better schools in some technical academic sense, but also to give them the *kind* of education they want—and in the process, to shift power from government to parents in deciding what values the schools will pursue.

The Early Years: Political Indifference

Friedman's voucher proposal slowly gained attention from academics and educators, largely because the idea was new and intriguing. But politically it was a nonstarter. Some conservatives gave the concept a sympathetic hearing, for they generally believed that choice and competition would be good for education. And some religious groups were sympathetic as well, because it would extend legitimacy to parents who prefer a religious education for their children and because it would give much-needed financial support for parochial schools. Yet the times were simply not right for vouchers to attract support from powerful political leaders or constituencies.

During the 1960s and 1970s, the prevailing ideology among American elites was one of government activism, and faith that democratic government could succeed in addressing the social problems of the time. This was the era of civil rights and affirmative action, the War on Poverty and the Great Society, huge growth in social and economic regulation, and expansion of the federal government's role in American society. Markets were clearly distrusted and out of favor. They were seen not as solutions to problems but rather as causes of them—of poverty, of segregation, of discrimination, of pollution, of inequity. A big part of the rationale for government action, in fact, was precisely that markets had created serious social problems that only government could correct.[6]

In the field of education, the federal government drastically increased its own spending during this period and created expansive new programs and regulations. Initially, government action was spurred by the launching of the Soviet sputnik in 1957, which convinced policymakers that America was falling behind in educational performance, particularly in the areas of math and science. But rather quickly, with the dawning of the 1960s, political emphasis shifted from performance to social equity, and government turned to the problems of unequal educational opportunity that, as many saw it, were endemic to a market society—a society that stacked the deck in favor of well-to-do families and denied needy children the most essential foundation for a productive life: a quality education. The political response, over the next decade or so, generated programs for compensatory education, bilingual education, and special education (among others) that vastly increased the federal government's role in state and local education.[7]

Even more significant, from the standpoint of the voucher issue, were the federal government's highly charged efforts to end racial segregation in the schools, following the Supreme Court's decision in *Brown v. Board of Education*.[8] Segregation was a vexing problem of social equity that civil rights supporters associated directly with choice and thus with the working of markets. For it seemed all too clear that, when whites were given the freedom to choose, they often chose not to go to school with blacks. There was, of course, much truth to this at the time, and its verity was well illustrated by the strategic use of "freedom of choice" plans in the South, which were obvious means of avoiding desegregation. In the North, where de jure segregation was far less common, the real problem was the de facto segregation of housing patterns, and thereby of neighborhood schools, that resulted from "white flight"—another indication to civil rights supporters that, when whites were given choice, they chose to separate themselves from blacks. The federal government's response during this period was to impose a top-down solution—mandatory busing—that corrected for the perceived abuses of markets and minimized the undesirable role of parental choice. To civil rights leaders and their allies in government, markets were the enemies of racial balance, choice was a formula for segregation—and government regulation was the answer.[9]

The Idea of Regulated Vouchers

Throughout this period, the voucher concept was relegated to the political wilderness. It was an idea whose time had not come. Indeed, that puts it too mildly. Vouchers were regarded within most education and policy circles as little more than a crackpot, right-wing notion unfit for serious discussion. There were several early signs, however, of the transformation that would take place over the next few decades.

One was that the public school system, largely in response to grassroots pressures and despite the prevailing antimarket ideology, was beginning to create schools of choice within its boundaries anyway. In the late 1960s and early 1970s, these tended to be alternative schools that offered children different (often more liberal or progressive) curricula and teaching styles from the regular public schools.[10] Choice, it turned out, was popular among parents. The more enduring development, however, was the proliferation of magnet schools, beginning in the mid-1970s. This represented an important shift in public policy and in the prevailing view of choice. It came about because the government's reliance on forced busing was generating passionate opposition, and because policymakers and even civil rights activists were prompted to rethink their preference for coercive methods of racial integration. What they realized now was that they might promote racial balance by means of a much more popular, entirely voluntary method—school choice—with magnet schools, boasting specialized themes and upgraded facilities and staff, serving to attract white children back into urban areas. Many liberals who had become accustomed to excoriating school choice as a symbol of segregation, therefore, were led to see it in a very different light. Their memories were not erased, nor were their suspicions entirely eliminated. But here was a concrete example that, under the right circumstances—an expressly designed context of governmental controls—choice could contribute to the fight for social equity.[11]

Vouchers are a far more radical reform than magnet schools. The latter are entirely public, and they offer a very limited brand of choice that is highly controlled by the government to engineer racial balance. It should come as little surprise, then, that liberals did not warm to vouchers the way they warmed to magnet schools. Nonetheless, there were some liberals during this time who did see real value in vouchers—and who were attracted to them in large measure because of their capacity for promoting social equity.

A well-known example is Christopher Jencks, a left-leaning professor of sociology from Harvard University who became disenchanted during the late 1960s with what he saw as the poor performance and bureaucratic unresponsiveness of the public schools, especially in urban areas, and who embraced vouchers as a means of bringing educational opportunities to disadvantaged families. Working on contract with the Office of Economic Opportunity (OEO) (a presidential agency charged with overseeing much of the War on Poverty), Jencks produced a detailed report in 1970 outlining his own version of a voucher system and calling for federally funded experiments that would put the proposal into operation and allow tests of its efficacy.[12]

Jencks picked up on Friedman's basic ideas, but modified them significantly and turned them toward liberal ends. What he proposed was a

regulated voucher system—a system in which choice and competition operate within a framework of government rules that embody social values,
impose requirements on private schools, and actively promote social equity. Under his plan, all children in a given area would qualify for vouchers, but low-income children would get bigger vouchers than everyone
else, making these kids especially attractive to private schools and compensating for the additional costs that might be involved in addressing
their disadvantages. Another equalizing element was that parents could
not add on to the vouchers with their own funds, and participating private
schools would be required to accept the voucher as full payment of tuition. These private schools, moreover, would no longer have full control
over their own admissions, which would be regulated in the interests of
fairness and equity: if more children applied than could be accommodated,
the schools would be required to select half their kids through a lottery,
thereby assuring all applicants an equal shot at admission. To make meaningful choice possible, schools would also have to provide detailed information to parents on their programs, teacher qualifications, and student
test scores. And transportation to schools of choice would be free to all
children, provided by the government.

The social ideals behind the Jencks proposal were in sync with the times.
But the proposal itself ran into a political buzz saw, as teachers unions and
other education groups vigorously opposed the OEO's efforts to initiate
voucher experiments. Ultimately, only a single pilot program came out of
all this (in Alum Rock, California), and it was a pale reflection of what
Jencks had in mind. Indeed, it was so compromised by politics that it did
not even allow private schools to participate, and thus was not a voucher
program at all.[13]

Jencks was not the only liberal to gain attention for regulated vouchers.
They were being promoted at the same time by law professors John Coons
and Stephen Sugarman—who were also, and more generally, pushing hard
for fundamental reform of school finance in the interests of the disadvantaged.[14] During the early 1970s, Coons and Sugarman gained prominence
by framing the legal arguments that ultimately led to the landmark California Supreme Court decision in *Serrano* v. *Priest,* which declared the
state school finance system unconstitutional and required radical equal-
ization of spending across districts.[15] Soon thereafter, they published a
major book, *Education by Choice,* that made a strong case for vouchers—
focusing less on the wonders of the marketplace than on the value of vouchers in giving greater control to families and in helping ameliorate the social

inequities that, as they saw it, were profoundly rooted in the current system.[16] They followed up by launching a campaign in 1979 to put an initiative on the California ballot that, if enacted, would have established a regulated voucher plan for the entire state. The political campaign to put the initiative on the ballot, however, was a grassroots effort that lacked major funding sources, and it failed to collect the necessary signatures to qualify. Like Jencks before them, Coons and Sugarman tested the political waters with their novel ideas about vouchers—and went nowhere.[17]

Despite the fact that nothing was immediately achieved, the Jencks and Coons-Sugarman plans were important events in the history of the voucher movement. Like the proliferation of magnet schools, they demonstrated that choice-based reforms needn't go hand in hand with free markets, but instead could be embedded in a structure of government regulation whose purpose is to harness the power of markets to promote fairness, equity, and racial balance, as well as performance and efficiency. Conservatives could use vouchers to promote their own vision of the good society. But so could liberals. It was all a matter of how the programs were designed and what values were to be realized.

I should add, finally, that this nonlibertarian view of vouchers and markets was not an isolated strand of thinking unique to education. It was (and still is) entirely compatible with mainstream economics. Friedman and other libertarians believe that when markets are allowed to work freely with a minimum of government interference, society will be maximally productive and efficient. But this is an extreme position that few other economists share. The vast majority of economists would argue that while markets have great potential for promoting efficiency and other valued outcomes, how well they actually do depends on the real-world conditions under which they operate—and there are some conditions that can undermine their effectiveness and even lead to social problems. This can happen, for instance, if consumers are poorly informed, if the goods in question are public goods, if competition is inherently limited, or if some people are kept out of the marketplace (because they lack resources, for example, or are discriminated against). The solution among economists, however, is not to abandon markets, but rather to address their imperfections through an appropriately designed framework of governmental rules and then to put markets to good use within this framework. This, in fact, is the way most nations in the Western world have structured their economies, which are not free markets in any meaningful sense, but mixed systems in which governmental rules constrain and channel how markets work.

In effect, this is precisely the sort of thing that Jencks, Coons, and Sugarman were proposing for education. The traditional education system made no real use of markets and relied entirely on government. It was at one end of the spectrum. What Friedman proposed, on the other hand, was essentially a free market in education that made virtually no use of the regulatory powers of government. It was at the other end of the spectrum. Jencks, Coons, and Sugarman were charting out a middle path— and, from the standpoint of mainstream economics, a very conventional one. They wanted an education system that took greater advantage of what markets have to offer but relied on the regulatory powers of government to channel and direct the operation of markets toward socially desirable ends. What they wanted, in short, was a mixed system.

At the time, this kind of thinking was still a radical departure from traditional ideas about American education, and it failed to win many converts. It also did not sit well with Friedman and other libertarians, who chafed at the regulatory role of government and the emphasis on equity. It did, however, turn out to be an early indication of where the voucher movement was headed.

The Times Change

By the end of the 1970s, vouchers had attracted little support to speak of and were barely on the political map. But times were about to change. Three important developments would soon alter the landscape of American education politics and create fertile conditions for the rise of a dynamic voucher movement.

The first was that, in the United States and around the world, the theory of markets scored a resounding comeback. Political elites almost everywhere, even in communist nations, came to agree that traditional command-and-control approaches to economic and social policy were often highly inefficient, and that the key to better government lay with a greater, more innovative reliance on markets and the private sector. Communism soon crumbled, replaced by market economies. The international economic system became much more competitive, driven by the globalization of markets. And within countries that already had capitalist systems, state regulation and control fell out of favor, and market-based reforms that had been rejected out of hand in the recent past were seriously considered, and often adopted, across a whole range of policy areas—including education. Throughout the world, as a result, the idea that choice and competition might be good for schools—and good for children, and good for the national economy—suddenly had intellectual respectability and political currency.[18]

The second development was the election of Ronald Reagan as president in 1980. The Reagan administration put power and substance behind these ideals in the American context, seeking to usher in a new era of smaller government, lower taxes, decentralization, and greater reliance on markets. Reagan officials saw choice and competition as key mechanisms for improving American schools, and they actively pursued legislation promoting the use of vouchers (and tax credits for private schooling). But their voucher proposals—which were actually quite modest, simply allowing districts to use federal money to experiment—were defeated within Congress. Politically, it was still too early. What they did accomplish, though, was important. They put choice and vouchers squarely on the nation's policy agenda for the first time: drawing attention to their virtues, legitimizing them as policy options, and encouraging experimentation and reform within the states. Reagan officials also facilitated the emergence of a movement to support these ideals. In disseminating information, holding conferences, and encouraging contacts among choice supporters, they promoted a network of like-minded activists who in the near future would become central players in the struggle for choice. By the end of Reagan's second term in 1989, the foundation for a movement had been laid, and the issues that would drive it were highly visible and politically salient. Among elites, anyway.[19]

The third development was the publication in 1983 of *A Nation at Risk*, the report of a blue-ribbon panel of experts that has become one of the most influential studies of American education ever conducted.[20] The panel, particularly concerned about the nation's ability to compete in the global economy, issued a dire warning: the nation faced a crisis of educational performance—a "rising tide of mediocrity" in its schools—that called for immediate action. Policymakers responded with alarm, producing an avalanche of reforms aimed at improving school performance. Graduation requirements were increased, teacher certification was strengthened, more emphasis was placed on student testing, teacher pay was increased, and more money was spent overall. Policymakers, in other words, did all the obvious things that seemed likely to promote better schools. But by the latter part of the decade, the results were disappointing. Many experts, including those firmly in the education mainstream, began to argue that the real problem was the system itself and that major improvement called for much more fundamental innovations. School choice and vouchers, of course, were reforms of exactly this type—and the time had come for their emergence as truly powerful political ideas. Proponents had an ideal opportunity to push for bold, choice-based reforms. And policymakers and educators, more than ever before, had incentives to listen and respond.[21]

The Opposition

These developments set the stage for the rise of the voucher movement. They also sent a signal to opponents that they needed to take the voucher idea seriously and mobilize to defeat it before it had a chance to spread and take root. The leading opponents at that time were the same players who are leading the attack on vouchers today. These opponents believe in the public school system and what it stands for, and they are convinced that vouchers will undermine the quality of American education and the ideals on which it rests. But there is something else going on as well, something big, that deepens their opposition immeasurably. And this something is due precisely to the fact that vouchers, unlike virtually all other education reforms, actually do have the capacity to generate a profound transformation of the system.

There is a lot at stake. The current education system spends more than $300 billion annually, provides millions of jobs, and is a motherlode of power and resources for the public officials, administrators, and unions that are the established players in its operation. Vouchers threaten all this. They allow students and resources to leave the public sector for the private sector—which means a smaller public system, fewer public employees (particularly teachers), and less public money to spend on favored programs and constituencies. Vouchers replace the security and comfort of regulation with the insecurity, discipline, and performance demands of competition. They decentralize power, shifting many decisions from the establishment to parents. And they create problems of gargantuan proportions for the teachers unions, which would lose members, collect less in dues, and find themselves forced to operate in a newly competitive environment that makes their organizing tasks far more difficult.[22]

It is no accident that the education establishment—led by the two major teachers unions, the National Education Association (NEA) and the American Federation of Teachers (AFT)—is the vanguard of the opposition to vouchers. These organizations have vested interests in the status quo, and vouchers threaten those interests in the most serious ways. Because this is so, they put vouchers in a different category from virtually all other issues in the politics of education reform. Vouchers are public enemy number one, as they see it, and must be defeated at all costs.

The opposition is backed by formidable political power. As inside players, members of the establishment are privileged: they are integral parts of the very government whose policies they are trying to influence. Thanks to the unions, they are flush with financial resources—for campaign contributions, lobbying, and public relations. They are supremely well organized and can mobilize political armies of well-educated activists (teachers). They have technical expertise and know the arcane details of education policy and practice. And not least, they have the huge advantage of operating in a political system that, by design of the nation's founders, is built around a multiplicity of checks, balances, and veto points that make it much easier to block new policies than to enact them. And blocking, of course, is all they need to do to stop vouchers.[23]

The establishment also has powerful allies. Led by the teachers unions, its members contribute enormous amounts of money and manpower to Democratic politicians. The Democrats, in turn, work closely with them on all sorts of educational policy issues—and, given the intensity of the establishment's views, are especially willing to go to the mat for them in defeating vouchers. Liberal interest groups weigh into the balance as well. In general, they distrust markets and have agendas that call for extensive government regulation, so there is a natural inclination to oppose vouchers. The most active in voucher politics is the National Association for the Advancement of Colored People (NAACP), whose upper-level leaders tend to see vouchers as a thinly disguised strategy by which whites can avoid integration. Another active group is the American Civil Liberties Union (ACLU), which, under the banner of protecting constitutional rights, pursues a liberal policy agenda that frequently leads it into courtrooms and legislatures to fight against vouchers.[24]

Arguments and Counterarguments

Even in light of its financial and organizational advantages, one of the opposition's most powerful political weapons is simply its intellectual argument that vouchers are bad public policy. What the opponents have to say clearly touches on values, beliefs, and fears that stand to resonate with many Americans, as well as with the interest groups and policymakers who wield clout on education reform. Here are some of the themes they emphasize in the public debate:[25]

(1) Vouchers would harm the public schools. They would drain children and resources from the public sector, making it even more difficult for the schools to improve their performance, particularly in needy areas that are already strapped. They would also attract away the most moti-

vated parents and students, who are precisely the ones most likely to push for improvement and participate actively in school affairs. The schools would suffer in their absence.

(2) Vouchers would create inequities. It is the socially advantaged—higher in income and education, white, more highly motivated, better informed—who are most likely to put choice to aggressive use and to bail out of the public schools. This is all the more likely because private schools will favor children who test well, are well behaved, and come from well-to-do families. The upshot will be a two-tiered system, with advantaged kids escaping to the private sector and poor and minority kids isolated in public schools incapable of serving their needs or improving.

(3) Vouchers would promote racial segregation. The reasons are much the same, with one addition: many white parents (opponents argue) don't want their children to go to school with blacks, and they would use choice as a means of escaping diverse public schools to find more racially homogenous private ones. Existing problems of school segregation would get worse.

(4) Vouchers would threaten democratic control. The public school system is supposed to be about expressing the collective values of a democratic society, socializing the young to democratic citizenship, common schooling for all classes and races, and equal opportunity for all—and these objectives can only be realized through top-down control of the schools by democratic government. Vouchers would break the hold of democracy and its values, producing a system that exalts the individual over the community and promotes balkanization and self-interest.

(5) Vouchers would violate the "separation of church and state." Religion should be kept out of public education entirely, except as a subject of study, and no government funds should support schools that are affiliated with a church, or that allow religion to infect their teaching or moral climates. Religion is a private matter. To support it through vouchers, moreover, is not just bad policy: it is unconstitutional, violating the Establishment Clause of the U.S. Constitution.

(6) Vouchers would give too much power to parents. There are democratic reasons why society's preferences, rather than parent preferences, should take priority in a system of public education. But there are other reasons for giving parents a lesser role as well. Many parents are unlikely to know about their alternatives under school choice and are incapable of making competent choices for their children anyway. Moreover, many do not put primary emphasis on quality education and are inclined to make choices based on noneducational criteria—where friends go to school, for instance, or simple proximity. Because parents are such flawed consumers,

the alleged power of markets collapses. Schools will not have incentives to provide higher quality education in response to their demand.

Voucher advocates, of course, have responses to all these claims, but precisely how they respond depends on who is doing the talking. Libertarians such as Milton Friedman tend to respond by pushing hard on the advantages of free markets and attacking the problems of government.[26] Voucher supporters who believe in a regulated system (and in using it to promote equity), on the other hand, tend to approach the matter rather differently—and, in fact, are sympathetic to some of the criticisms. To them, choice and competition are highly beneficial and there are real problems with government, but it is precisely because there is something valid about the opponents' concerns that regulations are called for.[27]

While different voucher supporters may give rather different responses to the claims of opponents, then, the counterarguments below—which blend the libertarian and regulated approaches—are typical of those made throughout the 1990s.

(1) Would vouchers harm the public schools? No. They would indeed drain off some of the public sector's children and resources, but this is actually a good thing, because the loss of business is precisely what gives the public schools strong incentives to improve. It is misleading, moreover, to claim that the schools are being denied the resources necessary to improve, for they are only losing resources for kids they don't have to educate. The public sector will be smaller, but leaner and more driven to perform. Finally, while vouchers may (or may not) attract some of the more motivated parents and students, their leaving puts pressure on the schools to improve—and the students who stay behind will benefit as their schools push to reform themselves.

(2) Would vouchers create inequities? The fact is, the current system is already horribly inequitable, because it is based on a perverse form of choice: people with money can acquire better schools by moving to the suburbs or paying private tuition, but poor and minority parents often do not have these choices and get stuck in our society's worst schools. Social equity demands that real choice be extended to the disadvantaged, allowing them to leave bad schools, seek out better ones, and exercise the kind of control advantaged people already have. This alone would have huge, positive effects. And while it is possible, under free-market conditions, that some private schools might discriminate against the disadvantaged, or that choice would favor some parents over others, this is what regulations are for. The system can be designed to address these problems directly and to see that equity is aggressively pursued.

(3) Would vouchers promote racial segregation? The current system is already highly segregated. Vouchers would extend choice to minorities who historically have been denied it, and who have been concentrated in high-minority, high-poverty schools. This would give them the power to seek out other schools more to their liking and promote integration. And although a free market could allow some private schools to move toward white-only student bodies, or allow some whites to avoid going to school with minorities, regulations can be designed to see that this doesn't happen. Indeed, they can be designed to promote or even require racial balance.

(4) Would vouchers threaten democratic control? For the free-market version, the answer is yes. But other versions of a voucher system involve, at the very least, a basic framework of governmental controls that are determined by the democratic process, reflect basic community values, and impart the same public principles—of fairness and equity, for instance— that define the public school ethos. Government is not eliminated from the picture. It is simply less intrusive, pulling back to grant choice and competition much more central roles than in the past.

(5) Would vouchers violate the "separation of church and state"? Parents should be able to use their vouchers at religiously affiliated schools, such as Catholic schools, if that is what they want for their children. Their preferences deserve to be respected. Whether this is constitutional or not must ultimately depend on what the courts say. But many legal scholars argue that there is nothing in the Establishment Clause to prohibit vouchers, and that, so long as parents (rather than governments) are the ones who decide which schools get public money, it should be quite possible to design a voucher system that passes constitutional muster.

(6) Would vouchers give too much power to parents? The schools should be especially responsive to the children they are supposed to be serving, and thus to parents. Parents, more than politicians or administrators, want the best for their own children—and are far better decisionmakers than the condescending arguments of critics often suggest. Parents care about quality education. And in a choice system, where their participation actually matters, they will be informed enough and competent enough to make good decisions for their kids.

The New Politics of Education

Laying the two sides of the argument out in this way is helpful in providing a clearer, more complete picture of the intellectual debate. But because the debate really took shape and became an important political phenomenon during the 1990s, we have gotten a little ahead of our political story—which we left off in the late 1980s. Let's now return to it.

By the late 1980s, the important building blocks for the voucher movement had just been put in place. The theory of markets was held in high regard. The Reagan administration had legitimized the voucher issue and nurtured an early network of activists. And A Nation at Risk had uncovered a crisis in education performance, leading to calls for major reforms of the system. The time was ripe for change. With the dawning of the new decade, two events helped spark a sudden explosion of interest in vouchers that, with a foundation already in place, caused the movement to take off.

One of these events was the publication in 1990 of Politics, Markets, and America's Schools, which I coauthored with John E. Chubb. It is a bit awkward for me to comment with any objectivity on my own book, so I will deal with it only briefly. Until that point, the standard argument for vouchers was an economic one, emphasizing the superiority of markets over government. But there had been no serious attention to exactly how government operates and why. There was an underlying theory of markets but no theory of government to complete the case. Why, for instance, couldn't democratic government successfully respond to the kinds of incentive problems that Friedman points to—substituting, say, democratically based incentives for market-based incentives—and use its expertise and political will to bring about better schools? What kinds of schools should we really expect from democratic government? Chubb and I addressed these sorts of questions and provided new evidence as well.

Drawing upon an established theoretical tradition in political science, and extending work that each of us had done on political institutions more generally, especially on bureaucracy, we developed a theory of educational governance to show how politics affects the organization and performance of schools.[28] The bottom line is that, given the way incentives are structured in politics, the usual top-down forms of democratic control inherently tend to bury the schools in bureaucracy and erode their performance. Because the causes are rooted in the system itself, significant improvement is difficult or impossible if reforms leave the system intact. The only way to get real improvement is to shift away from top-down control to a very different type of system, based largely on markets rather than politics. Having made this argument, we went on to conduct an extensive empirical analysis, based on a large survey of students, teachers, and administrators. This study did not test the efficacy of vouchers per se, as there were no voucher programs to study. But it did suggest that democratic control promotes bureaucracy, that bureaucracy is bad for schools (and autonomy good for them)—and that the basic elements of our thinking were consistent with the facts.

At the time, the reaction was both heartening and horrific. There was tremendous media attention, which suddenly gave marked political salience to the voucher issue. There was a noticeable surge of energy, enthusiasm, and confidence within the voucher movement. And from some academic quarters, there was respect for a social scientific job well done. But the backlash was brutal. Leaders of the education establishment denounced the book as a conservative diatribe, and certain education researchers (usually from education schools) argued that our empirical analysis was flawed and implied that we were essentially ideologues who manufactured theory and manipulated facts to arrive at our own preferred policy solutions.[29]

Today, ten years later, the book arouses less emotion and vitriol and is more likely to be seen for what it always was: an exercise in social science that offered a genuinely theoretical argument, was rooted in a respected scholarly literature (which at the time represented the cutting-edge work on political institutions, and still does to this day), and carried out quantitative empirical tests. But be that as it may, it seems to be the consensus among those familiar with the politics of choice that this book was a pivotal event in the voucher movement—coming at just the right time and providing a forceful new argument for vouchers that generated national attention, stirred up controversy, and galvanized supporters into action.[30]

The second event that helped spark the takeoff of the modern voucher movement, however, was more important in its substantive impact. Until the late 1980s, the voucher movement was largely based in conservatism and religion. Both of these traditional pillars of the movement, moreover, had actually been strengthened as a result of recent social trends. Conservatives were much more numerous and powerful than in prior times, and their ideas more broadly popular. And religion, too, had experienced a comeback, with growing numbers of born-again Christians and a powerful "moral majority" holding sway within the Republican party. It is doubtful, however, whether conservatism and religion on their own could have ignited a movement powerful enough to challenge the education establishment, at least in the short term.

At any rate, we will never know. Because just before the publication of the Chubb-Moe book, the voucher movement was routed along on a very different political path by an event that may someday be regarded as among the most significant developments in the history of American education. What happened was that a new and radically different kind of voucher coalition formed in the city of Milwaukee and, in the spring of 1990, won a surprising victory over the powerful defenders of the existing system. The result was the nation's first public voucher program—reserved for low-income children in the inner city and dedicated to the goal of social equity.[31]

Milwaukee was similar to many other American cities. The school-age population was overwhelmingly poor and minority, mainly black, and the school system was clearly not educating them very well. Milwaukee's parents had a grassroots leader, however, in Polly Williams, a Democratic state legislator and former state campaign director for Jesse Jackson. Williams blasted the Milwaukee public school system for its failures. She also rejected the idea that inner-city kids should be bused into the suburbs in search of better schools. Milwaukee's children deserved good schools close to home, she argued, and if they couldn't get good schools in the public sector, the government should help them go to local private schools. Unlike traditional voucher supporters, her resort to vouchers was not motivated by a fervent belief in the wonders of the free market. It was about equity for the disadvantaged, and about finding a practical solution to a serious social problem in her own city.

The voucher idea met with an enthusiastic response from Milwaukee's parents, and attracted support from certain community leaders—notable among them Howard Fuller (soon to become superintendent of the Milwaukee public schools)—who fought alongside Williams for the new program. But the usual allies of low-income and minority constituents—Democrats, liberal interest groups, the unions—were vehemently opposed and vowed to do whatever it took to defeat them. Williams had to look elsewhere for support and found it on the other side of the political fence, where Republicans, conservatives, and business groups—led by Governor Tommy Thompson—agreed to back her cause.

After a bruising fight in the Wisconsin state legislature, this odd coalition won a first victory for vouchers. The new program was limited, hedged about by unavoidable compromises with opponents. Participation was limited to just 1,000 low-income children in a district of 100,000. And vouchers could not be used at religious schools, which meant that the vast majority of Milwaukee's private schools were eliminated as choice options. But despite its limitations, the victory had enormous political significance. For it not only created the nation's first voucher system. It also gave birth to a distinctly new politics, which in the years since has transformed the voucher movement and altered the landscape of American education.[32]

The hallmark of the new politics of education is a reconfiguration of alliances that turns traditional American politics on its head. The liberal coalition has long been the vanguard of change on behalf of the poor, and it has been their representative in politics. But in the case of vouchers, it finds itself defending demonstrably bad inner-city school systems against demands for reform by the very constituents it claims to represent—while these constituents, for lack of any other option, are driven to seek support from new conservative allies. These battle lines are politically embarrassing to the liberal coalition. They are also threatening: for under the right circumstances, the alliance between conservatives and the urban poor stands to be a very powerful political force indeed.

This new coalition for vouchers is unorthodox. But politics makes strange bedfellows, and it is difficult to deny that the urban poor are a natural constituency for vouchers. Poor and minority parents in the inner cities tend to be concentrated in schools that, by the accounts of even the most liberal observers, are among the worst in the nation; and the current system, busing aside, gives them few ways to escape or to seek out better opportunities.[33] It makes sense that they would find vouchers appealing. The political argument on their behalf, moreover, can obviously be a persuasive one, and can appeal to a broad audience. Part of its appeal is straightforwardly moral and linked to popular concerns for social equity: inner-city voucher plans are designed to aid the most disadvantaged children in the country. Another part of its appeal is purely practical: the inner cities are where America's educational problems are the worst, and where mainstream solutions have consistently failed, so something different and even radical would seem called for.[34]

Both members of this unorthodox coalition, then, have something to gain from working together. The urban poor get the benefit of vouchers, and a means of changing an entrenched system that has long been failing them. Conservatives get a visible and deserving new constituency, a strong set of moral and practical arguments for vouchers, and a more powerful movement for promoting fundamental change in American education.

There is nothing automatic about such a coalition, though. Leaders of the urban poor are reluctant to trust the motives of conservatives, who oppose them on most every social issue. They also fear that, once vouchers are provided to low-income children, conservatives would provide them to everyone and privatize the school system—which leaders of the poor do not favor. Many conservatives, on the other hand, are not as committed to vouchers as stereotypes would suggest. Conservative elected officials, for example, often have constituents who are in the suburbs, fairly satisfied with their schools, and not pressuring for radical reform. Outside the core of the voucher movement itself, the reality (for now) is that many conservatives are ideologically in tune with vouchers but not inclined to take tough political action. They talk a good game, but they don't do much.[35]

Because of these obstacles, the unorthodox coalition for vouchers has not emerged in all (or even most) contexts that seem to provide fertile ground for it. But in the years since Milwaukee's pioneering voucher program was first adopted, this alliance between conservatives and the poor has gained momentum throughout the country and become the most powerful force for change in American education. Milwaukee was the dawning of a new era.

The 1990s: Vouchers Make Progress

Since Milwaukee, the voucher movement has attracted a very different following: more egalitarian in outlook, less impressed with free markets, less concerned with religion. Many conservatives in its ranks continue to see vouchers in universalistic and market-oriented terms. In their view, all children should get vouchers, and the entire education system should be reformed via choice and competition. But to many of the newer supporters, vouchers are not just about choice, competition, and performance incentives. Nor are they necessarily for all children. They are about bringing equal opportunity to the children in greatest need, and about using regulations to channel markets in the right directions. The ideas of Jencks, Coons, and Sugarman, once on the periphery of the movement, are now fueling its growth and diversity.

This internal diversity is one key to understanding the modern voucher movement. Another is its profound lack of organization and weak financial support. Even with the advantages of its new politics, the movement has developed no coherent leadership or organization and is largely driven by the uncoordinated decisions of activists throughout the country, who, like Polly Williams, are usually focused on their own states or cities. And while big (usually conservative) donors do indeed play key roles on occasion, most contributions are sporadic, and the amount of political money pales by comparison to what the teachers unions can raise through their regular, institutional sources.

The diversity and disorganization of the movement, combined with the boundless enthusiasm of its devotees, help explain a central feature of the modern movement: there is a tremendous amount of political activity, happening all over the place and at all levels of government, without any overarching plan or strategy. While the movement would doubtless have more success if it could coordinate its actions and resources, a major virtue of this unrestrained decentralization is that it plays on the law of large numbers. The movement has launched so many attacks on so many fronts that the system's defenders, although usually much more powerful, have been unable to defeat each and every one of them. As a result, the voucher movement has lost almost all its battles, yet it has also made progress through highly visible victories. Even in defeat, the movement has sometimes come tantalizingly close, brought attention to its cause, and demonstrated that it is a political force to be reckoned with.

Increasingly, vouchers have been moving to center stage in national politics. President George Bush, a Republican, began his term pushing for public school choice rather than vouchers. But he eventually joined the voucher camp, and during the 1992 election year unveiled his "G.I. Bill for Children," which would have provided $1,000 vouchers to children from families with incomes below the national average. The idea went nowhere in the Democratic Congress, but it succeeded in attracting national attention.[36]

When Bill Clinton won the 1992 election, vouchers went out of official favor, as the new Democratic president, who had received strong campaign support from the teachers unions, vowed his opposition. The issue burst back onto the national scene with the 1996 election campaign, when Republican candidate Bob Dole came out with his own proposal for low-income vouchers—with Clinton adamantly against. The polarities in the 2000 presidential election shaped up in much the same way. George W. Bush, the Republican nominee, favored vouchers for children in failing schools, while Al Gore, the Democratic nominee, declared himself unalterably opposed to vouchers of any kind.

In Congress, the battle lines are similar, except that Republican legislators tend to be less dependable voucher supporters than their presidential standard-bearers. The reasons are rooted in constituency. Republican presidents, or candidates for president, need to put together a broadly based support coalition—not just of conservatives and suburbanites, but also of minorities, urban dwellers, and those lower in income—and they have seen the voucher issue as an attractive means of doing that. Republican legislators, on the other hand, tend to come from more homogeneous suburban constituencies, and for them (as I explained earlier) vouchers have less of an electoral connection.

It is not a coincidence that, when the Republicans took over Congress in 1995 for the first time in forty years, they quickly began crafting legislation on their Contract with America—but they ignored vouchers, even though school choice was part of the Contract. Most were sympathetic, but vouchers were low in priority. Eventually, as other agenda items were taken care of, and as vouchers began to score successes elsewhere, congressional Republicans became more active in pushing voucher and tax credit proposals. Of these, the most notable was their successful enactment, against vigorous opposition from the teachers unions, civil rights groups, and the Democrats, of a 1998 bill authorizing vouchers for low-income children in Washington, D.C. This bill was vetoed, to no one's surprise, by President Clinton.[37]

National politics is important and highly visible. But because education is largely a state and local matter in the United States, and because the voucher movement is radically decentralized, most of the political action has taken place at these lower levels. The first half of the 1990s was a period of unfocused activism during which the movement was getting its bearings and testing the political waters. Voucher proposals were introduced in many state legislatures and everywhere defeated—although in a few states, notably Pennsylvania, Arizona, and Texas, they came close to winning. Vouchers were also proposed through the initiative process in California and Colorado, as were tax credits in Oregon, but these were defeated as well.[38] In various cities, conservatives and the urban poor pushed for voucher plans, and in Jersey City, white Republican Brett Schundler was elected mayor in an overwhelmingly black, Democratic town by running on a platform of school vouchers. But even in Jersey City, where Schundler's efforts appeared bolstered by the election of Republican Christie Whitman as governor, vouchers were derailed when Whitman proved reluctant to take on the opposition.[39]

The early 1990s were, in some sense, just a string of losses. But this is to be expected, given the formidable strength of the opposition—and the experience served important purposes. It helped put vouchers on the policy agenda, it taught the movement's leaders about politics, it attracted new recruits to the movement. And as time went on, these foundations began to pay off. Three successes stand out, all of them outgrowths of the new politics of education.

—In Wisconsin, proponents won a major extension of the Milwaukee voucher program in 1995, raising the ceiling on student participation to 15,000 (a huge increase), and authorizing students to take their vouchers to religious schools for the first time (vastly increasing the number of private schools they could choose from).[40]

—In Ohio, led by Cleveland councilwoman Fannie Lewis (that city's Polly Williams) and Governor George Voinovich, proponents succeeded in 1995 in getting the state legislature to adopt a voucher program for some 2,000 low-income children in inner-city Cleveland. Here too, religious schools were allowed to participate.[41]

—In Florida, led by newly elected governor Jeb Bush, voucher proponents won the nation's first statewide program in 1999, this one making vouchers available to all children who attend "failing" schools. (The vast majority of these kids, in practice, will come from low-income families.) Initially, only two schools in the entire state met the criteria of "failing" performance, so few children qualified for vouchers. But as performance standards rise, the voucher population could easily become quite large. In this program, as in Milwaukee and Cleveland, religious schools are allowed to participate.[42]

While all this was happening in politics, the voucher movement was further bolstered by a development of profound importance occurring entirely outside of politics: the emergence of private voucher programs. The first of these programs was set up in Indianapolis in 1991 by J. Patrick Rooney, chief executive officer of the Golden Rule Insurance Company, whose idea was to use private funds to give vouchers immediately to low-income children in the inner city, without the need for political battle, and without the interference of government. By this route, vouchers couldn't be stopped. The movement for private vouchers grew steadily throughout the 1990s, as new programs sprouted in major cities around the country, and a new organization—CEO America—emerged to provide coordination, expertise, and seed money. As of 1998, private vouchers had reached more than thirty cities and included about 12,000 children. In that year, however, the movement skyrocketed into another realm when businessmen Theodore J. Forstmann and John T. Walton implemented an ambitious new program (funded, in part, by $100 million of their own money) that provided vouchers to some 40,000 low-income children throughout the nation. The vouchers were all awarded on a single day, through a lottery of all children who had applied. The number of applicants was an astounding 1.25 million—a figure that from this point on would be widely quoted as an indication of the demand for vouchers among the urban poor.[43]

The movement for private vouchers, therefore, is very much a political phenomenon. And, so far, a very successful one. Once in operation, these programs not only provide valuable benefits to needy families. They also bolster the movement for publicly supplied vouchers: attracting attention to the issue, mobilizing support among the urban poor, highlighting the role of vouchers in advancing social equity, and generating hard evidence on the actual impacts of vouchers. And they do all this through private action, without having to overcome the power of teachers unions and other opponents.

Looming over the recent successes of the voucher movement, however, is a great uncertainty almost beyond its control: how the courts will come down on the "separation of church and state" issue. In each of the movement's major political victories—Milwaukee, Cleveland, Florida— the liberal coalition simply brushed itself off from legislative defeat and shifted the fight into the courtroom, claiming that the voucher program in question was unconstitutional and should be struck down. Because there are two court systems of relevance to each program (one state, one federal), and because each court system has a multi-tiered hierarchy of courts, many judges of varied political stripes have been able to weigh in on the matter over the last several years—and the results, not surprisingly, have been mixed. Some courts have favored the voucher side, some have favored the opponents.

I will not summarize these court battles here.[44] They are an integral part of the politics of vouchers. They can also be enormously disruptive, creating uncertainty for program participants and possibly even shutting down the programs entirely pending higher-level decisions by other courts. But the reality is that these are all short-term skirmishes that do not settle anything. In the end, it doesn't matter much what a lower court judge says, because lower-court decisions are always appealed. What really counts is how the U.S. Supreme Court decides the issue—and, as of early 2001, it has yet to speak. (I will return to this important issue in the concluding chapter.)

Public School Choice

Other forms of school choice, from alternative and magnet schools to inter- and intradistrict choice plans to charter schools, also mushroomed in importance during the 1990s. The political conditions were favorable for choice, and these forms aroused far less opposition from the liberal coalition than vouchers. The reasons are pretty obvious. They were confined to public schools alone, and thus did not drain off students and resources. They excluded religion. They preserved the ethos of public schooling and typically involved regulations to ensure fairness, racial balance, and equity. And, not least, they left the traditional system of top-down control, along with the power positions of established players, largely intact.[45]

Of all forms of public school choice, charter schools hold the greatest potential for dramatic change. These are public schools of choice that operate independently (or largely so) of the district and most regulations. In the years since Minnesota (in 1991) and California (in 1992) first passed charter legislation, charter schools have taken the nation by storm. Most states now have charter bills of their own, and, as of this writing, there are over 2,000 charter schools in operation serving a population of more than 500,000 students. If this growth continues (and it almost surely will), the charter movement stands to generate far more choice and competition than currently prevails, and this, along with their relative autonomy from state and district control, could genuinely transform public education.[46]

But there is no guarantee that charters will work out as enthusiasts hope. The teachers unions, in particular, are not in favor of reforms that shift power to parents, force the regular public schools to compete for parental support, upset established routines, and threaten collective bargaining, as potent charter reforms would actually do. If the unions "support" charters on occasion, they tend to do so as a fallback position that, by offering citizens a moderate alternative, may help to stave off vouchers.

This is one reason charters have proliferated: because even the opponents of choice sometimes have incentives to support them. Yet there is a price to pay. The unions and (some of) their allies may go on record supporting charters, but they use their power in the legislative process to impose severe restrictions on the programs, so that there will actually be little choice or competition in practice, and little disruption to the system. Among other things, they typically seek to limit the total number of charter schools (the original Minnesota plan authorized only eight charter schools for the entire state), to require that the schools be unionized, and to require that districts and teachers give their consent before a charter is granted. A few states—the more conservative ones, such as Arizona, with weaker unions—have escaped these heavy restrictions. But in most states, charter reforms have barely made a dent in the existing system. So far.

Voucher proponents typically support charters, as well as other versions of public school choice. But they don't think these reforms go far enough. In their view, charters and other plans for public school choice are inherently limited, because they fail to take full advantage of the size, diversity, and dynamism of the private sector, cannot really escape the politics and bureaucracy that go along with being public, and cannot in the end provide the kind of choice and competition—and thus the incentives for quality, responsiveness, and innovation—that a voucher system could.[47]

Looking to the Future: The Battle over Public Opinion

With the dawning of the twenty-first century, the voucher movement could be on the verge of transforming American education. It has already achieved important victories, and the trajectory suggests that there will be more to come in the near future. But success is hardly assured. The opposition is still far more powerful overall, is dedicated to stopping vouchers in their tracks, and has been marshaling resources for a war it fully intends to win—and must, if it is to survive.

It is no accident that the two key actors within the opposing coalition, the National Education Association and the American Federation of Teachers, have been moving toward a merger of their organizations. This is a radical move in response to dire circumstances. They feel they need a unified front to win the voucher war and, more generally, to defend the public school system from what they see as growing threats from the outside.

The elite-level debate over vouchers is now an integral part of American politics. Vouchers are debated by presidential candidates. They are debated by members of Congress. They are struggled over by judges in widely publicized court cases. And they are the subject of heated battles that flare up sporadically but relentlessly in districts, cities, and states all around the country. As time goes on, moreover, there is far greater substance to the debate. For there are now real voucher programs in which real children and real schools have been participating, and there is a small but growing body of evidence on what the impacts of vouchers actually are in practice.[48] As the evidence has begun to trickle in, it has been enormously controversial, with scholars arguing vehemently about what the data properly mean and combatants using the findings to gird their own arguments for and against. Every new development seems to heighten the drama and bring salience to the debate.

As in the past, what happens to vouchers from here on out will be determined through the democratic political process. This process, however, is about to enter a new phase. Until now, it has largely been an elite-level struggle between coalitions of officeholders, unions, education organizations, prominent businesspeople, interest groups of various stripes, and grassroots activists. But as the movement gains in power, and as the issue moves to center stage in American politics, the scope of conflict is vastly increased—and this inevitably generates a brand of democratic politics in which public opinion will play an ever greater role. In this new phase, elites will continue to carry the fight, and their power will continue to determine whether vouchers get adopted and in what forms. But how much power each side can wield—and how much progress the voucher movement is able to make—will increasingly depend on what "the people" have to say.

What, then, do ordinary Americans think about vouchers? In the chapters that follow, we will try to learn something about that—and to determine, in the process, what public opinion can tell us about where the elite-level politics of vouchers is headed.

2 *Satisfaction with the Public Schools*

In 1983 *A Nation at Risk* warned of a performance crisis in America's public schools. Ever since, American education has been in a perpetual state of reform. Every president now aspires to be the "education president," every governor the "education governor."

Whether the schools are actually any better for all this is a matter of debate. Most experts agree that, while there has been modest progress in student achievement, hopes for significant improvement have gone unmet, and much remains to be done if even the most reasonable goals are to be achieved.[1] To be sure, not everyone is so gloomy. Indeed, in recent years there has been a backlash by data-wielding defenders of the public schools, who claim that public performance is—and has long been—much better than critics claim.[2] True or not, however, this view has yet to win many adherents. Among elites generally, whether liberal or conservative, disappointment remains the dominant mood, and it continues to feed the reformist fire.

The voucher movement clearly benefits from this kind of environment. From Milton Friedman on, its leaders have argued that the public system is not doing the job, and the great windfall of the reformist era is that so many influential elites tend to agree. But a windfall is no guarantee of victory, and the opponents of vouchers have tried to turn the performance issue to their own advantage as much as possible. They have essentially responded by playing a mixed strategy. On the one hand, they often argue (pointing to the aforementioned data) that the schools are actually doing rather well and are unfairly maligned. On the other hand, they often agree that the schools are in trouble and need to be improved—and use this to argue for more resources and greater political support for the existing system.

As the battle over vouchers shifts to the realm of public opinion, the success of the movement will turn on what ordinary Americans think about these matters, and thus on whether they accept the premise of most of our nation's elites: that the schools are not performing well. The prospects for the voucher movement are brightest, obviously, if there is widespread dissatisfaction. If so, half the battle is already won and supporters can focus on convincing people that vouchers are an appropriate solution. But if Americans are happy with their schools, the political prognosis is very different.

In this chapter, we begin our study of public opinion on vouchers by exploring this most fundamental of issues. How satisfied are Americans with the performance of their public schools?

General Evaluations of Performance

Opinion on public education has been studied annually since the late 1960s through polls conducted by the Gallup organization. The sponsor of these polls is Phi Delta Kappa (PDK), a mainstream association of educators whose widely read journal, the *Phi Delta Kappan*, publishes the survey results every fall. This is the most comprehensive set of public opinion data currently available on education.

The PDK survey has regularly asked its respondents to evaluate the performance of the public schools by giving them a grade of A, B, C, D, or F. The results over the years provide strong, consistent evidence that the American public looks more favorably on the public school system than one might expect given the hypercritical perspective so widely shared by elites. In 1984, for instance, in the midst of the critical fervor caused by *A Nation at Risk*, 42 percent of the public gave their community's schools a rating of A or B.[3] In 1990 the corresponding figure was 41 percent.[4] And in 2000 it was 47 percent.[5] The full time-series suggests that satisfaction is a bit higher now than it was during the 1980s, which in turn suggests that the reformist era may be having some positive effect, either on actual performance or on popular perceptions of it.

It is important to recognize, then, that the standard impression one gets from the media and many elites—that the American people are highly dissatisfied with the public schools—is misleading. Clearly, many people are fairly happy with what they are getting. On the other hand, it is also important not to make too much of this and infer that the public as a whole is highly satisfied, for there is ample evidence that satisfaction varies quite a bit and is rather modest overall.

Consider the 2000 figures.[6] It is true that 47 percent of the public gave the schools an A or a B. But only 11 percent actually gave them an A. And more significantly, an ominous 46 percent gave them a C, D, or F—which is hardly good news, and suggests a substantial block of people who range from underwhelmed to totally dissatisfied. When these figures are broken down, the vast majority of the American public, fully 71 percent, is in the middle somewhere, giving the schools either a B or a C, and this single statistic probably sums it up better than any other. Judging from the PDK data, most Americans think the schools are doing a "passable" job—with much room for improvement.

Two important patterns also emerge from these data. The first is that public school parents are consistently more satisfied with the schools than nonparents are. (By "nonparents," I am referring here—and will, throughout this book—to people who don't currently have children in school, whether or not they are actually parents.) In 2000, for instance, 56 percent of public parents gave their local schools an A or B, compared to 44 percent of nonparents. The second is that people express higher levels of satisfaction the closer the schools are to their own lives. As I just noted, 56 percent of public parents gave their local schools an A or B in 2000, but this figure jumps to 70 percent when these same parents are asked to rate the specific school their oldest child attends. And it falls to a dismal 22 percent when they are asked to evaluate the quality of the nation's schools as a whole. The same pattern applies for nonparents as well, with the interesting corollary that, when evaluating the nation's schools rather than the local schools, the satisfaction gap between parents and nonparents disappears, and both emerge as extremely critical.

The PDK researchers have argued that these patterns have a common explanation.[7] A key difference between parents and nonparents, they say, is that parents have direct experience with the local public schools, while nonparents are much more removed and rely more heavily for information on the media, whose accounts have tended to be quite negative. At the local level, this should make nonparents more critical of the schools than parents are. Which is consistently the case. When assessing the nation's school system as a whole, on the other hand, both parents and nonparents are likely to be quite uninformed and heavily reliant on the media. This should lead both to see the national schools more negatively than the local schools, and to be about equally negative. Which, again, is just what happens.

There are really two prongs to the PDK argument. One is a claim about the negative role of the media: much of the media coverage is disparaging in tone, so the more reliant people are on the media, the more negative their views of the schools. The second is a claim about the positive role of knowledge: the more people actually know about the public schools, the more satisfied they are with them. In the researchers' words, "familiarity with the public schools breeds respect for them."[8] For defenders of the public schools, these two claims fit together nicely and suggest that the public schools are getting a bad rap. The bottom line is a provocative asymmetry: criticism of the schools is rooted in lack of information and media biases, while support for the schools is rooted in objectivity and facts.

This argument can easily be overstated, but there is a measure of validity to it. The media *does* emphasize the negative, and almost surely influences many people to see the national and state school systems more negatively than they otherwise would. And while the "familiarity breeds respect" notion is a bit glib and one-sided—the differences between parents and nonparents are not large enough to justify this kind of cheerleading—it does appear that personal knowledge leads (on average) to more positive views of the schools, a point that bodes well for the public system, and legitimately so.

This PDK argument is worth keeping in mind. But we can't really test its validity here, because our survey doesn't contain items that measure exposure to the media or factual knowledge about the schools. Be this as it may, the PDK findings and the issues they raise provide a useful introduction to the analysis that follows.

New Data: How Satisfied Are Americans with Their Schools?

Now let's turn to our own data, beginning with the most general of performance issues: how satisfied are the American people with the public schools? This is not as straightforward as it might seem, because there are many ways of thinking and asking about school performance. What people have to say about the schools could vary considerably depending on what aspects are touched upon. This is typical of the problems involved in measuring any concept: all survey questions are imperfect measures, capturing only part of what we want to know. Because of this, it is helpful to measure performance (and other concepts) in several different ways, and then to use these multiple indicators in combination to take advantage of the greater information they provide.

The responses to four of our survey's performance measures are set out in table 2-1. For the most part, the simple aggregate findings displayed

Table 2-1. *Overall Satisfaction with Public School Performance*
Percent, unless otherwise indicated[a]

Survey item	Nation	Non-parents	Public school parents
"Which of the following best describes how you feel about the schools in your district?"			
Doing well	34	31	45
Need minor changes	31	30	32
Need major changes	26	27	20
Don't know	9	11	2
"Which of the following best describes how you feel about the schools in your state as a whole?"			
Doing well	21	20	24
Need minor changes	33	31	37
Need major changes	35	36	28
Don't know	11	12	10
"If the very best schools in your state were given a score of 10 on a scale of 1 to 10, and the worst were given a score of 1, what score would you give your local schools?"			
1–4	13	13	10
5	11	11	10
6	11	12	8
7	19	19	21
8	23	22	28
9–10	16	15	20
Don't know	7	9	4
"In our community, we are very proud of our public schools."			
Strongly agree	47	46	52
Weakly agree	27	28	25
Weakly disagree	12	12	10
Strongly disagree	10	10	10
Don't know	4	5	3
N[b]	(4,700)	(1,617)	(2,553)

a. Percentages are based on weighted data. They may not sum to 100 due to rounding.
b. N is the unweighted number of respondents.

here tend to reinforce what the PDK polls have been showing for some time, both in terms of public satisfaction and in terms of the basic patterns. If there is a difference, it is that the public actually appears somewhat more positive about the schools than the PDK figures suggest, at least in these very general assessments (more on this later).

The first item asks respondents whether their local schools are "doing well," "need minor changes," or "need major changes." The public is fairly evenly split across these categories, but the largest portion, 34 percent, say the schools are doing well, and the smallest portion, 26 percent, call for major changes. There is clearly a desire for improvement here, with a large majority supporting some kind of reform. And it is important not to dismiss the fact that fully one-fourth of the American public thinks the local schools need a major overhaul, which is indicative of real dissatisfaction. Nonetheless, the larger picture is a reasonably positive one, suggesting modest but widespread support for the existing system. And the picture for public parents is more positive still. As in the PDK polls, they are more satisfied with the local public schools than nonparents are. Fully 45 percent of them say their schools are doing well, compared to 31 percent of nonparents.

A second measure is identically worded, but asks respondents to evaluate their state school systems as a whole. Now that their focus has shifted up a level, from local to state, they become more critical. The most common response, given by 35 percent of the general public, is that the state schools are in need of major changes, while only 21 percent say the schools are doing well. And although parents are somewhat more supportive than nonparents, the gap between them is much smaller here than it was for the local schools. All of this, once again, is consistent with the PDK findings. And although it does not point to extraordinary discontent with the state system, it does suggest that the hypercritical environment, framed by the media and elites, has its greatest impact on people the more remote the system is from their own experience.

The other two performance measures bring the focus back to the local schools—which, it seems, ought to be the prime concern in an analysis of vouchers. When parents are thinking about whether they want to go private, it is the quality of the local public schools, not of the state or national school systems, that is most relevant to their decisions. And when people think about whether vouchers would make good public policy, it is again the local schools that are presumably most relevant, because this is the system they know and care most about, and the best indicator of their own needs and those of their community for educational reform. "All politics is local," as the saying goes, and there is no reason to think vouchers are any different.

The two remaining measures of local performance are very different from the first, and from one another. One item asks, "If the very best schools in your state were given a score of 10 on a scale of 1 to 10, and the worst were given a score of 1, what score would you give your local schools?" The advantage of this approach is that respondents are asked to quantify the performance of their schools.

The resulting scores are weighted toward the high end of the scale, with only 13 percent giving their local schools a score of less than 5. The distribution shows that most people believe their local schools are better than the typical school statewide. Objectively speaking, of course, there is something perverse about this. Unlike in Lake Wobegon, where everyone is above average, this can't be true for the great majority of schools, as people claim. Assuming a normal distribution of school quality, and assuming that people accurately evaluate their own schools relative to schools statewide, we should have gotten responses that are normally distributed about the midpoint (5.5) on the scale.

Part of the reason for our results, most likely, is that negative media effects taint people's opinions of the more remote state school system. In view of this, the absolute level of support implied by this method should not be exaggerated. It appears high because it is judged relative to the less admired state school system—and even so, only 16 percent of people are enthusiastic enough to give scores of 9 or 10. Nonetheless, it is difficult to avoid the conclusion that the vast majority of Americans are at least moderately positive about how their local schools are performing. And this is especially true for public parents, who again are more positive than nonparents.

The third measure of performance gets at public evaluations from an altogether different angle. This item does not ask people to say how well the schools are doing, nor does it even suggest that the issue is performance. It simply asks whether they agree or disagree with the following statement: "In our community, we are very proud of our public schools." Although pride may stem from various sources, people are more likely to be proud of good schools than bad ones, and their responses should tell us something about how they evaluate performance. The difference is that this measure encourages people to reflect not only on their own evaluations, but also on the way others in the community feel as well.

Responses to this measure reveal a strikingly high level of support for the public schools. Almost half the general public, 47 percent, strongly agree that their communities are "very proud" of the local schools, with another 27 percent indicating weaker agreement. Only 22 percent disagree. Parents and nonparents both indicate a great deal of pride in their schools—but once again, parents are the more positive group.

The Emphasis on Academics

When people give these summary evaluations of the schools, what are they really thinking about? Among reformers, including voucher advocates, there is a heavy emphasis on academics. But there is also great concern about other aspects of schooling more directly tied to what many see as troubling declines in American culture. There are strident complaints, for instance, about lack of discipline, about violence and other threats to safety, about the inability or unwillingness to teach moral values, and about the impersonal, bureaucratic treatment of students and the absence of "community." These sorts of issues can have a direct bearing on academic performance, of course. But they also reflect a constellation of social concerns that have grown in political importance during recent decades—as witnessed by the resurgence of conservatism, religious fundamentalism, and the movement for "family values." These are constituencies commonly associated with the voucher movement.

The question is: do ordinary Americans seem responsive to these sorts of cultural concerns when they evaluate their schools, or are they mostly thinking about academic performance? The survey cannot offer definitive answers, but the evidence it provides is helpful. Respondents were asked not only to give general appraisals of their local schools, but also to evaluate them (on a scale from 1 to 10) with respect to several specific criteria: academics, safety, discipline, moral values, and individual attention to students. Results are displayed in table 2-2.

Interestingly, to the extent people express dissatisfaction with specific aspects of the schools, they are much *less* likely to be dissatisfied with academics than with the other dimensions. Only 13 percent of the public give the schools low ratings (scores of less than 5) for poor academic performance, but nearly 30 percent give them low ratings for their failure to teach moral values and keep discipline. When people see the schools as having problems, then, they seem to emphasize the kinds of social concerns that gained so much attention over the last few decades and have been particularly important with a segment of the voucher movement.

But how do these concerns translate into overall assessments of the schools? While people are especially critical of the schools on social grounds, as opposed to academic grounds, it doesn't follow that they see these factors as the key components of school quality. A parent may think the schools do a bad job of teaching moral values and at the same time believe that the schools' central task is to provide a good academic education. What appears to be a problem may in fact have little to do with a

Table 2-2. *Satisfaction with Specific Aspects of the Public Schools*
Percent, unless otherwise indicated[a]

Survey item	Nation	Non-parents	Public school parents
"Using a 10-point scale, where 10 is truly outstanding and 1 is very poor, tell me how you think your local public schools are performing on the following dimensions"			
Academic quality			
1–4	13	12	11
5	14	15	11
6	11	11	10
7	19	20	19
8	21	20	25
9–10	15	13	21
Don't know	7	8	2
Safety			
1–4	17	16	13
5	11	11	12
6	9	9	8
7	13	13	12
8	20	19	23
9–10	24	22	30
Don't know	7	9	2
Discipline			
1–4	28	30	30
5	16	17	13
6	9	9	9
7	13	13	14
8	13	12	18
9–10	14	11	22
Don't know	7	8	3
Teaching moral values			
1–4	29	31	21
5	15	16	14
6	10	9	11
7	12	11	14
8	14	13	16
9–10	11	8	19
Don't know	10	12	6
Providing individual attention to students			
1–4	25	25	23
5	16	16	15
6	10	10	9
7	13	12	15
8	14	14	17
9–10	12	10	9
Don't know	10	13	3
N[b]	(4,700)	(1,617)	(2,553)

a. Percentages are based on weighted data. They may not sum to 100 due to rounding.
b. N is the unweighted number of respondents.

Table 2-3. The Academic Basis of Performance Evaluations[a]

Variable	Nation		Nonparents		Public school parents		Public school parents (academic)		Public school parents (values)	
	Coefficient	[Impact]	Coefficient	[Impact]	Coefficient	[Impact]	Coefficient	[Impact]	Coefficient	[Impact]
Academic quality	.15***	[.40]	.16***	[.41]	.14***	[.37]	.16***	[.40]	.13***	[.35]
Safety	.03***	[.10]	.04***	[.13]	.02**	[.07]	.04***	[.13]	.02	[.06]
Discipline	.02**	[.07]	.02*	[.06]	.03***	[.11]	.04***	[.11]	.01	[.05]
Moral values	.02**	[.07]	.02**	[.08]	.01	[.03]	-.00	[-.01]	.04**	[.13]
Individual attention	.07***	[.22]	.06***	[.18]	.08***	[.27]	.08***	[.25]	.07***	[.24]
Constant	-1.90***		-1.96***		-1.81***		-1.98***		-1.67***	
N[b]	(2,065)		(1,239)		(1,570)		(834)		(553)	
Adjusted R²	.56		.56		.54		.58		.51	

* Significant at .1 level
** Significant at .05 level
*** Significant at .01 level

a. The dependent variable is an index of parents' satisfaction with public school performance that includes the first, third, and fourth items from table 2-1. Ordinary least squares regressions were estimated using weighted data. Coefficients are unstandardized regression coefficients. For each independent variable, the impact coefficient represents the estimated change in the dependent variable (measured in standard deviations) when the independent variable shifts by two standard deviations, holding all other variables constant.

b. N is the unweighted number of respondents.

respondent's *overall* level of satisfaction. It all depends on what weights are attached to the various dimensions of school performance.

We can estimate these weights by using simple regression, and modeling overall satisfaction as a function of the respondents' scores on the five dimensions they were asked about. Results are presented in table 2-3 for an analysis that takes as its dependent variable an index of satisfaction (combining into one variable the three measures of performance discussed in the previous section).[9] The table presents the resulting regression coefficients, which tell us how a one-unit increase on a particular dimension affects overall satisfaction with the local schools, holding all the other dimensions constant. The table also presents a set of "impact" coefficients, which convert these effects into standard deviation units. This approach is adopted here and throughout the book to provide a standard frame of reference for judging the size of effects. The impact coefficient tells us the effect on the dependent variable—the number of standard deviations it increases or decreases—when the independent variable in question shifts from a "low" value (one standard deviation below its mean) to a "high" value (one standard deviation above its mean).[10]

A look at the impact coefficients reveals that, when respondents offer summary assessments of how well their local schools are performing, *academic quality* is far and away the most important factor (of the five considered here) that enters into their thinking. The second most influential factor is *individualized attention*—which, of all the "nonacademic" criteria, is arguably the most immediately connected to student learning in people's minds. The criterion that is certainly the most social here, and the most clearly connected to the socially conservative wing of the voucher movement—the teaching of moral values—is at or near the *bottom* in its impact on overall evaluations. People complain about the lack of moral values in the schools, but it barely affects their overall evaluation of performance.

We can explore this a bit further. At one point in the survey, parents are asked, "If you had to pick, which would you say is more important in a school? High academic quality or emphasis on the right values?" A majority of public parents, 52 percent, choose academic quality, while 36 percent say that values are more important than academics. This in itself is an interesting result. It shows that most Americans give priority to academics, consistent with the notion that this is what they really care about. But it also shows that a remarkably large percentage think the teaching of values should be given greater weight than academics. This raises questions about how widespread the importance of academics really is. It also seems to signal a good deal of support for the social conservatism that has caused so much political trouble for the education mainstream.

Do values really matter to people in their overall assessment of the schools? The initial quantitative results tend to suggest they don't. But this analysis was carried out for broad populations, and perhaps it hides an intensity that is felt by a sizable minority. A way to get beneath the surface is to carry out separate analyses for the two types of public parents, those emphasizing academics and those emphasizing values, to see what actually accounts for their overall evaluations of the schools. The results are presented in the far columns of table 2-3. They show that for *both* sets of parents, academic quality is considerably more important than any other factor. While the impact coefficients show that the values parents do indeed put much more emphasis on the teaching of moral values than the academic parents do (the latter put no emphasis on it whatever, it appears), the values parents still assign much more weight to academics than to moral values. Indeed, even individualized attention turns out to be more important than moral values in explaining their overall evaluations.

An interesting conclusion emerges from all this. It appears not only that people are modestly satisfied with the public schools, but also that the aspects of schools they point to most often as major problems—moral values, discipline—are not given great weight in their overall assessments. They may complain about these things. And if given a choice, they may well choose schools with these criteria in mind. But the dominant factor in their minds when they offer general evaluations of the public schools is academic performance—and it is precisely with regard to academics that they are the most satisfied.

Another interesting conclusion emerges as well. In the voucher debate, opponents often argue that parents cannot be trusted with choice, because academics have little to do with the way they evaluate schools. Our own analysis does not take account of all the nonacademic factors—proximity, sports teams, friends—that opponents think corrupt parental judgment. But it does suggest, given the high weight consistently attached to it, that academic performance is probably the key criterion on which parents form their views. And the same conclusion applies for nonparents, who make up the bulk of the electorate and are thus crucial to the politics of vouchers. Despite the disparaging view one often gets from critics, then, the American public comes off as quite academically oriented. And this can only shape the way they respond to the concept of vouchers and to the political appeals of both sides.

The Seeds of Discontent

There is good news and bad news here for the voucher movement. The bad news is that, on the whole, Americans hold fairly positive views about their public schools and are clearly not raw material for a radical reform movement aimed at transforming the entire school system. The good news is that few people think the schools are doing a terrific job, most think there is considerable room for improvement, and a significant minority are truly dissatisfied—which means that the voucher movement still has a lot to work with here.

In this section, we will see that there is more good news here than meets the eye. Once we look beyond general measures of satisfaction to specific issues of relevance to the politics of vouchers, it appears the movement may have a broader constituency within the American public than the evidence so far implies.

Private Schools

To support vouchers, Americans needn't think their public schools are awful. What vouchers really offer is a choice: parents can choose to take their children out of public schools and place them in private schools if they think the private schools are better. So the essential question may not be whether people think the public schools are doing well on some absolute scale, but rather how they think the public schools *compare* to the alternatives.

Objectively, what do these alternatives look like? While critics tend to portray private schools as high-cost, college preparatory academies, the fact is that the vast majority of private schools are small, modestly funded, and affiliated with a religion. About 85 percent of the children in the current private sector attend religious schools of this sort, and more than half of these are enrolled in Catholic schools.[11] When people are asked to compare public and private schools, we cannot know exactly what private schools they are using for comparison. But they probably base their opinions on what they know, have heard, or have read about the schools that exist in the private sector—and the vast majority of these schools are religious. Indeed, a recent study by Public Agenda suggests that these are the schools most Americans think of when "private" schools are referred to.[12]

Our survey asks respondents to compare public and private schools (with the latter referred to as "private and parochial") on the same five performance criteria discussed above: academics, safety, discipline, moral

Table 2-4. *Comparisons of Public and Private School Performance*
Percent, unless otherwise indicated[a]

Survey item	Nation	Non-parents	Public school parents
"How do you think private and parochial schools usually compare to public schools on these same dimensions—better, worse, or about the same?"			
Academic quality			
Better	57	58	50
About the same	27	28	28
Worse	5	5	5
Don't Know	11	9	17
Safety			
Better	55	56	48
About the same	29	29	31
Worse	4	5	3
Don't know	12	10	18
Discipline			
Better	64	66	55
About the same	20	20	24
Worse	4	4	4
Don't know	11	10	17
Teaching moral values			
Better	63	64	55
About the same	21	21	24
Worse	4	5	4
Don't know	12	10	18
Providing individual attention to students			
Better	60	62	53
About the same	23	23	25
Worse	4	4	4
Don't know	12	11	18
Which type of school is better able to teach democratic values?			
Public	14	13	16
Equally able	52	53	53
Private	29	29	26
Don't know	5	6	6
N[b]	(4,700)	(1,617)	(2,553)

a. Percentages are based on weighted data. They may not sum to 100 due to rounding.
b. N is the unweighted number of respondents.

values, and individual attention.[13] The results are set out in table 2-4. By a wide margin, Americans clearly think the public schools—however satisfactory in absolute terms—do *not* measure up to the competition.

When comparing the two sectors on academic grounds, 57 percent of respondents view the private schools as superior, while only 5 percent think the public schools do a better job. (The rest either see the two sectors as about the same or say they don't know.) Even among public school parents, 50 percent see the private schools as better, while again just 5 percent give the nod to the public schools. For parents and nonparents alike, the perceived advantages of private sector education are even greater when other criteria, such as moral values or discipline, are the grounds for comparison.

Another measure puts the spotlight on a public-private comparison that would seem to give a distinct advantage to the public schools. The received wisdom among defenders of the public system is that its common-school ethos and democratic governance make it a far better setting for socializing the nation's children to the norms of democratic citizenship. They portray private schools as elitist and inherently unsuited to performing these crucial integrative functions for a democratic society. But do ordinary people see it this way? Do they think that a public school education is more conducive to democracy?

The survey asks the following question: "Most people believe that schools should teach children about tolerance, democracy, and social responsibility. Do you think that public schools are better able to teach these values, that private and parochial schools are better able to teach these values, or that they are equally able to teach these values?" The responses are indicated in table 2-4. What they show is that the conventional wisdom among the system's defenders is decidedly *not* shared by the American public. About half see no difference between public and private schools in their capacity for socializing children to democratic norms. Of those who think one sector does a better job than the other, private schools are actually favored over public schools by a 2-to-1 margin. This is true even of public parents, albeit by a somewhat smaller margin.[14]

Were we to pursue this issue in more depth, we would find some areas in which people think public schools outperform private schools. A 1995 survey carried out by Public Agenda, for instance, showed that Americans believe public schools do a better job of teaching kids how to deal with diversity and of teaching children with special needs (for example, those who are physically handicapped). It is noteworthy, however, that these are the only dimensions—out of thirteen that Public Agenda asked about—on which Americans saw public schools as superior. On the other eleven, which ranged from academics to class size to teaching, private schools were seen as better and by wide margins.[15]

Whatever positive views Americans may have of their public schools, then, they hold private schools in much higher esteem generally, and even see them as superior in functions often portrayed as inherently public. In this sense—a relative sense—Americans are not satisfied with their public schools. They think they have better options, and these options are precisely the ones the voucher movement makes available to them.

Social Equity

Much of the modern politics of vouchers is driven by concerns about social equity. Voucher advocates see vouchers as a powerful tool for bringing about better educational opportunities for poor and minority children. Opponents think vouchers will only make existing social inequities worse—but they do agree that poor and minority children are getting a substandard education. The conflict is over what to do about it.

As we have seen, most Americans appear to be much more favorably disposed toward the public schools than elites are. Do their positive views extend to issues of social equity? Or do they agree that the public education system is inequitable? If the latter, this would suggest that Americans are less satisfied than the broader measures seem to imply, and that equity concerns have the potential for generating support for vouchers among the broader public.

The survey offers three useful measures of how people see these equity issues. The first is simple but starkly revealing. It asks respondents to agree or disagree with the following statement: "Families with low incomes often have little choice but to send their children to schools that are not very good." Almost two-thirds of Americans agree with this statement, 41 percent of them strongly (see table 2-5). These are large numbers, implying that ordinary people seem to be in substantial agreement with elites on the failure of public schools to provide equal educations to children regardless of social class.

Two indirect measures are derived from a set of items asking respondents to indicate, on a scale of 1 to 10, the quality of education they think different groups of children in their state receive in the public schools. The groups are defined by reference to income (upper, middle, lower) and race (white, black, Hispanic). A measure of race-based equity can be derived by subtracting the respondent's score for blacks from the score given to whites. If the remainder is positive—that is, if whites are believed to receive a better education than blacks—then the respondent is pointing (indirectly) to a race-based inequity. A measure of class-based equity can be derived analogously, by comparing the scores for lower-class children to those for middle-class children.

Table 2-5. *Perceptions of Inequality*
Percent, unless otherwise indicated[a]

Survey item	Nation	Non-parents	Public school parents	Whites	Blacks	Hispanics
"Families with low incomes often have little choice but to send their children to schools that are not very good"						
Strongly agree	41	40	43	39	52	43
Weakly agree	23	24	21	25	16	19
Weakly disagree	16	17	15	17	10	18
Strongly disagree	16	15	17	15	19	17
Don't know	4	4	4	4	3	2
Assessment of class-based equity in public education						
Equitable	40	38	44	41	38	34
Inequitable	50	51	47	48	56	55
Don't know	10	11	8	11	11	11
Assessment of race-based equity in public education						
Equitable	50	49	53	53	46	37
Inequitable	34	35	32	31	43	46
Don't know	16	17	14	17	11	17
N[b]	(4,700)	(1,617)	(2,553)	(3,289)	(763)	(408)

a. Percentages are based on weighted data. They may not sum to 100 due to rounding.
b. N is the unweighted number of respondents.

The results for class-based inequity are not quite as strong as those for the more direct measure, perhaps because people are not as comfortable giving quantitative scores. But the findings reported in table 2-5 tend in the same direction, with 50 percent of respondents indicating (by their relative scores) that the school system gives a better education to middle-income kids than to lower-income kids, and 40 percent seeing no problem in this regard. Taken together, then, the two measures suggest that a belief in class-based inequity is indeed widespread.

The race issue is another matter. A notably smaller fraction, 34 percent, believe that blacks are provided with lower-quality public schools than whites. This is still a pretty big number given the seriousness of the charge. But it is revealing that Americans are more inclined to think of educational inequities in terms of class than race.

A closer look at these responses helps to clarify matters a bit. As table 2-5 shows, minorities are more likely than whites to see the system as inequitable, whether the issue is class or race. It is the preponderance of whites in the population that keeps the figures on inequity from being higher than they already are. This also helps explain why, in the aggregate, class inequities are more salient than racial inequities: when whites do see inequities, they are much more likely to perceive class differences than racial differences.

It is important to add, however, that the salience of class over race is not exclusively associated with whites. In fact, it applies to a lesser degree for blacks and Hispanics too: all three groups are more inclined to see inequities in terms of class than race. Indeed, while a large majority of blacks think that the schools are inequitable on class grounds, a small majority actually think they are *not* inequitable on racial grounds—quite the opposite of what many observers might predict. Overall, then, it appears that class is America's dominant concern when it comes to issues of educational equity. Not race.

Important as this is, the more general point deserves emphasis: large numbers of Americans believe that our public education system does not treat children of different social groups equally. Minorities are especially likely to feel this way, which is hardly surprising, as they are on the receiving end of both racial and class inequities and can be expected to be more sensitive to them than whites. But a majority of whites agree that the system fails to treat kids equally on one or both of these grounds. Given that Americans believe deeply in equality, the public's apparent satisfaction with the schools needs to be interpreted with these equity concerns in mind. Under the surface, there is dissatisfaction with the current state of educational equity—and this stands to have a big impact on the politics of vouchers.

In principle, equity concerns could work to the benefit of either side. People who care about equity might be inclined to sympathize with the thrust of the present-day voucher movement and see vouchers as a means of empowering the disadvantaged. Or they might agree with critics that vouchers would only make existing inequities worse. In later chapters, we will see what the survey evidence says about this. But for now, one thing is certain: the movement's emphasis on equity makes this one of the key battlegrounds—and there appears to be a receptive audience out there.

Diversity (Racial Balance)

Traditionally, the ideology of American public education has extolled the virtues of common schooling, which aims to bring children from different social groups together into the same schools for common training and the building of a common culture. Another bedrock principle is that children should be provided with a good school close to home—a neighborhood school—that is easy to get to, invites participation by parents, and is based on personal relationships among people who interact with one another frequently.

There is tension between these two traditions. In the distant past, this tension was dealt with (in effect) by making trade-offs that worked against common schooling, and thus against diversity. Children attended neighborhood schools, but residential patterns, income differentials, and official laws and practices produced widespread segregation. Since *Brown v. Board of Education*, there has been slow, uneven progress in moving toward the common school ideal, as courts, legislatures, and the education community have sought to promote diversity. But this has come at the expense, inevitably, of the neighborhood school. The most visible symbol of this tension is mandatory busing. Children are bused away from their neighborhoods to schools in distant communities, so that the mix of students in the schools will better approximate their mix in the local population.

These are volatile issues, and they could clearly affect how satisfied people are with the public schools. One scenario, put forward by the critics of vouchers, goes as follows. People who believe in diversity will generally support the public system and its efforts to promote racial balance. People who want to avoid diversity (because they are racists, perhaps), or who simply put low value on diversity (because they care more about other things, such as neighborhood schools), will tend to be dissatisfied with the public schools and interested in leaving for the private sector. According to this scenario, vouchers are a way for anti-diversity whites to avoid minorities by going private.

Voucher advocates portray the issue very differently. They argue that the current system remains highly segregated, and that it is the supporters of diversity—especially minorities—who are likely to be frustrated and dissatisfied. They will be the ones who want vouchers, as a way of escaping segregated, low-performing schools. Advocates recognize that people who oppose diversity, including avowed racists, may want vouchers too. But they believe (or at least want to believe) that this is not a serious problem these days, and that the main effect of expanded choice is to empower the disadvantaged.

We cannot determine whether people are racists or not. But we can get a sense of where they stand on diversity, and we can see how this influences their satisfaction with the public schools, their desire to go private,

Table 2-6. *Attitudes toward Diversity*
Percent, unless otherwise indicated[a]

Survey item	Nation	Non-parents	Public school parents	Whites	Blacks	Hispanics
"In some cities, children are bused to schools outside their neighborhoods in order to promote racial balance. Do you support or oppose such a policy?"						
Support	35	35	37	31	54	49
Oppose	55	56	53	60	36	41
Don't know	10	9	11	9	10	10
"Which of these statements is closer to your point of view?"						
Schools should promote common culture	39	39	40	35	57	54
Children should attend schools near their homes	52	52	52	57	32	39
Don't know	9	9	8	8	11	7
N[b]	(4,700)	(1,617)	(2,553)	(3,289)	(763)	(408)
"If you had to choose between these two schools, which would you pick for your own child?"						
Good, diverse school	...	...	67	62	74	76
Outstanding, homogenous school			26	29	22	19
Don't know			7	9	4	5
N[b]			(2,553)	(1,998)	(620)	(331)

a. Percentages are based on weighted data. They may not sum to 100 due to rounding.
b. N is the unweighted number of respondents.

and their willingness to support vouchers. Our survey provides a few measures that are helpful in this regard.

One has to do with school busing. Here, there should be no surprises about where most Americans stand. Other surveys have found that people are generally opposed to busing, often by huge margins. Our survey asked respondents the following question: "In some cities, children are bused to schools outside their neighborhoods in order to promote racial balance. Do you support or oppose such a policy?" We too find that most people, 55 percent, are opposed to busing, with 35 percent in support and 10 percent undecided (see table 2-6). If there is any surprise, it is that the level of opposition measured here is not higher than it is. Perhaps it is due to the wording of the question. Whatever the case, it is clear that busing—a common, legally enforced practice for decades—is not the majority sentiment. It is a basis for dissatisfaction.

A second item measures attitudes toward diversity by highlighting the tension between common schooling and neighborhood schools. Here is the question: "Which of these statements is closer to your point of view? (a) Public schools are an important means of building a common culture, so more effort should be made to put children of different backgrounds into the same schools, or (b) It is best for children to attend public schools near their homes and families, even if this means children of different backgrounds may not get to attend school together." In this direct measure of competing values, 52 percent choose neighborhood schools and 39 percent put the emphasis on common schooling—which suggests, again, that most people dissent from the modern thrust of education policy.

It is only reasonable to suspect that whites and minorities will come down very differently on these diversity-related issues. As table 2-6 shows, most African-Americans and Hispanics think common schooling is more important than preserving the tradition of neighborhood schools. And they tend to support busing. They largely agree, therefore, with the education system's basic responses to problems of diversity during the modern era. It is whites who are in marked disagreement with the system. The proportion of whites supporting neighborhood schools and opposing busing is in each case almost 60 percent.

It would be wrong, however, to characterize the position of whites as a simple reflection of racism. While racism has surely not been eliminated in American society, other studies have shown that whites are actually supportive of diversity (if not as strongly as minorities), and that what appears to be racism is often due to the relevance of other, quite legitimate values[16]—in this case, the value of neighborhood schools. Our own survey provides some additional information on this score. It comes from an item that factors out the neighborhood school issue and asks parents to choose between diversity and academic excellence. Here is the question: "If you had to choose between these two schools, which would you pick for your own child: (a) A good academic school whose children happen to come from many races and ethnic groups, or (b) An outstanding academic school whose children happen to come from the same racial or ethnic background as your child?"

I suspect that many well-educated, politically liberal people (most of my academic colleagues, in other words) would have a hard time choosing between the two, and that a good portion would ultimately opt for the better school, despite its homogeneous student body, because a high-quality education is so important to them. But this is not how most public parents approach the issue. Whatever weight they attach to academic excellence, the fact is that fully two-thirds of them choose the socially diverse school of lesser academic quality, and only 26 percent opt for the academically excellent, socially homogeneous school. White parents are somewhat less likely than minority parents to choose the socially diverse alternative (see table 2-6), but they still prefer diversity over academic excellence in this example by a 2-to-1 margin.

While there is surely some degree of racism among whites (and minorities, for that matter), the most reasonable conclusion is that both whites and minorities support diversity but that whites tend to give it lower priority relative to other values. They are less willing to make trade-offs. As a result, they are more likely to oppose school policies—such as mandatory busing—that achieve diversity through sacrifices they think are not worth the price.

In any event, diversity is a clear basis for dissatisfaction with the current system. On the one hand, the people who are most supportive of diversity—minorities—have every reason to be dissatisfied, because their schools remain highly segregated. On the other hand, most Americans—whites—object to the way the education system has tried to remedy the situation, through busing at the expense of neighborhood schools. Either source of dissatisfaction, or both, could influence people to see private schools as attractive options and to support vouchers. Voucher advocates think that the diversity issue works to their advantage on both scores. Voucher opponents think that anti-diversity whites are the ones most likely to support vouchers, but that people who support diversity will join them in defending the public schools.

Our survey evidence will help to sort things out and determine who (if anyone) is right about how racial issues come into play. For now, however, it is clear that race is an important basis for dissatisfaction with the educational status quo, and could well have a profound influence on the politics of vouchers.

Religion

The public education system has been struggling with religion for a long time. In the late 1800s and early 1900s, religion was an integral part of the curriculum and climate of the public schools. Religion, however, meant Protestantism, and members of other religions were forced to attend public schools infused with Protestant teachings or to seek out alternatives in the private sector—which goes a long way toward explaining the emergence of the Catholic school system. With time, religion fell out of official favor in the public sector. The courts moved toward the view that religion in the public schools violates the constitutional separation of church and state, even when it does not embrace Protestantism or any other sect and even when it is voluntary. The schools have complied. Today, the firm consensus among mainstream education leaders is that religion is entirely improper in public education. And Democratic officeholders are generally quick to back them up.[17]

What do ordinary Americans think about the proper role of religion in the public schools? Do they support the official position against religion that has so shaped public policy in modern times? The survey does not explore this issue in any depth, but it appears the answer is an emphatic no. The most general measure comes from a simple agree-disagree item: "Prayer should be allowed in the public schools if it is voluntary." As table 2-7 indicates, the public believes overwhelmingly in the legitimacy of voluntary prayer in the schools—with 85 percent agreeing, 67 percent strongly. Public parents, who have "chosen" the nonreligious option of public schooling, feel exactly the same. This is about as supportive as people get on any policy issue. Later on in the survey, in the section on vouchers, respondents are asked whether parents should be allowed to use their vouchers in religious schools, or be restricted to using them only in nonreligious schools. The results for this item are discussed in chapter 8, but here it suffices to say that they point in the same direction—underlining the public's apparently strong belief that religion should be included (on a voluntary basis) in education.

This is another key issue, then, on which a sizable portion of the American public appears dissatisfied with the current public school system. And at the elite level, of course, it is also an issue that has been at the heart of the voucher movement from the beginning, and the source of intense political fireworks. Whether religion is salient enough among ordinary people to give the movement a major political boost is not guaranteed. That depends on how it translates into the desire to go private, and into support for vouchers. But it seems clear that, on the religion issue, the arguments of voucher advocates are likely to resonate with the public.

Parent Influence

The public schools are governed by a complicated array of democratic authorities—among them state and local school boards, state and local

Table 2-7. *Attitudes toward School Prayer, Parent Influence, School Size, and Markets*
Percent, unless otherwise indicated[a]

Survey item	Nation	Non-parents	Public school parents
Voluntary prayer should be allowed in public schools			
Strongly agree	67	67	68
Weakly agree	18	18	18
Weakly disagree	5	5	5
Strongly disagree	7	7	7
Don't know	3	3	2
Appropriate amount of parent influence			
Trust teachers and administrators	27	31	19
More parental influence	66	62	73
Don't know	7	7	7
Preferred school size			
Large better	18	19	12
Small better	74	74	81
Don't know	8	8	7
To give incentives, need to reward and punish schools			
Strongly agree	25	25	24
Weakly agree	20	21	19
Weakly disagree	19	18	20
Strongly disagree	29	29	31
Don't know	7	8	6
Competition and choice would make schools more productive			
Strongly agree	38	37	40
Weakly agree	31	33	28
Weakly disagree	11	11	12
Strongly disagree	10	10	11
Don't know	9	9	9
N[b]	(4,700)	(1,617)	(2,553)

a. Percentages are based on weighted data. They may not sum to 100 due to rounding.
b. N is the unweighted number of respondents.

superintendents, legislatures, governors, state and local bureaucracies, state and local courts, and the three branches of national government—all of which are responsive to large and diverse political constituencies. The parents of any given school are but a tiny part of this and have no special claim to influence.

Within the education community, moreover, there is no great desire to enhance parent influence over important education policies and practices. Educators want parents to "participate" in their children's educations by helping out with homework and otherwise supporting the schools' efforts. But there is a strong belief that education is properly conceived and carried out by those who know best. At the higher levels, this means public officials and education professionals. At the school level, it means administrators and teachers.[18]

What do Americans think about the role that parents should play in public education? The survey explores this issue by asking respondents to choose between the following alternatives: "(a) Parents should have more influence over the schools than they do now, or (b) Parents should trust the judgment of administrators and teachers, because they know more about education than parents do." Americans overwhelmingly believe that parents ought to have more influence than they currently do (see table 2-7). Sixty-six percent of the general public feel this way, and the figure rises to 73 percent for public parents, who are the ones most directly affected.

The implications for the politics of vouchers are pretty obvious. The voucher movement has long argued that the current system gives parents too little influence and that vouchers are a way to put more power in parents' hands. The evidence suggests that many Americans are likely to be receptive to this kind of appeal.

School Size

Public schools are much bigger now than they were many decades ago, the result of a historical trend toward the consolidation of schools and school districts into larger units. School officials did this in order to economize on costs and enhance administrative management, not to please parents and students. This is not to say that big schools have no academic or social advantages, for they offer a greater variety of classes, services, and extracurricular activities from which students might benefit. Some people prefer them. But large schools also tend to be bureaucratic and impersonal, and to lack some of the key elements—individual attention, informal cooperation, a shared mission, a sense of community and belonging—that research has consistently associated with effective schooling. Small schools are better able to provide these things. And there is now rather broad agreement, within both the research and the education communities, that small schools are desirable. Be that as it may, however, consolidation is a reality, and the system remains built around schools that are larger than many experts think is best.[19]

In the voucher debate, the issue of school size comes up quite a bit. Voucher supporters argue the private sector is filled with small schools and that vouchers would give parents access to them. Voucher opponents are essentially in a bind on this issue, because they often agree that schools ought to be smaller. Their recourse is to argue that, with enough community support, public systems can move in this direction over time (although it is difficult to see how, in most communities, the current generation of kids has any hope of benefiting from it).

How do ordinary Americans come down on this issue of school size? The survey asks respondents to choose from the following two statements: "(a) Large schools are better, because they provide students with more variety, resources, and activities, or (b) Small schools are better, because they provide students with more attention and a greater sense of belonging." As the American public sees it, there is no contest between the two. Seventy-four percent prefer small schools, only 18 percent large schools.

Here is another basic issue, then, that is quite central to the struggle over vouchers, and on which the American public appears to be dissatisfied with the current state of affairs in public education. People who see the value of smaller schools may well see the attraction of private schools—and of vouchers.

Markets

When voucher advocates raise the kinds of issues we've been discussing here, they don't see them as wholly independent of one another and don't present them that way. There is a common thread running through many of the charges they bring, because their thinking tends to be rooted in an underlying rationale: the theory of markets. Specifics aside, they believe that top-down control of schools by government is inherently unproductive, and that choice and competition—by transforming the incentives and opportunities at the heart of the system—will generate superior outcomes for schools, parents, the disadvantaged, and society as a whole.

Inevitably, markets are just as fundamental to the arguments of voucher opponents, whose intellectual case is built around the theme that markets will not work well, at least for schools. They claim that choice and competition will actually hurt the public schools rather than improve them, that markets will exacerbate social inequities—and that a system of governmental control, with enough support from the public, is a far better solution.

Ordinary Americans are not economists, and most of them probably have little understanding of how markets work (or don't work). Still, choice and competition are woven into the fabric of American culture. People are familiar with them as ideas and as everyday realities. They can be expected, then, to have opinions on whether choice and competition are desirable, and whether it seems wise to extend them to public education. The views they express may not be well developed or deeply held. But they do give us a sense for the general orientations that people bring to the voucher issue.

The survey does not explore this in much detail, but it does contain two items that are helpful. The first asks respondents to agree or disagree with the following statement: "Competition and consumer choice make business firms more effective and cost-conscious, and they would help do the same for schools." The results, displayed in table 2-7, suggest that Americans are quite supportive of the idea that choice and competition would help improve the schools. Almost 70 percent give a positive response. We have to be cautious not to make too much of this, since the question makes positive mention of how markets work for business, and does nothing to remind respondents of the downsides of markets or the advantages of government control. But it is reasonable to suggest, on the basis of these responses, that the public is a receptive audience for market-based appeals.

The second survey item asks respondents to agree or disagree with the following: "To give schools strong incentives to improve, we need a system that rewards good schools and punishes bad schools." Strictly speaking, this is a question about accountability that does not require markets. Nonetheless, the current public school system is clearly not built around these incentives, and they are the essence of what a more market-based system would provide. When presented with this version of a general, pro-market argument, Americans turn out to be almost equally divided. Forty-five percent agree that such an approach would improve the schools, while 48 percent disagree. The contrast with the previous item is instructive: here there is no positive reference to business, and people are reminded that a system of incentives might actually involve punishments for schools that are performing poorly, something many respondents may not feel comfortable with.

The market issue is ultimately a very complicated one, and we should resist drawing any but the broadest conclusions about where Americans stand. It is reasonable to suggest, however, that many Americans come to the voucher issue with a general orientation to markets that is positive. They may be less satisfied with the current system than they would otherwise be, because it lacks the kind of incentives, as well as the kind of choice and competition, that they think a good system should have. To the extent this is so, there is a rather large constituency within the American public that is willing to listen and open to change.

Conclusion

How satisfied are Americans with their public schools? As we've seen, this is a simple question that doesn't have a simple answer.

If Americans are asked to give an overall assessment of how the schools are doing, they appear on average to be fairly satisfied. To be sure, few people are enthusiastic, and nontrivial numbers think the schools are doing a mediocre or poor job. Nonetheless, ordinary citizens come across in these summary evaluations as much less critical of the public schools than elites are, and much more content with what they have. And this is a fact of great political significance. The American population is hardly a seething mass inclined toward revolution, and political movements aiming to attract them on that basis—as some voucher advocates would like to do—seem destined to fail.

There is, however, much more to the story than this. If we look beyond simple summary measures of support and ask people about specific aspects of system performance—aspects that are very basic and represent key points of contention in the debate over vouchers—it turns out that there are many sources of dissatisfaction. In particular, most Americans think that the current public school system

(1) is outperformed by schools in the private sector,

(2) is inequitable, particularly on class grounds

(3) adopts undesirable means of promoting diversity

(4) is too intolerant of religion

(5) gives parents too little influence

(6) has schools that are too large and

(7) should make better use of market-like mechanisms.

What should be made of this? One interpretation is that summary measures of public support, which tend to be more positive, are barely scratching the surface—and that once we take a deeper look at what people really think, we get a very different view indeed, and a much more negative one. This is the conclusion of Public Agenda, based on a thoughtful, widely read study of the public's views on the local schools. "American support for public education is fragile and porous," the report argues. "Although many people voice initial approval of their own local public schools, this support disintegrates at the slightest probing."[20]

It is certainly true that the summary measures of satisfaction are hiding something. They are hiding specific dimensions, lots of them, on which people are dissatisfied. The ones highlighted by Public Agenda have to do with the public's concern with the "basics" and with safety and order, as well as its belief that private schools are superior. Our own analysis high-lights a number of issues central to the voucher debate, but we could have gone on to discuss survey results for other issues as well—relating, for instance, to teacher tenure, multicultural curricula, school spending, and education reform—that would offer additional evidence of the public's dissatisfaction with specifics.

It would surely be a mistake, then, to focus solely on the more positive measures of overall satisfaction and to ignore all these dissatisfactions. But it would also be a mistake, I believe, to dismiss the overall measures as some sort of superficial veneer. Another interpretation seems more plau-sible in this case: that the general measures of satisfaction are actually providing information that is just as important and meaningful as the information provided by the specific measures. Perhaps more so. Two possibilities point in this direction.

One is that the general measures are the respondents' attempts to sum-marize—by weighting and averaging, in effect—all the various consider-ations that affect their assessments of the schools (and that come to mind). If these summary measures turn out to be positive relative to the specific measures, respondents may be saying that the latter are not that impor-tant to their overall satisfaction. On this account, the summary measures are probably the best indicators of what they think, and cannot be dis-missed as hiding the "real" information beneath the surface. If people appear more positive by these measures, they probably *are* more positive.

The second possibility is that when people are asked to give an overall evaluation, they may tend to think in terms of academic performance—while most other issues, even if truly important to them, don't have much influence on their response. Our survey provides some tentative evidence that this may be so, and thus that the general measures are largely mea-sures of academic performance. If this is the case, we have another reason not to dismiss the general measures as misleading or superficial, for they provide information that is both fundamentally important and different in content from what the more specific measures are providing.

We cannot resolve this puzzle entirely, although further analysis will shed a bit more light on it. It is reasonable to suggest, however, that we learn something important about public opinion from *both* the general measures and the more specific measures, and that both need to play roles in our subsequent analysis.

As far as substance is concerned, the picture is still a fairly optimistic one for the voucher movement. Revolution is probably out. But the indict-ments leveled by voucher advocates against the current system—on grounds ranging from inequity and religion to parent influence and school size—are precisely the dimensions on which the American public is dissatisfied. And even though the public is modestly content overall, most people appear unenthusiastic and very open to change. There is a lot for the voucher movement to work with here. Just not as much as its leaders might have liked.

3 *Why So Much Satisfaction?*

AMERICANS ARE CRITICAL of the public schools on a whole range of specific issues, from equity to religion to parent influence, yet they are fairly satisfied overall. Why would this be so? Why don't they give the system a resounding vote of disapproval?

Part of the answer seems to be that people emphasize academics when giving their summary judgments of school performance, and they are more positive about academics than about other things. But there is much more to the story. In this chapter, we will explore a number of other factors that, like academics, are central to how Americans see their public schools and help explain why their assessments are more positive than we might otherwise expect.

These sources of overall satisfaction have great political relevance. They tend to counterbalance the specific issues on which people are dissatisfied, and dispose Americans to be more content with the existing public school system—and more resistant, presumably, to vouchers and other proposals for radical change.

The District Context

Let's start with the obvious. People in districts with high-performing schools ought to be much more satisfied than people in districts with low-performing schools. The objective quality of schools is fundamental and should explain a lot about people's views.

Actual performance is notoriously difficult to measure. But our data set does contain measures that are reasonable proxies—district test scores and socioeconomic characteristics—and these measures can be combined into a general index to represent the local context (see appendix A). Education researchers would be quick to point out that test scores and socioeconomic characteristics can be misleading indicators of true school quality. A good school in a disadvantaged district, for instance, may still have low test scores. This is because test scores are largely reflections of student socioeconomic backgrounds and only partly a reflection of school quality. An index based on test scores and socioeconomic characteristics, then, will do an imperfect job of measuring objective performance.[1]

Nonetheless, an index of this sort is both useful and meaningful. The great majority of citizens, including those who are well educated and informed, regard test scores and socioeconomic characteristics as reliable proxies for the quality of district schools. When education-conscious people consider moving into a district, these are the things they want to know. Any real estate agent will verify as much. But more important, researchers widely agree that disadvantaged areas—notably, areas with high concentrations of poor and minority families—do tend to have schools that are low in quality, indeed often abysmally and shockingly inadequate, compared to the schools in well-do-do suburbs.[2] It is possible to find good schools in disadvantaged districts and bad schools in advantaged districts. But on the whole, advantaged districts seem to have much better schools than disadvantaged districts do.

Substantively, our index is a direct measure of how advantaged the various districts are, and I will usually refer to it in this way throughout the book. If the index is used to divide districts into quartiles, they can be arranged from the least advantaged to the most advantaged, and compared on that basis. In the least advantaged districts, 80 percent of the public parents live in urban areas, most of them large cities. About three-fourths of these parents are minorities. Seventy percent have a high school education or less, and 64 percent have total family incomes of less than $30,000 (which doesn't go far in urban areas). For the most part, then, the least advantaged districts are urban, low income, minority, and uneducated. The most advantaged districts represent another world entirely. Almost half of public parents in these districts live in the suburbs, while only 4 percent are in large cities. Eighty-six percent are white. Thirty-three percent have college educations. And fifty-five percent have household incomes above $40,000 (or did, in 1995).

Table 3-1. *Performance Evaluations across Districts*
Percent, unless otherwise indicated[a]

"Which of the following best describes how you feel about the schools in your district?"	District Context			
	Least advantaged 1	2	3	Most advantaged 4
Public school parents				
Doing well	41	40	45	55
Need minor changes	31	36	34	34
Need major changes	28	24	21	11
N[b]	(883)	(433)	(523)	(494)
Nonparents				
Doing well	32	32	33	42
Need minor changes	28	34	35	36
Need major changes	40	35	33	23
N[b]	(198)	(304)	(343)	(392)

a. Percentages are based on weighted data. They may not sum to 100 due to rounding.
b. N is the unweighted number of respondents.

Now let's look at how the people in these districts evaluate their schools. The obvious expectation is that people in disadvantaged districts ought to be far less satisfied with their schools than people in advantaged districts are. Indeed, the belief that this is true has become conventional wisdom among American political elites and a virtual mantra within the voucher movement. Poor and minority parents, concentrated in troubled inner-city schools, are seen as highly dissatisfied and clamoring for change, while parents in the suburbs are rather content.

This scenario is eminently reasonable, but there is a slight problem: the facts do not entirely support it. Consider, for instance, how people respond to the survey item that asks whether the local schools are doing well, need minor changes, or need major changes. As the figures in table 3-1 suggest, satisfaction is indeed lower in the least advantaged districts. But the differences across districts are not nearly as dramatic as one would expect, given the enormous disparities in objective conditions.

If any single finding stands out, it is that so many people in disadvantaged districts, particularly public parents, think their schools are doing well. Forty-one percent of the public parents in the least advantaged districts are satisfied, by this measure. The comparable figure for parents in the most advantaged districts is 55 percent—not that much higher, all things considered. The pattern for nonparents is much the same except,

because they are more critical in general, the whole scale is shifted down—
32 percent think their schools are doing well in the least advantaged districts, versus 42 percent in the most advantaged districts.

There clearly *is* a connection between how advantaged the context is
and how satisfied people are with their schools. Moreover, people in the
least advantaged districts are considerably more likely to say that their
schools are in need of "major changes" than people in the most advantaged
districts are—by 28 percent to 11 percent for public parents, and by 40
percent to 23 percent for nonparents. Still, especially for parents, the absolute level of dissatisfaction is low. Most observers, and certainly most
voucher advocates, would expect many more parents in the least
advantaged districts to be calling for massive reforms.

What is going on here? Why does satisfaction seem so uniform across
districts that are so very different? And, in particular, why does satisfaction seem so high in the least advantaged districts, especially among parents who seem to have so much to be unhappy about?

Direct Experience

Most people probably have some sense of their district's demographics,
and they probably know something about how its test scores stack up to
those of other districts. All of this is indirect evidence about school quality. Parents of school-age children, however, also have access to a *direct*
source of information that is not available to everyone: they experience
firsthand what the schools are doing. Through the involvement of their
children, their own participation, and word of mouth, parents get a sense
for how well the schools are handling their basic academic and social
tasks and for how well teachers seem to be doing their jobs.

This does not mean that parents are highly knowledgeable. Studies indicate that many parents are only marginally involved in the public schools
and only dimly aware of what goes on inside them.[3] Nonetheless, whatever parents' direct experiences with the schools may be, those experiences are likely to shape their satisfaction with the local school system
generally. There should also be important spillover effects, for parents will
surely talk to nonparents about their personal experiences, and nonparents,
having less direct bases for arriving at judgments themselves, may be
strongly influenced by what they hear.

Our survey includes a small battery of measures that tap parents' direct
experiences with their schools. It asks parents to focus on their oldest
child's school, and poses questions about whether (1) they find the school

Table 3-2. *Direct Experiences of Public School Parents*
with Their Children's Schools
Percent, unless otherwise indicated[a]

Survey question	Agree	Disagree	Don't know	N[b]
"I am often frustrated with the school."	38	59	3	(2,553)
"The school gives me a sense of belonging and feels almost like a family."	58	38	4	(2,553)
"I don't feel as though my participation at school can make a difference."	30	67	3	(2,553)
"The school provides my child with an exciting learning environment."	73	23	3	(2,553)
"Teachers don't care as much as they should."	48	48	4	(2,553)

a. Percentages are based on weighted data. They may not sum to 100 due to rounding.
b. N is the unweighted number of respondents.

frustrating, (2) the school gives them a sense of belonging, (3) they feel that their participation makes a difference, (4) the school provides an exciting learning environment, and (5) the teachers are sufficiently caring. The actual items, along with the responses of public parents, are set out in table 3-2.

The responses are remarkably positive. Despite all the talk about apathetic, uninvolved parents, 67 percent say they feel their participation makes a difference. Despite the elite consensus that public schools are stumbling in pursuit of their academic missions, 73 percent say that their schools provide an exciting learning environment. And despite the common claim that the schools are too bureaucratic and impersonal, 58 percent say their own school "feels almost like a family," while just 38 percent say they are "often frustrated." The only real indication of concern is that about half of these parents feel that teachers don't care as much as they should.

The obvious conjecture is that public parents have fairly positive assessments of their local school systems because their views are shaped by direct, quite positive experiences with their own children's schools. Table 3-3 reinforces this notion. Refer first to the top half of the table. If we combine the five separate indicators of direct parental experience into a single index, representing the quality of their firsthand experiences with the schools, we find that direct experience is very strongly related to the way parents evaluate the entire local school system—much more than objective context is.[4] Parents who have the worst experiences with their

Table 3-3. *Direct Experiences, School Satisfaction, and District Context (Public School Parents Only)*
Percent, unless otherwise indicated[a]

	Direct experience			
	Worst			Best
Survey item	1	2	3	4
"Which of the following best describes how you feel about the schools in your district?"				
Doing well	23	41	54	65
Need minor changes	32	39	35	27
Need major changes	44	20	11	8
N[b]	(582)	(544)	(595)	(591)

	District context			
	Least advantaged			Most advantaged
	1	2	3	4
Rating of direct experiences with child's school				
1 (Worst)	26	29	24	20
2	26	22	27	25
3	24	25	28	25
4 (Best)	25	24	21	29
N[b]	(664)	(483)	(493)	(539)

a. Percentages are based on weighted data. They may not sum to 100 due to rounding.
b. N is the unweighted number of respondents.

children's schools are far less likely to say the local schools are "doing well" than parents who have had good experiences, by 23 percent to 65 percent, and they are much more likely to say the local schools need major change, by 44 percent to just 8 percent. How public parents see the local system is very much a product, it appears, of their own experiences with particular schools.

This is hardly surprising. Direct experience ought to have a big influence on perceptions. What *is* surprising—although it makes perfect sense, given the evidence of the last section—is that the kinds of experiences parents have with their children's schools (along the five dimensions we have measured) are very much the *same* regardless of the objective context. As the bottom half of table 3-3 shows, public parents in disadvantaged districts—notwithstanding the horror stories about violence, drugs, low standards, and miserable performance—are almost as pleased with their own children's schools as parents in the most advantaged districts. There is tremendous uniformity in parental experience across districts (at least on the five measures we have used).

This flies in the face of conventional wisdom, and it raises the obvious next question: why are parents' experiences with their children's schools so much the same, regardless of how advantaged or disadvantaged the context? What's wrong with this picture? Ardent defenders of the public schools would say there is nothing wrong at all—that, in fact, the evidence simply confirms that the schools are doing a good job, even in socially depressed areas, and that much of the elite-level hype is ill informed and undeserved. Those closest to the schools, the public parents whose children attend them, know them to be good. As the Phi Delta Kappa researchers have been arguing: familiarity breeds respect.

To some extent, our new evidence is consistent with this line of thinking, and it needs to be taken seriously. Still, most informed observers, including researchers, would agree that schools in the least advantaged districts are *not* (on average) as good as schools in advantaged districts. So even if familiarity does breed respect in some sense, the issue is not just why evaluations seem to be so positive across districts. They should be positive anyway in the best districts. The more perplexing question is: why are residents of disadvantaged districts so satisfied with schools that experts have reason to believe are low in quality?

The factors discussed in later sections will help shed light on this. At the level of direct parental experience, however, our survey does not allow us to go much further in providing an answer. We cannot measure true school quality, and the data do not tell us what the foundations of parental experiences really are. The best we can do is to recognize that these experiences, whatever accounts for them, seem to have a big—and positive—impact on how parents see the public schools generally. And this helps explain why so many people in the least advantaged districts are surprisingly satisfied with their local school systems.

Residential Mobility and Private School Choice

Another part of the explanation may have to do with the way choice operates under the current system and with the kinds of "selection effects" that result from it. These factors seem fundamental to the larger puzzle we are trying to piece together here.

Consider, for example, a district widely known to have low-quality schools. In principle, parents can avoid these schools in one of two ways:

they can choose to live somewhere else, or they can send their kids to private schools. Both forms of choice, however, are costly and not equally available to everyone. They are most likely to be exercised by those who can pay the price, and who are sufficiently motivated to pursue expensive options. Families without money or motivation are the ones who should tend to get left behind in low-quality schools. Simply because of the operation of choice, then, the parents in low-performing public school systems should tend to be *socially* different from the parents in high-performing districts. It may be that these social differences lead them to evaluate their schools differently and to be more satisfied with schools of lower quality. We will explore this issue later on.

Choice also has effects on satisfaction, however, that are much more direct. People who choose their neighborhoods on the basis of school quality are simply more likely to wind up in public schools they are satisfied with. Similarly, private school choice drains off parents who are dissatisfied with the public schools—and when such parents leave, the average satisfaction within the public sector cannot help but be higher (other things being equal). In both respects, the self-selection of parents works to the public schools' advantage, increasing satisfaction beyond what it would otherwise have been.

These selection effects may help explain the surprisingly high satisfaction levels within low-quality districts. The people who move out of these districts, who never move in, or who send their kids to private schools are precisely the ones who would be the most dissatisfied with poorly performing schools. Satisfaction within these districts measures the satisfaction of only the parents who remain—and they are a select group, shorn of their most critical members and likely to be more positive because of it.[5]

Residential Mobility

Under the existing school system, the vast majority of children are assigned to schools on the basis of where they live. Because this is so, parents with money and motivation can move to neighborhoods with good schools, and thus exercise choice through residential mobility. Parents who lack money or motivation are unlikely to choose their public schools in this way—and they are more likely to find themselves concentrated in areas with lower-quality schools.

Nonparents (our term, remember, for adults who don't now have school-age children) are affected by all this. Some may have moved into their current neighborhoods because, at an earlier stage of life, they were seeking out high-quality schools. But whether or not this is so, the fact is that

Table 3-4. *Residential Mobility by District Context, Education, and Income*

Percentage (weighted) in each category that moved into their neighborhoods at least in part because of the quality of the public schools	District Context				
	Least advantaged 1	2	3	Most advantaged 4	N[a]
Public school parents	27	29	42	60	(2,328)
Nonparents	18	19	25	33	(1,402)

	Education					
	Less than high school	High school	Some college	College graduate	Post-graduate	
Public school parents	32	36	43	50	58	(2,481)
Nonparents	23	24	22	28	26	(1,537)

	Annual income ($)					
	20,000 or less	21,000–30,000	31,000–40,000	41,000–60,000	Over 60,000	
Public school parents	36	33	38	45	55	(2,171)
Nonparents	18	20	29	23	35	(1,294)

a. N is the unweighted number of respondents.

property values are strongly influenced by the quality of the local schools: education-conscious parents bid up housing prices in order to live in areas with desirable schools, and they guarantee that property values will appreciate at higher rates than in other areas. Buying a house in an area with good schools, in short, is a good investment, even if one has no children in school.

In our survey, respondents are asked whether they moved into their neighborhoods at least partly because of the quality of the public schools. 40 percent of public parents responded that they did, compared to 28 percent for nonparents. Most Americans, then, have not been able to choose their schools on the basis of residence—which is not too surprising, given how costly and difficult this kind of choice is. Nonetheless, a fairly large percentage of public parents actually do, and this is likely to have important "selection effects" across districts.

Table 3-4 begins to offer a closer look at this. As expected, there is a strong relationship between residential choice and how advantaged the district is. In the most advantaged districts, 60 percent of public parents say they have chosen their residence with an eye to the schools, compared to just 27 percent of parents in the most disadvantaged districts. The same is true, on a reduced scale, for nonparents. Thirty-three percent of them chose their neighborhoods for educational reasons in the most advantaged districts, versus 18 percent in the least advantaged districts.

There is a distinct class bias at work here, particularly among public parents. Parents with higher educations and incomes are more likely to choose their residences on the basis of school quality. Fifty-eight percent of parents with postgraduate degrees exercise this kind of choice, while 32 percent of parents with less than a high school education do. Similarly, 55 percent of parents whose annual incomes exceed $60,000 exercise residential choice, while 36 percent of parents with incomes below $20,000 do.

These figures are not as lopsided as they could be, and they probably hide much larger disparities. For example, the poor may often "choose" by moving among neighborhoods in low-performing districts, whereas the rich can choose to live almost anywhere they want. But the bias even in these figures is still marked and could hardly have been otherwise. For income reasons, the poor and the uneducated are obviously less able to use residential location as a way of seeking out better schools.

The class bias affects nonparents too, but in a somewhat different way. For nonparents, the discriminating factor is income alone. Those with incomes over $60,000 are about twice as likely to exercise residential choice as those with incomes under $20,000. Education, however, makes no difference at all. This is intriguing, because it tends to reinforce the notion that parent education is a proxy for motivation. Parents who are highly motivated by school quality will obviously want to live in neighborhoods with good schools for their kids. But nonparents have no kids in school. Their residential decisions probably have more to do with property values or the general quality of life, things they will buy if they can afford them.

Residential choice, then, has selection effects across districts and generates a class bias. The question is: does it also lead to higher satisfaction with the public schools? The logic connecting residential choice to satisfaction with the schools is a bit more complicated than it might seem. Earlier, I argued that residential mobility promotes satisfaction by allowing parents (and nonparents) to seek out areas with schools they like. This means, however, that their *own* satisfaction should increase—not that they will necessarily be more satisfied than *other* parents. Consider a parent, for instance, who is highly motivated by education and thus quite critical of schools that don't measure up to her high standards. She is prone, by

Table 3-5. *Satisfaction with Local Schools by Residential Mobility*
Percent, unless otherwise indicated[a]

"Which of the following best describes how you feel about the schools in your district?"	Chose residence because of school?			
	No	Yes, one of many reasons	Yes, an important reason	Yes, most important reason
Public school parents				
Doing well	42	46	52	55
Need minor changes	32	35	38	32
Need major changes	25	19	10	13
N[b]	(1,481)	(396)	(266)	(319)
Nonparents				
Doing well	34	43	33	48
Need minor changes	33	38	32	33
Need major changes	33	19	36	19
N[b]	(1,017)	(165)	(98)	(108)

a. Percentages are based on weighted data. They may not sum to 100 due to rounding.
b. N is the unweighted number of respondents.

virtue of her high standards, to be less satisfied than other parents. Because of residential mobility, she can improve her own satisfaction level by moving to more desirable areas. But wherever she lives, she may be less satisfied with the schools than most other parents are.

Residential mobility, then, is a means by which individual parents can increase their own satisfaction levels. But whether they are more satisfied than other parents turns on the syndrome of factors that go along with residential choice (such as high motivation). Were all these factors controlled, and thus were we comparing people who are identical in all respects but residential mobility, then the choosers ought to be more satisfied than the nonchoosers. But in simple, aggregate comparisons of the two groups we may not see the full effects.

The aggregate results are presented in table 3-5. They suggest that, even without controls, there is a moderate relationship between residential mobility and satisfaction with the local schools. Among public parents, those who say that the schools were an important reason for their residential decision are more likely, by 55 percent to 42 percent, to claim that the local schools are doing well than are public parents who did not take the schools into account in deciding where to live. They are also only half as likely, 13 percent versus 25 percent, to say that the schools are in need of major change. The effect is less consistent for nonparents, as we might expect, but the relationship still holds. Those for whom education was important to their residential choice are more supportive of the schools, by 48 percent to 34 percent, than those saying education did not affect their choice. And they are less likely, by 19 percent to 33 percent, to call for radical reform.

To some degree, obviously, residential choosers are more satisfied because they are moving into better districts. But this is not all there is to it. Were we to control for district context, the same basic pattern would obtain: however advantaged or disadvantaged the district, residential choosers are more satisfied than nonchoosers. This holds for nonparents as well as for public parents. Even within district types, then, residential choice—the choice of specific neighborhoods or specific schools—promotes greater satisfaction.

We will get a better picture of its impact in the multivariate analysis later on. Even in the aggregate, though, residential mobility appears to promote satisfaction with the schools. This brand of choice thus works to the schools' advantage by promoting higher levels of support. It also reinforces the class and racial biases of the system.

Private School Choice

Parents who go private must seek out the schools they want, enroll their children, and pay tuition. Presumably, they go through all this because, on whatever grounds—academic quality, discipline, moral values—they find private schools preferable to public schools. In addition, of course, they need to meet an income constraint: they must be able to afford it.

Private school parents are not the only parents who make choices about sector. Many public school parents can afford to send their children to private schools but prefer the local public schools. Other public school parents, however, do not really wind up in the public sector because they think its schools are better. They "choose" public schools by default—because they can't afford to go private, because they don't know about private options, or because they don't care much about education and simply accept whatever schools are dealt them.

However explicit these choices, there is a selection process going on here that allocates parents to sectors and ensures that the two populations will be systematically different. As the education system is currently set up, the private sector should attract parents who tend to be better educated, better off financially, and more motivated than those who stay in the public sector. We will be comparing private parents to public parents in chapter 5, and data on their social differences will be presented there. What the evidence shows, not surprisingly, is that private parents are in-

Table 3-6. *Satisfaction with Local Schools by Sector and District Context*
Percent, unless otherwise indicated[a]

"Which of the following best describes how you feel about the schools in your district?"	All districts	District Context			
		Least advantaged 1	2	3	Most advantaged 4
Public school parents					
Doing well	45	41	40	45	55
Need minor changes	34	31	36	34	34
Need major changes	21	28	24	21	11
N[b]	(2,333)	(704)	(517)	(536)	(576)
Parents with children only in private school					
Doing well	27	23	28	27	31
Need minor changes	25	19	18	31	35
Need major changes	48	58	54	43	34
N[b]	(333)	(134)	(77)	(43)	(79)
Parents with children in both sectors					
Doing well	27	19	23	27	36
Need minor changes	32	37	31	33	26
Need major changes	41	44	45	40	38
N[b]	(138)	(42)	(24)	(31)	(41)

a. Percentages are based on weighted data. They may not sum to 100 due to rounding.
b. N is the unweighted number of respondents.

deed more advantaged in these respects, and that the selection process associated with private school choice does produce social biases across sectors.

Whatever the backgrounds of parents who go private, however, the thing they have in common is that they find their children's private schools to be more attractive than the public schools in their local area. This does not mean that they are highly critical of the public schools. But it is reasonable to expect that, on average (and particularly once other factors are controlled), private parents will turn out to be more critical of the public schools than public parents are—and that this higher level of dissatisfaction, in many cases, is precisely why they are going private.

The figures in table 3-6 tend to bear this out. Parents with children solely in private schools are a good bit less likely than public parents to say the schools are doing well, by 27 percent to 45 percent, and more inclined to say the schools are in need of major changes, by 48 percent to 21 percent. Parents with kids in both public and private schools look very much like private-only parents in this regard: they are quite critical of the public schools.

These differences could arise from the fact that private parents are not evenly distributed across districts. In fact, private parents are more likely to be found in the least advantaged districts than anywhere else, and this could make them appear more critical overall. While 25 percent of public parents are located in such districts (in our four-way categorization), some 33 percent of private-only parents are a reflection of the greater demand for private schools in areas where the public schools are doing poorly, and a reflection of the greater availability of private schools in urban areas (which is surely, in part, a response to the demand).

Do private parents still appear to be especially critical of the public schools once their district contexts are taken into account? The answer is yes. The same patterns hold, as the district breakdowns in table 3-6 indicate. Perhaps the most striking finding here is that private parents are so much more inclined to call for major changes than public parents are, whatever the district type. Within the least advantaged districts, fully 58 percent of the private-only parents think the public schools need major changes, compared to just 28 percent of the public parents. And even in the most advantaged districts, where one would think satisfaction would be uniformly high, more than a third of all private parents want major changes, versus just 11 percent of the public parents. In a relative sense, private parents come across as quite discontent with the public school system.

Like residential mobility, then, private school choice is a selection mechanism that is closely tied to satisfaction with the public schools. Residential choice allows people to seek out better districts and neighborhoods, while private school choice allows people who are dissatisfied with the public schools to leave. Both promote higher levels of satisfaction among the existing pool of public parents—one by directly raising satisfaction among mobile parents, the other by draining off the discontented and raising the average satisfaction among those who remain—and both may have a lot to do with why satisfaction appears so high in the least advantaged districts.

Public School Ideology

While to my knowledge no one has tried to measure or study it, it seems clear that there is something tantamount to a public school ideology among a substantial segment of the American population. Anyone familiar with the politics of education is faced with evidence of this ideology time and again.[6] Many Americans simply like the idea of a public school system. They see it as an expression of local democracy and a pillar of the local community, they admire the egalitarian principles on which it is based, they think it deserves our commitment and support, and they tend to regard as subversive any notion that private schools should play a larger role in educating the nation's children.

What they have, in effect, is a normative attachment to the public schools—and an affective inclination to see the public schools in a sympathetic light, whatever the latter's actual performance might be. This is another basic reason, I suspect, why satisfaction with the public schools is as high as it is, and why it does not vary dramatically as objective conditions change. Public school ideology keeps it propped up—everywhere.

Three survey items offer possible measures of public school ideology. The first asks respondents to agree or disagree with the following statement: "The public schools deserve our support, even if they are performing poorly." While some people who are not ideologically wedded to the public schools might agree with this statement, it probably does a reasonable job of separating those who take a utilitarian view of the schools from those with a deeper, more value-laden attachment. And to the extent it does so, the breakdowns are impressive.

As table 3-7 suggests, two-thirds of Americans say the public schools deserve support even when they are performing poorly, and the figures are much the same whether we look at public school parents (64 percent) or nonparents (67 percent). We even find, in fact, that many private parents share this same attachment to the public school system. Of the parents we would expect to be most alienated, those with children solely in private schools, 49 percent embrace this version of the public school ideology. And of parents with children in both public and private schools, 68 percent do. These kinds of responses begin to suggest that public school ideology may indeed be quite widespread.

The second item proposes that "The more children attend public schools, rather than private or parochial schools, the better it is for American society" and asks respondents to agree or disagree. This item is more extreme, posing a strong, even provocative claim that should tend to attract support only from people with a very strong (and rather one-sided) attachment to the public schools. In view of this, the level of support is surprisingly high. Forty percent of public school parents and 41 percent of nonparents agree that society is better off to the extent that children go to public rather than private schools. Private parents are less apt to embrace this

Table 3-7. *Public School Ideology*
Percent, unless otherwise indicated[a]

| | | Parents | | |
Survey item	Non-parents	Public only[b]	Private only[c]	Both[d]
"The public schools deserve our support even if they are performing poorly."				
Agree	67	64	49	68
Disagree	31	33	49	29
Don't Know	3	3	3	3
"The more children attend public schools, rather than private or parochial schools, the better it is for American society."				
Agree	41	40	26	28
Disagree	49	49	69	66
Don't know	9	11	5	6
"I believe in public education, and I wouldn't feel right putting my kids in private or parochial school."				
Agree	...	43	17	31
Disagree	...	49	75	66
Don't know	...	8	8	3
N[e]	(1,589)	(2,553)	(381)	(149)

a. Percentages are based on weighted data. They may not sum to 100 due to rounding.
b. *Public only* refers to parents who send their children only to public schools.
c. *Private only* refers to parents who send their children only to private schools.
d. *Both* refers to parents who send their children to both public and private schools.
e. N is the unweighted number of respondents.

anti-private version of the ideology, of course, with 26 percent of those with children solely in private schools and 28 percent of those with children in both sectors indicating agreement. But even this level of support is surprisingly high—suggesting that at least a quarter of these parents may well carry a measure of guilt or personal anguish for going private.

The third item was asked only of parents, as part of a battery of questions addressing the voucher issue. It asks them to agree or disagree with the following statement: "I believe in public education, and I wouldn't feel right putting my kids in private or parochial school." This seems an especially good measure of the affective bond that some parents feel for the public schools.

Forty-three percent of public parents say they wouldn't feel right putting their kids in private schools—a profoundly important fact, given that so many of these same parents think that private schools are actually *better* than public schools. Interestingly enough, moreover, a surprisingly high portion of private parents—17 percent of those with kids in private school only and 31 percent of those with kids in both sectors—indicate that they have the same kind of feelings toward the public schools and don't feel right about having to go private. Although performance may argue for private schools, there is apparently a strong, value-based tug that pulls people toward the public schools and makes them feel badly if they don't go along with it.

If we look over American society more generally, what types of people seem to embrace this public school ideology, and what types don't? Perhaps the most obvious expectations are that support for public school ideology would be

(1) greater among Democrats,

(2) greater among people who exercise residential mobility,

(3) greater among those located in the better districts, and

(4) lower among the religious groups—Catholics and born-again Christians—that seem most interested in private schools.

A multivariate analysis would show that all these expectations are supported by the data. The effects, however, are rather modest. Moreover, the findings about residential mobility and advantaged districts—which may seem to suggest that public school ideology is largely an upper-middle-class phenomenon—are balanced by the fact that, when relevant factors are controlled, it is actually the people *lower* in education and income who are more inclined to have public school ideology. And these people, of course, are concentrated in less advantaged districts and are less apt to exercise residential choice. The result is that, in the aggregate, public school ideology is very evenly distributed across districts. It is everywhere in almost equal amounts.

Now let's turn to the satisfaction issue. On balance, it seems obvious that public school ideology should have a positive impact on satisfaction. But the connection is more subtle than it might appear.[7] For if people have a normative attachment to the public schools, they can decide that the schools are doing a poor job—that is, they can express dissatisfaction—and continue to see the schools as valuable institutions that deserve our support. Thus, while people who embrace public school ideology will probably be more satisfied with the public schools—and, in general, less critical in evaluating them—the most important impact of public school ideology is probably not on satisfaction per se, but on how people see vouchers, privatization, and other departures from the traditional public system.

All these relationships will be explored in later chapters. For now, we can get an initial sense for how public school ideology bears on satisfaction by

Table 3-8. *Public School Ideology and School Satisfaction (Parents Only)*
Percent, unless otherwise indicated[a]

"Which of the following best describes how you feel about the schools in your district?"	"I believe in public education and I wouldn't feel right putting my kids in private or parochial school."	
	Agree	Disagree
Public only[b]		
Doing well	53	38
Need minor changes	31	36
Need major changes	16	26
N[c]	(1,062)	(1,272)
Private only[d]		
Doing well	31	24
Need minor changes	43	23
Need major changes	26	53
N[c]	(98)	(366)

a. Percentages are based on weighted data. They may not sum to 100 due to rounding.
b. *Public only* refers to parents who send their children only to public schools.
c. N is the unweighted number of respondents.
d. *Private only* refers to parents who send their children only to private schools.

looking at the figures in table 3-8, which focuses on the survey item asking parents whether they "wouldn't feel right" putting their kids in private schools. The bottom line is that parents who have public school ideology are indeed more satisfied with their local public schools. Among public parents, 53 percent of those with public school ideology think that their local schools are doing well, compared to 38 percent of parents without public school ideology. A similar connection exists for private parents. Some private parents, as we noted earlier, do indeed seem to have a normative attachment to the public schools, despite their having gone private. These parents are more likely to say the public schools are doing well, by 31 percent to 24 percent, than private parents who don't have the ideology—and they are much less likely, by 26 percent to 53 percent, to call for major changes.

As these figures begin to suggest, public school ideology is a phenomenon of potentially great significance for American politics and education. It has long gone unappreciated by education researchers, and in the years ahead it deserves to be studied seriously. For now, we can simply note that public school ideology is widespread within the American population, it is equally present in advantaged and disadvantaged districts, and it almost surely works to the great benefit of the public school system: generating support and satisfaction for normative reasons that have little to do with the actual performance of the system.

Social Class and Expectations

I have left the most provocative argument for last. Earlier, I underlined a rather obvious fact of American social life: that people in the least advantaged districts are socially different from people in advantaged districts—among other things, they rank lower in education and income (and perhaps in motivation)—and I raised the question of whether these social differences might lead them to evaluate their schools differently. The question, more specifically, is whether there is something about these social characteristics that might prompt people to be satisfied with schools that are low in quality. In this section, I suggest that the answer appears to be yes, although the issue clearly needs further research.

One of the most consistent findings in social science is that education plays a profound role in shaping social behavior. It is the single most important determinant of political participation: better-educated people are more likely to vote, to engage in campaigns, to belong to interest groups, to be involved in community affairs. It is also a factor of overwhelming significance in structuring how people fashion their opinions on issues of public policy: better-educated people are more likely to know about important policy issues, to evaluate them in coherent ways, to have positions or viewpoints, and to think in ideological terms that link the various issues together.[8]

It is reasonable to suggest, then, that education may have something to do with how people evaluate the public schools. To explore this, we need to recognize that well-educated people are likely to live in the better districts, and so are likely to be more satisfied on objective grounds alone. Thus we need to control for district context and ask what effect education seems to have on satisfaction when people are faced with schools of roughly the same quality.

Consider the least advantaged districts, which are the contexts of greatest concern here. As the figures in table 3-9 indicate, satisfaction with the public schools does vary within these districts—and rather strikingly—depending on how educated people are. Forty-nine percent of parents with less than a high school education say their local schools are doing well, compared to just 20 percent of those with postgraduate educations. The same relationship holds for nonparents, for whom the analogous figures are 46 percent and 9 percent.[9] *The less educated the respondents, the*

Table 3-9. *Satisfaction in the Least Advantaged Districts, by Education*
Percent, unless otherwise indicated[a]

"Which of the following best describes how you feel about the schools in your district?"	Education				
	Less than high school	High school	Some college	College graduate	Post-graduate
Public school parents					
Doing well	49	43	28	33	20
Need minor changes	30	28	35	29	48
Need major changes	21	29	37	38	33
N[b]	(97)	(295)	(171)	(101)	(33)
Nonparents					
Doing well	46	31	32	13	9
Need minor changes	30	30	25	29	7
Need major changes	24	38	43	58	84
N[b]	(21)	(68)	(54)	(44)	(10)

a. Percentages are based on weighted data. They may not sum to 100 due to rounding.
b. N is the unweighted number of respondents.

more likely they are to be satisfied with the schools. It is the better-educated people who are the most critical and the most inclined to call for reform.

If anything, the true relationship between education and satisfaction may be stronger than this suggests. Schools vary in quality within any district, and it is a good bet that educated people tend to find their way into the better schools. This is likely to be so even in the most disadvantaged districts. Thus quality is not really constant for all respondents within a district type: the better-educated parents probably tend to have higher-quality schools—and on objective grounds alone, therefore, should be *more* rather than less likely to say that the schools are doing well. Similarly, regardless of how good a given school is, well-educated parents are likely to get better treatment from school staff and to participate more actively; and on these grounds too they would seem *more* likely to give the schools positive scores. Were we able to control for all these factors, therefore, the relationship between education and satisfaction would probably turn out to be still more negative than our data indicate.

Now let's go a step further. Why does education seem to have this intriguing effect on satisfaction with the schools? The answer is doubtless complex, and our survey was not designed to explore the issue in any detail. There is, however, one measurable factor that is likely to be of great importance: the expectations people have about the kinds of schools they ought to be getting.

It makes sense to think that expectations about many social services, including schools, will be systematically related to social class—that, in particular, people who are lower in education and income will tend to receive services (whether public or private) of lower quality than better-off citizens receive, and that this normal state of affairs will be built into their expectations. If true, this could well account for some of the negative relationship between education and satisfaction with the schools. People with less education will tend to have low expectations about school quality—and for any given level of school quality, people with low expectations are more likely to be satisfied.

We can explore this idea, at least to a limited extent, by taking advantage of an item on the survey that offers a reasonable, if imperfect, proxy for expectations. The item asks respondents to agree or disagree with the following statement: "The government provides us with free schools, so we should try to be satisfied with them." This is a rough measure, and we have to be careful not to expect too much from it. But it is clearly a question that would tend to get affirmative answers from people with low expectations.

When we take this variable as our proxy, we find a striking relationship between expectations and social class (see table 3-10). Among nonparents, 51 percent of those with the least education (less than high school) can be categorized as having low expectations, while the corresponding figure for those with the most education (postgraduate degrees) is just 10 percent. The gap is smaller for public school parents, 37 percent to 15 percent, but overall there is clearly a difference in expectations across education groups. *Those with little education don't expect as much.* There is also a strong connection between expectations and income. For nonparents, 44 percent of those in the bottom income group (less than $20,000 a year) have low expectations, while just 16 percent of those making more than $60,000 per year can be so classified. For public parents, the comparable figures are almost the same: 42 percent and 17 percent, respectively. In general, then, there is good evidence here that having low expectations is a class phenomenon.

Finally, we need to know whether people who have low expectations are in fact more likely to say they are satisfied with the schools. The best way to do this, given all the variables that need to be controlled, is through a multivariate analysis, which the next chapter will carry out. Here, we can get a sense for what the relationship looks like by focusing on the least advantaged districts, controlling for education, and seeing how satisfaction varies with expectations.

Table 3-10. *Education, Income, and Expectations*
Percent, unless otherwise indicated[a]

"The government provides us with free schools, so we should try to be satisfied with them."	Education				
	Less than high school	High school	Some college	College graduate	Post- graduate
Public school parents					
Agree (low expectations)	37	34	24	21	15
Disagree	63	66	76	79	85
N[b]	(244)	(899)	(637)	(489)	(188)
Nonparents					
Agree (low expectations)	51	36	22	19	10
Disagree	49	64	78	81	90
N[b]	(148)	(465)	(399)	(365)	(162)

	Annual income ($)				
	20,000 or less	21,000– 30,000	31,000– 40,000	41,000– 60,000	Over 60,000
Public Parents					
Agree (low expectations)	42	32	24	25	17
Disagree	58	68	76	75	83
N[b]	(448)	(478)	(386)	(518)	(331)
Nonparents					
Agree (low expectations)	44	35	27	26	16
Disagree	56	65	73	74	84
N[b]	(260)	(258)	(252)	(294)	(227)

a. Percentages are based on weighted data. They may not sum to 100 due to rounding.
b. N is the unweighted number of respondents.

The data, set out in table 3-11, clearly suggest that people with low expectations are more likely to be satisfied with their schools. Among poorly educated parents in the least advantaged districts, for instance, 58 percent of those with low expectations say the schools are doing fine, while 36 percent of those with high expectations say the same. The corresponding figures (in this same context) are 48 percent versus 20 percent for parents with some college, and 29 percent versus 28 percent for parents with at least a college education. The same basic pattern holds for nonparents. Given that our measure of expectations is fairly rough, these are surprisingly consistent results.

It appears, then, that there is a class bias in the way Americans evaluate their schools. When objective conditions are held constant, people with little education are more likely to say they are satisfied with their schools

Table 3-11. *Influence of Education and Expectations on Satisfaction with Public Schools (Least Advantaged Districts)*

Percentage (weighted) of respondents in each category who believe that the schools are doing well	High expectations	Low expectations	N^a
High school education or less			
Public school parents	36	58	(377)
Nonparents	32	50	(88)
Some college			
Public school parents	20	48	(165)
Nonparents	26	39	(53)
College degree			
Public school parents	28	29	(131)
Nonparents	13	17	(53)

a. N is the unweighted number of respondents.

than better-educated people are—and they do this, at least in part, because they have lower expectations about the quality of schools they should be getting.

These findings need to be documented by future research if they are to be embraced with confidence. Nonetheless, there is a good logical case for them. And if true, they may help explain why satisfaction is surprisingly high in disadvantaged districts, as well as why satisfaction does not vary dramatically across advantaged and disadvantaged districts. Part of the story is that disadvantaged districts have proportionately large numbers of people who are poorly educated and low in expectations—and who, for any given level of school quality, are especially likely to say the schools are doing well.

If we follow this rationale through, moreover, it has a natural extension for the full range of districts. As districts become more advantaged, and thus as objective conditions improve, more of their residents are likely to be well educated and to have higher expectations; and, because such people tend to be more critical, they may tend to be less enthusiastic about their schools than the latter's high quality would seem to justify. Thus the effects of education and expectations may raise the level of satisfaction within the least advantaged districts—but also lower it within advantaged districts. And it may be the combination of the two, not just the former by itself, that is making the aggregate relationship between satisfaction and district context less dramatic than it presumably ought to be.

From a political standpoint, the implications of all this are far reaching, at least potentially. For it appears that the people in American society who are the most desperately in need of educational reform are precisely those who are the least likely to demand it—and the most likely to say instead that they are satisfied. To the extent that this is so, the public schools are spared heavy criticism from the people who surely seem to have the most to complain about. And the voucher movement, which has long targeted its programs at the disadvantaged and cultivated them as a prime political constituency, may find that a big part of this population is more content with the current system than voucher leaders have assumed.

Conclusion

Despite near-universal criticism of the public schools among elites, ordinary Americans are fairly satisfied with their local schools overall, and this satisfaction is surprisingly widespread across district contexts. Context does make a difference: the less advantaged the district, the less satisfied people are with the schools and the more they call for major change. But the conventional wisdom—that people in disadvantaged districts are highly dissatisfied by comparison to people in advantaged districts—is an exaggeration. In fact, many people in disadvantaged districts appear to be reasonably satisfied with schools that most experts would characterize as seriously inadequate.

If we want to understand how Americans evaluate their schools, we have to gain perspective on all this. Why is satisfaction as high as it is? Why does it appear so uniform across districts? And why is it so common within the least advantaged districts, where people seem to have so much to be dissatisfied about? We cannot provide definitive answers, and, perhaps not surprisingly, a more extensive analysis reveals a few loose ends (see appendix B). Still, this chapter's analysis suggests that several factors have important roles to play.

(1) *Direct experience.* Public parents have positive experiences with their own children's schools, even in the least advantaged districts, and this shapes their evaluations of the school system as a whole. Nonparents may also be affected, for they are likely to hear about school quality through their conversations with parents. The direct experiences of parents, then, keep satisfaction high in general and reasonably uniform across districts.

(2) *Residential choice.* Many parents (and nonparents) who would otherwise be dissatisfied with their local schools are able to seek out districts and neighborhoods whose schools they like better. This raises the overall satisfaction level within the system. It may also promote a kind of balance

across districts, because the dissatisfied will disproportionately tend to move out of bad districts (or not move in), raising the average satisfaction levels of those districts and perhaps pushing them close to the already high levels of good districts.

(3) *Private school choice.* Parents who send their children to private schools tend to be more critical of the local public schools than public parents are—and when they leave, average satisfaction within the system goes up. The existence of the private sector thus serves as a safety valve for the public schools, draining off the more critical parents and raising average satisfaction in the smaller pool that is left. Private parents are also disproportionately located in the least advantaged districts, and their leaving gives a bigger boost to satisfaction in these contexts.

(4) *Public school ideology.* Many Americans adhere to a public school ideology that prompts them to support the public schools regardless of their actual performance, and to believe that, despite the perceived superiority of private schools, public schools are better for society and worthy of their commitment. Across all contexts, from the least advantaged to the most advantaged, people often have normative attachments to the public system that predispose them to be positive and sympathetic.

(5) *Education and Expectations.* People who are poorly educated and have low expectations are especially likely to be satisfied with the local schools. Because such people are over-represented in the least advantaged districts, those who suffer under the worst educational conditions are the most inclined to be satisfied with them and thus not to complain or demand political reform. The flip side is that people who are well educated and have high expectations are the least inclined to be satisfied with any given level of service—but because they tend to be concentrated in the best districts, they have less to complain about and come across as satisfied too. The net result is a leveling effect that promotes fairly high levels of satisfaction across all types of districts, from the least advantaged to the most advantaged.

These are not the only influences on how people evaluate the public schools. But, as the next chapter's analysis will show, they are among the most important—and in every case but one, they tend to promote a very supportive environment *even if the schools are not performing well.* Residential mobility, private school choice, public school ideology, social class, and expectations are all factors that promote higher, more uniform levels of overall satisfaction with the schools—and in doing so, they reinforce the status quo by defusing discontent and inhibiting demands for political change.

One influence on public satisfaction, however, does hinge on whether the schools are performing well: the direct experiences of parents. Parents have positive views of the school system in part because, even in the least advantaged districts, they have favorable direct experiences with their own children's schools. Experts largely agree that school quality varies considerably across advantaged and disadvantaged districts, so there is reason to suspect that these parental assessments are not simply measuring the true underlying quality of the schools. Other factors (such as education and expectations) are at work to keep satisfaction higher than it ought to be, especially in the least advantaged districts. Nonetheless, it is almost surely the case that their direct experiences are to some extent a function of true quality.

The data on direct experiences, then, reflects well on the public schools. The schools are clearly doing something right, even in the least advantaged districts, or they wouldn't evoke such positive responses from parents. Thus, while it is important to recognize how residential mobility, private school choice, public school ideology, social class, expectations, and perhaps other factors can create a highly supportive environment for the schools for reasons other than performance, it is also important to recognize that there *is* a performance component to the public's satisfaction, and perhaps a large one.

If this perspective on satisfaction with the public schools is basically correct, it points to a political environment that may be troublesome for the voucher movement. Each prong of the argument I've made here, in fact, is troubling for its own reasons. The first prong suggests that there are fundamental forces at work that keep satisfaction with the public schools reasonably high and widespread regardless of the schools' actual performance—which, if true, means that voucher leaders may have a difficult time capitalizing on performance problems to mobilize public disaffection. The second prong suggests that many people have concrete reasons for being satisfied with public school performance, and may not be prime candidates for mobilization anyway.

From a voucher standpoint, the combination is sobering.

4

Explaining
Satisfaction

To SAY THAT AMERICANS are fairly satisfied with their public schools is to say something about average satisfaction levels, and averages hide a great deal of variation. Some Americans are clearly not satisfied with the public schools. Some are quite enthusiastic about them. And most are somewhere in-between. What we want to know is why Americans see the schools as they do, whether positive, negative, or indifferent. What explains satisfaction?

Our previous chapters offer the building blocks for a broader analysis. Chapter 3 establishes a simple baseline: satisfaction ought to reflect the district's objective context (a proxy for school quality). It goes on to argue that there are a number of important influences—from residential mobility to public school ideology to low expectations—that promote satisfaction, and thus help to engineer a more supportive environment for the public schools. In all these respects, then, we know what variables to look for in explaining satisfaction, and we know what to expect.

Similarly, chapter 2 points out that many Americans are dissatisfied on specific dimensions of public school performance—having to do, for instance, with equity, diversity, religion, parent influence, school size, markets, and the superiority of private schools. Although their critical views have not prevented them (in the aggregate) from being fairly satisfied overall, it is reasonable to think that some or all of these specific issues may affect their general assessments—and that the impact on satisfaction will be negative. Again, we know what to look for, and we know what to expect.

Finally, chapter 1, as well as the discussions throughout, makes it clear that certain social and political characteristics—income, race, political party, and others—may affect what people want from the public schools, how they experience them, and whether they are satisfied with them. When these factors are included, they help round out the picture and connect it more explicitly with important groups in American society.

The current chapter pulls all these elements together into a single analysis. In doing so, it forces them to compete with one another for explanatory power—allowing us to determine which influences seem to matter most in explaining how Americans view their schools, and whether the ideas from previous chapters seem to hold up.

Method

Most readers, I suspect, are not eager to wade through a methodological discussion about why the statistical analysis is carried out as it is. Some amount of this is necessary, though, if the path we'll be following is to make sense and if the findings are to be interpreted properly. I'll try to keep it brief and simple.

The task in this chapter is to estimate a broader model of satisfaction. The most straightforward approach would be to include all relevant variables in a single, fully specified model and then to estimate their impacts all at once. Doing so would give us the effect each variable has on satisfaction, controlling for the effects of all other variables. And it would force all variables to compete with one another for explanatory power.

This is where we are headed. But rather than jumping immediately to a fully specified model, it is more enlightening to get there in step-by-step fashion, beginning with a smaller model and building toward a comprehensive one. By doing this, we can gain a better appreciation of the roles that the different variables play.

Consider an example. We have good reason to think that income and race will be related to how people evaluate the public schools. But in each case the rationale has something to do with district context. Parents who are minority and low in income are more likely than other parents to be stuck in disadvantaged districts, and thus (especially when expectations are controlled) to be less satisfied with their schools' performance. To some extent, then, income and race are important not because they have direct effects on satisfaction, but because they help determine which contexts people live in—and the context shapes their satisfaction. Context has a direct effect. The effects of income and race are (to some extent) indirect. They operate through their prior effects on context.

All these variables are important to the story that needs to be told. And knowing something about their direct and indirect effects helps us arrive at a more refined understanding of how they affect people's evaluations of the schools. But here is the dilemma: if we enter all the variables in a single model and estimate their impacts, only the direct effects will show up. Thus, when district context is included, variables such as income and race may appear to have much smaller effects than if district context were omitted.

This sort of thing is quite common. It is especially common in an analysis that combines background variables with attitudinal variables. For then there is a clear causal hierarchy at work. Background variables—education, income, race, religion, and the like—may have direct impacts on how people evaluate the schools. But they may also shape people's attitudes: their belief in diversity, their perceptions of inequity, their public school ideology. To the extent that these attitudes affect how people see the schools, then, the background variables may be having indirect effects, channeling some of their influence through attitudes. When background and attitudinal variables are included in the same model, however, these indirect effects of the background variables will not show up. As a result, the background variables—especially one as broadly relevant as education—may appear to be have little effect, even if its underlying influence is substantial.

We could follow a modeling strategy that maps out all causal connections and estimates the numerous direct and indirect effects. But given all the variables involved, this would be tedious and distracting. The approach I have settled upon, both here and in subsequent chapters, is a much simpler way of ensuring that, in moving toward a comprehensive model, we don't lose sight of the roles certain variables may be playing behind the scenes. It involves a step-by-step estimation of the following models.

(1) The first step is to estimate a model consisting entirely of background variables, but without variables representing the district context or attitudes. Some indirect effects remain hidden even here. The effects of race, for instance, may be channeled through education and income. Indeed, it is often because blacks and Hispanics are lower in education and income that we expect racial effects at all. When these factors are controlled, race may therefore appear to have no effect, even in the background model alone. In general, though, this first-step model gives us a much better sense of the impacts of background variables than a more comprehensive model would.

(2) The second step is to add variables representing district context to the background model. The new set of variables includes residential mobility, which is closely associated with context (and strongly influenced by education and income, which are clearly prior to it in the causal chain). This allows us to see whether contextual variables add significantly to the explanation. It also tells us something about the roles that various background factors seem to be playing, by showing how their impacts are altered (or not) when context is controlled.

(3) The next step is to add a set of attitudinal variables, measuring the public's views on issues ranging from diversity to prayer to school size.[1] When these variables are incorporated, we can see what they contribute to the overall explanation and determine which attitudes seem to be playing important roles. The direct effects of background and context may be reduced or altered here, because some of their effects may now be channeled through attitudes, which are the more proximate causes.

(4) The last step is to introduce factors that come at the end of the causal chain. In subsequent chapters, these are usually measures of satisfaction with school performance. It should be pretty obvious why satisfaction comes last. If we want to explain why parents go private (chapter 5), for example, or why they would support vouchers (chapter 7), satisfaction with the performance of public schools should play an important role in the explanation, as should background, context, and attitude variables. But some of the latter variables are also causes of satisfaction (as this chapter's analysis will show), and when all are included in the same model, some of their effects will be channeled indirectly through the effects of satisfaction—and thus be hidden. By introducing satisfaction only at the last stage, therefore, we allow the other variables to demonstrate their effects in the earlier models, and we get a more complete sense of what is going on.

This approach may sound complicated, but it really isn't. A typical analysis consists of several estimated models, arranged in a simple hierarchy: each fully incorporates the one before it and adds some new variables of its own. The estimates for all models are presented in the same table, so that they are easily compared and the basic patterns stand out. Together, they constitute a single analysis, and they make good sense when viewed as a whole.[2]

Throughout this book, we will be covering a range of topics. But whatever the topic, the analysis will be carried out according to the framework outlined above, and it will be built around the same basic set of background, contextual, and attitudinal variables. In this section, I briefly indicate what these variables are. (This is a bit tedious, but it only has to be done once. For a discussion of how the variables are measured, see appendix A.)

The main background variables include demographics that come up again and again in any discussion of private school choice. I also include in this category certain value and perceptual orientations (party identification and expectations) that are so basic that they are likely to be causally prior to other attitudes and beliefs. Here is the list:

(1) education
(2) income
(3) religion (Catholic, born-again Christian)
(4) race (northern black, southern black, Hispanic)
(5) age
(6) party identification (with a high score indicating Republican)
(7) low expectations

Another candidate for this list was liberal-conservative ideology, which, along with party, has played a major role in the elite-level politics of education. But the problem is that, as survey research has long shown, many Americans do not really know what the terms *liberal* or *conservative* mean or how to categorize themselves; and only a small percentage of the population structure their thinking in ideological terms. So I have simply omitted it from the analysis and retained its cousin, political party.

In addition to the background variables listed above, other background variables (such as gender and region) are included in the actual analysis for purposes of statistical control.[3] Because these variables are not really central to the argument, however, they are omitted from the tables of empirical findings. This keeps the tables as simple as possible.

Now let's consider the contextual variables—which, I should note, do not reflect survey responses per se, but have been incorporated in the data set by matching respondents (via their zip codes) to the school districts in which they reside. The focus here is on two variables that are clearly relevant to parental choice:

(1) district context
(2) residential mobility

Recall that the first uses demographics and test scores to measure how advantaged or disadvantaged a district is, while the second measures how much weight (if any) respondents attached to school quality in deciding where to live. The actual analysis includes a number of additional contextual variables (such as revenue per student) for purposes of statistical control.[4] Like the background controls, they are not included in the tables.

The attitude portion of the analysis is an attempt to explore the influence of a small number of basic attitudes that, for reasons set out in chapters 2 and 3, seem especially relevant to the way Americans evaluate schools. They deal with the following:

(1) diversity (support for racial integration in the public schools)

(2) inequity (a perception that public schools provide an inferior education for low-income and minority kids)

(3) school prayer (support for voluntary prayer in the public schools)

(4) parent influence (support for more of it, versus trusting teachers and principals)

(5) school size (a preference for smaller over larger schools)

(6) public school ideology (a normative attachment to public schooling and its ideals)

(7) markets (a general belief that choice and competition are likely to make schools more effective)

(8) moral values (a concern that moral values are poorly taught in the public system)

The only wrinkle here is that the effect of diversity is estimated separately for white and nonwhite respondents, and, to keep things simple, only the estimate for whites is presented in the tables. The reason for this is pretty obvious: in the politics of education, a standard fear is that many whites are racially motivated in their approach to schooling and that, in particular, they will choose to separate themselves from minorities if given a chance. By singling out whites for attention, we can see whether this fear is borne out.

The final model typically introduces one or more variables that measure satisfaction with school performance. Because these variables are sometimes different from chapter to chapter, they will be discussed at the time they are introduced. In this chapter, where satisfaction is actually the dependent variable, the final independent variable is direct experience, which is the most proximate cause of how people (parents) see their local schools.

What Accounts for Overall Satisfaction?

Now let's get down to business. Why do people evaluate the schools as they do? The task is to pull together the ideas from earlier chapters, investigate their relative importance, and see whether they add up to a coherent perspective that can tell us something about the politics of vouchers and of education more generally.

Our focus here is on overall satisfaction, which is measured as an index of several survey items. In chapter 2, our discussion centered on three items that tap satisfaction in different ways: one asks respondents whether the schools are "doing well," one asks them to rate their schools' performance from 1 to 10, and one asks them about their community's pride in the schools. The findings indicate, not surprisingly, that these items are correlated with one another and are prime candidates to be averaged into a summary index of overall satisfaction. We went on, however, to show that responses to these items are heavily shaped by academic considerations. In view of this, it makes sense to include the survey item on academic performance as an additional component of the index. The measure of overall satisfaction employed in this chapter, then, is an average of four separate indicators: the three initial measures, plus the academic item.

One more preliminary point. It might seem natural to carry out this analysis by using the entire national sample of 4,700 respondents. But it is better not to. Parents have different stakes in the schools than nonparents do, and the two groups may well think rather differently about the issues (including vouchers) and show different patterns of effects. Similarly, public parents are likely to think about things differently than private parents. And inner-city parents are likely to be different from parents who live in the suburbs.

Accordingly, here and throughout the book, I will break the analysis down by group. Usually, I will give separate attention to public parents, nonparents, and inner-city parents. The survey gives us large numbers of respondents in each category, and each is clearly important to the politics of vouchers. Private parents are important too, of course, but there are far fewer of them and their opinions are usually less central to the themes we are developing here. So to keep things simple, I have chosen not to present separate estimates for them in the multivariate portion of the analysis (except in chapter 5, which is about going private). They will, however, be included in each chapter's descriptive statistics.

Let's begin with the findings for public parents, which are set out in table 4-1. There is a lot of information here, and it is important not to get hung up on all the details. We should instead be alert to basic patterns and remain focused on whether the ideas developed in earlier chapters seem to have explanatory value.

By way of introduction, note how useful it is to have incrementally different models to compare. The background model, for instance, shows that parents with higher incomes are more satisfied with their schools.

Table 4-1. Satisfaction with Public Schools (Public School Parents)[a]

Variable	Background model		Context model		Attitude model		Performance model	
	Coefficient	[Impact]	Coefficient	[Impact]	Coefficient	[Impact]	Coefficient	[Impact]
Background								
Education	-.02	[-.08]	-.05***	[-.17]	-.04***	[-.13]	-.05***	[-.17]
Income	.04***	[.21]	.02*	[.09]	.02*	[.08]	.00	[.00]
Catholic	.07*	[.09]	.06	[.08]	.07*	[.09]	.03	[.04]
Born-again	-.03	[-.04]	-.01	[-.01]	.02	[.03]	-.03	[-.04]
Black (north)	-.24***	[-.31]	-.04	[-.05]	-.05	[-.07]	-.07	[-.09]
Black (south)	-.02	[-.03]	.10	[.13]	.11	[.14]	.02	[.03]
Hispanic	-.02	[-.03]	.10*	[.13]	.10*	[.13]	.08	[.13]
Age	.00	[.02]	.01	[.06]	.01	[.05]	.00	[.02]
Party identification	-.01	[-.03]	-.01	[-.05]	-.01	[-.04]	-.01	[-.06]
Low expectations	.05***	[.20]	.06***	[.23]	.06***	[.22]	.05***	[.20]
Context								
Residential mobility			.10***	[.29]	.10***	[.29]	.08***	[.23]
Advantaged district			.16***	[.36]	.14***	[.33]	.13***	[.29]

	(1)		(2)		(3)		(4)	
Attitudes								
Diversity (whites)					.03	[.07]	.02	[.04]
Inequity					−.09***	[−.19]	−.04**	[−.08]
School prayer					.03**	[.09]	.03**	[.08]
Parent influence					−.10***	[−.20]	−.06***	[−.12]
School size					−.05**	[−.10]	−.05***	[−.10]
Public school ideology					.08**	[.15]	.06***	[.11]
Markets					−.05**	[−.09]	−.01	[−.02]
Moral values					.01	[.04]	.02**	[.09]
Performance								
Direct experience							.49***	[.88]
Constant	−.03		.07		.12		.34	
N[b]	(2,553)		(2,304)		(2,304)		(2,304)	
Adjusted R^2	.05		.10		.13		.31	

* Significant at .10 level.
** Significant at .05 level.
*** Significant at .01 level.

a. The dependent variable is an index of satisfaction with public school performance that is based on five performance items discussed in chapter 2 (see appendix A). Ordinary least squares regressions estimated using weighted data. Unstandardized coefficients reported. For each nondichotomous independent variable, the impact coefficient represents the estimated change in the dependent variable (measured in standard deviations) when the independent variable shifts by two standard deviations, holding all other variables constant; for each dichotomous variable, the impact coefficient represents the estimated change in the dependent variable (measured in standard deviations) when the independent variable shifts from 0 to 1, holding all other variables constant. Models control for the full range of background and context variables, not all of which are reported in the tables.

b. N is the unweighted number of respondents.

Indeed, next to race (northern blacks), income is the most powerful determinant of satisfaction, judging from the impact coefficients.[5] This makes perfect sense and attests to the importance of money under the current system. People with money get what they want. The context model, however, reveals that the impact of income on satisfaction is drastically reduced—cut by more than half—when controls are introduced for district context and residential mobility (as well as other contextual variables). This too is as it should be. What it says is not that income is less important, but rather that the *reason* income is so predominant in the background model is that people with money are able to exercise residential mobility and locate themselves in desirable districts (among other things).

The same is true for race. The background model suggests that, even when income, education, and expectations are controlled, northern blacks are more likely than whites to be dissatisfied with their schools. Yet from the context model we can see that, when the usual contextual variables are controlled, this racial effect goes away entirely. Again, this doesn't mean that race is irrelevant. It means that the reason northern blacks are especially dissatisfied is due to their context: they are more likely to be located in disadvantaged districts than whites, and they are less able to exercise residential mobility.

While we're on the topic: these findings about race also caution against overgeneralizing about how minorities view the schools. Once education, income, expectations, and context are taken into account—the things that many minorities have in common, and that tend (in the aggregate) to give them common views on many issues—the differences across minority groups become more apparent. Here, northern blacks emerge as considerably more critical of the schools than southern blacks are, and considerably more critical than Hispanics as well. The reasons are probably rooted in culture and experience—factors that are not taken into account in this analysis. Blacks and Hispanics, in particular, are literally worlds apart. The latter tend to come from cultures that are more deferential toward authority and more paternalistic, and many are recently arrived from countries in which basic services are barely provided. It is not very surprising, then, that Hispanics turn out to be less critical of the schools than northern blacks; and it wouldn't be surprising if they were less eager to go private and less interested in vouchers. Whatever the case, minority groups are sometimes very different, and generalizing about them—once we get beyond the social disadvantages they often share—can be misleading.

Now let's turn to the basic ideas from previous chapters and see how they stand up to the data. Several conclusions deserve to be highlighted:

(1) The direct experience parents have with their own children's schools is by far the most important determinant of their satisfaction with the local school system. This only makes sense. Indeed, because direct experience is so "close" to the dependent variable, the former might even be regarded as another satisfaction measure that doesn't really belong in the equation as an independent variable like the others. The point it drives home, though, is worth remembering: much of the satisfaction parents express for the local public schools appears to be rooted in their own experiences—which tend to be positive and probably reflect (if imperfectly) the actual quality of their schools, especially when other variables (such as low expectations) are controlled. There is a rational basis for their satisfaction.

(2) Aside from direct experience, the most important influence on satisfaction with the schools is district context, followed closely by residential mobility—both of which are presumably reflections of school quality. Here again, there seems to be a rational basis to the way Americans evaluate their schools. On the surface, this may seem out of keeping with the earlier finding that satisfaction is rather uniform across districts, surprisingly high in the less advantaged districts, and subject to perverse influences that keep it higher than it objectively ought to be. But there really is no inconsistency. In this chapter's analysis, unlike the earlier one, we try to control for the factors (such as low expectations) that account for these countervailing effects—and when we do, the objective context emerges as a more powerful explanation than it appeared to be at first blush.[6]

(3) A look at these other factors, however, strongly suggests that there are indeed forces at work within the education system, as argued in chapter 3, that generate satisfaction regardless of whether the system is performing well. Even in the presence of countless controls, for instance, education and expectations continue to have perverse effects on how parents see the public schools. Parents who are poorly educated and have low expectations are more likely to be satisfied with their local schools, whatever their quality, than other parents are. Low expectations, in fact, turns out to be one of the most important influences in the entire model. This is an especially troubling phenomenon that may keep satisfaction artificially high in all districts. But poor education and low expectations are more prevalent in disadvantaged districts, so there is reason to think that these factors have disproportionately propped up satisfaction in those areas and prevented parents from complaining about their schools.[7]

(4) The other factors explored in chapter 3 also work as expected, and thus to boost systemwide satisfaction. One is public school ideology. As the attitude model shows, parents who adhere to the ideology—which encourages support for the public system, even if it performs poorly—do indeed express more satisfaction with their schools; this normative commitment to the public schools, in fact, is one of the top attitudinal influences on their satisfaction. Another positive factor is residential mobility, which keeps satisfaction high by allowing people who exercise choice to locate themselves in areas where they are happier. Yet another factor is private school choice. This one is not included in the current analysis because of the focus on public parents only. But a more inclusive analysis would show, as expected, that private parents are indeed significantly less satisfied with the public schools than public parents are—and thus that their removal from the public system keeps the average satisfaction level higher than it would otherwise be, especially in less advantaged districts (where many private parents are located). The bottom line: every one of chapter 2's expectations is confirmed.[8]

(5) We showed in chapter 2 that many people are dissatisfied with the public schools on specific policy dimensions, and it is only reasonable to think that these concerns should spill over to affect their overall satisfaction with the schools. While it is true that their overall assessments of the schools appear to give special weight to academics, some of these specific dimensions—parent influence, school size, markets—are directly related to the academic performance of schools. The others may be only tangentially related to academics, but the concerns they bring to bear—about race, equity, religion, moral values, normative commitment—are surely important ones, and may also contribute to the level of satisfaction people express.

As table 4-1's attitude model indicates, most of the specific dimensions we have singled out for attention—inequity, public school ideology, prayer, parent influence, school size, and markets—are indeed related to overall satisfaction. Three stand out as especially salient. One is public school ideology, as noted above. The other two are inequity and parent influence. People who see the public system as inequitable are particularly inclined to express dissatisfaction in their overall judgments, as are people who think parents should have more influence. These two dimensions have been central themes of the voucher movement over the last decade, perhaps more than any of the other attitudes we explore here, and their salience in this analysis suggests that the movement may find a supportive audience on these grounds.

I do not want to get ahead of myself. But it is worth pointing out, to avoid confusion, that the parent influence factor does *not* prove to be very influential in the analysis of subsequent chapters. It has only weak influence, for example, on why parents want to go private (see chapter 5) and on why they support vouchers (see chapter 7). In view of this, I have to wonder about the strength of its impact here. One possibility is that there is some mutual causality at work that inflates this variable's true effect. Parents who are satisfied with their schools, for instance, may be more trusting of their schools' administrators and teachers, and thus less concerned with the need for parent influence—inducing a negative correlation that is actually not due to the causal arrow our model presumes. Whatever the explanation, this chapter's analysis is the only one in which parent influence appears important.

The inequity dimension is another matter. Here, it proves to be among the top influences on parental satisfaction with the public schools, and in subsequent chapters, it *consistently* stands out as a major and often the predominant attitudinal influence on how parents (and usually nonparents) think about the schools.[9] Because the modern wing of the voucher movement is fundamentally based on equity concerns, and because this is so central to its political appeals and its prospects for political success, the consistent strength of equity concerns throughout this analysis will turn out to be one of the key findings of the book.

(6) With equity so important, it is worth pursuing in more detail. Specifically, we might think that equity concerns should be especially salient to parents who are disadvantaged and less so to parents who are advantaged—which, if true, would say a lot about the political role of equity in attracting a constituency for vouchers. To test for this, we can simply adjust the model to see whether the impact of equity on satisfaction varies with parental income. The results (for the attitude model only) are reported in table 4-2. They show that equity concerns *are* much more salient among low-income parents than among parents in the middle- and upper-income groups. Judging from the impact coefficients, low-income parents put more than twice as much weight on equity as the other parents do. The modern voucher movement's emphasis on the equity issue, then, may strike a very responsive chord among the less advantaged.

(7) Equity has a lot to do with the way parents evaluate their schools, but race—or at least the aspects of race we have measures for—apparently does not. As we saw in chapter 2, many parents are against busing and oppose the current system's policy of promoting common schooling at the expense of neighborhood schools. Yet these racial issues don't prompt

Table 4-2. *Effects of Inequity on Satisfaction with Public Schools (Public School Parents)*[a]

	Attitude model	
	---	---
Variable	Coefficient	[Impact]
Attitudes		
Diversity (whites)	.03	[.06]
Inequity (low income)	−.13***	[−.28]
Inequity (middle income)	−.06**	[−.13]
Inequity (upper income)	−.06	[−.12]
School prayer	.03**	[.09]
Parent influence	−.10***	[−.20]
School size	−.05**	[−.10]
Public school ideology	.08***	[.15]
Markets	−.05**	[−.09]
Moral values	.01	[.03]
Constant	.12	
N[b]	(2,304)	
Adjusted R^2	.13	

** Significant at .05 level.
*** Significant at .01 level.
   a. The dependent variable is an index of satisfaction with public school performance that is based on five performance items discussed in chapter 2 (see appendix A). Ordinary least squares regression estimated using weighted data. Unstandardized coefficients reported. For each nondichotomous independent variable, the impact coefficient represents the estimated change in the dependent variable (measured in standard deviations) when the independent variable shifts by two standard deviations, holding all other variables constant; for each dichotomous variable, the impact coefficient represents the estimated change in the dependent variable (measured in standard deviations) when the independent variable shifts from 0 to 1, holding all other variables constant. Model controls for the full range of background and context variables, not all of which are reported in the tables.
   b. N is the unweighted number of respondents.

them to be less satisfied with the public schools overall—nor, looked at the other way, does it prompt parents who support diversity to think more highly of the public schools. This may seem odd, given the racial history of American education. But it is the first of a series of similar findings throughout this book, which together suggest that race—as we have measured it—may not be as salient to the way Americans view their schools as has commonly been assumed.

(8) Among parents, satisfaction with the schools also seems little influenced by the kinds of partisan, religious, and moral concerns that are so prevalent in the politics of education. Republicans express just as much satisfaction with the schools as Democrats do. Parents who are critical of the way moral values are taught are actually no more inclined to give the schools low performance ratings than other parents are. Catholics and born-again Christians are no less satisfied than the baseline group (regular

Protestants)—and Catholics, by this estimation, are actually more satisfied. Indeed, across all groups, the people who support school prayer are more satisfied with their schools than the people who are against prayer. All in all, there is no evidence that some sort of social conservatism is at work among parents to undermine their satisfaction with the schools.

Nonparents may be quite different from parents. They don't have an immediate stake in the schools, they don't have ongoing direct experiences with them, they have less incentive to seek out school-related information, and as a result they may be more susceptible than parents to whatever comes across in the media—much of which is negative and framed by elite-level concerns and conflicts. On the other hand, many have had school-age children in the recent past and are not very removed from the education scene. During their everyday lives, moreover, they may find themselves talking to parents and picking up what parents know and think about the schools. Thus, in some respects, they may turn out to see the schools much as parents do. People in the same community may view things rather similarly, whether parents or nonparents.

Both these perspectives are probably valid to some extent. There are reasons to expect differences, and reasons to expect similarities. Here is what the data have to say (see table 4-3).

(1) While income is a major determinant of satisfaction for parents, it has nothing to do with satisfaction for nonparents. Although we might have expected some effect, given the connection between school quality and property values, it makes sense that income should play a smaller role for nonparents than for parents because they have much less need to "purchase" good public schools than parents do.

(2) Regarding race, the data for nonparents reinforce the earlier finding for parents: northern blacks are more critical of the schools than are whites (and other minorities), even when education and income are controlled. Southern blacks, on the other hand, are actually more satisfied than whites—an odd result that may say something, again, about their distinctive culture and experience.

(3) Although income plays a weaker role for nonparents, their evaluations of the schools are just as sensitive to their contexts as those of parents are. Indeed, district context and residential mobility are the most powerful determinants of satisfaction for public parents (aside from their direct experiences)—and basically the same is true of nonparents. It appears universal, then, that context is the prime shaper of satisfaction. This reinforces the notion that, despite certain perversities, there is a rational core to the way Americans evaluate the schools.

Table 4-3. *Satisfaction with Public Schools (Nonparents)*[a]

Variable	Background model		Context model		Attitude model	
	Coefficient	[Impact]	Coefficient	[Impact]	Coefficient	[Impact]
Background						
Education	−.00	[−.01]	−.00	[−.01]	.01	[.02]
Income	−.00	[−.02]	−.01	[−.06]	−.01	[−.05]
Catholic	−.06	[−.08]	−.05	[−.06]	−.04	[.05]
Born-again	−.18**	[−.23]	−.22***	[−.28]	−.20**	[−.25]
Black (north)	−.23**	[−.29]	−.12	[−.15]	−.16	[−.20]
Black (south)	.14*	[.18]	.22**	[.28]	.17*	[.22]
Hispanic	−.07	[−.09]	.03	[.04]	−.03	[−.04]
Age	−.01	[−.08]	−.01	[−.06]	−.01	[−.08]
Party identification	−.03***	[−.14]	−.03***	[−.16]	−.03**	[−.13]
Low expectations	.09***	[.33]	.08***	[.29]	.07***	[.26]
Context						
Residential mobility			.13***	[.28]	.13***	[.28]
Advantaged district			.15***	[.29]	.15***	[.30]
Attitudes						
Diversity (whites)					.03	[.06]
Inequity					−.09***	[−.17]
School prayer					.02	[.08]
Parent influence					−.07***	[−.17]
School size					−.01	[−.02]
Public school ideology					.09***	[.16]
Markets					−.05*	[−.09]
Moral values					−.00	[−.01]
Constant	.03		−.13		−.21***	
N[b]	(1,589)		(1,439)		(1,439)	
Adjusted R^2	.09		.14		.16	

* Significant at .10 level.
** Significant at .05 level.
*** Significant at .01 level.
   a. The dependent variable is an index of satisfaction with public school performance that is based on five performance items discussed in chapter 2 (see appendix A). Ordinary least squares regressions estimated using weighted data. Unstandardized coefficients reported. For each nondichotomous independent variable, the impact coefficient represents the estimated change in the dependent variable (measured in standard deviations) when the independent variable shifts by two standard deviations, holding all other variables constant; for each dichotomous variable, the impact coefficient represents the estimated change in the dependent variable (measured in standard deviations) when the independent variable shifts from 0 to 1, holding all other variables constant. Models control for the full range of background and context variables, not all of which are reported in the tables.
   b. N is the unweighted number of respondents.

(4) Chapter 3's arguments about factors that tend to keep satisfaction uniformly high, even in the least advantaged districts, are once again confirmed here. While low education does not seem to promote satisfaction among nonparents (which I find surprising and may just be a quirk in the data), low expectations do play an influential role in boosting satisfaction—and the perverse effects appear to be even stronger for nonparents

than for parents. Public school ideology also has a significant effect on nonparents' satisfaction, suggesting that this normative commitment to the schools has a positive influence that is widespread throughout the population. And finally, as noted above, residential choice also proves to be a key factor. Its availability makes satisfaction higher among nonparents than it would otherwise be and keeps quality-conscious people out of districts where they would be dissatisfied.

(5) When we turn to the specific policy dimensions discussed in chapter 2, we find another striking similarity. Aside from public school ideology, the satisfaction of nonparents is most strongly influenced by the same two dimensions that are salient for public parents: inequity and parent influence. As I discussed earlier, there is reason to question the generality of the parent influence factor (as well as its impact in this particular analysis), but the strength of the inequity factor deserves emphasis—because it will be repeated again and again in later analysis. It is a prime determinant of the way Americans think about their schools.

(6) If, however, we pursued a more detailed analysis of the inequity variable, asking—as we did for parents—whether its impact is greater for low-income respondents than it is for those in the middle- and upper-income groups, we would find that there is *not* such a differentiated impact for nonparents. Inequity is a salient concern for them, but its salience does not vary by social class, as it does for parents. We would find the same thing, moreover, in subsequent chapters. What this is telling us, most likely, is that the inequity of the current public school system has a direct bearing on the lives of low-income parents, far more so than it does for parents who are better off and for people who don't have kids in school. Of all members of society, low-income parents pay the highest price for educational inequities, and it is not surprising that they are the ones who attach the most weight to it in evaluating the system's performance. Nonparents attach weight to it too, but for them there is less reason for it to be closely tied to their own social class.

(7) As was true for parents, the salience of equity is not paralleled by the salience of racial attitudes. Support or opposition to diversity seems to have little to do with how satisfied nonparents are with their local schools.

(8) While school prayer and moral values seem to have no relevance among nonparents, there is some evidence of other influences of social conservatism. Republicans are more critical of the schools than Democrats are. Born-again Christians also stand out as especially critical. And the coefficient of the Catholic term, while weak, is also negative. It is simply unclear, however, why these influences should play a more prominent role

for nonparents than they do for parents. Partisanship may play a greater role for nonparents because they rely more heavily on the media for information about the schools. But the same thing would not explain the other results. If anything, we would expect Catholic and born-again parents to be the ones who are especially dissatisfied, not Catholic and born-again nonparents.

In any event, these details are not of great moment. The more general and important result is that, when it comes to the key influences—district context, residential mobility, low expectations, inequity, public school ideology—the thinking of parents and nonparents is structured in much the same ways.

Inner-City Public School Parents

In this section, we take a separate look at inner-city parents. Here and throughout the book, our attention focuses on those inner-city parents who are low in income (earning less than $30,000 per year) and whose children are in the public schools. (See appendix A for a discussion of the sample.)

What accounts for the way inner-city parents evaluate their schools? The results are presented in table 4-4. Some of the estimates—for income, race, and district context—may seem surprisingly weak at first. But we have to remember that we are dealing here with a very restricted sample: all parents are low in income, most are minority, and almost all live in disadvantaged districts. So when we look *within* the inner city, rather than at the population at large, there is not much scope for these factors to demonstrate their impacts, and their impacts are more difficult to measure with confidence (as reflected in low levels of statistical significance).[10]

The rest of the findings are more straightforward and offer some useful comparisons to public parents generally.

(1) For inner-city parents, direct experience with their own children's schools is by far the most important influence on their overall satisfaction. Its impact appears to be roughly the same as it is for parents generally.

(2) Inner-city parents are responsive to their objective contexts. Those who exercise residential mobility (which could mean, in the inner-city context, just moving from neighborhood to neighborhood) are more likely to give their schools positive evaluations, and the same is true of parents whose inner-city districts are more advantaged than most (although the district context factor is not always statistically significant). These find-

ings provide additional evidence, in conjunction with the evidence on direct experience, that there is a rational core to their evaluations.

(3) The perverse effects of education and low expectations, which operate among parents generally to promote higher levels of satisfaction regardless of school quality, prove to be especially powerful—and especially perverse—within the inner city. In fact, for inner-city parents, low expectations stand out as the single most important influence (aside from direct experience) on satisfaction with the schools.

(4) The attitude model suggests that inner-city parents attach weight to a number of attitudes—having to do with inequity, prayer, public school ideology, and markets—in their evaluations of the public schools. Of these, inequity is among the strongest influences. This is consistent with earlier findings about the special salience that low-income parents attach to equity issues—and suggests, once again, that the voucher movement's recent emphasis on equity is likely to strike a responsive chord within this constituency.

When it comes to evaluating the public schools, then, inner-city parents have a lot in common with other public parents. They are highly responsive to direct experience. They are responsive to residential mobility and district context. They are especially concerned about social equity. And they are burdened by the perverse effects of lack of education and low expectations.

Conclusion

When Americans judge how well their schools are doing, the most important influences on their thinking arise from the substantive context of education—from how advantaged or disadvantaged the district is, from the decision to locate in a district or neighborhood because of the schools, and from the direct experiences of parents. The predominance of context, moreover, is universal. It shapes the assessments of nonparents, parents, and inner-city parents alike. This is not to say that Americans are well informed about the schools, nor that their thinking is entirely focused on school quality. It is to say, rather, that there is a substantive basis for much of what they think, one that is anchored in the reality of schools as they experience it.

For the voucher movement, the dynamics of public opinion are encouraging in some respects, discouraging in others. On the plus side is the simple fact that people *are* less satisfied with schools of lower quality. This

Table 4-4. Satisfaction with Public Schools (Inner-City Public School Parents)[a]

Variable	Background model		Context model		Attitude model		Performance model	
	Coefficient	[Impact]	Coefficient	[Impact]	Coefficient	[Impact]	Coefficient	[Impact]
Background								
Education	-.08**	[-.21]	-.08**	[-.22]	-.08**	[-.20]	-.08**	[-.20]
Income	.05	[.07]	.08	[.09]	.11	[.13]	.09	[.10]
Catholic	.02	[.02]	.05	[.06]	.07	[.08]	.00	[.00]
Born-again	-.08	[-.10]	-.11	[-.13]	-.14	[-.17]	-.21	[-.25]
Black (north)	.08	[.10]	.13	[.16]	.07	[.08]	.01	[-.01]
Black (south)	-.16	[-.19]	-.04	[-.05]	-.00	[-.00]	-.12	[-.15]
Hispanic	-.06	[-.07]	-.01	[-.01]	-.01	[-.01]	-.03	[-.04]
Age	.03*	[.17]	.01	[.08]	.02	[.12]	.01	[.09]
Party identification	-.01	[-.04]	-.02	[-.08]	-.02	[-.08]	-.03	[-.13]
Low expectations	.07***	[.29]	.08***	[.30]	.08***	[.32]	.08***	[.31]
Context								
Residential mobility			.08**	[.18]	.09**	[.19]	.07*	[.14]
Advantaged district			.09	[.16]	.10*	[.18]	.08	[.15]

	Model 1		Model 2		Model 3	
Attitudes						
Diversity (whites)			.01	[.01]	-.00	[-.00]
Inequity			-.14***	[-.25]	-.04	[-.06]
School prayer			.07**	[.18]	.06*	[.15]
Parent influence			-.02	[-.03]	-.01	[-.02]
School size			-.13***	[-.26]	-.12***	[-.24]
Public school ideology			.11**	[.19]	.05	[.09]
Markets			-.10**	[-.20]	-.06	[-.11]
Moral values			.03	[.10]	.03	[.10]
Performance						
Direct experience					.51***	[.82]
Constant	.19		.29		.58	
N[b]	(539)		(506)		(506)	
Adjusted R^2	.07		.12		.28	

* Significant at .10 level.
** Significant at .05 level.
*** Significant at .01 level.

a. The dependent variable is an index of satisfaction with public school performance that is based on five performance items discussed in chapter 2 (see appendix A). Ordinary least squares regressions estimated using weighted data. Unstandardized coefficients reported. For each nondichotomous independent variable, the impact coefficient represents the estimated change in the dependent variable (measured in standard deviations) when the independent variable shifts by two standard deviations, holding all other variables constant; for each dichotomous variable, the impact coefficient represents the estimated change in the dependent variable (measured in standard deviations) when the independent variable shifts from 0 to 1, holding all other variables constant. Models control for the full range of background and context variables, not all of which are reported in the tables.

b. N is the unweighted number of respondents.

is something the movement can try to capitalize on. The people who are less satisfied, moreover, tend to be groups that the modern movement has seen as its prime political constituency: low-income parents, northern blacks, people in disadvantaged districts.

The movement may also benefit from attitudes prevalent within the broader population. A central theme of the modern voucher movement is that the current education system is inequitable. In chapter 2, we saw that large numbers of Americans agree. And in this chapter, we find that perceptions of inequity are universally important influences on public satisfaction—shaping the thinking of nonparents, parents, and inner-city parents, and taking on special salience for parents who are low in income. In models containing large numbers of possible influences, including a long list of competing attitudes, perceptions of inequity consistently come out near the top. Politically, this is a finding of great significance. For inequity is capable of igniting political action and driving educational reform, and it is an issue on which the current education system is vulnerable. If people see vouchers as a means of bringing greater equity to the system, the movement may find that this is one of its most attractive appeals.

But all the news is not encouraging. To begin with, the satisfaction of parents with the public system is heavily influenced by their own direct experiences, which are quite positive. And this positive glow almost surely spills over to affect the perceptions of nonparents as well. It is difficult to avoid the conclusion that this is a real obstacle, given its rooting in concrete experience, and one that the movement may have to labor to overcome.

In addition, the public school system benefits from a whole array of forces that generate higher levels of satisfaction even if the system doesn't perform very well. Many Americans embrace what I have called the public school ideology, and thus have a normative commitment to the public schools that causes them to see the system in a positive light. The availability of residential choice allows many people to sort themselves into better districts and to stay out of low-performing ones, thus raising their satisfaction. And the availability of private school choice allows parents who are dissatisfied with the public schools to leave, thus raising the average satisfaction levels within the system by draining off the discontented. All of these factors, this analysis shows, do indeed have significant effects on satisfaction—and do, it appears, work as chapter 3 suggests in promoting a nurturing, protective environment for the public schools.

One satisfaction-promoting factor stands out as especially perverse in its effects. That factor is low expectations, which, together with low education, generates an unfortunate sociological phenomenon in which certain people are inclined to be satisfied with low-quality schools. The perverse impact of low expectations is felt throughout the population, among parents and nonparents alike, and is especially problematic for inner-city parents. This does not turn inner-city parents into fanatical supporters of the system, for they are sensitive to their objective contexts as well, and, precisely because they are, they remain less satisfied with their public schools than other parents. Nonetheless, they are more satisfied than their contexts would lead us to expect—and thus, presumably, less likely to complain about their situations and less open to proposals for change. This is clearly not a good thing for the voucher movement, which is counting on the dissatisfaction of inner-city parents to fuel the fires of reform.

All in all, these findings paint a mixed picture for the movement and its prospects. There are important opportunities here for picking up support among the dissatisfied, especially on grounds of social equity. But there are also major forces at work that keep satisfaction reasonably high, even in the least advantaged districts, and provide the public schools with a supportive environment that would seem well suited to a political defense of the status quo.

The question is: can the voucher movement make progress in such an environment? The answers will become clearer in subsequent chapters, as we begin to take a look at how people view private schools and what they think about vouchers.

5   *The Attraction*
of Private Schools

IF VOUCHERS ARE to take hold in American education, private schools must be popular with parents. This is obviously true on practical grounds alone, for there would be little point to vouchers if parents didn't want to use them to go private. But parents are also crucial for political reasons. When parents want to go private, they have a self-interest in supporting vouchers, and their self-interest is likely to translate into political power for the movement. In addition, a parental interest in going private is a potent source of evidence to the public at large, as well as to political elites, that a voucher program would benefit lots of people and be good for society as a whole. In important respects, then, parents are the key to the whole thing. The more they want to go private, the brighter the movement's prospects for success.

What accounts for the desire to go private? From Milton Friedman on, voucher proponents have largely put the emphasis on performance. Given the freedom to choose, they argue, parents seek out the best schools they can for their children. Under current arrangements, where private schools are costly, only people with enough money are really able to improve their opportunities in this way. But were vouchers extended to public parents, making private schools available to them at low (or zero) cost, many of them would do the same. They would use their new powers of choice to seek out better-performing schools.[1]

To the extent proponents are right, and performance is at the heart of why parents might be interested in going private, our own data are already of some relevance. From the previous chapter, we know that most public parents have positive experiences with their own children's schools and are reasonably satisfied with the public system's performance overall. This seems to imply that they are not eager to escape into the private sector for performance reasons and that proponents might be in for a disappointment. On the other hand, we know from chapter 2's analysis that most public parents actually think private schools are *better*, and that there are specific issues—such as social equity—on which they find the public system wanting. This second side of the equation puts things in a different light, for it suggests that even a fairly satisfied population of public parents could still generate a strong demand for private schools— not because they are abjectly unhappy with what they have, but because they want something better.

To many critics of vouchers, however, this sort of discussion misses the reality of private school choice. They argue that going private often has little to do with the quality of the public schools, or with how their academic performance compares to that of private schools. The real motivations are largely social—and the impact on the public interest pernicious. The private sector, they contend, has a special appeal to people with money and education, who want their children to be separated from ordinary kids. It has a special appeal to whites, who want to avoid sending their children to school with blacks. It has a special appeal to the devoutly religious, who seek a church-based education they cannot find in the public sector. And in general, it has a special appeal to separatists of all kinds, whatever the grounds of separation might be.[2]

So far, critics argue, the social downside of choice has been kept in check by the fact that, under current arrangements, only 10 percent of American children go private. But if private school choice were expanded, these same motivations would be unleashed to an even greater extent, and the negative effects on society would only get *worse*, resulting in an education system that is more inequitable, more segregated, more penetrated by religion.

As the scope of these arguments can only suggest, the simple question of why parents want to go private is in fact one of the most fundamental that can be asked about the voucher issue, with far-reaching consequences for the way we understand its effects on society and politics. There is a small body of research that sheds a measure of light on these matters. But for the most part, there is surprisingly little evidence to go on.

This chapter is an attempt to do something about that. In part, the analysis will explore who goes private under the current system and why they choose to do so. But this is just part of a broader foundation for understanding the more interesting point at issue here: what would happen if money were taken out of the equation, and *all* parents were granted the choice of sending their kids to private schools? Then how would parents and students distribute themselves across the two sectors? Would there be a class bias? A religious bias? A racial bias? Would performance be the dominant concern for most parents, or would social considerations, including pernicious ones, heavily shape their choice of schools? Would a private sector based on free choice help promote social equity, or would it deepen existing problems? This analysis is an effort to provide at least some tentative answers.

The Logic of Choice

Before turning to the data, let's begin by thinking rather abstractly for a moment about the demand for private schooling. We need to recognize, for starters, that the way parents currently sort themselves into public or private schools is not an immutable fact of life. Rather, it is inevitably shaped by the fact that public schools are free, while parents must pay if they want to send their children to private schools.

Under such a system, parental choice is governed by a simple calculus. Parents tend to go private if they can afford the tuition, and if the value they associate with going private—whether this value derives from performance, religion, race, or other sets of concerns—exceeds the costs. This calculus does *not* tell us what parents actually value. They may value performance, or they may not. They may value racial separation, or they may not. And so on. These are empirical issues. But the simple fact that parents must weigh any benefits against the financial costs points to basic implications that should guide our thinking.

Most obviously, private schools under this system are more accessible to the financially well-off because they are better able to afford the tuition. The same applies for the well educated, both because education is highly correlated with income and because better-educated parents tend to be more motivated by educational concerns. For these reasons, the current system should tend to promote a class bias in the types of parents going private, much as the critics of choice contend. This bias would only be enhanced, of course, if some of these parents were elitist and sought separation for its own sake. But even if none were elitists, a class bias would be an inherent part of the system.

To some extent, this class bias is mitigated by the fact that advantaged parents also tend to have the best public schools, thanks to residential choice, and thus the least incentive (on performance grounds alone) to seek out private alternatives. The parents with the most to gain (on performance grounds) are the ones who are stuck in the worst districts, and these parents are often poor and minority. The connection between private schooling and social class may be weaker, therefore, than some critics might lead us to believe. But some class bias is still likely, owing to the cost barriers that prevent most poor people from taking action.

In addition to the class bias, we should expect the current system to promote another kind of bias—namely, that the people who go private should tend to be somewhat extreme in their values or in the salience they attach to them. The reason is that parents who are unusually concerned about particular values—academics, religion, race—are more likely to think that the benefits of going private outweigh the financial costs. This is especially true at higher levels of tuition. The higher the costs, the more motivated parents have to be in order to justify paying them, and the greater the bias separating them from the average parent in the population.

Here too, however, there are mitigating factors at work. One is that tuition is rather modest at most private schools (the religious ones).[3] A second is that, to the extent there is value-heterogeneity among parents, the parents who feel intensely about a given value (such as religion) may be quite moderate on other value dimensions (such as race), so that the average position of private parents along all dimensions, or the average salience they attach to them, may be far more centrist than an extremist stereotype would suggest. Still, even with these mitigating factors, private schools should attract more than their share of parents at the extremes.

Now let's consider what would happen if choice were vastly expanded, and parents were allowed (via vouchers) to send their children to private schools at no cost. The most immediate implication is that even the poorest parents would now be able to pursue private schooling for their kids. Unless other factors—discrimination, for instance, or lack of information, or low expectations—prevent them from following through, the income biases associated with the current system would thereby be reduced, perhaps dramatically. Biases due to education (controlling for income) might remain, because the better-educated parents would continue to be more motivated to seek out new opportunities. But with income and education so highly correlated, and income no longer much of a factor, many more people with low educations would tend to find their way into the private sector.

Vouchers should also tend to reduce whatever "extremism" today's tuition-based system builds into private school choice. For with tuition effectively zero, parents' values can be quite moderate and still give them reason to go private. They merely need to think that private schools are marginally better on the dimensions they care about. As a result, the parents who go private under an expanded choice system should tend to look more like average citizens in their positions on key values and the salience they attach to them.

Moderation aside, however, many of the same values should continue to provide the motivation for going private. If the parents who currently go private are highly motivated by religion or moral values, for example, public parents who value the same things would be especially likely to seek out private schools if choice were expanded. In general, the public parents who express an interest in going private should be rather similar on value grounds to the parents who already go private. The former should simply be more moderate.

Sameness should be the norm, but there could be exceptions. This is most likely to happen if certain values are bound up with social class, particularly income—because it is the income constraint that is being relaxed when choice is expanded. People who are low in income, for instance, may attach more weight to equity than more advantaged people do and see this as an important reason for going private; but their lack of resources, under current arrangements, may prevent them from taking action. Thus an expansion of choice could bring a flood of low-income recruits into the private sector who are motivated by "new" values that play little role under the existing private system.

In sum, if we think in analytical terms about the demand side of school choice, there are logical reasons for thinking that an expansion of choice will have certain effects. Under the current system, in which choice is costly, private school choice can be expected to produce social biases that mirror some of the concerns of voucher critics. Judging by its effects on parental demand, however, an expansion of choice should not make these biases worse, as critics tend to argue. Rather, it is more reasonable to expect that precisely the opposite will happen, and that the biases of the existing system will actually be moderated, perhaps substantially.

The Research Literature

To date, there is little research on why parents go private, or on the larger consequences of an expanded system of school choice. Still, a measure of progress has been made, and in this section I will summarize some of the more relevant findings—all of which, at this stage, should be regarded as tentative.

There is a small body of research on who goes private under the current system. The typical study relies exclusively on background and contextual data (without data on attitudes) to compare private and public parents and ultimately to draw inferences about the motivations for choice. Most of this work is carried out at the individual level. Some of it, however, is entirely based on aggregate data, and essentially tries to explain the percentage of parents in a district that go private by reference to an array of district-level variables (such as average education or average income). It is a risky business to draw individual-level inferences from aggregate data, so the latter studies have to be regarded with caution.

Details aside, here is what this literature tends to suggest about the workings of private school choice under the current system:

(1) There is a class bias. Parents who are higher in education and income are the most likely to go private. The results on race are mixed: some studies show that minorities are less likely to go private than whites (controlling for class), while others show the opposite.[4]

(2) Parents appear to be motivated by academic performance: the lower the perceived or actual performance of their public schools (as measured, for example, by test scores), the greater the tendency of parents to go private.[5]

(3) Catholics are more inclined to go private.[6]

(4) Attitudes toward race may or may not matter. Early research argued that the racial composition of the student population has an effect on going private and, in particular, that whites tend to go private when minorities constitute a majority of students.[7] The (presumed) implication was that racial separation is a key attraction of private schooling. These early results have received a measure of subsequent support,[8] but this support has not been consistent, and some studies show that racial composition has no clear or systematic effect on going private.[9]

In addition to this research on who goes private, another body of research is relevant as well. This one has emerged in response to the school choice movement and is an effort to go beyond a focus on the current private system to understand the dynamics of choice more generally. Some are public opinion surveys that simply ask people about their support for choice. Others survey parents participating in specific types of school choice programs—from publicly funded vouchers to privately funded vouchers to various arrangements for choice among public schools—in an attempt to understand how choice gets exercised in practice. Both take advantage of attitudinal data that are lacking in the literature on private schools.

This is a diverse body of work, still in its formative stages, but on some issues the evidence seems reasonably consistent:

(1) Support for choice is greatest among low-income and minority parents.[10] Even when choice is restricted to low-income populations, however, there remains a bias due to education. It is the more educated who tend to use choice most aggressively.[11]

(2) Parents, including those who are low in income, appear to make their choices based largely on academic performance. While early work argued the contrary,[12] this emphasis on academics has now been supported in studies of public voucher programs,[13] private voucher programs,[14] and public school choice.[15]

(3) While religion and moral values are relevant for many parents, they appear less important to parents newly recruited to choice (via new voucher programs) than to the types of parents who have traditionally gone private.[16]

(4) Racial attitudes do not appear to be strong motivators for parental choice. There is some evidence, however, that they do matter. In a study of magnet schools, for instance, Jeffrey Henig shows that whites tend to request transfers to schools with low concentrations of minorities and that minorities tend to do the opposite.[17]

Discussion

These literatures are still developing, and we are advised not to embrace any of their conclusions with too much confidence. New work could prove them wrong. For now, though, they represent what social scientists "know" about parental choice, and they provide a useful empirical background for our own analysis.

The evidence suggests, first of all, that private school choice under the current (costly) system does indeed lead to biases on grounds of income and education—but that, given the popularity of choice among low-income and minority parents, an expansion of choice could well lead to a moderation and perhaps even a reversal of the income bias. Similar moderating effects would appear to apply for race (to the extent that there is a racial bias per se, which is unclear). As we should expect, however, education appears to be a different story. An education bias appears endemic to parental choice regardless of income. The question is: does this bias get moderated, in the aggregate, when more parents are freely able to choose? We would expect as much, but the existing evidence can't say.

As far as it goes, then, the evidence is consistent with our expectations about class and race. What about values? The existing literature does not have much to say about some of the values of concern to us here—those having to do with inequity, for instance, or parent influence. But it does explore a number of others. It suggests that religion and moral values are important reasons why many parents currently go private, and that they would continue to be influential concerns—albeit less so—if choice were expanded. It tends to support, in other words, our expectation that values would be moderated under an expansion of choice.

One of the most consistent conclusions to emerge from this research is that parents put primary emphasis on performance, especially academic performance, in choosing where to send their kids to school. Given the logic of choice, it is reasonable to think that this emphasis on performance would be especially strong among those already in the private sector, and would be moderated—but still strong and of primary importance—if choice were expanded to greater numbers of parents. For now, however, the evidence does not shed much light on whether this sort of moderation occurs, or to what extent.

Overall, then, it appears that our expectations are basically on the right track. But there is a lot that remains unknown, and a continuing need for new research—both to determine whether the tentative findings of existing work are valid, and to go beyond them in building a more complete understanding of parent choice.

The Hidden Interest in Private Schools

Now let's turn to our own survey and see what it can tell us about these matters. The first step is to get the lay of the land. We know that nationwide about 10 percent of American children are in private schools, and the rest are in public schools.[18] This lopsided division of families, however, is almost surely influenced in a big way by the simple fact that private schools are costly and public schools are free, and it hides whatever constituency for private schooling might exist within the public sector. It is clear that parents who actually do go private also want to go private. It is *not* clear that parents who go public are really doing what they want. Many may be interested in sending their kids to private schools but be unable to do so.

What is the extent of this hidden interest in private schools? There are various ways to get at this, but our survey provides one measure by asking all public school parents the following question: "If you could afford it, would you be interested in sending your children to a private or parochial school?" The results are striking. They show that *most* public parents, 52 percent, would indeed be interested in sending their kids to private schools if money were not a problem, compared to 43 percent who say they would stay in the public sector. This is consistent with the results of a 1999 survey by Public Agenda, which asked public parents a similar question and found that 55 percent were interested in going private.[19]

How about inner-city parents? If the logic we developed earlier is on target, they should be even more interested in private schooling than other public parents are. This turns out to be quite true. Sixty-seven percent of these parents express such an interest, compared to just 29 percent who say they would rather stay in the public sector.

The latent demand for private schooling is good news for the voucher movement, suggesting that there is a potentially large constituency for vouchers within the public sector, especially among parents who are less advantaged. It also suggests that, despite fairly high levels of overall satisfaction, many public parents seem to be quite interested in having new educational options. This is an indication that relative (dis)satisfaction is in the driver's seat—arising from their belief that private schools are of better quality—and that the good feelings parents tend to have about the public system will not necessarily protect it from vouchers.

Some Descriptive Data

Let's begin the analysis with some simple descriptive comparisons. The focus will be on two subjects of special importance. One has to do with the social biases usually attributed to choice and whether they would be moderated if choice were expanded. The other has to do with the parental value of greatest interest to us here—school performance—and the role it seems to play in attracting parents to private schools.

Bias and Moderation: A First Cut

Probably the most common way of thinking about bias and moderation is in terms of simple averages. It is reasonable to say that the existing private system exhibits an income bias, for example, when the average income for private parents is higher than the average for the population of parents as a whole. Similarly, an expansion of choice could be said to bring about moderation if the new recruits to the private sector have lower average levels of income than existing private parents, causing the average for the private sector as a whole to shift toward the population mean.

Table 5-1. *How Choice Affects Bias and Moderation*[a]

Variable	All parents	Current private school parents	Current public school parents	Public school parents interested in going private	Public school parents not interested in going private
Background					
Education	.00	.42	−.08	−.06	−.07
Income	.00	.43	−.08	−.13	−.00
Catholic	.29	.44	.26	.28	.23
Born-again	.08	.09	.08	.08	.07
Black	.15	.12	.15	.18	.11
Hispanic	.12	.06	.13	.16	.09
Party identification	.00	.21	−.04	−.04	−.05
Low expectations	.00	−.22	.05	.02	.09
Context					
Residential mobility	.00	−.17	.03	−.01	.08
Advantaged district	.00	−.04	.01	−.10	.13

a. Figures represent group averages. All nondichotomous variables have been standardized over the entire parent population to have a mean of 0 and a standard deviation of 1. Dichotomous variables are: Catholic, born–again, black, and Hispanic.

Here, we will use this approach to get an initial sense (to be augmented later) of the biases of the current private system and how they would appear to be affected by an expansion of choice. To keep things simple, our focus will be on the various social biases—particularly class, race, and religion—that have been salient in the public debate over vouchers. (We could readily extend the analysis to the full range of attitudes as well, but this would require a much lengthier discussion.)

The data are set out in table 5-1. For each of the various groups of parents, it provides average scores for the key background and contextual variables in the model. Except for the dichotomous variables (Catholic, born-again, black, Hispanic), these variables have been standardized across the parent population as a whole. For each nondichotomous variable, then, the population average is 0 (and the standard deviation is 1)—making it easy to see how the various groups compare to the average, as well as to one another.

What are the social biases associated with going private under the current system? There are good reasons, logical and empirical, for expecting parents who currently go private to be socially advantaged. And our survey documents as much. Private parents have higher incomes and educations than the average American parent, higher expectations, and are more likely to be white. They also display the religious and partisan characteristics commonly associated with private schooling: they are more likely to be Catholic or born-again, and Republican.

For clarity's sake, we can be a little more concrete about this. Consider education. The table indicates that the average education for private parents is .42, compared with 0 for parents as a whole, indicating that private parents are almost half a standard deviation above the population mean. Were we to look at the underlying distributions in more detail, we would see that 43 percent of private parents have a college education or better, versus 25 percent for parents as a whole. At the other end of the spectrum, just 11 percent of private parents have less than a high school education, compared with 23 percent for parents generally. These are the kinds of differences that the two population means summarize. Similar differences obtain for income. Overall, then, there is a pronounced class bias at work here. It is not as dramatic as some critics might have expected, but it is substantial.

There are also clear differences on religion and partisanship, although they are less substantial than those for class. In our sample, private parents are more likely to be Catholic than most parents are, by 44 percent to 29 percent, a reflection of the pervasiveness of Catholic schools within the private sector (where they enroll more than half of all the children), and an indicator of the central role that religion has traditionally played in private school choice. Still, these differences are not as striking as critics might have expected. The same is true for partisanship. The table indicates that private parents have a Republican score of .21, relative to the population baseline of 0, which means that they are about one-fifth of a standard deviation above average in Republican partisanship. If we look at the actual distributions, we find that 39 percent of private parents are Republicans, compared to 27 percent of parents as a whole.

The biases on other grounds appear even smaller (at least on the surface). Despite the upsurge in fundamentalist Christian schools over the last two decades, born-again Christians are not prominently represented in the private sector. Only 9 percent of private parents are born-again, compared to 8 percent of parents generally. Nor are there big differences on race. Among the private parents in our survey, 12 percent are black and 6 percent Hispanic, while among parents generally the comparable figures are 15 percent and 12 percent. It is notable, in fact, how many minorities are represented in the private sector, given its distinct class bias and the high correlation between class and race.

If we view these comparisons in relative rather than absolute terms, the differences are perhaps more impressive. The differential for Hispanics, for instance, is 6 percent (private) and 12 percent (all parents), which may seem rather small. But in relative terms it means that Hispanics are only half as likely to show up in the private sector as their numbers in the general population would predict—which makes the bias seem much more consequential.

Nonetheless, given all the hype associated with the biases of private school choice, the differences across the two populations of parents turn out to be less striking than many observers would expect. If this is what extremism looks like, it is not especially extreme. The reasons, as I suggested earlier, may well have to do with certain factors that operate naturally within the American education system to keep the bias down somewhat—the low tuitions of private schools, the reduced incentives of advantaged parents to go private (since they already tend to have the best public schools), the heightened incentives of disadvantaged parents to go private (since they tend to have the worst public schools), and the heterogeneity of parent preferences.

The bottom line, however, is that costly school choice *does* lead to social biases. And these biases are consistent—in less exaggerated form— with some of the charges that have long been leveled against private choice by its critics. The question is: would these same biases be present if money were factored out of the equation, and choice were expanded to the broader population of public parents?

The key to an answer rests with what I will call the "swing" public parents, those who are interested in switching from public to private. In reality, of course, it is unreasonable to think that all swing parents would actually go private if given the chance. I will have more to say about this later on. Nonetheless, they *are* a distinct group of private-inclined public parents. And if we look at how they compare to existing private parents, as well as how they compare to the remaining public parents who are not interested in switching, we can get an initial sense for the kinds of changes an expansion of choice might bring.

The figures in table 5-1 clearly suggest that the biases associated with the existing private sector—class, race, religion, partisanship—would all be drastically reduced if the swing parents were actually to go private. Compared to existing private parents, the swing public parents are considerably lower in education and income, and less likely to be Catholic, Republican, or white. Expanded choice, it appears, would promote social moderation.

Indeed, the figures suggest that more than just moderation is going on here. For on grounds of income and race in particular, the swing parents are not just less advantaged than existing private parents. They are disadvantaged relative to the population as a whole, and, more telling still, they are disadvantaged relative to the public parents who *don't* want to go private—many of whom prefer to stay public because they are advantaged enough to have bought themselves good public schools. Of all these parent groups, the swing parents stand out as the *most* likely to be low in income, and to be black or Hispanic. Moreover, if we look down the table, we can see that they are also the most likely to come from disadvantaged districts.

This association of choice with the disadvantaged, of course, is consistent with the logic we laid out earlier. Indeed, all of the basic results here are consistent with that logic. The only wrinkle is that education, which we would expect to have some continuing (if moderated) association with going private—a continuation of the original bias—seems to wash out. The swing parents are not more educated than most. They are below average in education and no different on this score than the public parents who aren't interested in going private. But this comes about because the swing parents tend to be lower in income, more minority, and from less advantaged districts—and in the aggregate, people with these characteristics tend to be lower in education as well. When these factors are statistically controlled (as they are in the analysis to follow) it turns out that the partial effect of education is indeed positive, as our logic would lead us to expect.

Performance

Now let's carry out another descriptive comparison of parent groups, this time focusing on the value-dimension that, more than any other, stands at the center of the voucher debate: school performance.

According to critics, the major attraction of private schools is not that they are better than public schools, but that they cater to parental values that aren't about performance at all, such as religion or race. If the critics are right, the fundamentals of the school choice movement would be thrown into doubt. It would imply, first, that parents cannot be counted upon to make educationally astute judgments in choosing schools for their children, and that an expansion of choice is unlikely to get kids into better schools. It would also imply that a system of parental choice cannot provide schools with incentives to improve their performance, and that the much-touted competition that accompanies choice will not in fact lead to better schools—but rather to schools that are good at providing the other, noneducational (and sometimes pernicious) values on which parents place a premium.

In later sections we will examine how performance stacks up to other values in motivating parents to go private. But first, we can gain a better feel for the issue by taking a closer look at some of the survey responses of parents.

Let's begin with data on how parents directly experience their own children's schools.[20] We know from chapter 3 that public parents have quite positive experiences with their own children's public schools. We can now see that on all five dimensions of direct experience tapped by the survey, private parents—who have chosen to be where they are—are distinctly *more* satisfied with their private schools than public parents are with public schools. The results are set out in table 5-2. While 32 percent of public parents strongly agree that their school gives them "a sense of belonging and feels almost like a family," 60 percent of private parents see their schools this way. Similarly, while 43 percent of public parents strongly agree that their school provides an "exciting learning environment," 65 percent of private parents give their schools the same positive endorsement. And when asked whether "teachers don't care as much as they should," 29 percent of public parents strongly disagree, compared to 58 percent of private parents. Questions about frustration with the school and the value of participation show comparable differences.

These sorts of findings provide another basis for thinking that, as we try to explain the attraction of private schools, the real issue is not satisfaction per se, but *relative* satisfaction. Public parents are fairly satisfied with their public schools. But private parents are even more satisfied with their private schools—and many public parents are likely to think they are missing out on something. Almost surely, it is not just myth or legend that convinces so many public parents that private schools are better. All they have to do is talk to their neighbors.

The data in table 5-2 allow for another important comparison, this one between the two groups of parents within the public sector. The question at issue is whether the swing parents have a hidden interest in going private because they have had less positive experiences with their own children's public schools. The evidence is consistent with exactly that. The public parents who say they'd be interested in going private are clearly *less* satisfied with their current schools than public parents who say they want to stay public. The differences on the five test items are not quite as great as those between private and public parents, but they are comparable, and

Table 5-2. *How Parents Evaluate Their Own Children's Schools*
Percent, unless otherwise indicated[a]

Survey item	Private school parents[b]	Public school parents interested in going private	Public school parents not interested in going private	All public school parents
"The school gives me a sense of belonging and feels almost like a family."				
Strongly agree	60	26	40	32
Weakly agree	20	26	28	27
Weakly disagree	8	22	18	20
Strongly disagree	9	23	12	18
Don't know	3	3	3	4
"The school provides my child with an exciting learning environment."				
Strongly agree	65	34	54	43
Weakly agree	21	34	27	31
Weakly disagree	5	16	9	13
Strongly disagree	7	14	7	11
Don't know	2	2	3	3
"Teachers don't care as much as they should."				
Strongly agree	12	32	21	27
Weakly agree	9	24	19	21
Weakly disagree	17	18	20	19
Strongly disagree	58	23	37	29
Don't know	4	3	4	4
"I am often frustrated with the school."				
Strongly agree	13	28	16	22
Weakly agree	10	19	13	16
Weakly disagree	18	21	25	23
Strongly disagree	55	29	45	36
Don't know	4	3	2	3
"I don't feel as though my participation at school can make a difference."				
Strongly agree	10	20	13	17
Weakly agree	8	15	13	14
Weakly disagree	15	25	23	24
Strongly disagree	65	38	48	43
Don't know	3	2	2	3
N[c]	(381)	(1,380)	(1,041)	(2,553)

a. Percentages are based on weighted data. They may not sum to 100 due to rounding.
b. *Private school parents* refers to parents who have children only in private school.
c. N is the unweighted number of respondents.

they are consistent across all five items. Fifty-four percent of parents who prefer the public sector, for example, strongly agree that their public school provides an "exciting learning environment," while only 34 percent of parents interested in going private say the same. Forty-five percent of parents who'd stay public strongly disagree that their public school frustrates them, versus 29 percent for parents interested in going private. And so on. The desire to go private, then, appears to be rooted at least partly in the way parents believe their own children's schools are performing.

Now let's move from these in-the-trenches assessments of school performance to the way parents evaluate the performance of their local school system as a whole. Does overall satisfaction with the public schools seem to be associated with the inclination to go private?

We already know from chapter 3 that private parents are more critical of the public schools than public parents are. The figures in table 5-3 simply document this point in greater detail. When asked whether their local schools are "doing well" or need to be changed, only 25 percent of private parents say they are "doing well," compared to 45 percent of public parents. When asked to give their local schools a score from 1 to 10, 33 percent of private parents give them a score of 8 or above, while 48 percent of public parents do so. And when asked whether their communities take pride in the local public schools, 27 percent of private parents strongly agree that they do, compared to 52 percent of public parents.

This is not too surprising. But if we take a closer look at just the public parents, we find internal divisions of opinion along exactly the same lines. The swing parents are consistently more critical of the local public schools than the parents who want to remain in the public sector. Only 35 percent of the swing parents think the schools are "doing well," for instance, compared to 57 percent of the parents who want to stay put. Similarly, 40 percent of them give the schools high marks on a 10-point scale, compared to 58 percent of the stay-put parents. And 42 percent strongly agree that their communities take pride in the schools, compared to 66 percent of the others. Here again, there is a clear connection between the desire to go private and (relatively) low assessments of public school performance.

This same evidence is consistent with the moderation hypothesis. In general, whatever measure of performance we use, the same finding emerges: the existing private parents are the most critical, followed by the public parents who are interested in going private, followed by the public parents who want to stay put. Under the current education system, then, it is the parents who are most critical of public school performance who tend to go private. If choice were expanded, the people interested in leaving

Table 5-3. *How Parents Evaluate Their Local Public School System*
Percent, unless otherwise indicated[a]

Survey item	Private school parents[b]	Public school parents interested in going private	Public school parents not interested in going private	All public school parents
"Which of the following best describes how you feel about the school in your district?"				
They are doing well	25	35	57	45
Need minor changes	24	35	30	32
Need major changes	45	27	12	20
Don't know	7	3	1	2
"Our community is proud of our public schools."				
Strongly agree	27	42	66	52
Weakly agree	21	28	20	25
Weakly disagree	19	13	6	10
Strongly disagree	27	13	6	10
Don't know	5	3	2	3
Using a 10-point scale, where 10 is truly outstanding and 1 is very poor, rate local public schools:				
1–4	30	14	5	10
5	13	13	6	10
6	10	10	7	8
7	8	21	20	21
8	18	25	31	28
9–10	15	15	27	20
Don't know	6	3	4	4
N[c]	(381)	(1,380)	(1,041)	(2,553)

a. Percentages are based on weighted data. They may not sum to 100 due to rounding.
b. *Private school parents* refers to parents who have children only in private school.
c. N is the unweighted number of respondents.

would tend to be more critical than other public parents—but they would not be as critical as the parents who have already left. Were all the swing parents to go private, the expanded private sector would thus be more moderate on this count than the existing private sector. It would attract new recruits who are more positive toward the public schools than private parents currently are.

Both sets of measures we've look at so far—direct experience and satisfaction with the local school system—involve absolute assessments of the public schools. The items ask parents to say how well the public schools are doing, but not by comparison to any alternatives. If our earlier reasoning is correct, however, the way parents think about choice and vouchers is likely to be influenced as well, and perhaps more heavily, by their assessments of relative performance. How do our three groups of parents evaluate the relative performance of public and private schools?

Table 5-4 sets out the relevant figures, which show that the groups are different in exactly the way we would expect. Consider the figures for academics. Private parents are more inclined than public parents to think that private schools are superior, by 86 percent to 50 percent. And among public parents, 65 percent of those interested in going private think private schools are better, as against just 33 percent of the public parents who want to stay put. These results, while not surprising, suggest again that (relative) performance is an important motivation for going private. The rankings, moreover, are again consistent with the moderation thesis: private parents are the most convinced of the superiority of private schools, followed by public parents interested in going private, followed by public parents who want to stay put.

Why Do Parents Go Private—Or Want To?

If we want to understand why parents go private (or want to), simple comparisons are not enough. We need to fashion causal models that include a full range of influences, and we need to estimate the impact of each variable when the effects of all others are held constant. The results may turn out to be consistent with what the simple comparisons already show. But we can't know that until we do the analysis.

Methodologically, the approach here is virtually the same as in chapter 4, except that, because the dependent variables are dichotomous—for example, whether the parent chooses to go private or public—we will be shifting from regression analysis to probit analysis, which is designed for such situations. As before, impact coefficients have been calculated for all variables, this time showing their effects on the probability of going private. A comparison of impact coefficients offers a simple basis for judging relative importance.[21]

Going Private under the Current System

Let's begin by estimating a model of why parents go private under the current system. At a theoretical level, this is an effort to determine which variables influence whether a parent will go private or not, taking as our

Table 5-4. *How Parents Compare the Performance of Public and Private Schools*
Percent, unless otherwise indicated[a]

"How do you think private and parochial schools usually compare to public schools? Better, worse, or about the same?"	Private school parents[b]	Public school parents interested in going private	Public school parents not interested in going private	All public school parents
Academic quality				
Better	86	65	33	50
About the same	8	20	39	28
Worse	2	3	8	5
Don't know	3	13	21	17
Safety				
Better	85	60	36	48
About the same	9	23	41	31
Worse	2	2	3	3
Don't know	4	14	20	18
Discipline				
Better	91	68	41	55
About the same	4	16	34	24
Worse	2	3	4	4
Don't know	3	13	21	17
Teaching moral values				
Better	90	68	42	55
About the same	4	16	32	24
Worse	3	3	5	4
Don't Know	3	14	21	18
Providing individual attention to students				
Better	87	65	41	53
About the same	7	19	34	25
Worse	3	3	4	4
Don't know	3	13	21	18
N[c]	(381)	(1,380)	(1,041)	(2,553)

a. Percentages are based on weighted data. They may not sum to 100 due to rounding.
b. *Private school parents* refers to parents who have children only in private school.
c. N is the unweighted number of respondents.

population the entire set of parents with school-age children. More practically, however, we are essentially involved in a more sophisticated comparison (than the one carried out above) of two groups: current private parents and current public parents.

To make sense of the results, we need to keep one crucial fact in mind: the group of public parents *includes* the swing public parents who are interested in going private. This is an interesting thing, really. What we want to do is to understand the phenomenon of going private, and it may seem obvious that the way to do this is to focus on the parents who actually *do* go private and explore why. Yet the comparison is to public parents—and many of these parents, it turns out, would like to go private, and in important respects (their attitudes, mainly) are similar to the parents who are already in the private sector. Thus, when we compare current private parents to current public parents, we are not really getting a measure of "going private" in some general sense, but of the factors that can account for why, *under a system of costly choice*, some parents actually do go private while others (many of whom would like to) don't.

This is the way the following analysis needs to be understood, then, and the same would be true of any analysis in the broader research literature that tries to explain private school choice. The analysis is specific to the current system: it explains who goes private when choice is costly. And because it is system-specific, some of the factors that actually make private schools attractive to parents—including many public parents—may not show up. Indeed, the more the swing parents share the same values as private parents, the less likely these factors will emerge as significant.[22]

With these considerations in mind, let's turn to the statistical results reported in table 5-5. The multivariate analysis reveals the same social biases we uncovered earlier in the simple comparisons. The parents most likely to go private are those who are higher in education and income, Catholic, born-again, Republican, and (when context is controlled) white.

The contextual model indicates that, despite their social advantages, the parents most likely to go private are also less likely to exercise residential mobility and more likely to come from disadvantaged districts than public parents are. This makes good sense, especially once income, education, and other factors are controlled: many parents who go private probably do so because they cannot change their residence, because they live in low-performing districts, or both, and thus see private schools as attractive options. But the magnitude of these "impacts" needs to be interpreted with caution, because causality almost surely works the other way as well: if parents know they want to send their kids to private schools from the outset, they do not need to exercise residential mobility, and can locate in low-performing districts without affecting their children's educations. In principle, this process of mutual causation should be modeled as such, but our data are too limited to allow this to be done adequately. The best we can do is simply to note that mutual causation is probably at work here,

Table 5-5. Why Parents Go Private under the Current System[a]

Variable	Background model Coefficient	[Impact]	Context model Coefficient	[Impact]	Attitude model Coefficient	[Impact]	Performance model Coefficient	[Impact]
Background								
Education	.14***	[7.42]	.15***	[7.27]	.14***	[5.70]	.13***	[5.56]
Income	.07***	[5.67]	.12***	[8.94]	.12***	[7.18]	.13***	[8.34]
Catholic	.49***	[11.26]	.49***	[10.83]	.47***	[8.37]	.53***	[10.37]
Born-again	.39***	[9.53]	.41***	[9.56]	.34***	[6.53]	.41***	[8.61]
Black (north)	.01	[.14]	-.43***	[-6.75]	-.38***	[-4.79]	-.33**	[-4.70]
Black (south)	-.00	[-.03]	-.26	[-4.33]	-.24	[-3.28]	-.09	[-1.43]
Hispanic	-.36***	[-6.18]	-.60***	[-8.69]	-.53***	[-6.28]	-.52***	[-6.71]
Age	.00	[.40]	.00	[.10]	-.01	[-.36]	-.00	[-.08]
Party identification	.06***	[4.56]	.06***	[4.70]	.04**	[2.59]	.04*	[2.33]
Low expectations	-.03	[-1.96]	-.03	[-1.66]	-.02	[-2.79]	.01	[.58]
Context								
Residential mobility			-.18***	[-7.22]	-.15***	[-5.07]	-.09***	[-3.37]
Advantaged district			-.22***	[-7.56]	-.21***	[-5.91]	-.14***	[-4.12]

	Model 1	Model 2		Model 3	
Attitudes					
Diversity (whites)		-.02	[-.57]	-.00	[-.01]
Inequity		.03	[.64]	-.04	[-1.13]
School prayer		.05	[1.68]	.03	[1.12]
School size		.05	[1.25]	-.01	[-.17]
Public school ideology		-.18***	[-4.36]	-.11**	[-2.87]
Markets		.12***	[2.82]	.07	[1.86]
Moral values		.07***	[3.41]	.07***	[3.85]
Performance					
Public performance				-.62***	[-15.38]
Constant	-2.62***	-2.97***		-2.99***	
N[b]	(3,111)	(2,803)		(2,803)	
Pseudo R^2	.11	.18		.24	

* Significant at .10 level.
** Significant at .05 level.
*** Significant at .01 level.

a. Probits estimated using weighted data. The dependent variable is coded 1 if parents have any children in private schools and 0 if they have children solely in public schools. The impact coefficient is the change in the estimated probability of going private as the independent variable shifts from one standard deviation below its mean to one standard deviation above its mean (for nondichotomous variables), or from 0 to 1 (for dichotomous variables), holding all other variables constant at their means. Models control for the full range of background and context variables, not all of which are reported in the tables.

b. N is the unweighted number of respondents.

recognize that it will tend to inflate the estimated "impacts," and adjust for it in our interpretations.

Now consider the attitude model. This model introduces the full range of attitudes we discussed earlier, with one exception: the parent influence item is omitted. Parent influence is surely relevant to why parents currently go private, but our survey item may be misleading for the specific comparison we are making here. We want to understand why some parents have chosen to go private, but we are measuring their attitudes well *after* they have done so and been shaped by their private-school experiences. For most attitudes in our study, this doesn't cause serious problems. But for parent influence, it may. Private parents have especially good experiences with their children's private schools, and this is likely to make them more willing to trust administrators and teachers, and thus to appear *less* supportive of parent influence (which is the trade-off our survey item gives them). The attitudes we are measuring, then, may be quite different from the attitudes that led them to go private in the first place. In the (later) parts of our analysis that involve just public parents, though, attitudes toward parent influence should continue to work as expected: they should be associated with the desire to go private.

This problem aside, the attitude model generates some interesting findings about parental values and beliefs. The most notable is that *none* of these attitudes rival the background influences of class, race, and religion. Attitudes don't seem to play a big role in distinguishing private from public parents. Performance issues aside, going private under a costly system is more about social advantage and religion than it is about particular attitudes.

But attitudes are still of some relevance. And when they are, three attitudes stand out in explaining why some parents go private—or, to look at it the other way around, why many public parents *don't* go private. These attitudes are public school ideology, moral values, and markets. Of these, public school ideology has the largest impact. The fact that public school ideology emerges from the pack in this way testifies to the importance of the normative commitment that many public parents have to the public school system. In effect, public school ideology is not so much something that private parents lack as something that many public parents have, and that inhibits them from going private. The importance of moral values and markets should be noted as well. The former reinforces the notion that religion and moral concerns are fundamental attractions of the current private school system. The latter suggests that ideas about competition, incentives, and accountability, while ultimately rather abstract, are not lost on ordinary people and have genuine relevance to the way many think about education.

The attitude model also conveys important information about race. While we know that white parents are more likely to go private than minority parents are, attitudes toward racial diversity do *not* appear to be important factors in the decision to go private. It is possible that better measures of racial attitudes would pick up bigger effects. But to the extent that our measures—which focus on busing and common schooling—are tapping important aspects of the race issue, the findings are provocative. They contradict the persistent claims of private-school critics, who argue that racism and separatism are key motivations for going private. They also contradict a portion of the research literature, which makes similar arguments based on demographic data.

We need to remember, though, that all these findings are telling us something about why parents go private *under the current system*, and may be somewhat misleading in what they seem to say about the phenomenon of going private generally. A literal reading of table 5-5 suggests that public school ideology, moral values, and markets have significant influence on going private, while all the other attitudes potentially associated with going private—diversity, inequity, prayer, school size—don't. The implication is that the latter "don't matter" to current private parents, and have nothing to do with why they find private schools attractive.

But this is not quite right. Although the figures in table 5-5 cannot reveal it, the reason some attitudes fail to pass muster here is not that they are irrelevant to the thinking of private parents, but that they are *also* relevant to the thinking of the swing parents—who find private schools attractive, and who are part of the group against whom private parents are being compared. To get a better view of what attitudes matter to private parents, then, let's temporarily eliminate the swing parents from the comparison and take a brief look at how private parents compare to the public parents who do *not* find private schools attractive. When we do this, as table 5-6 shows, we find that public school ideology, moral values, and markets continue to have significant influences on the attraction of private schooling—but that inequity, prayer, and school size turn out to be significant as well. With the swing parents out of the analysis, the relevance of these attitudes to the phenomenon of going private is no longer hidden.[23]

Under this new comparison, moreover, racial diversity continues to have no impact—which indicates that attitudes toward race not only fail to explain going private under the current system, but that they seem to have

Table 5-6. *A Comparison of Private School Parents to*
Public School Parents Not Interested in Going Private[a]

Variable	Attitude model	
	Coefficient	[Impact]
Attitudes		
Diversity (whites)	.02	[1.11]
Inequity	.11**	[5.38]
School prayer	.09**	[6.35]
School size	.19***	[8.89]
Public school ideology	−.24***	[−11.01]
Markets	.21***	[9.53]
Moral values	.15***	[12.53]
Constant	−2.95***	
N[b]	(1,522)	
Pseudo R^2	.28	

** Significant at .05 level.
*** Significant at .01 level.
   a. Probit estimated using weighted data. The dependent variable is coded 1 if parents have any children in private schools and 0 if they have children in public schools only and are not interested in going private. The impact coefficient is the change in the estimated probability of going private as the independent variable shifts from one standard deviation below its mean to one standard deviation above its mean (for nondichotomous variables), or from 0 to 1 (for dichotomous variables), holding all other variables constant at their means. Model controls for the full range of background and context variables.
   b. N is the unweighted number of respondents.

little to do with the underlying attractiveness of private schools. This is one relationship that wasn't hidden by the presence of the swing parents. It just wasn't there to begin with (at least by our measures).

Now let's return to the original analysis, described in table 5-5, which explains going private under the current system. With attitudes already included, the final step is to add the performance variable into the equation. This allows us to see how parent satisfaction with public school performance stacks up to all the other influences on going private. The results show that performance is in fact the most powerful determinant of private school choice in the entire model. It we compare it to the other attitudinal concerns that motivate parents, it wins hands down; its impact coefficient is more than triple the size of its nearest attitudinal competitors (even if we look at their impacts before the introduction of performance). Its impact is quite large in absolute terms as well: when parental satisfaction with performance drops from high to low, the probability of going private increases by 15 percent—a big shift, given the small percentage of parents going private overall.

Performance appears less dominant if we recognize that some of these other factors may often work together. For example, if we combine the effects of being Catholic or born-again, supporting school prayer, and concern for moral values, and if we think of these as a syndrome of religious effects, then we might make a case that religious effects rival performance in impact. There is something to this, and it underlines the importance of religion as a motivational basis of the current system. Nonetheless, it is clear that performance is a major concern in the minds of parents and far more consequential than critics are claiming. Even as things now stand, with a costly system of choice built mainly around religious schools, parents seem to put substantial emphasis on academics and school quality.

Public Parents: Who Is Interested in Going Private?

What would happen if choice were no longer costly and all parents were given the option of sending their kids to private schools? Which parents in the public sector would be most likely to go private and why?

In theoretical terms, the population for analysis here is the entire group of public school parents, and our model seeks to determine which variables influence the desire to go private within this population. More practically, we are involved in a controlled comparison of two groups: the swing parents and the public parents who want to stay put.

The probit results are displayed in table 5-7. The background model confirms what the descriptive analysis suggested earlier: that an interest in private schools is especially high among low-income and minority parents. When choice is freely available to all and income is no longer a constraint, private schools have disproportionate appeal to those who are less well off and whose need for new opportunities is clearly much greater. This association of choice with the disadvantaged is reinforced by the results of the contextual model, which show that public parents in disadvantaged districts are the most likely to be interested in going private.

Still, the more traditional social influences associated with the current system continue to be relevant when choice is expanded. It is the public parents who are better educated, Catholic, born-again, and Republican who tend to be interested in going private. None of this is surprising. For the most part, we should expect the same sorts of values and beliefs to continue influencing the desire to go private once choice is expanded.

Overall, then, our findings are strikingly consistent with the elite-level composition of the voucher movement. The public opinion data show that, when we explore the motivations for going private, both its traditional and modern wings find their reflection at the mass level among public parents. There is a constituency of parents who reflect the traditional values of religion and (Republican) partisanship. And there is a

Table 5-7. *Why Public School Parents Are Interested in Going Private*[a]

	Background model		Context model		Attitude model		Performance model 1		Performance model 2	
Variable	Coefficient	[Impact]	Coefficient	[Impact]	Coefficient	[Impact]	Coefficient	[Impact]	Coefficient	[Impact]
Background										
Education	.05*	[4.68]	.06**	[6.23]	.06**	[5.65]	.05	[4.93]	.04	[3.58]
Income	-.05***	[-7.46]	-.05***	[-7.17]	-.05**	[-6.73]	-.04*	[-6.05]	-.03	[-4.35]
Catholic	.09	[3.45]	.16*	[6.29]	.14	[5.56]	.10	[3.93]	.18**	[7.07]
Born-again	.20*	[7.95]	.32***	[12.13]	.27**	[10.36]	.14	[5.42]	.31***	[11.75]
Black (north)	.63***	[22.91]	.42***	[15.79]	.51***	[18.74]	.44***	[15.97]	.50***	[18.56]
Black (south)	.12	[4.71]	.03	[1.20]	.03	[1.11]	-.06	[-2.48]	.08	[3.22]
Hispanic	.31***	[11.86]	.21**	[8.33]	.27**	[10.25]	.19	[7.37]	.33***	[12.54]
Age	-.03**	[-5.07]	-.03*	[-4.43]	-.03*	[-4.78]	-.04**	[-5.91]	-.03**	[-5.09]
Party identification	.03**	[5.13]	.04**	[5.52]	.03*	[4.21]	.03*	[5.09]	.03	[3.94]
Low expectations	-.02	[-2.48]	-.02	[-1.77]	-.01	[-.61]	.01	[.97]	.02	[2.08]
Context										
Residential mobility			-.04	[-3.10]	-.04	[-3.58]	-.01	[-1.01]	-.02	[-1.47]
Advantaged district			-.07*	[-4.51]	-.03	[-2.33]	.01	[.72]	.03	[1.77]

Attitudes				
Diversity (whites)		-.01 [-.36]	.02 [.94]	-.00 [-.13]
Inequity		.28*** [17.22]	.21*** [12.93]	.21*** [13.40]
School prayer		.06** [5.21]	.05** [4.48]	.06** [5.49]
Parent influence		.08** [4.88]	.08* [5.01]	.04 [2.61]
School size		.16*** [9.69]	.11** [6.46]	.12*** [7.39]
Public school ideology		-.23*** [-13.28]	-.21*** [-12.17]	-.21*** [-12.27]
Markets		.18*** [11.22]	.13*** [7.94]	.16*** [9.78]
Moral values		.06*** [6.96]	.08*** [9.83]	.07*** [7.86]
Performance				
Academic (absolute)			-.08*** [-12.51]	
Academic (relative)			-.64*** [-28.97]	
Public school performance				-.71*** [-37.32]
Constant	.21	-.77***	.69**	-.60***
N[b]	(2,421)	(2,201)	(1,850)	(2,201)
Pseudo R^2	.05	.12	.19	.20

* Significant at .10 level.
** Significant at .05 level.
*** Significant at .01 level.

a. Probits estimated using weighted data. The dependent variable is coded 1 if public parents are interested in going private and 0 if they are not. Impact coefficient is the change in estimated probability as the independent variable shifts from one standard deviation below its mean to one standard deviation above its mean (for nondichotomous variables), or from 0 to 1 (for dichotomous variables), holding all other variables at their means. Models control for the full range of background and context variables, not all of which are reported in the tables.

b. N is the unweighted number of respondents.

constituency of parents who are less advantaged and from low-performing districts.

Viewed from another angle, these findings also reinforce one of the basic themes from the research literature: the parents who want to go private tend to be low-income and minority, but also (controlling for income and race) better educated. Choice advocates laud the equity-promoting effects of expanded choice, and point to evidence that low-income families have a strong interest in going private. Yet opponents point to the fact that, even within programs restricted to the poor, it is the educated, more motivated poor who take greatest advantage of choice. And this, critics argue—not without reason—may give rise to inequities. The results of our probit analysis provide empirical support for both sets of claims.

We can also go a step further. The question is not just whether there is an education bias, but how this bias would be *changed* by an expansion of choice. A look back at table 5-1 tells us something about that. Because the swing parents are lower in income (and in other ways less advantaged), they are actually much lower in education, as a group, than existing private parents are. Their incorporation into the private sector, or even the incorporation of just some of them, would thus bring about considerable moderation. Overall, the education bias would be reduced.

Now let's turn to the attitude model. What values seem to affect the desire to go private among public parents? Several findings deserve emphasis:

(1) It appears that racial attitudes (as we have measured them) do not have a significant role to play in determining which public parents are interested in going private. This is consistent with our earlier finding about race and private choice under the current system. Together, they suggest that the critics' claims about the pernicious effects of racial attitudes, while perhaps justified a few decades ago, may be overstated today.

(2) *All* of the other attitudes in our model—regarding inequity, public school ideology, prayer, moral values, parent influence, school size, and markets—do appear to have an influence on the desire to go private. In each case, the impact is in the direction we ought to expect.

These findings on the full range of values point to two important conclusions. First, public parents interested in going private are influenced by the *same* basic values that are important to current private parents. Second, the consistent relevance of these values suggests that there is a *structure* to the way parents think about their choice of schools—and that there is some systematic thinking going on. Parents (or at least many of them) are not simply giving superficial answers when asked whether they are interested in going private.

(3) Of all the attitudes in the model, attitudes toward inequity stand out as the most salient. This finding dovetails nicely with the earlier findings on social bias. There we discovered that although current private parents are socially advantaged, it is the less advantaged public parents who especially want to go private. Now we find that, while equity concerns are only modestly important to private parents under the current system, they are strongly associated with the desire to go private among public parents. Although the current system is tilted toward the advantaged, then, and puts little emphasis on equity, it appears that an expansion of choice opens the private sector to a kind of parent whose demand has heretofore been almost totally stifled: those who are less advantaged, who see the public system as inequitable, and who want to change their situations.

(4) The estimates indicate that, as perceptions of inequity rise from low to high, the probability that a public parent is interested in going private increases by 17 percent (relative to a baseline of 55 percent). This is a big shift, but it is just the average effect across all public parents. If we carry out a more detailed estimation, we find—as in chapter 4's analysis of performance—that the salience of the equity issue varies systematically by social class, and that low-income parents are even more strongly influenced by equity concerns than this average effect tends to convey (see table 5-8). The detailed estimation shows that, for low-income parents, an increase in perceptions of inequity leads to a comparatively large 26 percent increase in the probability of being interested in going private. For parents with higher incomes, the corresponding probability change is 11 percent—still significant, but not in the same ballpark. The equity issue, then, seems to matter a great deal to public parents, particularly low-income parents, and they appear to connect it to private-school choice in a way that is entirely consistent with the argument voucher advocates have been making for the last decade: that choice is a way of promoting social equity.

(5) On the other side of the ledger, it is important to recognize that, at least in terms of average effects over all public parents, public school ideology is almost as influential as inequity. In the attitude model, parents who score high on public school ideology are 13 percent less likely to be interested in going private than parents who score low. This underlines, once again, the pervasive role that normative commitments seem to play in wedding parents to the public system and making them resistant to arguments for vouchers.

(6) In chapter 4's analysis, parent influence appeared to be one of the most important attitudinal determinants of how Americans evaluate the

Table 5-8. *Inequity, Class, and Public School Parents' Interest in Going Private*[a]

	Attitude model	
Variable	Coefficient	[Impact]
Attitudes		
Diversity (whites)	–.00	[–.21]
Inequity (low income)	.42***	[25.86]
Inequity (middle income)	.18***	[11.50]
Inequity (upper income)	.17**	[10.87]
School prayer	.06**	[5.05]
Parent influence	.08**	[5.29]
School size	.16***	[9.33]
Public school ideology	–.23***	[–13.68]
Markets	.18***	[11.21]
Moral values	.06***	[7.19]
Constant	–.75***	
N[b]	(2,201)	
Pseudo R^2	.12	

** Significant at .05 level.
*** Significant at .01 level.
   a. Probit estimated using weighted data. The dependent variable is coded 1 if public parents are interested in going private and 0 if they are not. The impact coefficient is the change in the estimated probability of going private as the independent variable shifts from one standard deviation below its mean to one standard deviation above its mean (for nondichotomous variables), or from 0 to 1 (for dichotomous variables), holding all other variables constant at their means. Models control for the full range of background and context variables, not all of which are reported in the tables.
   b. N is the unweighted number of respondents.

public schools, the others being perceptions of inequity and public school ideology. When it comes to explaining which public parents are interested in going private, however, inequity and public school ideology still stand out—but parent influence does not. It seems to carry no more weight than most of the other attitudes. While this may be a statistical quirk, it could also indicate that parent influence is actually not as important as one might think in shaping the way parents approach issues of school choice. (This is a conjecture, I should note, that will be supported in the chapters to follow.) If so, political appeals based on parent influence may have less impact in recruiting support for the voucher movement than chapter 4's analysis would seem to suggest.

Finally, let's turn to satisfaction with public school performance and see how it does by comparison to all these other variables. Throughout this chapter, and indeed since we first began thinking about performance in a systematic way in chapter 2, we have recognized two sides to the way public parents view their schools. On the one hand, most say they are reasonably satisfied with the public schools. On the other hand, they often think that private schools are better. The first is an absolute judgment about how well the public schools are doing. The second is a relative judgment about how well the public schools are doing compared to private schools. Both are conveying important information, and both presumably have something to do with the way people think about issues of school choice.

How these two types of evaluations come into play is crucial to the future of the choice movement. If public parents are fairly satisfied with their public schools, and if their absolute judgments were all that mattered to them, then they would presumably have little interest in going private. But if they think largely in terms of relative performance, this would change everything. For even "satisfied" public parents might be interested in going private if they were motivated by the desire to seek out better alternatives.

We already know that more than half of public parents *do* express an interest in going private. This is prima facie evidence that absolute satisfaction is not the only factor at work and that relative satisfaction is probably at least as important. But we needn't just speculate about it. The survey gives us a means to test it out. Let's take a detour from our usual path and introduce variables that represent each perspective on school performance: one a measure of how parents evaluate the academic performance of the public schools, the other a measure of how parents compare the academic performance of public and private schools. (Both were discussed in chapter 2.) When we force them to compete against one another in explaining parental interest in going private, which measure of performance—absolute or relative—does the better job?

The results are included in table 5-7. Estimates indicate that both perspectives on performance are quite important, but that relative satisfaction has more than twice the impact that absolute satisfaction has. Indeed, relative satisfaction with academic performance is by far the most influential factor in the entire model (rivaled only by the impact of inequity for low-income parents).[24] Our ongoing speculation, then, appears to be quite valid. The reason so many "satisfied" public parents express interest in private schools is that they are largely thinking in relative rather than absolute terms about their choices. They like their public schools. They like private schools better. Given the positive aura that surrounds the public schools, this is good news for the choice movement.

Now let's return to the original path and take the final step, which is to explore the impact of performance on the desire to go private. We want to use a single measure of overall satisfaction with performance, as before, to summarize its impact. But given the results on relative versus absolute assessments, it makes sense to alter our previous measure somewhat. The performance index in chapter 4 was based entirely on items representing absolute assessments of performance. From now on, we will use an index that takes account of both absolute and relative assessments. It simply averages the original index from chapter 4 and the measure of relative academic satisfaction referred to above.[25]

When this is done and the estimation carried out, the results (see table 5-7 again) show that performance is far-and-away the most powerful explanatory factor in the model. Its impact coefficient indicates that, when satisfaction with public performance drops from high to low, the probability that a public parent will be interested in going private increases by 37 percent—which dwarfs the effects of all other variables. Whether we talk about going private under the current system, then, or about who would be interested in going private under an expanded system of choice, performance looms as the number-one consideration. The familiar arguments to the contrary appear to be quite wrong.

Low-Income Inner-City Parents:
Who Is Interested in Going Private?

We already know that inner-city parents are especially inclined to want to go private, and that the same is true more generally for public parents who are low in income, minority, and from disadvantaged districts. In this section, we will carry out a more detailed analysis of inner-city parents in order to get a better sense for what motivates their interest in private schools.

In some respects, the background and contextual models will be limited in what they can tell us, because we are looking only at the effects of variables *within* this specialized population: where everyone is low-income, and the vast majority are poorly educated, minority, and from disadvantaged districts. Thus the basic background and contextual variables—income, education, race, district context—do not vary much and are unlikely to explain as much as they would in a more broadly based data set. Variables having to do with attitudes and performance should be more revealing.

The results, set out in table 5-9, are consistent with this. For the most part, the background and contextual models tend to wash out—except that the impact for northern blacks is extraordinarily large. Even education and expectations, which we have good reason to think are important for this group, do not turn out to be influential by these estimates. This could signal that something different is going on for inner-city parents and that education and expectations don't play the roles we expect. But more than likely it is simply due to the fact that we are dealing with a restricted sample, making it more difficult to get good estimates.[26]

The attitude model is more straightforward and generates two interesting findings. The first is about race. To this point, racial attitudes have had little relevance to the way parents evaluate performance or think about going private. Among low-income inner-city parents, however, it appears that race *does* matter, and in just the way that critics have argued: white parents who are opposed to diversity are especially interested in going private. The obvious interpretation is that, because race is a more salient issue in the inner city than elsewhere, many whites see private schools as a way to avoid integration with minorities.

This is the first evidence (within our own study) that separatism and possibly even racial bigotry may be motivating some of the parental interest in private schools. And it makes sense that such effects would show up, if they show up anywhere, for low-income whites in the inner city—for these are the whites who are most directly affected by policies of diversity. Whites in the suburbs, and whites with money, are much more removed from the reality of integration.

There is another interpretation, however, that is more benign. It may be that our diversity variable has little to say about racism per se, but is really measuring the extent to which respondents put positive value on diversity. People who score low are not necessarily racists. They just don't put as much value on diversity as people who score high. Thus the model's results may simply be telling us that whites who *support* diversity are especially inclined to *stay* in the public sector. Whites who lack that positive motivation are less wedded to the public schools and more open to private options, but this does not mean they are actively seeking to flee blacks and Hispanics.

We should be careful, then, about jumping to the conclusion that inner-city whites are racists. There are other explanations for the model's results. Nonetheless, it appears that race *is* relevant to the way inner-city whites approach going private, and this raises a red flag that choice advocates (and policymakers and program designers) need to be concerned about. On this count, the critics may be right.

The attitude model also contains a second important finding, this one confirming the basic thrust of the prior analysis. Both in chapter 4's analysis of satisfaction and in this chapter's analysis of going private, we found

Table 5-9. Why Low-Income Inner-City Parents Are Interested in Going Private[a]

Variable	Background model		Context model		Attitude model		Performance model	
	Coefficient	[Impact]	Coefficient	[Impact]	Coefficient	[Impact]	Coefficient	[Impact]
Background								
Education	-.01	[-.51]	-.01	[-.97]	-.02	[-1.70]	-.05	[-3.60]
Income	-.03	[-.91]	.03	[1.03]	.03	[1.02]	.11	[3.49]
Catholic	-.01	[-.26]	.24	[7.94]	.21	[6.95]	.14	[4.48]
Born-again	-.06	[-2.17]	.17	[5.42]	.12	[3.80]	.03	[.85]
Black (north)	.69***	[20.86]	.71***	[21.15]	.84***	[23.87]	1.00***	[25.89]
Black (south)	-.11	[-3.70]	-.26	[-9.41]	-.23	[-8.10]	-.16	[-5.50]
Hispanic	.26	[8.85]	.22	[7.37]	.22	[7.18]	.28	[8.87]
Age	-.01	[-2.39]	-.02	[-2.81]	-.03	[-4.55]	-.03	[-3.95]
Party identification	-.01	[-1.22]	.03	[3.02]	.03	[2.82]	.04	[3.77]
Low expectations	.00	[.07]	.00	[.40]	.02	[2.42]	.07	[7.77]
Context								
Residential mobility			.13*	[8.24]	.11	[6.93]	.16*	[9.63]
Advantaged district			-.03	[-1.63]	-.04	[-2.07]	.01	[.28]

	Model 1	Model 2	Model 3
Attitudes			
Diversity (whites)		−.33* [−17.74]	−.37** [−18.93]
Inequity		.35*** [17.17]	.29*** [13.78]
School prayer		−.01 [−.53]	.02 [1.32]
Parent influence		.07 [3.66]	.04 [1.97]
School size		.19** [10.42]	.17* [8.83]
Public school ideology		−.09 [−4.34]	−.05 [−2.36]
Markets		.14 [7.25]	.10 [5.17]
Moral values		.07 [7.54]	.08 [7.88]
Performance			
Public school performance			−.65*** [−29.83]
Constant	.52	−1.30***	−1.21***
N[b]	(512)	(483)	(483)
Pseudo R^2	.05	.14	.21

* Significant at .10 level.
** Significant at .05 level.
*** Significant at .01 level.

a. Probits estimated using weighted data. The dependent variable is coded 1 if public parents are interested in going private and 0 if they are not. The impact coefficient is the change in the estimated probability of going private as the independent variable shifts from one standard deviation below its mean to one standard deviation above its mean (for nondichotomous variables), or from 0 to 1 (for dichotomous variables), holding all other variables constant at their means. Models control for the full range of background and context variables, not all of which are reported in the tables.

b. N is the unweighted number of respondents.

that inequity consistently stands out as a salient concern for parents—and that it is especially salient for low-income parents, who are the ones most disadvantaged by the current system's inequities. We would expect, then, that inequity should play a key attitudinal role in explaining why low-income inner-city parents might be interested in going private. And as the figures in table 5-9 indicate, that is what we find. While its impact is rivaled by that of diversity (for whites), inequity is far more powerful than any other attitude in the model—and indicates, once again, that low-income people are especially driven by equity concerns when they think about school choice.[27]

Now let's take a look at performance and see whether it plays the same important role for low-income parents in the inner city that it plays for parents generally. The critics of choice have long argued not simply that parents put little emphasis on performance in considering whether to go private—a claim that appears incorrect—but also that low-income parents in the inner city are particularly unlikely to be guided by performance criteria. The image they construct is one of parents who need the help of school administrators and government agencies if they are to make good choices for their children, and who, left to their own devices, would make ill-informed decisions that are not motivated by a fundamental concern for school quality.

So far, the early work on school choice programs suggests that this perspective on low-income inner-city parents is not correct either. The evidence seems to show that these parents put first priority on academic performance. Our own evidence is consistent with that. Even among low-income inner-city parents, performance turns out to be the most powerful factor in the entire model. When satisfaction with school performance drops from high to low, the probability that a parent will express interest in going private increases by 30 percent, which is quite a large shift indeed. In this key respect, they look a lot like all the other parents.

Bias and Moderation Revisited

As a final step, let's return briefly to the issues of bias and moderation, armed with some new information that helps us take the earlier analysis a bit further.

As we've seen, it is a fairly easy matter to determine whether the existing system of private school choice is biased. If we think of bias in terms of how the average characteristics of private parents differ from those of parents generally, then the relevant comparisons can readily be carried out. They show that the current system clearly *is* biased, and in precisely the ways we should expect from a system that makes choice costly.

Determining how these biases might change if choice were expanded, and thus whether there would be moderation, is far less straightforward. We are dealing, after all, with a hypothetical. Choice has not in fact been expanded, but we want to study what might happen if it were. We can only do that by making assumptions about which parents would be doing the switching and how many of them there would be. Obviously, there are various assumptions that might seem reasonable, and different assumptions would tend to yield different conclusions.

The earlier analysis took the simplest possible approach. It differentiated between three groups of parents—current private parents, the swing public parents, and the public parents who want to stay put—and its assessments of moderation were essentially pegged to the limiting assumption (which was not actually embraced) that all the swing parents shift from public to private. The results were enlightening, and suggested that an expansion of choice could reduce existing social biases quite substantially, and even reverse some of them.

This approach gives us a baseline for understanding what would happen if choice were implemented to the fullest. As a practical matter, however, there is good reason to think that many swing parents would not actually wind up going private. In the first place, it is likely that only some of them would ultimately *want* to. They have merely indicated an interest in going private, not that they would actually do so, and there may be all sorts of reasons they would eventually stay put. In the second place, even if just a sizable fraction of them actually decided to go private, the private sector would have to expand tremendously to absorb them—which it could not immediately do. For the short run, demand would likely exceed supply, leaving many swing parents in the public sector.

A more general approach to the moderation issue, then, would recognize that only a portion of the swing parents are likely to go private, and it would derive conclusions about the consequences of choice based on a whole range of scenarios, in which various subsets of the swing parents make the switch. We obviously don't have the luxury of launching into such an exercise here. But we can take a step in that direction by exploring one scenario that seems eminently reasonable.

If just some of the swing parents actually go private, which ones are most likely to do so? The place to start is by recognizing that all swing parents are not alike. While all say they are interested in going private, some are surely more interested than others. In principle, they can be arrayed along a continuum, from tepid interest to enthusiastic interest, and it is the parents who fall toward the enthusiastic end of the continuum who are the best candidates for actually going private.

Fortunately, the earlier probit analysis provides us with estimates of where parents fall on this kind of continuum. Probit's underlying logic actually assumes that such a continuum exists, and the predicted probabilities it generates are a positive function of where individuals are estimated to fall along the continuum. The greater the underlying degree of interest or enthusiasm, the higher the predicted probability.

In the analysis that follows, I will take a predicted probability of .70 as the cut-point. For simplicity, all swing parents with estimated probabilities at or above .70 are assumed to be interested enough to go private, and all those below are assumed to stay in the public sector. Under this scenario, about half of the swing parents switch from public to private, half remain in the public sector—and the public sector thereby retains about 75 percent of its families overall. Empirically, this seems very plausible.

Now let's look at the data for this scenario, which are set out in table 5-10. When we consider how the expansion of choice affects the social composition of the private sector, the basic pattern under this new scenario turns out to be the *same* as it was in the earlier analysis: a pattern of moderation. Compared with existing private parents, the new recruits are substantially lower in income and education, more likely to be black or Hispanic, more likely to come from disadvantaged districts, less likely to be Catholic or Republican, and more likely to have low expectations. The usual biases associated with private schooling, then, continue to be moderated when only the most interested swing parents go private. There is just one exception: the new recruits are no less likely to be born-again than current private parents are.

While the basic pattern is one of moderation, the details reveal some interesting shifts from the earlier scenario in which all swing parents go private. The new recruits are somewhat more Catholic and born-again than under the earlier scenario (although they are still less likely to be Catholic than private parents are). But they are also even lower in income than before, more likely to come from disadvantaged districts, and more likely to be minority. Indeed, a stunning 45 percent of the parents now switching to the private sector are either black or Hispanic (compared to 34 percent under the earlier scenario). Thus, when we stipulate that only the most interested swing parents actually go private, the new recruits are drawn *even more heavily* from the ranks of the socially less advantaged— precisely the opposite of what critics have feared.

Table 5-10. *How Choice Affects Bias and Moderation When Only the Most Interested Public School Parents Go Private*[a]

Variable	Existing system — Private school parents	Scenario 1: All swing parents go private		Scenario 2: High-interest swing parents go private	
		Public school parents going private	Public school parents staying public	Public school parents going private	Public school parents staying public
Background					
Education	.42	−.06	−.07	−.01	−.10
Income	.43	−.13	−.00	−.22	−.02
Catholic	.44	.28	.23	.32	.24
Born-again	.09	.08	.07	.11	.07
Black	.12	.18	.11	.23	.13
Hispanic	.06	.16	.09	.22	.09
Party identification	.21	−.04	−.05	−.03	−.04
Low expectations	−.22	.02	.09	−.03	.06
Context					
Residential mobility	−.17	−.01	.08	−.13	.08
Advantaged district	−.04	−.10	.13	−.31	.11

a. Figures represent group averages. All nondichotomous variables have been standardized over the entire parent population to have a mean of 0 and a standard deviation of 1. Dichotomous variables are: Catholic, Born-again, Black, and Hispanic.

As a final step, let's follow through on the thought experiment and get direct measures of what the public and private systems might look like if choice were expanded. Given our assumptions, the new private system would consist of the existing private parents plus the swing parents most interested in going private, while the new public system would consist of the swing parents who are less interested plus the remaining public parents. The question is: how do the new systems compare to the original ones? In particular, how do the social gaps that separate public and private under expanded choice compare to the gaps that prevail under the current system?

The data are set out in table 5-11. They show that, even when just half of the swing parents go private, an expansion of choice dramatically transforms the private sector along almost every social dimension. The income and education biases prevailing under the current system are substantially reduced (especially the income bias), the percentage of families coming from disadvantaged districts is larger, and the representation of blacks

Table 5-11. *How Choice Affects the Composition of Public and Private Sectors (Assuming High-Interest Swing Parents Go Private)*[a]

	Existing system			New system		
Variable	Private	Public	Gap	Private	Public	Gap
Background						
Education	.42	−.08	.50	.19	−.10	.29
Income	.43	−.08	.51	.07	−.02	.09
Catholic	.44	.26	.18	.37	.24	.13
Born-again	.09	.08	.01	.10	.07	.03
Black	.12	.15	−.03	.18	.13	.05
Hispanic	.06	.13	−.07	.15	.09	.06
Party identification	.21	−.04	.25	.08	−.04	.12
Low expectations	−.22	.05	−.27	−.12	.06	−.18
Context						
Residential mobility	−.17	.03	−.20	−.14	.08	−.22
Advantaged district	−.04	.01	−.05	−.19	.11	−.30

a. Figures represent group averages. All nondichotomous variables have been standardized over the entire parent population to have a mean of 0 and a standard deviation of 1. Dichotomous variables are: Catholic, Born-again, Black, and Hispanic.

and Hispanics is greatly increased; indeed, these minorities make up 33 percent of the new private sector. As these changes almost dictate, there is also a shift in political partisanship: for with the socially disadvantaged comes a big influx of Democrats, and the original Republican bias is reduced considerably.

There is one social bias, however, that is reduced only slightly: religion. The parents making up the new private sector are almost as likely to be Catholic as they currently are (37 percent versus 44 percent), and they are just as likely to be born-again (10 percent versus 9 percent). Even with the influx of less advantaged parents, therefore, the private sector retains much of its religious character. And the voucher movement, to the extent it succeeds in appealing to private-inclined parents, retains much of its traditional constituency. As we suggested earlier, the new private sector emerges as a remarkably faithful reflection of the two-sided structure of the modern voucher movement—which is built both around a traditional constituency and a constituency mainly concerned about equity for the disadvantaged.

This same expansion of choice does not lead to major changes in the public sector. It remains pretty much as before on all relevant counts, except that it is somewhat higher in income, contains proportionately fewer minorities, and retains more parents who are from better districts and who exercise residential mobility. Again, this happens because many of the less advantaged choose to leave, and the parents who stay tend to be rather advantaged. But overall, the public sector is not affected by the expansion of choice to nearly the extent the private sector is—and the reason is pretty obvious. The current private sector is small and relatively select (due to the tuition requirement), and it is transformed by the influx of large numbers of new recruits. The public sector is already large and heterogeneous, and it remains so even after many parents leave. It is affected at the margins.

What is the bottom line, then? Given the changes occurring in both sectors, how does an expansion of choice appear to affect the social gap between public and private? As the figures in table 5-11 indicate, the transformation of the private sector does not succeed in eliminating all vestiges of the original gap. The new private sector is still somewhat higher in education and income than the public sector, higher in expectations, and more Catholic and Republican. This is due to the fact that the new recruits (many of them less advantaged) have been averaged in with current private parents (many of them fairly advantaged), and there are not enough of the former—under our assumption—to outweigh the latter.

Nonetheless, the changes are considerable. For the effect of choice, as the figures show, is to *reduce* the social differences between public and private—and thus to promote moderation—on every one of the dimensions we just listed. Moderation is weakest for religion, testifying to the tenacity of religion in the private-school equation. But the degree of moderation is strong and consistent for variables related to social class: income, education, and expectations. The income gap, in particular, is dramatically reduced, leaving only slight differences between public and private. With regard to race, moreover, the expansion of choice goes farther than this and actually reverses the traditional association of private schooling with social advantage. Remarkably, parents in the new private sector are actually more likely to be black or Hispanic than parents in the new public sector are.

These results, of course, are not chiseled in stone. Were we to make somewhat different assumptions about how many parents switch from public to private, and exactly who they are, the details of the analysis would be somewhat different. It is reasonable to suggest, however, that its thrust would remain essentially the same: that choice tends to break down existing biases of social advantage.

Conclusion

The political prospects of the voucher movement are directly tied to the demand for private schooling and to its social consequences. If the movement is to attract substantial political support, enough public parents must be interested in going private, and there must be good reason to believe that, if many of them actually shift to the private sector, the impact on society would be beneficial.

Our analysis speaks to both issues. Regarding the first, we find that most public parents say they would be interested in going private if money were not a problem. This does not mean that, when given an actual choice, all interested parents would decide to switch sectors. But it does suggest that the constituency for vouchers is large, and that the self-interest of parents may provide a bedrock of political strength for the movement.

The second issue, regarding social consequences, is more complex. But here too, our analysis points in directions that auger well for the voucher movement. It is true, as critics have argued (and as logic suggests), that the current system of costly choice is biased in favor of the socially advantaged: the parents who now go private are higher in education, higher in income, and more likely to be white. They also tend to be Republican and Catholic or born-again. The standard claim of critics, however, is that an expansion of choice would worsen these social biases. On this point, the logic of parental demand suggests otherwise. And our data do too.

The fact is, the appeal of private schools is especially strong among parents who are low in income, minority, and live in low-performing districts: precisely the parents who are the most disadvantaged under the current system. While we cannot know exactly how many parents will actually go private when given the choice, the direction of change is toward very substantial moderation of existing social biases and a considerable closing of the existing social gaps between public and private. Moderation is the rule, moreover, for *every* social dimension, from income to race to religion. The effects are especially dramatic for race: under reasonable assumptions about which parents are most likely to switch sides, the new private sector winds up being more ethnically diverse than the public sector does.

Our data also contradict familiar claims about the motivations for going private. Critics argue that performance has little to do with why parents find private schools attractive, and that the real reasons are rooted in elitism, racial separatism, and religion. It is true that religious and moral values have important roles to play under the current system and would continue to do so under a system of expanded choice. But on other counts, their claims appear to be quite wrong. Most generally, here is what the evidence suggests:

(1) When parents think about going private, performance is by far the most important consideration. This is the case even for low-income parents from the inner city, in whom the critics have least confidence. The evidence suggests that public parents, regardless of class, care a great deal about the quality of their children's schools, particularly their academic quality, and that this more than anything else is what shapes their decision about whether to go private. The dilemma raised in chapter 4, moreover, appears to have a simple answer: while public parents tend to be reasonably satisfied with their schools, they often think private schools are better—and it is relative performance that plays the primary role in their calculations.

(2) Race, the most pernicious of social motivations, appears to have little to do with going private, at least by our measures. There is one sub-population for whom race may be salient (and the critics' fears realized): low-income whites in the inner city. Policymakers and choice advocates are advised to take note. But this racial effect, as we discussed earlier, may not actually be due to racism. And more important, there seems to be little racial effect within the broader population of parents generally. Indeed, among all the attitudes tested in our analysis, the racial variable has the weakest overall connection to going private.

(3) Aside from performance, the most powerful attitudinal influence on going private among public parents, especially those who are low in income, is the perception that the public system is inequitable. In fact, because equity concerns are tied to social class, these are the concerns that are most forcefully expressed—liberated, really—when choice is no longer costly, and anyone, including the poor, can go private. As a result, it is the equity issue that, more than any other attitudinal dimension, most clearly distinguishes an expanded choice system from the system we have now.

(4) Generally speaking, whether we talk about parents who already go private or about public parents who are just interested in going private, the attitudes associated with the attractiveness of private schools tend to be the same (although they vary in salience). Aside from diversity, *all* of the attitudes at the center of our analysis—regarding inequity, prayer, public school ideology, parent influence, school size, markets, and moral values—appear to play roles in shaping how parents think about going private, and all work in the direction we would expect. This tells us something about the kinds of political appeals that are likely to attract support for

vouchers. It also tells us something about parents: for evidence of a clear, reasonable *structure* of attitudes is further evidence that their expressed desire to go private is a thoughtful reflection of their underlying values and beliefs. Like the findings on performance, it suggests that parents tend to take their educational choices seriously.

Some of the concerns that critics of vouchers raise, however, do find limited support in our data. One is that, even among the less advantaged, the parents most likely to go private are those who are better educated: a finding confirmed by other studies in the research literature. According to critics, this threatens to create inequities, as the most motivated parents take greatest advantage of the benefits of choice. They are right. Choice advocates and program designers need to take this into account in crafting voucher plans that are truly equitable. Nonetheless, it is important to note that the education bias is dramatically *reduced* when choice is expanded—for, in the aggregate, the people who go private under expanded choice are still quite a bit *less* educated than the people who already go private. By this measure, equity is promoted.

We also need to recognize that there is more to the critics' argument than our data can address. Throughout this chapter, our focus has been on the demand for private schools, and thus on what parents want. But parents who want to go private might not be able to do so in their everyday lives for reasons that choice advocates too often dismiss. In the real world, even if everyone had the right to choose their schools, parents who are educated and financially well-off are likely to be more motivated than other parents, to have better information about their alternatives, to have more resources at their disposal for getting their way, to have better social connections and more attractive opportunities, and to have children who are easier and less costly to teach. On the supply side, moreover, private schools may find these advantaged parents (and their children) desirable, and may discriminate against poor and minority families.

These are legitimate concerns. Critics are right to emphasize them, and choice advocates need to take them into account as they think about the proper design of choice systems. With the right designs, these problems may be mitigated and parental demand more freely pursued. In any event, the analysis of this chapter is an analysis of the demand side of the equation only, and what it has to tell us about the social effects of choice should be understood to hold as long as "other things are equal." It tells just part of what must ultimately be a much larger story.

The part that it tells is quite fundamental, however, and quite revealing. It is also quite positive for the voucher movement. For despite chapter

4's rather gloomy message about how supportive parents are of their public schools, an analysis of parental demand shows that there is plenty of political potential out there. An interest in going private is widespread throughout the American population, and especially strong among parents who are less advantaged and reacting against the inequities of the current system. This constituency's attraction to private schools gives the voucher movement a persuasive argument—on moral grounds that transcend the usual arguments of free-market economists—that an expansion of choice would be good for society.

The question is: can the movement convert this potential into political support for a major change in public policy?

PART TWO

PUBLIC OPINION
ON VOUCHERS

CHAPTER

6

Who Knows
About Vouchers?

W<small>HEN PEOPLE THINK</small> about public school performance, or about whether they want to send their kids to private schools,
they are thinking about issues that are close to home. Literally. They may
not be experts on these topics, but they are likely to read about the schools
in their newspapers, hear about them on television, and pick up information as they talk with friends, neighbors, and relatives in the course of
their everyday lives. Virtually all, moreover, have experienced schools firsthand as students, and many are parents who have (or have had) direct
contact with the schools through their children. The level and quality of
information surely varies, but there is a lot of it. And as a result, most
people are likely to have reasonably coherent opinions about schools and
some sense of where their own interests lie.

It only makes sense that these opinions and interests should have a
direct bearing on what people think about vouchers. This is what voucher
leaders are banking on. In their eyes, it is the people who are dissatisfied
with the performance of the public schools and the parents who want to
go private who represent the prime constituency for vouchers. For dissatisfied parents, vouchers offer an immediate means of exit from public
schools and immediate access to new educational opportunities: attractive benefits that flow directly to them, personally. And for all citizens
convinced that the public schools are not measuring up, whether parents
or not, vouchers offer a new system of choice, competition, and incentives
to promote better schools for society as a whole.

Yet there is a fly in the ointment. A proposal for vouchers is an abstract idea about how to transform public policy. It is a concept that few citizens have any experience with, that is typically justified by theoretical arguments, and that is genuinely complex in its consequences for schools and society. There is no guarantee, then, that many people will know anything at all about vouchers, nor that those familiar with the concept will have thought about it in any but the most superficial ways. As a result, even people who are prime candidates for becoming voucher supporters may be unable to *connect* their underlying opinions and interests to the voucher issue. To make matters worse, there is an underlying incentive problem at work. Information is usually costly to collect, and people will get informed on a topic only to the extent that knowing more is worth the price. In the case of consumer goods, the connection is quite direct: an individual who gathers information about automobiles, bread, or stereo systems can put that information to use in purchasing products that will make her better off. This payoff is what gives her an incentive to become informed. But the connection is far weaker in the case of public policy. An individual who becomes well informed on a policy is *not* in a position to provide that policy for herself. The policy can only be provided, if at all, through a political process in which everyone in the community, state, or nation gets to participate—and in which, once the policy is provided (if it is provided at all), all who qualify are able to reap the rewards whether they have participated in the decision process or not. As a result, there is little connection between what the individual knows and the policies she gets. And because this is so, there is little incentive to get informed in the first place. The upshot, in the language of political science, is that people are likely to be "rationally ignorant" about public policy.[1]

This problem is not unique to vouchers. As political scientists have been showing for decades, it is pretty typical of most policy issues. In fact, one of the keys to understanding public opinion on vouchers lies precisely in this commonality: the voucher issue is in most respects *just like any other issue.* And what this means, among other things, is that we should expect most Americans to be very poorly informed about it—because that is the norm for public policies in general. Americans just don't know much about government and politics, aren't much interested in them, and don't have much incentive to get informed about even the most salient national issues. To elites caught up in the voucher debate, it may seem that Americans are surely watching, thinking, and taking sides. But political scientists would say that this is quite unlikely, and that most people are largely unaware of the whole thing.[2]

This raises questions that strike to the heart of any analysis of public opinion. For what can it mean to say that people have opinions on an issue such as vouchers, when in fact they are poorly uninformed and may never have thought about it until it was posed on a survey? How can there be any real connection between these survey responses and the values, beliefs, and interests that genuine opinions are supposed to reflect?

We will pursue these matters in the next chapter, when we explore public opinion on the voucher issue. In this chapter, we will begin at the beginning by addressing some basic questions about information. This serves, of course, as a useful preface to the analysis that follows. But it also sheds light on the politics of vouchers more directly—telling us how many Americans are actually aware of the issue, what types of people tend to be informed or uninformed, and whether the social transmission of information seems to help or hinder the voucher movement in its effort to recruit constituencies to the cause.

An Uninformed Public

In the first half of our survey, respondents are asked general questions about public and private schools, and about a variety of educational issues and possible reforms. The concept of vouchers is never mentioned. After respondents have had a chance to consider education in larger perspective, the survey introduces them to vouchers for the first time and asks a long battery of questions designed to explore their thinking on a broad range of voucher-related issues. The second half of the survey is all about vouchers.

As the survey moves from the general portion to the voucher portion, the shift is introduced in the following way. The interviewer says, "So far, I have asked your opinions on a number of different approaches to school reform. Now I would like to focus on one particular type of reform and get your views on it. Have you heard anything about the use of vouchers for education?" This is the key informational question, and what we find is enormously important. Despite all the political turmoil at the elite level, *fully 65 percent of Americans say they have not heard about vouchers.* This should come as no surprise, but the implications are at once troubling and fascinating. At one extreme, it may mean that most people have no idea what is going on: they aren't aware of proposals to promote parental choice through the use of vouchers, they haven't picked up on the controversy, they don't know about the arguments for and against, and so on. It's not on their radar screens. There is, however, a more charitable interpretation that is worth entertaining: that many people aren't familiar with the term *voucher* but still may be reasonably informed about the ideas and controversies surrounding the issue itself.

Some studies of public opinion seem to support this more charitable view. The 1995 Phi Delta Kappa survey, for instance, asks Americans how much they have heard (if anything) about proposals for parental choice programs involving private schools, and 51 percent claim they have heard a lot, or at least a fair amount, about them.[3] These results are interesting and shouldn't be discounted. But they may exaggerate the extent to which people are actually informed. In the first place, someone who is even half-way familiar with parental choice programs involving private schools should at least have heard of the term *voucher*—and so, if the Phi Delta Kappa figures are meaningful measures of what people know, our own survey should have turned up more than 35 percent who say they recognize the concept. In the second place, it is well known that respondents don't want to appear ignorant of public issues when being surveyed, and will often claim to be better informed on issues than they really are. Phi Delta Kappa is clearly asking respondents how well informed they are, and this bias may be a problem. Our own survey item comes across as a transition question (moving from one part of the survey to another), not as a test of how much respondents know about public policy, and seems a better measure. Ignorance about vouchers appears to be widespread.

This suspicion is supported by other polls that test people for their knowledge of which parties and candidates favor vouchers and which oppose them. In polls jointly sponsored in 1996 by the *Washington Post,* the Kaiser Foundation, and Harvard University, for instance, such questions were asked of registered voters—who are likely to be much *more* knowledgeable about policy issues than the public as a whole. When asked "which party . . . favors government vouchers to allow parents the choice of sending their children to public, private, or parochial schools?" 49 percent said the Republicans, 36 percent the Democrats, and 13 percent didn't know. When asked the same questions about the presidential candidates, 42 percent said that Bob Dole favored vouchers, 39 percent said Bill Clinton did, and 15 percent said they didn't know.[4]

Anyone remotely familiar with the voucher issue knows that it is a Republican issue and that most prominent Democrats are opposed. The positions of the 1996 candidates reflected as much and were readily discernible. Dole favored vouchers and put forward his own low-income voucher plan as a central part of his campaign, while Clinton came out strongly against.

The evidence suggests that most registered voters—again, a knowledgeable group in relative terms—were largely uninformed. On these very basic questions, half or more of the registered voters either gave the wrong answers or simply didn't know. And to make matters worse, we can't assume that those who gave the right answers actually knew what they were doing. The fact is, a voter who was totally uninformed still had a 50-50 chance of picking the right answer simply by guessing. Given the large numbers of people who did guess, and guessed wrong, it is only prudent to suspect that many people who gave right answers were also guessing. Indeed, the overall distribution of responses—with only slightly more people picking the right over the wrong answer—looks a lot like what we would expect from a population of uninformed guessers. In light of this evidence, our own figures suggesting that only one-third of the larger population has even heard about vouchers seems to be perfectly reasonable.

A recent survey by Public Agenda, which, aside from our own, is the most comprehensive poll yet conducted on the voucher issue, points to the same conclusion.[5] It finds that 63 percent of the general public claims to know "very little" or "nothing" about vouchers, and thus that only 37 percent claim to be informed. This is a telling result. For not only is it statistically indistinguishable from ours, but it also suggests that, despite the increased salience of the voucher issue over the last several years— from 1995, when our own survey was carried out, to 1999, when the Public Agenda survey was—the level of public awareness appears to have stayed very much the same. And very low. So far, the political firefight among elites has done little to raise the consciousness of ordinary citizens.

Logic: Who Is Likely to Get Informed?

Now let's put this measure to use in taking a closer look at who knows about vouchers and who doesn't. Generally speaking, what should we expect to find?

As a baseline, we need to recognize that, in the study of public opinion generally, the most fundamental of all patterns is that political knowledge is a function of social class. People are likely to be better informed about politics the higher their education and (to a lesser extent) their income. Another common pattern is that knowledge varies with age: young adults are typically not as well informed about politics as their elders are.[6]

Are these the people, then, who should be most knowledgeable about vouchers? Political scientists have been studying citizen information for many years, and they have different views on how attentive people are to specific issues. One view is that citizens tend to be generalists. For any given issue, almost whatever its substance, the people most likely to be knowledgeable—a distinct minority of the population—are the ones who tend to be broadly knowledgeable about politics generally. A person who knows about crime is also likely to know about foreign policy and abortion. And about vouchers.[7]

This theory represents the gloomy side, as far as the voucher movement is concerned. The people who tend to be generally knowledgeable, and thus knowledgeable about vouchers, should tend to have precisely the characteristics we just outlined: they should be higher in social class and not young. If so, the people the movement sees as its prime constituents— poor and minority parents (many of whom are young and most of whom are poorly educated)—are precisely the ones who, in the natural order of things, are the *least* likely to be informed about the issue. More generally, the threat to the choice movement here is that there may be a disconnect between need and knowledge, so that the people who stand to benefit most from school choice are the least likely to find out about it and take supportive action.

The alternative view among political scientists, which seems to be the predominant one, is more optimistic. It argues that people tend to be specialized in their knowledge of political issues. The notion is that, even though most people may be quite uninformed, the people who do acquire and process information will tend to do so on policy issues in which they are especially interested or have a personal stake or involvement. Depending on their interests, certain people may know a good deal about foreign policy— or vouchers—but very little about abortion or crime. And because this is so, different policy issues will tend to have different "issue publics" of citizens who are informed and capable of developing meaningful opinions.[8]

If the specialist theory is correct, the movement should find its informational task easier to accomplish. The specialist theory is compatible with the notion that, when all is said and done, knowledge is ultimately linked to incentives. Of course, as we discussed earlier, the incentives to get informed about public policy are weak by comparison to those for consumer goods, and for this reason "rational ignorance" about vouchers and other public policies is likely to be widespread. But the specialist theory argues, in effect, that incentives should still make a difference in explaining what issues people pay attention to, and why some people are better informed about particular issues than others are. Most obviously, the people who are directly affected by a policy, or who stand to gain (or lose) from it, are more likely to pay attention to it—when it is presented through the media, for instance—and to get informed. By this logic, senior citizens might be expected to know much more about Social Security or Medicare than they do about other policies, and they are likely to be better informed on these issues than other people are. Something analogous should be true for people with a special stake in the voucher issue.

This means that the people who have the most to *gain* from vouchers, at least potentially, would have incentives to know something about it. Thus parents should be more informed about vouchers than nonparents. Private parents should be more informed than public parents. Swing public parents should be more informed than the remaining public parents. Parents who are dissatisfied with public school performance should be more informed about vouchers than those who are satisfied. Catholics and born-again Christians should be more informed than other religious groups. And so on.

Things are not necessarily so simple, of course. In principle, people who are negatively affected by vouchers could have just as much incentive to learn about the issue as people who are positively affected. Thus, just as poor parents might be open to information about vouchers because they could directly benefit, so parents from the suburbs might want to learn about the issue because they feel threatened. Similarly, people attracted to vouchers on religious grounds might seek to become better informed about them, but people who strongly oppose the public funding of religious activities, or who want to protect the separation of church and state, may have compelling incentives to get informed too.

As these examples suggest, the logic of incentives can be ambiguous. When a policy has a clear clientele group and no clear opponents, as is true for Social Security and Medicare, ambiguity is not a problem: the beneficiaries (senior citizens) are the ones who have the strongest incentives to get informed. But when the issue is characterized by opposing groups, as the voucher issue is, both sides could have incentives to get informed, and there is no purely logical reason for thinking that either side should have the advantage.

Empirically, however, the most reasonable presumption is that the potential beneficiaries of vouchers ought to have the strongest incentives to get informed. If the movement were large, powerful, and threatening to the status quo, there would be more reason for people who oppose it to start paying attention. But the voucher movement is still in its formative period, and the people who find it most relevant to their lives are almost surely the people who think that it has something positive to offer them and speaks to their values and interests.

Table 6-1. *Information and Social Background*
Percent, unless otherwise indicated[a]

	Public school parents			Nonparents		
Background variable	*Have heard of vouchers*	*Have not heard of vouchers*	*N*[b]	*Have heard of vouchers*	*Have not heard of vouchers*	*N*[b]
Education						
Less than high school	16	84	(246)	26	74	(152)
High school graduate	26	74	(903)	23	77	(479)
Some college	39	61	(645)	37	63	(400)
College graduate	52	48	(496)	48	52	(371)
Postgraduate	76	24	(194)	71	29	(168)
Annual Income ($)						
Less than 20,000	16	84	(449)	27	73	(268)
21,000–30,000	20	80	(478)	34	66	(262)
31,000–40,000	39	61	(390)	31	69	(257)
41,000–60,000	41	59	(528)	42	58	(303)
More than 60,000	59	41	(331)	49	51	(232)
Age						
18–24	9	91	(91)	15	85	(208)
25–29	21	79	(211)	34	66	(196)
30–34	26	74	(378)	42	58	(120)
35–39	30	70	(548)	48	52	(96)
40–44	44	56	(529)	30	70	(105)
45–49	46	54	(354)	41	59	(118)
50 and over	48	52	(342)	40	60	(705)

a. Percentages are based on weighted data. They may not sum to 100 due to rounding.
b. N is the unweighted number of respondents.

This is bolstered by the operation of social networks. The people who might benefit from vouchers do not necessarily have to seek out information on their own. There are organizations that have a stake in telling them about vouchers and promoting the growth of the movement. Two organizational networks are well situated for playing this kind of role: churches and private schools. It is well known that some churches and private schools have been active in conveying information to their constituents about vouchers. While it is unclear at this point how widespread a practice this is, or how effective, there is a potential here for using social organization to get the word out—and an incentive for voucher leaders to see that it happens.

Once again, however, there is ambiguity that must be recognized. Elite opponents also have an important social network for conveying information: the public school system. This network is public, so it is more difficult and controversial to use—and illegal in some respects. But the audience is huge, and the education establishment clearly has incentives to get its message out through all the various channels, official and unofficial, that the school system puts in their hands. So far, it appears opponents have not invested seriously in such a strategy, except in cases when the voucher issue has become a salient local issue (due to the initiating pressure of advocates).[9] In the future, however, their use of the public schools as information networks could become much more common.

Despite the ambiguities, these considerations help to guide our thinking about vouchers and information. The voucher movement is best off if the specialist theory of information is correct, if incentives play a role in explaining who gets informed and who doesn't—and if the beneficiaries and latent supporters of vouchers are the ones with the strongest incentives and networks. If the generalist theory is correct, on the other hand, people will tend to get informed about vouchers (if they get informed at all) for reasons that have little to do with the issue itself or with their incentives. And this will make life difficult for the movement. The people most receptive to information will tend to be high in social class and older, and this means that the movement's key constituencies will be especially difficult to reach and recruit.

Who Knows about Vouchers?

Let's begin with the descriptive data in table 6-1. While we have to be careful about drawing conclusions in the absence of controls, the figures here suggest that social class is a very powerful determinant of who gets

Table 6-2. *Information and Incentives*
Percent, unless otherwise indicated[a]

Type of respondent	Have heard of vouchers	Have not heard of vouchers	N[b]
Nonparents	34	66	(1,589)
Private school parents	53	47	(530)
Inner-city parents (public)	21	79	(539)
Public school parents	32	68	(2,553)
Public school parents who			
are Catholic	31	69	(637)
are born-again	42	58	(187)
think schools need "major changes"	38	62	(582)
think schools are "doing well"	29	71	(1,053)
are interested in going private	34	66	(1,380)
are not interested in going private	32	68	(1,041)

a. Percentages are based on weighted data. They may not sum to 100 due to rounding.
b. N is the unweighted number of respondents.

informed about vouchers. Among public school parents, only 16 percent of those with less than a high school education have heard of vouchers, compared to 76 percent of those with postgraduate training. The figures are much the same for nonparents, ranging from 26 percent to 71 percent. Income tells a similar (but less dramatic) story.

The other component of the natural baseline, age, also appears to be an important influence on who gets informed. Young people are far less knowledgeable about the voucher issue than their elders are. Among public parents, for instance, only 9 percent of those between the ages of 18 and 24 have heard of vouchers, compared to about 46 percent of parents who are beyond the age of 40.

Our data suggest, then, that the joint effects of class and age do indeed paint a troubling picture for the voucher movement. It is precisely the people targeted by the movement as needing vouchers the most, the parents who are poor and uneducated (and mainly young), who are the least likely to have heard about vouchers—by a long shot.

This is strikingly illustrated by our data on the inner-city poor, set out in table 6-2. As we saw in the last chapter, these parents are highly interested in private school options for their children. Yet almost 80 percent of them do not know what vouchers are. At least in the short term, therefore, the choice movement has a lot of educating to do before it can count on support from the very people it presumes to be serving. These parents can't get engaged and can't exert political pressure if they don't even know about the issue.

This begins to suggest that incentives may not be major factors in explaining who gets informed. It is hard to tell by looking only at the inner-city poor: they ought to be less informed than everyone else, purely because their levels of education and income are so low. The rest of the evidence in table 6-2, however, reinforces the notion that incentives are only weakly relevant to who gets informed, and pale by comparison to class and age.

The best evidence for incentive effects is that private parents, the most immediate beneficiaries of a general voucher program, are indeed more likely to be knowledgeable about vouchers than public parents. Fifty-three percent of private parents know about vouchers, compared to 32 percent of public parents. But the margin of difference is smaller than one might expect, given the obvious stake private parents have in getting vouchers, given that they are part of a social network capable of getting the word out, and given that they are higher in education and income than public parents are (and thus should be more knowledgeable anyway). Despite these advantages, almost half of private parents have never heard of the concept—hardly an impressive demonstration of incentives at work.

And this is as impressive as it gets. While public parents are much more directly affected by the voucher issue than nonparents are, the two groups are about equally informed on the topic. The greater incentive of public parents does not, apparently, motivate them to learn more about the issue. Both Catholic and born-again parents have incentives to look into vouchers and are tied into social networks capable of providing them with information. But Catholic parents are no better informed (at 31 percent) than other public parents are (at 32 percent). And while born-again parents (at 42 percent) are somewhat better informed than the others, the differences are still more modest than one might expect if incentives were a strong determinant.

The final nails in the coffin, it would seem, come with the evidence on performance and the desire to go private. From chapter 5's analysis, we know that performance plays a huge role in shaping who wants to go private, and appears to be quite important in the thinking of parents. Yet, as table 6-2 shows, it does not seem to have much to do with whether they know about vouchers: of the parents who believe the schools need "major changes," 38 percent are informed, compared to 29 percent of parents who think the schools are "doing well"—pretty modest, all things considered. Even more compelling is the evidence on public parents who express an interest in going private. They, of all public parents, have the clearest incentive to learn about vouchers. But the fact is, they are virtually as ignorant (34 percent informed) as the public parents who have no interest at all in going private (32 percent).

Descriptive evidence, then, suggests that the generalist theory is on the mark and that the specialist theory—or at least the gainer (that is, one-sided) version of it highlighted here—is not. The biggest influences on the acquisition of information, class and age, appear to be generic factors that dispose people to pay attention to public policy in general, and need have nothing to do with vouchers per se. The people with the greatest incentives to know about vouchers are usually no better informed than anyone else.

Multivariate Analysis

These conclusions are only tentative, because the findings could change when controls for other variables are introduced. The main suspect here is social class, which is a powerful determinant of who gets informed about vouchers, but is also related to most of the other variables we are interested in. It is entirely possible, for instance, that private parents are better informed than other parents because they are higher in education and income, and not because they have stronger incentives. Conversely, it is possible that inner-city parents are grossly uninformed about vouchers because of their social class, and not because of the weak role of incentives. A multivariate analysis, by controlling for class (and other things), allows us to arrive at more confident conclusions.

A Comparison of Groups

Table 6-3 sets out the results for two background models. Each allows us to determine whether, as the specialist theory maintains, particular groups of parents—those with incentives to get informed—are in fact better informed than other groups, once class and other background variables are controlled. They also allow us to see whether class and age stand out as the prime determinants of who gets informed, as the generalist theory maintains.

The first model is estimated over all respondents, and thus includes nonparents as well as parents. It contains a variable representing all parents (public and private), and another representing private parents—but the presence of the latter means that the coefficient of the parents variable is actually telling us solely about *public* parents. Specifically, the coefficient of the parents variable indicates whether public parents are better informed than nonparents, and the coefficient of the private par-

Table 6-3. *Who Gets Informed: A Comparison of Groups*[a]

Variable	Model 1 (total population)		Model 2 (parents)	
	Coefficient	[Impact]	Coefficient	[Impact]
All parents	.06	[1.95]		
Private school parents	.28***	[10.43]	.30***	[11.18]
Inner-city parents			.10	[3.59]
Swing parents			.06	[2.03]
Background controls				
Education	.19***	[17.55]	.24***	[21.04]
Income	.10***	[12.89]	.14***	[18.04]
Catholic	−.03	[−1.16]	−.08	[−2.65]
Born again	.08	[2.71]	.25***	[9.39]
Black (north)	.11	[3.77]	−.03	[−1.13]
Black (south)	−.10	[−3.48]	−.05	[−1.61]
Hispanic	−.02	[−.52]	−.29***	[−9.66]
Age	.09***	[18.99]	.09***	[12.88]
Party identification	.02**	[3.21]	.00	[.61]
Low expectations	−.06***	[−6.16]	−.02	[−2.29]
Constant	−1.89***		−1.98***	
N[b]	(4,597)		(3,045)	
Pseudo R^2	.13		.16	

** Significant at .05 level.
*** Significant at .01 level.
  a. Probit models estimated using weighted data. The dependent variable is coded 1 if the individual has heard of vouchers and 0 otherwise. Impact coefficient is the change in estimated probability as the independent variable shifts from one standard deviation below its mean to one standard deviation above its mean (for nondichotomous variables), or from 0 to 1 (for dichotomous variables), holding all other variables constant at their means. Models control for the full range of background variables, not all of which are reported in the tables.
  b. N is the unweighted number of respondents.

ents variable indicates whether private parents are better informed than public parents.

The results show that two of the basic results from the descriptive analysis continue to hold when background is controlled. Public parents, who have far greater incentive to know about vouchers than nonparents do, are *not* in fact better informed—which of course contradicts the incentives hypothesis. Private parents, however, *are* better informed than public parents (and nonparents too) even when their socioeconomic and religious characteristics are taken into account—indicating that there is at least one major group of parents for whom incentives seem to work (either directly via their own motivation to get informed, or indirectly through the operation of social networks). Still, the effect is not large. Compared to public parents, private parents have a 10 percent greater probability of being informed.

The second model of table 6-3 looks only at parents, and introduces a finer breakdown of parent beneficiaries—private parents, swing public parents, and low-income inner-city public parents—for exploring the role of incentives. The results for private parents are what we would expect, given the prior model. But the results for other groups add important new details. The swing parents, who clearly have strong incentives to learn about vouchers, are only slightly more likely to be informed than public parents who don't want to go private, and the difference between them is too small to be statistically significant. This confirms the earlier result in the presence of controls for social class, and is a major failure for the incentives hypothesis. Much the same conclusion emerges when we look at the results for the inner-city poor: here too the coefficient is statistically insignificant, and the incentives hypothesis is not borne out.

In the case of the inner-city poor, however, there is a silver lining that deserves to be appreciated. These parents are extremely low in social class, and almost certainly (judging from political science research) quite low in their general knowledge about politics and public policy. It is not surprising that 79 percent of them have never heard of vouchers (see table 6-2). Still, it is important to recognize that, once education and income (and other background factors) are controlled, they are actually a bit *more* likely to be informed than other public parents are. These differences are not statistically significant. But this may be an indication that, as of 1995 (when our survey was carried out), the voucher movement was beginning to get the word out among inner-city parents, and that incentives were beginning to work (against great social odds).

Still, the incentives hypothesis does quite poorly overall. And if we look at the background portion of the statistical results, we can see very clearly that education, income, and age are the primary determinants of who gets informed. The evidence is consistent, then, with the generalist theory of knowledge, and argues that what people know about the voucher issue usually has little to do with vouchers per se, or their stake or interest in it. They know about vouchers, it appears, simply because they tend to know about politics generally.

More Detail

Now let's shift over to the same framework employed in previous chapters, and take a look at the effects of background, context, attitudes, and performance on who gets informed. This provides a nice parallel with the rest of the book and a level of detail that sheds additional light on the connection between information and incentives.

To simplify matters, table 6-4 sets out the results only for the most comprehensive version of the model. (The coefficients change so little across models in this case that there is no reason to present them all.) Here is a brief summary of the basic findings:

(1) Education, income, and age continue to be major determinants of who gets informed about vouchers, whether we are talking about parents or nonparents.

(2) As these factors imply, people who are less advantaged are less likely to know about vouchers, despite their greater interest in going private. Other findings, when relevant at all, tend to point in the same direction. Among inner-city parents, for example, blacks and Hispanics are significantly less likely to know about vouchers than whites are. In addition, residential mobility and district context do not seem to be very important in determining who gets informed, and, to the extent they have any effects at all, being uninformed is associated with living in more advantaged districts and with the exercise of residentially based choice. All of this is the opposite of what one would expect if incentives were operating and the beneficiaries of vouchers were seeking out information.

(3) Religious affiliation has little effect on who gets informed. For nonparents, there are no effects whatever. For parents, whose incentives are arguably much greater, the effects are as we described earlier: Catholics are no better informed than other parents are; born-again parents are better informed—although the boost they get is rather modest. There is some indication, then, that religion-based incentives (bolstered by social networks) might be operating, but they are far weaker than most observers would have expected.

(4) The desire to go private, which would seem on the surface to be the prime reason parents might want to learn about vouchers (to the extent incentives work at all), once again proves to have no impact on information. This is true for public parents generally, and for inner-city parents as well.

(5) Satisfaction with public school performance appears to have more to do with who gets informed—although there is no logical reason it should have a greater impact than the desire to go private. The results on this factor are actually mixed. For public parents as a whole—arguably the critical group on this count—there is no significant connection between dissatisfaction with the schools and getting informed about vouchers. This is another major defeat for incentives. Yet there is such a connection for inner-city parents. And surprisingly, given their relatively weak incentives, there is a connection for nonparents as well. It would be wrong, then, to

Table 6-4. The Determinants of Who Gets Informed[a]

Variable	Public school parents performance model		Nonparents performance model		Inner-city parents performance model	
	Coefficient	[Impact]	Coefficient	[Impact]	Coefficient	[Impact]
Background						
Education	.21***	[18.19]	.16***	[15.43]	.21***	[11.72]
Income	.14***	[18.40]	.08***	[11.41]	.23	[6.14]
Catholic	-.01	[-.23]	-.05	[-1.61]	.13	[3.43]
Born-again	.21*	[7.72]	.09	[3.21]	-.10	[-2.59]
Black (north)	.05	[1.66]	.13	[4.96]	-.56**	[-12.62]
Black (south)	.07	[2.32]	-.03	[-1.20]	-.22	[-5.24]
Hispanic	-.19***	[-6.24]	.07	[2.57]	-.69***	[-16.56]
Age	.09***	[11.90]	.10***	[24.04]	.08**	[10.13]
Party identification	-.01	[-1.30]	.04*	[5.07]	-.01	[-.80]
Low expectations	-.02	[-2.47]	-.09***	[-8.86]	-.00	[-.18]
Context						
Residential mobility	.04	[3.07]	.12**	[7.17]	.00	[.10]
Advantaged district	.09*	[5.25]	.07	[4.04]	.10	[3.77]

	Coefficient	Impact	Coefficient	Impact	Coefficient	Impact
Attitudes						
Diversity (whites)	-.12**	[-6.51]	-.00	[-.12]	-.01	[-.32]
Inequity	.08*	[4.18]	.14**	[7.43]	.22**	[8.37]
School prayer	-.16***	[-12.45]	-.16***	[-13.32]	-.16**	[-9.17]
Parent influence	.11***	[6.16]	-.15***	[-9.77]	.14	[5.47]
School size	.04	[2.06]	.02	[1.02]	-.02	[-.80]
Public school ideology	.03	[1.63]	-.11**	[-6.03]	.23***	[9.13]
Markets	.09**	[5.08]	.08	[4.35]	.06	[2.51]
Moral values	.16***	[16.66]	.04	[4.37]	.08*	[6.69]
Performance						
Public performance	-.07	[-3.61]	-.16***	[-8.37]	-.25**	[-9.25]
Desire to go private	-.08	[-2.82]			-.00	[-.07]
Constant	-1.27***		-.74**		-1.72**	
N[b]	(2,161)		(1,407)		(475)	
Pseudo R^2	.20		.18		.18	

* Significant at .10 level.
** Significant at .05 level.
*** Significant at .01 level.

a. Probit models estimated using weighted data. The dependent variable is coded 1 if the individual has heard of vouchers and 0 otherwise. Impact coefficient is the change in estimated probability as the independent variable shifts from one standard deviation below its mean to one standard deviation above its mean (for nondichotomous variables), or from 0 to 1 (for dichotomous variables), holding all other variables constant at their means. Models control for the full range of background variables, not all of which are reported in the tables.
b. N is the unweighted number of respondents.

conclude that performance has no incentive value in prompting people to get informed about the voucher issue. In fact, were our models specified a bit differently (by dropping attitudes, for example), performance would have a statistically significant impact in the public-parents equation as well, and the results would be consistent. Nonetheless, the overarching fact here is that the impacts are much more modest than the incentive hypothesis would lead us to expect, especially given the weight parents attach to performance in thinking about going private. Incentives just don't seem to be having much impact.

I have left a discussion of attitudes for last, largely because the results are difficult to interpret. If the gainer version of the incentive theory is correct, then people who hold the kinds of attitudes and beliefs that have figured prominently in the analysis of previous chapters—those related to social equity, parent influence, moral values, and the like—should be especially interested in the voucher issue and inclined to get informed. The evidence suggests that there may be something of the sort going on.

Public parents provide the strongest support for the incentives hypothesis—as they should, because they have the biggest personal stake in the issue. Of the eight attitudinal variables tested, six have effects on information that are statistically significant. Only one of these—school prayer—has an impact whose direction is clearly the opposite of what the incentives hypothesis would suggest. All of the other effects are consistent with the notion that attitudes associated with criticism of the public schools, or with sympathy for private schools, should encourage higher levels of information about vouchers.[10]

But other findings don't make much sense. Parent influence, for example, has a significant effect for nonparents, but in the wrong direction: those who support parent influence are less likely to be informed about vouchers than those who don't. Similarly, public school ideology has a significant impact among inner-city parents that is also in the wrong direction, and no impact at all for public parents generally. And then there is the finding on diversity among whites. We showed in chapter 5 that this factor has nothing to do with going private among public parents generally, but that it does among the inner-city poor—yet the results here suggest that it has an informational effect among public parents and no effect among the inner-city poor.

The major departure from the expected pattern, however, arises from a startling but robust result on school prayer: it is the people who *oppose* school prayer who are especially likely to get informed about vouchers. This is true for public parents. It is true for inner-city parents. It is true for nonparents. And for each group, school prayer stands out as an attitude of genuine salience in explaining who gets informed. For nonparents and inner-city parents, it is the most important attitudinal influence, and for public parents it is second in importance only to moral values.

This finding, which comes right out of the blue, could be a statistical quirk. All researchers know that this happens on occasion, due to sampling error, misspecification, and the like, and that all findings cannot be believed. Nonetheless, the sheer consistency and magnitude of the school prayer effect suggests that it may be telling us two things of real importance.

The first is substantive. In the public debate over vouchers, the religion issue may be more than just a force that motivates pro-religious types to support the voucher movement, as is commonly assumed. It may also be a force that activates equally strong or stronger opposition to vouchers among (the distinct minority of) people who are antagonistic to religion, or who believe it has no place in the schools, or who don't want any of their tax money flowing to the churches. The statistical results of previous chapters, then, which show that support for school prayer is associated with lower satisfaction with public school performance, as well as with a greater desire to go private, may be driven by intense motivations on *both* sides of the religion issue. Indeed, it is even possible that the anti-religious people are the ones who are especially intense, and that the earlier findings are really driven by the tendency of these people to be supportive of public schools and unsympathetic to private schools. If so, there may be an important (if relatively small) political constituency here that elite opponents of vouchers can put to good use in their campaign to stop the spread of vouchers.

The second implication is essentially theoretical. The pure logic of the incentives argument, of course, allows for incentives to arise on both sides of an issue. As we discussed earlier, it is reasonable to think that, especially in the early stages of a movement, the supporters are the ones who are likely to pay the most attention. But this is an empirical judgment and may be wrong. The finding on school prayer is a stark reminder that the people who have incentives to get informed about vouchers (or any issue) may *not* simply be those who would benefit or who have positive attitudes. The opponents may also have incentives to get informed. If so, then our focus in this chapter on the gainer (one-sided) version of the incentives hypothesis does not really do justice to the broader theory of incentives, and could even be misleading.

If the incentives were actually two-sided on the voucher issue, then for many of the attitudes in our model there can be no clear expectation about the net impact on information. It could go either way, positive or negative, since people at either extreme presumably have strong incentives to get informed. Mixed results would presumably be common, and certainly not a sign that incentives fail to operate. Indeed, even statistically insignificant results (given our models) would be consistent with the theory, because if people on both sides of an issue were about equally motivated to learn about vouchers, the net effect would be zero.

With better data it would be possible to carry out more discriminating tests, and thus to determine whether the broader theory of incentives has merit in explaining who gets informed about vouchers. Until such research can be carried out, judgments about the link between incentives and information need to be qualified: the link may in fact be somewhat stronger than we have determined here.[11] Nonetheless, we *do* have evidence that is quite relevant to an assessment of the theory, and we needn't throw up our hands just because it isn't definitive or comprehensive.

Most of the ambiguities arise when we consider attitudes, many of which could be two-sided in their incentives, and which generate empirical findings that fail to reflect a simple pattern. These results are difficult to interpret. Most of the other results, however, are more straightforward. When we compare public parents to nonparents, for example, or swing parents to other public parents, or inner-city parents to non–inner-city parents, there is no ambiguity about how the incentives should work. If incentives are important to information, and if the broader theory is correct, then we *know* in these cases which group should be better informed. And the evidence suggests that the impact of incentives is weak at best. These results reflect badly not just on the gainer (one-sided) version of the theory, but also on the broader incentive theory as a whole (which logically implies it)—and thus suggest that, even if we could successfully test out the two-sided version, it would probably not emerge as a powerful explanation of who gets informed.

Conclusion

In previous chapters, we found that the way Americans think about close-to-home educational issues—the performance of public schools, the attractiveness of private schools—gives the voucher movement a lot to work with in mobilizing support for its cause. While Americans tend to look favorably on the public schools, they often think that private schools are better, and most parents would consider going private if given the opportunity. Moreover, most Americans are dissatisfied with specific aspects of the public school system—on issues ranging from inequity to religion to parent influence—and all of these concerns have a natural connection to vouchers. The potential for public support is out there.

For the movement, however, building on this potential is not so simple. This is not just because its opponents are powerful or because politics is filled with obstacles. It is also because there is something about most public policy issues, vouchers included, that makes the mobilization of strong, meaningful public support very difficult. The problem is twofold. First, policy proposals tend to be remote from the everyday lives of most people, complicated to think about, and abstract and theoretical in their arguments—and most Americans are not interested enough to pay close attention. Second, public policies are adopted (if at all) by the polity as a whole, and their benefits are available to anyone who qualifies, regardless of whether they have played an informed role (or any role) in the decision process; this dilutes the incentives of individuals to pay the costs of getting well informed. In the realm of public policy, ignorance is usually quite rational.

Given these problems, we should not expect Americans to know much about vouchers. And they don't. Our survey shows that only 35 percent say they have even heard of the concept. So the voucher movement does indeed face a major challenge: somehow its leaders have to break through the "rational ignorance" of the American public, communicate their message, and mobilize support, especially among constituencies that have the greatest stake in the issue.

This challenge would be easier to overcome if there were a strong connection between stakes and information, and thus if the constituencies with the greatest stakes in getting vouchers had strong incentives to become informed. In view of the problems that plague public policy generally, we know that these incentives are going to be weaker than they would be for consumer goods, as well as for issues that are local and familiar. But this doesn't mean, at least in principle, that incentives won't still play *some* role in determining who gets informed—and in prompting the movement's target constituencies to find out about vouchers.

The evidence from our survey, however, paints a pretty grim picture here as well. The people who get informed about vouchers are the people who tend to be more knowledgeable about public policy in general: those who are higher in education, income, and age. For the most part, people appear to be generalists and learn about vouchers for reasons that have little to do with the substance of the issue or their stake in it. The idea that people are often specialists, and thus that constituencies with stakes in the issue will become better informed, finds little support. Public parents should be better informed than nonparents, but they are not. Swing parents should be better informed than other public parents, but they are not. And so on. There are some groups—notably, private parents—for whom incentives seem to work. But even with them, the effects are modest.

Overall, then, it appears that the voucher movement faces an uphill battle against the "rational ignorance" of the American public. Most people are not paying much attention, and even constituencies with the greatest stakes in the issue tend to be uninformed about it. This may well change over time, as the movement succeeds on a case-by-case basis in winning new programs, gaining publicity, and involving more parents and children in the actual use of vouchers. But as the recent Public Agenda survey indicates, it apparently hasn't changed over the last several years, even though the movement has made a good deal of progress during this time. "Rational ignorance" is simply a pervasive fact of life in the American polity, the incentives to get informed about public policy are weak—and even if the movement is making progress, the task of gaining the attention and support of the American public almost surely remains a formidable challenge.

7 *Support for Vouchers*

IN A BOOK ABOUT vouchers and public opinion, one question would seem to stand out from all others. To what extent do Americans support vouchers?

This is the question elites on both sides of the issue care about most. They all recognize that, in a democracy, the polling numbers matter—for the numbers tell elected officials what decisions are likely to meet with public approval, and thus what positions they can take to enhance their own popularity and reelection prospects. The more Americans support vouchers, the more inclined policymakers will be to move in that direction.

But what exactly *are* the numbers? On this there is disagreement. Advocates want to argue that most Americans support vouchers. Critics want to argue the opposite. And both point to scientifically designed polls, carried out by reputable organizations, that seem to bolster their positions.

To some extent, this conflict over the facts is a natural outgrowth of politics. On virtually any policy issue, partisans can be expected to take a selective approach to the evidence and to use it strategically in trying to win over the uncommitted. In politics, evidence often has little to do with the search for truth. It is just another weapon in the struggle for victory.

With the voucher issue, however, and with many other policy issues as well, there is another reason why the truth is so elusive and competing claims so prevalent. The reason is that there *isn't* a simple truth to be discovered. This may sound a bit melodramatic, but the problem is unavoidable. For if most Americans have never heard of the concept, much less thought about it in any depth, they cannot have well-developed opinions. Indeed, it is not even clear that they can have opinions at all. And once we question the meaning and validity of their opinions and recognize how easily their views can change, the notion that there is a true level of public support—a true level that surveys are supposedly measuring—becomes untenable.

To understand support for vouchers, then, we cannot take public opinion at face value. We need to think more fundamentally about what public opinion is and what it represents. In the process, we need to go beyond the raw numbers to see if we can explain *why* people take the positions they do, and whether they appear to be thinking in a reasonable, structured way about the subject at all. The challenge is to determine whether, in a population of people who are largely uninformed about vouchers, public opinion tells us much of anything about what Americans really want for themselves, their communities, and their country.

This chapter will try to provide some answers. It is an effort to direct attention *away* from simple questions of support and opposition—the questions that have so monopolized attention in politics and the media—and to construe the subject in a way that helps us understand what is actually going on.

What Is Public Opinion?

Political scientists began to study public opinion and voting behavior in the 1940s. When they did, their findings were troubling.[1] While theorists had long argued that successful democracy requires an informed citizenry, the facts pointed to an electorate that does not even remotely measure up. The typical American, they found, is poorly informed about government and public policy and lacking in coherent, stable attitudes about important public issues.

The seminal work on the subject was done by Philip Converse. Converse argued that, while a sophisticated stratum of the American public is capable of thinking in an informed, coherent, ideological way about public policy, the masses of ordinary people are not, and in fact "do not have meaningful beliefs, even on issues that have formed the basis for intense political controversy among elites for substantial periods of time."[2] On any given issue, there is likely to be a small "issue public" that is knowledgeable and has genuine attitudes, and a mass public that is largely unaware and without meaningful attitudes.[3]

What, then, are surveys measuring when they try to gauge public opinion? Converse's answer is that people don't want to appear ignorant to the interviewer, and feel obligated to provide some kind of response—so they manufacture an attitude on the spot. This is not a real attitude that reflects their underlying values and beliefs. It is just a means of getting through the interview. Were they to be interviewed again at a later time, they might give the opposite response. The opinions that surveys tend to measure, then, are often just "nonattitudes" that are to a large extent randomly chosen, inconsistent and unstable over time, and not a meaningful reflection of serious thinking.

More recent work has painted a more charitable picture, but not by a lot. Americans, while poorly informed, are probably not as "wretchedly informed" as Converse and others have claimed.[4] And a number of scholars have argued that ordinary citizens can function well with low levels of information: they are selective in what they pay attention to, and capable of using simple cues and cognitive shortcuts to arrive at policy positions that reflect their own interests and values.[5] Even so, the dominant view among political scientists remains a pessimistic one that is not far from the stark position set out by Converse.

Today, probably the most influential framework for thinking about attitudes and public opinion comes from John Zaller.[6] Zaller agrees that ordinary people are poorly informed about public policy issues, largely incapable of thinking in a consistent, coherent way about them, and, when answering questions on a survey, are essentially just making up their opinions as they go along. Yet unlike Converse, he does not claim that nothing significant is going on inside the respondent's mind. Quite the contrary: a great deal is going on, and it is quite meaningful.

In Zaller's view, people may see all sorts of interests, values, and beliefs as relevant to a given policy issue, and their response to a survey item depends on which "considerations" come to mind during the interview process. Among people who are politically knowledgeable, many considerations often come to mind, and these considerations are integrated to produce attitudes that are meaningful, consistent, and relatively stable over time. For the great majority, however, things are not so neat. Many considerations may be relevant, but they exist as separate concerns that are never fully reconciled with one another, and only a few of them (if that) actually come to the "top of the head" during the interview. Those that do, moreover, will often emerge not because of the substance of the issue being raised (for people are too poorly informed to make the connection), but because of specific cues contained within the survey itself—due especially to the wording of questions. In effect, most people use the survey and its cues to figure out what considerations are relevant, and then to figure out what their position on issues ought to be.[7]

Zaller argues that, beneath the surface, people tend to be ambivalent. On a given policy issue, they could come down positively or negatively. It all depends on what considerations happen to be evoked by the survey, and on the cues embedded in the survey itself. From one survey to the next, then, individuals might well express very different positions on the same issue. And even within a single survey, individuals may give inconsistent responses as they react to newly emerging considerations and cues during the course of the interview. Nonetheless, the opinions they express are not random, as Converse implies, and not simple attempts to please the interviewer or avoid appearing ignorant. Opinions arise from considerations that matter, and they tell us something about people's interests, values, and beliefs.

Zaller's framework has much to recommend it, and I will use it to guide some of the analysis in this book. Its simplest message is that, in exploring where Americans stand on vouchers, we need to get away from the notion that people have true attitudes. People are likely to be uninformed and ambivalent when it comes to vouchers, and their opinions will be a function of whatever considerations come to the "top of the head" during the interview. These considerations may vary from survey to survey, depending on the specific wording of questions and the broader content of the surveys themselves. And because this is so, support for vouchers may seem to jump all over the map.

If we want to know what people think about vouchers, then, it is a mistake to focus on simple measures of support or opposition. We need to look beneath the surface. For even if their opinions are poorly thought-out and subject to change, we can gain insight into their thinking by determining which considerations influence their views and what their relative importance is. Indeed, some of the prime candidates are precisely the concerns we have been dealing with all along: performance, inequity, religion, public school ideology, and other dimensions that have already proved their relevance. Granted, people may not know much about vouchers. But if the positions they take are related to particular values, beliefs, and interests—if we know what matters to them as they try to sort things through—then we can say we understand something more fundamental about public opinion on the issue.

At this point, we are getting to the outer reaches of Zaller's theory of public opinion. Indeed, I may have pushed it too far. The reason is that, according to Zaller, most people do not really engage in a process of reasoning to come up with their opinions. They mechanically average whatever considerations pop into their minds without mulling them over or trying to integrate them into a more coherent viewpoint. There isn't much thinking going on.

As I noted above, however, other scholars are more sanguine on this point. In their view, people *do* engage in genuine reasoning about policy, and use their limited information in ways that make sense. This implies, among other things, that when people are presented with new information on an unfamiliar topic such as vouchers—as they are during the survey—they would use the opportunity to *learn*, and their thinking on the topic would become more coherent and structured as a result. They would be actively engaged in an intellectual process of connecting their values, beliefs, and interests to a compatible position on vouchers. Indeed, James Fishkin has argued that this kind of learning is not only common, but should be built into the operation of American democracy—through, for instance, community forums for the collective deliberation of important policy issues.[8]

This debate bears on our own efforts to understand how Americans think about vouchers. Are ordinary people, despite their informational and cognitive limitations, able to think about vouchers in a coherent, structured way, and does their thinking become more coherent and structured as the survey (or more generally, their worldly experience) provides them with new opportunities to learn? Simply put: is there "real thinking" going on? Moreover, are ordinary people so different from the more sophisticated members of the population? Do they apply the same sort of intellectual structure that elites do, especially after having a chance to learn about the issue—or do they think about it in a different, wholly unsophisticated way?

Our analysis will not be able to settle this debate. In fact, it is not so obvious where the dividing line between the two sides should actually be drawn. Zaller's theory, depending on how one interprets it, may be compatible with some degree of "real thinking" on the part of ordinary people—since they are, after all, giving weight to relevant considerations as they fashion their opinions. Scholars on the other side, moreover, are not saying that ordinary citizens are truly sophisticated at thinking things through, only that they are not as pathetic as some political scientists make them out to be. Still, there are important differences in theoretical perspective at work here, and our analysis will give us a basis for judging whether Americans are engaging in "real thinking" about the voucher issue.

Evidence from Other Surveys

Before getting to our own data, it is instructive to look at what other surveys have had to say about support for vouchers. These surveys are part of the history of the issue, used by advocates and critics alike to back up their claims about what the American people presumably want. They are politically important, and for this reason alone are worth paying attention to. They are also worth paying attention to, however, because they give us an opportunity to see that the concerns raised by Zaller and other political scientists do in fact have a central bearing on the information surveys generate, and on how useful—or misleading—the "facts" can be.

Different surveys, as we will see, often yield very different results on support for vouchers. This is what we should expect, given an uninformed public, and given that different surveys tend to word their questions differently and embed them in contexts that give off different cues. Still, we needn't throw up our hands and regard all surveys as somehow equal in the evidence they produce. We are not trapped in a relativistic world without baselines or standards. Some surveys are better at evoking meaningful responses than others are—and a lot of it has to do with how well their questions are worded. Well-worded questions provide enough (balanced) information to give people a sense of the key elements of an issue and a basis for bringing their own concerns to bear. Poorly worded questions give people little to go on and may contain cues that systematically push them in one direction or another. Although public opinion on an issue may often be shallow and changeable, then, we learn more about it from some surveys than others.

The most prominent surveys tapping public opinion on vouchers have been carried out by the Gallup organization, acting on behalf of the *Phi Delta Kappan*. The Phi Delta Kappa (PDK) polls, which began in 1969, have explored a wide range of educational issues, particularly those salient at the time of the survey. The focus has always been on the public school system. Opinion on vouchers was first measured in 1970 and 1971, around the time some academics and policymakers (notable among them Christopher Jencks) showed a fleeting interest in the subject. The voucher issue did not appear on the survey again until 1981, when rising interest in school choice, coinciding with the early years of Ronald Reagan's presidency, opened a new era in which vouchers would become a continuing topic of debate and controversy. Since 1981 voucher questions have been included on most PDK surveys. The findings have regularly found their way into major newspapers and are by far the most frequently quoted figures available on the public's support for or opposition to vouchers.[9]

Through 1991 the PDK voucher question was always the same. It read: "In some nations, the government allots a certain amount of money for each child's education. The parents can then send the child to any public, parochial, or private school they choose. This is called the 'voucher system.' Would you like to see such an idea adopted in this country?" The pattern of results for the years 1970 through 1991 suggested that there had been a clear shift in public sentiment over time. In 1970 and 1971 more Americans opposed vouchers than supported them—at least by this particular measure. In 1981, however, the very same measure showed that more Americans expressed support than opposition, and this plurality was maintained throughout the next decade. By 1991 the figures stood at 50 percent in support, 39 percent opposed, and 11 percent undecided.[10]

At about this time, the voucher movement was beginning to take off politically. 1990 was the first year of the Milwaukee voucher program and the year in which Chubb and Moe's *Politics, Markets, and America's Schools* was published. Before then, the debate over vouchers had largely been a matter of intellectual sparring. Afterwards, the debate suddenly became very real, with consequences enormously threatening to the educational status quo.

With the voucher movement picking up steam, it is natural to wonder what was happening to public opinion during this period. But we will probably never know the answer. Because at just the time vouchers were bursting onto the national scene, PDK decided to drop its traditional voucher question. This is a big thing for pollsters to do, because they lose a valuable time-series of data in the process and, in this case, the only empirical basis for assessing change over time in public opinion on vouchers. PDK's rationale was that the question was positively biased—that is, it implicitly encouraged respondents to give supportive answers—because of its reference to other nations having adopted voucher-like systems.[11]

In its place, PDK substituted a very different question. Here is its wording: "Do you favor or oppose allowing students and parents to choose a private school to attend at public expense?" This question was first asked in 1993, and it produced a dramatically different picture of public opinion. By this new measure, Americans emerged as overwhelmingly opposed to vouchers. The level of support was only 24 percent in the population as a whole—not even close to the 50 percent figure that the "in some nations" measure had yielded just two years earlier. According to the new

measure, in fact, even *private* parents were opposed to vouchers: an outcome almost no one familiar with the issue would be prepared to believe,
given any reasonable definition of *support* and *opposition*.[12] PDK has held
onto this version of the voucher question, however, and used it every year
from 1995 to the present.

Let's reflect a bit on the wording of these two questions. The original
question may indeed have encouraged more positive responses, if implicitly, by introducing the consideration (to use Zaller's term) that other nations have voucher systems. On the other hand, it contains some good
features too—features that, in a population that is largely uninformed,
help people get a better sense of the issue by underlining its most fundamental, defining elements. As worded, it clearly indicates that

(1) vouchers would be available to parents generally, not just to existing private school parents,

(2) vouchers would enable parents to choose among public, parochial,
and private options in deciding where their children go to school, and

(3) vouchers would be financed by the government and thus paid for
out of taxes.

These, it seems to me, are basic pieces of information that any well-
worded question on support for vouchers should try to convey, and as neu-
trally as possible, in order to ensure that people are able to give meaningful
responses. PDK's "at public expense" question, however, fails on each count.
It makes no attempt to point out that a voucher program would allow all
parents to choose their children's schools, and to select among both public
and private options. Instead, it rivets attention on the benefits that would
accrue to private parents. Among unsophisticated respondents who are
not familiar with the issue, the proposal can easily come off as a narrow,
special-interest program for existing private parents, rather than as a program that extends choice to everyone. Moreover, the phrase "at public
expense" is a pejorative way of telling respondents that the program is
government financed. The wording implicitly portrays the program as a
raid on the public treasury—which may be the way voucher critics think
of it, but is hardly a neutral description of government funding.

In 1992 two polls were conducted that dramatically illustrate how consequential these measurement issues can be. In that year, the Carnegie Foundation for the Advancement of Teaching, under the direction of Ernest
Boyer, came out with a highly negative study of school choice that was
released to the media with much fanfare just one week before the presidential election.[13] As part of that study, Carnegie had hired the Wirthlin
Group to carry out a national survey of public school parents. One of the

questions was on vouchers, and its format followed the "at public expense" wording that PDK would subsequently adopt. What Carnegie found, not surprisingly, was that public school parents opposed vouchers by a lop-sided 2-to-1 margin. This finding received extensive publicity in the na-tional media and was put to forceful political use by the critics of vouchers.

Another study of school choice was conducted in the same year. This one was carried out by Gallup under contract with the National Catholic Educational Association (NCEA).[14] It included two questions on vouch-ers. One was PDK's original "in some nations" wording of the voucher question, and it led to findings strikingly at variance with Carnegie's. By this measure, vouchers were supported by 70 percent of American adults and 76 percent of parents with children in public schools. These results were embraced by voucher advocates as convincing evidence that the public was strongly on their side and became part of their arsenal in the political struggle for choice.

This story is symbolic of how tenuous the connection often is between surveys and the "truth"—and how close the connection (partly as a re-sult) between surveys and politics. Both the Carnegie and NCEA surveys were authored by respected education organizations and carried out by reputable polling groups. Yet because their voucher items were worded very differently, they came up with starkly different findings on the public's support for vouchers, findings that were then put to selective use by advo-cates and critics in the political arena. Advocates discounted the Carnegie results and embraced those of the NCEA. Critics did the opposite. Any semblance of objectivity got lost in the political shuffle.

Questions about vouchers have been included in many surveys over the years—with results that, like the ones we've just discussed, yield patterns of support and opposition that often vary quite substantially. In these cases too, the variance across surveys is usually a predictable function of the wording of the questions. Generally speaking, questions that portray vouch-ers as a narrowly targeted program for private school parents will usually lead to lower support scores than questions that portray vouchers as a broad program for all parents, allowing them to choose among public, pri-vate, and parochial schools. (Aside from PDK's use of the pejorative "at public expense" phrase, which no one else uses, the government-funding aspect does not seem to be a problem in these survey items. They deal with it in a neutral way.)

In recent years, for instance, polls jointly sponsored by NBC and the *Wall Street Journal* have asked questions about a range of political issues, including vouchers. Here are several versions of the voucher items they posed between 1996 and 1998. In each case, respondents were asked whether they favor or oppose the policy in quotes.[15]

(1) "Giving government vouchers to parents who send their children to private schools." Results: 44 percent favor, 53 percent opposed (December 1996).

(2) "Providing tax-funded vouchers or tax deductions to parents who send their children to private schools." Results: 45 percent favor, 52 percent opposed (March 1997). Additional results: 46 percent favor, 50 percent opposed (September 1997).

(3) "Providing taxpayer-funded vouchers to help parents pay for private school tuition." Results: 43 percent favor, 52 percent opposed (June 1998).

These items share one of the fundamental problems inherent in the PDK "at public expense" item: their wording does not make it clear that all parents would get vouchers and be able to choose their own schools, but instead gives the impression that vouchers are a special-interest program for existing private school parents. We would expect questions framed in this way to give low support scores. And they do. By 1997, in fact, PDK's "at public expense" item was itself yielding support scores of 44 percent—the same as the NBC–*Wall Street Journal* items.

Now consider the results of two Gallup Polls carried out during 1996.[16] While the official Gallup Poll does not usually ask questions about vouchers, these two presumably did because it was an election year in which vouchers were an issue. Here is their wording: "Suppose that on election day this year you could vote on key issues as well as candidates. After I read one proposal, please say whether you would vote for or against it. . . . A system giving parents government-funded vouchers to pay for tuition at the public, private, or religious school of their choice." In the Gallup wording, the purpose of a voucher is made clear: it is to pay for tuition at a school of the parent's choice. More important, the focus is not on private school parents, but on all parents, and on the connection between vouchers and expanded parental choice of schools. This corrects for the special-interest framing of the NBC–*Wall Street Journal* wording, and we would expect support for vouchers to be higher by this measure. Which it is—by a wide margin. In the first Gallup Poll (April 1996), 59 percent of Americans said they favor vouchers, while just 37 percent were opposed. In the second poll (September 1996), the results were almost identical: 59 percent in favor, 34 percent opposed.

There are some exceptions to this pattern of results. The most notable comes from the PDK surveys. Since PDK abandoned its "in some nations" format, its most influential and widely publicized substitute has been the "at public expense" version. But in 1994 it tried out yet another wording of the voucher question, and from 1996 to the present it has included both the "at public expense" version and this newer version in its surveys. Here is the wording of the newer item: "A proposal has been made that would allow parents to send their school-age children to any public, private, or church-related school they choose. For those parents choosing nonpublic schools, the government would pay all or part of the tuition. Would you favor or oppose this proposal in your state?"

This newer PDK item has all the properties we should look for in a well-worded question. Yet it leads to support scores that are much lower than we might expect, given the results from other well-worded items on other surveys. In 1996, for example, it shows that just 43 percent of Americans expressed support for vouchers, which is far below the 59 percent scores from the Gallup Polls administered in the same year.[17] What could be going on here?

It is impossible to know for sure. But these kinds of differences on well-worded questions suggest that we need to look beyond the wording of items and consider other sources of cues to respondents—notably, the broader content of the survey and the ordering of its questions. It may be that the PDK survey as a whole, because it is so clearly focused on the public schools, implicitly encourages a more sympathetic stance toward them, and more negative responses to voucher questions. It may also be—indeed, it seems quite likely—that how people respond to PDK's well-worded voucher question has been influenced by exactly where it appears on the survey: for it is asked immediately after the "at public expense item," and this could infect it with a negative bias.

There is no perceptible reason, on the other hand, why the Gallup questions—which appear on broadly based surveys that are not even about education—should be suspected of producing a bias in either direction. It is a reasonable (if uncertain) bet, therefore, that the PDK results are lower than we ought to expect for well-worded questions, not that the Gallup results are too high, and that this explains most of the discrepancy.

Perhaps the best thing about the PDK surveys, given our purposes, is that they ask the same items repeatedly over time, and thus allow for useful comparisons we can't get from other surveys. Table 7-1 sets out the results for both the "at public expense" item and the well-worded item for the period 1993–2000. Two conclusions are worth underlining.

The first is that the well-worded item always produces higher support for vouchers than the "at public expense" item does. This is true for every year in which both questions were asked, and it is consistently true for

Table 7-1. *Phi Delta Kappa Polling Results on Vouchers, 1993–2000*

Percent

"At public expense" item[a]

Survey item	National							Nonparents							Public school parents						
	2000	1999	1998	1997	1996	1995	1993	2000	1999	1998	1997	1996	1995	1993	2000	1999	1998	1997	1996	1995	1993
Favor	39	41	44	44	36	33	24	36	38	41	44	33	30	21	43	45	48	45	39	38	27
Oppose	56	55	50	52	61	65	74	57	58	54	54	63	68	76	55	50	46	50	59	59	72
Don't know	5	4	6	4	3	2	2	7	4	5	2	4	2	3	2	5	6	5	2	3	1

Well-worded item[b]

Survey item	National						Nonparents						Public school parents					
	2000	1999	1998	1997	1996	1994	2000	1999	1998	1997	1996	1994	2000	1999	1998	1997	1996	1994
Favor	45	51	51	49	43	45	43	45	48	46	38	42	47	60	56	55	49	48
Oppose	52	47	45	48	54	54	54	52	48	51	59	57	51	38	40	43	49	51
Don't know	3	2	4	3	3	1	3	3	4	3	3	1	2	2	4	2	2	1

Source: *Phi Delta Kappan*, 1993–2000.

a. The item reads: "Do you favor or oppose allowing students and parents to choose a private school to attend at public expense."

b. The item reads: "A proposal has been made which would allow parents to send their school-age children to any public, private, or church-related school they choose. For those parents choosing non-public schools, the government would pay all or part of the tuition. Would you favor or oppose this proposal in your state?"

parents, nonparents, and the nation as a whole. The consistency of these findings is good evidence that the "at public expense" item is particularly negative in its portrayal of public opinion on the voucher issue. If we compare the percentages supporting vouchers, the differences between the two items are not enormous—although, as the Gallup scores imply, the differences might be more dramatic if the items could be compared in another survey context. Still, the differences are hardly trivial. For the nation as a whole, the well-worded question yields results that are from 5 percent to 10 percent more favorable than the "at public expense" item. And if we look at parents, the differences vary from 8 percent to 15 percent. In 1999, in fact, the "at public expense" item tells us that only 45 percent of public parents support vouchers and that 50 percent are opposed—while the well-worded item indicates that fully 60 percent support vouchers and only 38 percent are opposed.

The second conclusion is that, especially if we focus on the well-worded item, things don't seem to have changed that much over time. One might have expected, given the growing success of the voucher movement, that public support would have grown as well. And for 1993 through 1998, the figures do seem to show a slight upward trend. Yet in 1999 the well-worded measure obtained the same level of support as in 1998, and in 2000 it registered a decline, pointing to support levels about the same as five years earlier.

PDK sees an important new development here: that support for vouchers "may have peaked and has begun to trend downward"[18]—a claim widely publicized in the national media. This interpretation, however, is based on year-to-year comparisons that are probably misleading. A major source of confusion is that the 2000 survey framed the voucher issue very differently—and more negatively—than the 1999 survey did. The 2000 survey led up to its voucher items by first asking several items that implicitly portrayed vouchers as anti–public school, and that highlighted the positive ideals public schools are supposed to stand for—prefatory material that was absent from the 1999 survey.[19] This shift in survey content could easily explain the apparent decline in support for vouchers from 1999 to 2000. Indeed, without the negative framing, the slight upward trend might even have continued.

There are two other studies of vouchers that merit brief discussion. The first is a 1999 educational survey jointly sponsored by National Public Radio, the Kaiser Foundation, and Harvard's Kennedy School of Government. It is interesting for our purposes because it introduced creative twists into the usual survey format.[20]

The first twist involved asking just half the respondents a typical question about support for vouchers, and asking the other half the identical question—but with the addendum "or haven't you heard enough about that to have an opinion?" Of the respondents who were simply asked the usual voucher question, only 4 percent declined to give an opinion. But of the respondents who were given the second version, 33 percent said they did not have an opinion. This only confirms what Zaller and other political scientists have been arguing all along: that many people are expressing views on subjects they haven't heard or thought much about, and are probably more ambivalent than anything else.

This is further illustrated by the second twist. Here, the survey designers followed the voucher question with another, whose content turned on whether the respondent had expressed support or opposition. To supporters, they asked: "Would you still favor this if it meant there would be less money for public schools in your area?" The result: 44 percent of the supporters changed their position and said they would now oppose vouchers. To respondents who had initially expressed opposition, they asked: "Would you still oppose this if it meant that children from less well-off families might not be able to attend better schools?" The result: 43 percent of the opponents changed their position, saying they would now support vouchers.[21]

This is a debatable technique. It gives respondents a one-sided reason for changing their position and clearly puts them on the spot. Many may feel that they will look unreasonable if they don't make a change. Nonetheless, it does offer one indication of how uncommitted people are to their positions and how variable their positions might be when different considerations are raised by the survey. And the results are what Zaller would lead us to expect. For they show that many respondents feel justified in portraying themselves as either supporters or opponents, depending on the circumstances. Even if the technique exaggerates the degree of ambivalence and instability, there is clearly a good deal of slack in public expressions of support and opposition.

The final study that warrants discussion is Public Agenda's *On Thin Ice*, released in late 1999. This study, like the others, is very brief and presents only simple aggregate data (the percentages of people giving particular responses). But it stands out because it explores the voucher issue in some depth: asking people not just whether they would support vouchers, but also about the consequences for schools and society and the features a voucher system ought to contain. In subject matter, then, it covers some of the same ground that we do in this book, and I will take advantage of this by using its findings to supplement our own results. Indeed, I have already done that in chapter 6 (regarding how poorly informed Americans are) and will do so again in chapters 8 and 9.

The Public Agenda study is well done and recommended reading. What it offers, above all, is a clear-headed appraisal of public opinion that simply makes good sense. The authors note that Americans seem to be quite sympathetic to vouchers, at least on the surface. The survey's support item (which is fairly well worded) suggests that support for vouchers is 57 percent among the general public, with 36 percent opposed: almost identical to the Gallup figures from three years earlier and a good bit higher than the PDK results. Support among parents is 68 percent with just 27 percent opposed, which again puts support at a much higher level than PDK does. The theme of the Public Agenda analysis, however, is that these high support levels do not tell us much about what the public really thinks: because Americans are poorly informed about the issue, do not have well-developed views, and are not firmly committed to the idea. Their support is based on "thin ice" and could change.

If we take all these surveys into account, then, there is one bottom line: we are right to be wary of simple support scores. These scores do tell us something of value. It is clear, for instance, that well-worded questions should generate more meaningful results than poorly worded questions, and that well-worded questions point to higher levels of support than the often-used poorly worded questions do. But still, even well-worded questions can lead to very different results. When people are poorly informed about an issue and basically ambivalent, they can easily come down on either side depending on which considerations are evoked by the survey. The real action is in the considerations. What we want to know is not whether people express support for vouchers during a particular survey, but what matters to them. The existing surveys don't tell us much about that.

The Approach of This Study

It would make an interesting project to see how question-wording and context affect the way people respond to surveys on vouchers. But this sort of enterprise is ultimately limited: if people are largely unfamiliar with the issue and don't have well-developed views, then we shouldn't put much stock in questions that measure their support or opposition. Even a well-worded question hides more than it reveals. The purpose here, therefore, is not to nail down the "true" figures on public support for vouchers. It is to understand what matters to people as they think about the issue, and whether they seem to be engaging in "real thinking" about it at all.

The survey helps us do this. Here is the approach it takes. As I pointed out in chapter 6, the first part of the survey is about a broad range of educational issues and does not mention vouchers. Midway through the interview, the concept is first introduced through the informational question. To repeat, the interviewer says: "So far, I have asked your opinions on a number of different approaches to school reform. Now I would like to focus on one particular type of reform and get your views on it. . . . Have you heard anything about the use of vouchers for education?" With the subject of vouchers thus raised, respondents are then presented with an initial support question that defines the concept of vouchers in clear, simple terms and asks them how they would feel about such a reform. This is how it is worded: "According to reformers, the general idea behind a voucher plan is as follows. The parents of each school-age child would be eligible for a grant or voucher from the state, representing a certain amount of tax money. They would then have the right to send their child to a public school, just as before. Or they could use the voucher to help pay for the child's education at a private or parochial school of their choosing. Would you favor or oppose such an idea?" Note that this question refers to all parents, makes it clear that they would be able to choose from public, private, and parochial schools, and indicates in a neutral way that the program would be government financed. We needn't believe that this wording is somehow the best possible (whatever that might mean). It is enough to believe that it is reasonable and meets the basic properties of a good question.[22]

The survey doesn't put all its eggs in this one basket. The idea is to get away from an exclusive reliance on single indicators by moving toward a richer empirical base for evaluating public opinion, one that gets beneath the surface. This is done by following up the initial support item with a large number of additional questions about vouchers—about forty of them (for parents, somewhat fewer for nonparents)—addressing the full range of issues in the national debate, from competition to race to religion to social class.

Once respondents have had a chance to reflect more fully on the issue, they are presented with the same support question they were asked at the beginning. The interviewer says: "Now let me ask you just a few concluding questions about education reform and school choice. First, I want to ask you again about the general idea behind vouchers. Under a voucher plan, the parents of each school-age child would be eligible for a grant or voucher from the state, representing a certain amount of tax money. They would then have the right to send their child to a public school, just as before. Or they could use the voucher to help pay for the child's education at a private or parochial school of their choosing. Now that you've heard more about the idea, would you tend to support or oppose it?" This is a useful design. The initial question on support for vouchers serves as a baseline. While the first part of the survey primes respondents to think about educational issues, it does not give them any information at all about vouchers and does not link the issue to race, class, performance, or anything else. They are on their own, and their responses represent their first attempt—usually based on very little knowledge or sense of the issue—to take a stand. This is comparable to what happens on virtually every other survey currently available on the topic: people are asked a voucher question out of the blue.

One of the things we need to know is whether people are able to give responses to these out-of-the-blue questions that make good sense. Does the evidence suggest that there is a coherent structure to their thinking, and thus that the initial positions they take are reasonably connected to their own values, beliefs, and interests? Or are these initial positions essentially groundless, and little more than random choices by people who know nothing about the issue and can't relate it to things that matter to them?

After the initial support question is asked, the survey provides respondents with much more to work with: a whole range of new considerations that are related (they now know) to vouchers. From our own standpoint, the immediate advantage of these items is that people are asked to take positions on all of them—and when they do, they provide us with additional information about how sympathetic they are to the ideas and arguments that go along with vouchers. This information goes well beyond what we could ever hope to get from simple support scores, and gives us a better idea of respondents' basic propensities on the issue. We get a better sense of what matters to them.

These same items are also helpful for another reason. When people are presented with a host of voucher-related issues, and when they are forced to mull them over and recognize their relevance, they are put in a learning situation. They are being presented with new considerations, most of which they hadn't thought about when the initial voucher question was asked. And these new considerations may prompt them to see vouchers in a different light—and perhaps to shift away from their initial positions.

Because we have data on these considerations, and because respondents are re-asked the same support question at the end of the interview, we are able to gain new insights into their thinking on the issue. If their support for vouchers is now different, we can explore what accounts for the shift—and whether it is a sensible response to the considerations they have been asked to think about, or essentially a random movement of the kind Converse associated with the unsophisticated masses. More generally, we can examine whether respondents' final positions seem to be more solidly connected to their own values, beliefs, and interests than their initial positions were, and thus whether there seems to be "real thinking" going on.[23]

In the end, the survey cannot tell us everything we might want to know. But it will give us a better sense of what public opinion on the voucher issue means, why it takes the form it does, and what the implications seem to be for politics.

Initial Support for Vouchers

Now let's turn to the evidence, beginning with the first question on support for vouchers. Again, this item provides an important baseline, because it measures support for vouchers before people have had much opportunity to think much about the issue, which is the way it is typically measured on other surveys.

Simple Aggregate Results

The aggregate results are set out in table 7-2. They show that 60 percent of the general public express support for the idea of vouchers, with 32 percent opposed and 7 percent undecided. We have to be careful not to view these results as measuring the "true" level of popular support for vouchers. They would have been different had the question been worded differently or even asked on a different survey. Nonetheless, they are almost identical to those of the two Gallup Polls from 1996, whose questions were well worded and similar in informational content to ours.

It seems fair to say that Americans are open to the general concept of vouchers, at least when they first think about it, and when it is defined as a means of expanding choice for all parents. Their commitment to the idea is probably rather weak, and they could probably be swayed—as people clearly were in the National Public Radio survey—by one-sided arguments from the other side. But at the outset, their basic take on the issue is positive.

We should be less interested in the level of support per se, though, than in how support *varies* across groups, and in what this can tell us about

Table 7-2. *Who Supports Vouchers? Initial Responses*
Percent, unless otherwise indicated[a]

Position on vouchers	Total population	Non-parents	Public school parents	Private school parents	Inner-city parents
Oppose	32	36	26	13	14
Support	60	57	66	81	77
Don't know	7	7	8	6	9
N[b]	(4,700)	(1,617)	(2,553)	(530)	(539)

a. Percentages are based on weighted data. They may not sum to 100 due to rounding.
b. N is the unweighted number of respondents.

why people see the issue as they do. Existing surveys provide almost no analysis along these lines, but they do offer a glimpse of what is going on beneath the surface. They reveal patterns that are much the same for all surveys, whether or not the questions are well worded and regardless of how high or low the level of support seems to be. What they show, notably, is that parents are more supportive of vouchers than nonparents, that private parents are more supportive than public parents, and that blacks and Hispanics are more supportive than whites. This begins to suggest that people with the strongest *incentives* are the ones who are the most sympathetic, and that there is an underlying *structure* to the issue that makes sense. Our job is to pursue this in greater depth.

For starters, our own survey shows that public parents are more supportive of vouchers than nonparents are, by 66 percent to 57 percent. This in itself is a noteworthy result, because we know from chapter 2 that public parents are actually more satisfied with the public schools than nonparents are. We also know, however, that parents tend to think in relative rather than absolute terms about performance, that many public parents are interested in going private even though they are reasonably satisfied—and that a voucher plan would directly affect their lives. Parents, as a result, have incentives that nonparents don't have, and these incentives show up in their greater support for vouchers. (For more perspective, refer back to table 7-1, which gives the PDK figures for 1993 to 2000. In every year, parents are more supportive of vouchers than nonparents are. For the well-worded PDK measure, the average difference is 9 percent. For our measure, the difference is also 9 percent.)

This difference between parents and nonparents is a mixed blessing for the voucher movement. On the one hand, parents have a greater stake in vouchers, and their support is crucial if policymakers are to go along. On the other hand, nonparents make up some two-thirds of the electorate, and their more negative inclinations—especially if played upon by critics during political campaigns—may threaten the movement's success.

Another basic finding from table 7-2 is that private parents are enthusiastic about vouchers, with 81 percent of them expressing support. This is hardly surprising. Private parents would immediately benefit from a universal voucher program, and they have reason to be supportive. It is worth noting that at the elite level the issue is not so straightforward. Private school leaders sometimes express concern about vouchers (and even oppose them in some cases) because they fear the regulations that often go along with government money. As we will see in chapter 9, however, private parents don't have the same fears. The issue is apparently an easy one for them.

Table 7-2 also shows that low-income public parents from the inner city are much more sympathetic toward vouchers than public parents are in general. Seventy-seven percent of them express support, with just 14 percent opposed. This is another indication that incentives are shaping how people view the voucher issue. Inner-city parents face the most troubled educational contexts, and we know from chapter 5 that they are eager to gain access to the private sector. Vouchers allow them to do that, and these parents are highly supportive of a policy that would put vouchers in their hands. It is reasonable to presume, moreover, that these results for the inner city are just the tip of the iceberg, and that vouchers are attractive to disadvantaged populations generally.

Table 7-3 bears this out. Among public parents, vouchers are supported by 73 percent of those with family incomes below $20,000 per year, compared to 57 percent of those with incomes above $60,000. For education, the story is much the same: voucher support is 70 percent among parents with less than a high school education, but 49 percent among those with postgraduate educations. Minority parents also tend to be more supportive: 75 percent of black parents and 71 percent of Hispanic parents express sympathy for vouchers, compared to 63 percent of white parents. And we find the same asymmetry across school districts: 72 percent of parents in the bottom tier of districts favor vouchers, while 59 percent of those in the top tier do.

Race aside, these relationships don't obtain for nonparents. But nonparents have less stake in the issue. Certainly for parents, however, the modern wing of the voucher movement—the wing that, over the last decade, has championed the cause of the socially disadvantaged—is very much reflected in the structure of public opinion. Somehow, even though most parents (particularly those who are less advantaged) are uninformed about the issue, they seem to be connecting their own concerns and interests to their positions on vouchers.

What about the traditional wing of the voucher movement? In the aggregate, at least, there is little evidence that political party matters much. Republicans are slightly more supportive of vouchers than Democrats, but the differences are small: a 6 percent margin among nonparents and a 1 percent margin among public parents. A multivariate analysis will show that, once class and other factors are controlled, party is more consequential than these figures imply—and that it is very consequential among the stratum of people who are informed (and thus more tuned into the national debate). Nonetheless, its role in shaping public opinion is but a pale reflection of its role in structuring the political battle among elites.

Religion seems to be more influential. Among public parents, 72 percent of Catholics and 67 percent of born-again Christians express initial support for vouchers, compared to 62 percent of the baseline group of Protestants. Among nonparents, it is born-again Christians who are most supportive, at 70 percent, followed by Catholics at 59 percent and Protestants at 55 percent. These effects hardly testify to a religious fervor for vouchers at the grass roots. Religion is not as salient a consideration to ordinary people as it is to elites. Still, it is clearly relevant to many people and, even in the absence of much initial information about vouchers, it influences their stand on the issue.

A broad-brush look at the data, then, suggests that both the traditional and modern wings of the voucher movement are mirrored in the way Americans think about the issue. But what brings the two wings together, in the eyes of voucher leaders, is a shared concern about the performance of the public schools and a shared belief in the greater benefits of going private. These are the fundamental grounds on which the movement has always depended for attracting constituents to the political cause.

Do these fundamentals seem to work as leaders hope? Consider satisfaction with performance. If we take the performance index we've been using in previous chapters and divide it into quartiles, the data in table 7-3 show that there is a clear relationship between how people evaluate public school performance and what position they take on vouchers. Among public parents least satisfied with school performance, 75 percent express support for vouchers. Among those most satisfied with school performance, support drops to 57 percent. For nonparents, the differential is similar: voucher support is 61 percent among the least satisfied, 46 percent among the most satisfied. It appears, then, that many

Table 7-3. Background, Context, and Initial Support for Vouchers

Percent, unless otherwise indicated[a]

Background variable	Public school parents' position on vouchers				Nonparents' position on vouchers			
	Support	Oppose	Don't know	N[b]	Support	Oppose	Don't know	N[b]
Annual Income ($)								
Less than 20,000	73	19	8	(458)	53	38	9	(276)
21,000–30,000	70	21	9	(488)	60	32	8	(267)
31,000–40,000	67	28	5	(401)	57	40	3	(261)
41,000–60,000	61	32	6	(534)	62	33	5	(305)
More than 60,000	57	36	8	(336)	57	38	5	(237)
Education								
Less than high school	70	18	11	(254)	59	34	7	(157)
High school	70	23	7	(925)	56	36	7	(489)
Some college	64	27	8	(656)	59	33	8	(406)
College graduate	58	35	7	(501)	55	40	5	(383)
Postgraduate	49	47	4	(196)	50	45	6	(172)
Ethnic background								
White	63	30	7	(1,616)	55	39	7	(1,312)
Black	75	16	9	(529)	64	27	9	(146)
Hispanic	71	17	12	(286)	70	22	8	(79)

District context								
Disadvantaged 1	72	19	9	(720)	50	41	10	(229)
2	72	22	7	(526)	60	33	7	(406)
3	62	29	9	(545)	60	34	5	(389)
Advantaged 4	59	33	8	(583)	54	39	7	(401)
Party identification								
Democrat	66	27	7	(1,150)	55	38	7	(614)
Independent	69	24	7	(674)	55	38	7	(401)
Republican	67	26	7	(595)	61	34	4	(510)
Religion								
Catholic	72	20	8	(637)	59	33	7	(427)
Protestant	62	32	6	(731)	55	39	6	(536)
Born-again	67	26	7	(187)	70	24	6	(114)
Public school performance								
Low-performing 1	75	18	6	(535)	61	33	6	(458)
2	71	22	8	(589)	64	30	6	(400)
3	65	26	9	(634)	55	37	8	(392)
High-performing 4	57	33	10	(795)	46	47	8	(367)
Desire to go private								
Yes	78	15	7	(1,380)				
No	53	38	9	(1,041)				

a. Percentages are based on weighted data. They may not sum to 100 due to rounding.
b. N is the unweighted number of respondents.

people are able to make a connection between performance and their stand on public policy.

The same is true for the desire to go private. Only more so. As the figures in table 7-3 indicate, 78 percent of the public parents interested in sending their children to private schools—the swing parents from chapter 5's analysis—express support for vouchers, compared to 53 percent of public parents who aren't interested in going private. Again, people are able to make the connection. The size of the effect, moreover, is larger than any other we've seen thus far, and is the most direct indication yet that parental self-interest may in fact play an important role in shaping public opinion on this issue.

These are just aggregate results. But they strongly suggest that there is a structure to the way people are responding to the voucher issue, and that support is systematically related to incentives. The upshot is that, despite their lack of information on the topic, ordinary Americans seem to be responding to an out-of-the-blue question in a way that *is* connected to concerns that matter to them. Their responses make sense.

It is reasonable to ask at this point: why do incentives seem to affect support for vouchers when they don't have much to do with who gets informed about the issue? The reason is that the two behaviors are very different. Expressing a position on public policy is a costless act. If people feel that a policy would benefit or hurt them, or otherwise be desirable or undesirable, they can simply take a position on that basis. Actually getting well informed about it, on the other hand, usually involves making a costly investment in the collection of information. And as political scientists have long recognized, this investment often won't be worth it, because even an informed voter is likely to have little or no impact on the democratic decision process. Thus even respondents with incentives to support or oppose an issue, and who express themselves accordingly, may find they have no incentive to get informed about it.

A Multivariate Analysis

Now let's turn to a broader analysis. The dependent variable here is the entire four-point scale that respondents were presented with on the survey, which categorizes their position as one of strong support, weak support, weak opposition, or strong opposition. Our empirical analysis is an effort to explain where they fall on this scale.[24]

Recall that we are exploring the respondents' *initial* attempt, in the absence of much information, to stake out a position on vouchers. There may be gaps and oddities in the findings that could change later. Perhaps the most interesting overall question, at this point, has less to do with particular results than it does with the general patterns we observe. When we look at the determinants of respondents' initial support for vouchers, is there a *structure* to it—from background to context to attitudes to performance—that makes sense?

The answer is yes, especially for parents. Here is what the estimates, set out in table 7-4, suggest about how parents seem to be approaching the issue.[25]

(1) An interest in going private is by far the most important influence on support for vouchers among public parents. This does not mean that parents are unconcerned about the social impacts of vouchers. But self-interest clearly plays a key role.

(2) Performance is also important, but it is less salient than voucher leaders would expect. This may be a signal of something more fundamental: namely, that parents do not connect performance to the voucher issue in the same way they connect it to their personal interest in going private. The latter connection is easy and direct. But connecting performance to public policy is more complex, because there is a chain of social causation to consider—which may involve, for instance, pondering whether vouchers will stimulate competition (which many people may not realize at all) and whether competition will then improve the public schools (which, if they get this far, about half the people may not believe anyway). It is here that the connection may attenuate.

(3) This said, performance still matters quite a bit—and to the extent it does, the data suggest once again (see performance model 1) that it is *relative* rather than absolute performance that counts the most. Parents are reasonably satisfied with their public schools. But when it comes to vouchers (or going private), this is less important than the fact that they think private schools are better.

(4) The modern thrust of the voucher movement is very much in evidence here. As we found in the aggregate, the parents who most favor vouchers are those who are low in social class, black or Hispanic, and from disadvantaged school districts. (Note that minorities are especially favorable toward vouchers even though income and education are controlled.)

(5) The traditional sources of support for vouchers—religion and political party—also prove their relevance. With other variables controlled, Republicans are inclined to be sympathetic, as are Catholics. The only hitch is that born-again Christians do not quite measure up: the effect for them is small and statistically insignificant. (This is one of the oddities we will return to later.)

Table 7-4. *Initial Support for Vouchers:*
Public School Parents and Nonparents[a]

| | Public school parents | | | | | | | |
| | Background model | | Context model | | Attitude model | | Performance model 1 | |
Variable	Coefficient	[Impact]	Coefficient	[Impact]	Coefficient	[Impact]	Coefficient	[Impact]
Background								
Education	-.07***	[-.17]	-.05***	[-.13]	-.06***	[-.14]	-.06***	[-.14]
Income	-.05***	[-.15]	-.04***	[-.15]	-.04**	[-.12]	-.04**	[-.12]
Catholic	.16**	[.15]	.17**	[.15]	.17**	[.15]	.15**	[.14]
Born-again	.08	[.07]	.05	[.05]	.01	[.01]	-.07	[-.06]
Black (north)	.27***	[.25]	.15	[.14]	.15	[.14]	.16	[.15]
Black (south)	.40***	[.36]	.32***	[.29]	.29***	[.26]	.27**	[.25]
Hispanic	.13*	[.12]	.00	[.00]	-.02	[-.02]	-.04	[-.04]
Age	-.05***	[-.20]	-.05***	[-.17]	-.05***	[-.17]	-.04***	[-.13]
Party identification	.04***	[.13]	.05***	[.16]	.04***	[.14]	.06***	[.20]
Low expectations	-.02	[-.05]	-.00	[-.01]	-.01	[-.01]	-.01	[-.03]
Context								
Residential mobility			-.01	[-.01]	-.01	[-.02]	.01	[.01]
Advantaged district			-.10***	[-.16]	-.08**	[-.12]	-.07**	[-.12]
Attitudes								
Diversity (whites)					.01	[.01]	.03	[.04]
Inequity					.15***	[.21]	.08**	[.11]
School prayer					.04**	[.09]	.04**	[.08]
Parent influence					.04	[.06]	.02	[.03]
School size					.06**	[.09]	.05	[.07]
Public school ideology					-.12***	[-.16]	-.12***	[-.16]
Markets					.22***	[.31]	.20***	[.29]
Moral values					.04**	[.10]	.03*	[.09]
Performance								
Performance (absolute)							-.01	[-.04]
Performance (relative)							-.15***	[-.16]
Performance								
Go private?								
Constant	3.09***		2.92***		2.57***		2.91***	
N[b]	(2,366)		(2,146)		(2,146)		(1,813)	
Adjusted R^2	.08		.08		.13		.12	

* Significant at .10 level.
** Significant at .05 level.
*** Significant at .01 level.
  a. Ordinary least squares regressions estimated using weighted data. The dependent variable is the initial voucher support item, which is coded from 1 (strongly oppose) to 4 (strongly support). Unstandardized coefficients reported. For each nondichotomous independent variable, the impact coefficient represents the estimated change in the dependent variable (measured in standard deviations) when the independent variable shifts by two standard deviations, holding all other variables constant; for each dichotomous variable, the impact coefficient represents the estimated change in the dependent variable (measured in standard deviations) when the independent variable shifts from 0 to 1, holding all other variables constant. Models control for the full range of background and context variables, not all of which are reported in the tables.
  b. N is the unweighted number of respondents.

Parents (cont'd)				Nonparents							
Performance model 2		Performance model 3		Background model		Context model		Attitude model		Performance model	
Coefficient	[Impact]	Coefficient	[Impact]	Coefficient	[Impact]	Coefficient	[Impact]	Coefficient	[Impact]	Coefficient	[Impact]
−.07***	[−.16]	−.08***	[−.20]	−.06**	[−.14]	−.07***	[−.16]	−.07***	[−.17]	−.08***	[−.18]
−.03**	[−.10]	−.03**	[−.11]	−.02	[−.06]	−.02	[−.05]	−.01	[−.04]	−.01	[−.04]
.18***	[.16]	.15**	[.14]	.01	[.01]	.04	[.03]	.01	[.01]	.00	[.00]
.03	[.03]	.07	[.06]	.31**	[.26]	.41***	[.35]	.30**	[.26]	.26**	[.22]
.14	[.13]	.15	[.14]	.39**	[.33]	.38**	[.32]	.24	[.21]	.20	[.17]
.30***	[.27]	.34***	[.31]	.10	[.09]	.11	[.09]	.07	[.06]	.09	[.08]
−.00	[−.00]	−.01	[−.01]	.13	[.11]	.03	[.03]	.05	[.04]	.05	[.04]
−.04***	[−.16]	−.04***	[−.15]	−.05***	[−.30]	−.05***	[−.31]	−.05***	[−.29]	−.05***	[−.30]
.04***	[.13]	.04***	[.04]	.03**	[.12]	.04**	[.13]	.02	[.06]	.01	[.05]
−.01	[−.00]	−.02	[−.05]	.06***	[.15]	.05**	[.13]	.06**	[.14]	.06***	[.16]
.00	[.00]	.02	[.04]			−.02[	−.03]	−.01	[−.01]	.01	[.01]
−.06*	[−.09]	−.08**	[−.12]			.04	[.05]	.06	[.08]	.08*	[.11]
.01	[.01]	.02	[.03]					.01	[.01]	.02	[.02]
.12***	[.17]	.08***	[.12]					.07	[.09]	.04	[.05]
.04**	[.09]	.04*	[.08]					.05*	[.09]	.04*	[.09]
.03	[.04]	.03	[.04]					.07**	[.11]	.07*	[.11]
.06*	[.07]	.02	[.03]					.01	[.01]	.00[	.01]
−.10***	[−.14]	−.11***	[−.14]					−.10**	[−.13]	−.09**	[−.12]
.20***	[.29]	.21***	[.30]					.29***	[.39]	.28***	[.38]
.04**	[.10]	.03*	[.08]					.09***	[.21]	.08***	[.21]
−.18***	[−.22]	−.04	[−.05]							−.19***	[−.22]
		−.51***	[−.46]								
2.62***		2.56***		3.09***		3.24***		3.02***		3.02***	
(2,146)		(2,058)		(1,478)		(1,337)		(1,337)		(1,337)	
.14		.20		.04		.05		.10		.11	

(6) All the above are important elements of structure, indicating that parents are able to connect vouchers to considerations that matter to them. This is strongly reinforced by the attitude model. Aside from race and parent influence, all the other values and beliefs we expect to be relevant— inequity, public school ideology, prayer, school size, moral values, and markets—turn out to have statistically significant impacts, and in the expected directions. The three that stand out are markets (especially), inequity, and public school ideology, which were also the three standouts in chapter 5's analysis of going private.[26] Parents attach little weight to racial concerns (or at least to those we have measured in this survey), but this is consistent with prior results: for race had no effect on parents' interest in going private, nor did it affect their satisfaction with the public schools. Much the same is true for parent influence: we found earlier that it had little to do with why parents wanted to go private, and now we find that it has little to do with how they view the voucher issue.

(7) Inequity is a special part of our analysis, because it is an important measure of the connection between vouchers and the socially disadvantaged. In chapter 5, we found not only that perceptions of inequity prompt public parents to want to go private, but also that low-income parents put more weight on inequity than other parents do. The question is, does inequity have the same differential effects when we try to explain support for vouchers? To see, this section's model has been re-estimated with separate inequity variables for low-, middle-, and upper- income parents. The findings (taken from the attitudinal model) are presented in table 7-5. They show that the *same* ordering emerges once again, this time in the more removed realm of public policy: inequity has the greatest impact for low-income parents, a somewhat smaller impact for middle-income parents, and no impact for upper-income parents. This is another indication that vouchers are especially appealing to the less advantaged, and that perceptions of inequity are part of that syndrome.

(8) Finally, it is worth noting that age makes a difference here: younger parents are more supportive of vouchers than older parents are. This may be due to generational differences in attitudes toward choice, or perhaps to different stances toward taxes and risk, for as a rule older people are less open to change. It may also reflect a basic difference in self-interest: younger parents tend to have younger children, and vouchers may have greater value to them. From chapter 5's analysis, moreover, we know that younger parents are especially interested in going private. Whatever the precise motivations, age is an important factor here, and one that could

Table 7-5. *Inequality, Class, and Initial Support for Vouchers among Public School Parents*[a]

Variable	Attitude model	
	Coefficient	[Impact]
Attitudes		
Diversity (white)	.02	[.03]
Inequity (low)	.22***	[.29]
Inequity (medium)	.17***	[.23]
Inequity (high)	−.00	[−.00]
School prayer	.04**	[.09]
Parent influence	.04	[.06]
School size	.06**	[.09]
Public school ideology	−.12***	[−.16]
Markets	.21***	[.31]
Moral values	.04***	[.11]
Constant	2.57***	
N[b]	(2,146)	
Adjusted R^2	.13	

** Significant at .05 level.
*** Significant at .01 level.

a. Ordinary least squares regressions estimated using weighted data. The dependent variable is the initial voucher support item, which is coded from 1 (strongly disagree) to 4 (strongly agree). Unstandardized coefficients reported. For each nondichotomous independent variable, the impact coefficient represents the estimated change in the dependent variable (measured in standard deviations) when the independent variable shifts by two standard deviations, holding all other variables constant; for each dichotomous variable, the impact coefficient represents the estimated change in the dependent variable (measured in standard deviations) when the independent variable shifts from 0 to 1, holding all other variables constant. Model controls for the full range of background and context variables, not all of which are reported in the tables.

b. N is the unweighted number of respondents.

affect the politics of the issue—for younger people are less likely to be politically active, less likely to be informed about policy, and less likely to have the resources to be effective.

Now let's turn our focus from parents to nonparents (see table 7-4 again). Nonparents have much less stake in the voucher issue than parents do, and it shows up most clearly in the lack of a consistent structure associating vouchers with the socially less advantaged. Nonparents who are low in education are especially likely to be sympathetic toward vouchers. But the effect of income is weak (although in the right direction). Similarly, northern blacks are especially likely to support vouchers, but the effects for southern blacks and Hispanics are smaller (although, again, they are in the right direction—and we have to remember that, with controls for education and income, it is not so clear that racial effects should persist). The effects of district context, however, are actually in the wrong direction, and under the performance models become statistically significant.

In other respects, though, the responses of nonparents *do* follow a reasonable structure, one quite similar to what we found for parents. Most notably:

(1) Performance is a top determinant of support for vouchers, but does not play a dominant role.

(2) Religion and party have significant effects (although the religion effect is limited to born-again Christians—an oddity we'll come back to later on).

(3) Age is important, perhaps even more than for parents.

(4) Race aside, all the other values and beliefs in the attitude model have effects that are in the direction we would expect, and almost all of these effects are statistically significant. As with parents, attitudes toward race have no effect.

Overall, then, there is a definite structure to nonparent responses, and it looks very much like the structure for parents. Especially in light of their weaker stake in the issue, nonparents seem to do a reasonable job of connecting vouchers to their underlying values, beliefs, and interests—and they are able to do this even at the outset, when they have not had a chance to think about it much.

Finally, let's take a look at low-income parents from the inner city. Here, as we've noted in other chapters, there is less variation on the usual social and contextual variables, especially income, and we cannot expect to observe the kinds of effects we might see in the population generally. We are just looking at differences *among* inner-city parents, not at how they compare to everyone else, so the usual syndrome of disadvantage will not pop out as strongly or uniformly. Another problem is that, because these parents are so supportive of vouchers—only 14 percent are opposed—there is much less variance in their policy positions to explain.[27]

For these reasons, we can't expect to learn as much as we might like. Nonetheless, the results are enlightening in several key respects (see table 7-6).

(1) The desire to go private is by far the most influential determinant of voucher support among inner-city parents. They support vouchers, by and large, *because they want to use them.*

(2) Although it is difficult to get significant effects for income (as we are looking only at low-income people), the findings for income and edu-

cation both suggest that support for vouchers is greatest among those in the inner city who are the most disadvantaged.[28]

(3) As a rule, people who are low in income and education are less able to connect attitudes to public policy than more advantaged people are. Still, one attitude stands out for inner-city parents (see the attitude model) and has a significant effect on their thinking about vouchers: the belief that the public system is inequitable. This confirms what we have been finding all along. Social equity is a major concern of the disadvantaged, and they *do* connect it to private schools and vouchers.

Information and Political Sophistication

One of the basic findings in this analysis is that people who are low in education are especially supportive of vouchers. On the surface, this raises no eyebrows, for we have reason to think that the less advantaged look favorably on vouchers, and our findings—not just on education, but on income, race, and district context—seem to demonstrate as much.

Yet the findings on education are not so straightforward. In previous chapters, education was the one variable that didn't really fit the disadvantaged syndrome. Once controls were introduced for the other class and contextual variables, it was the *better*-educated parents who were most critical of the public schools and the *better*-educated parents who were most interested in going private. This is in line with other studies, which show not only that better-educated parents are the ones who want to go private, but that, even within voucher programs restricted to the poor, it is the better-educated poor who tend to apply.[29]

Our findings on support for vouchers, however, point in the other direction. And they are quite consistent on this score: whether we look at parents, nonparents, or inner-city parents, low education is always associated with support for vouchers. Why would this be? Two arguments are relevant here, both of which may be valid at once.

The first is that education is a class variable that does double duty. On the one hand, despite our imperfect attempts to control for other class influences, education unavoidably captures the profound effects of social class, and cannot help but be a measure of the many disadvantages that shape the lives of people with little education. These disadvantages restrict their access to quality schooling and give them incentives to be interested in private schools and vouchers. On the other hand, education is also a proxy for motivation: people with better educations

Table 7-6. *Initial Support for Vouchers: Inner-City Parents*[a]

Variable	Background model		Context model		Attitude model		Performance model 1		Performance model 2	
	Coefficient	[Impact]	Coefficient	[Impact]	Coefficient	[Impact]	Coefficient	[Impact]	Coefficient	[Impact]
Background										
Education	-.05	[-.12]	-.09**	[-.20]	-.11**	[-.26]	-.12**	[-.26]	-.12***	[-.27]
Income	-.06	[-.07]	-.06	[-.06]	-.07	[-.07]	-.06	[-.06]	-.07	[-.07]
Catholic	.05	[.05]	-.03	[-.03]	-.00	[-.00]	.01	[.01]	-.02	[-.02]
Born-again	.16	[.16]	.06	[.06]	.08	[.08]	.08	[.08]	.03	[.03]
Black (north)	.05	[.05]	.03	[.03]	-.06	[-.06]	-.05	[-.05]	-.09	[-.09]
Black (south)	.14	[.15]	-.02	[-.02]	.01	[.01]	.03	[.03]	.07	[.07]
Hispanic	.13	[.14]	.08	[.08]	.01	[.01]	.02	[.02]	.05	[.05]
Age	-.01	[-.07]	-.02	[-.11]	-.02	[-.11]	-.02	[-.10]	-.02	[-.12]
Party identification	-.01	[-.02]	-.00	[-.00]	.00	[.00]	.00	[.00]	-.01	[-.02]
Low expectations	.01	[.03]	.02	[.06]	.02	[.06]	.02	[.08]	-.01	[-.02]
Context										
Residential mobility			.03	[.05]	.01	[.03]	.02	[.03]	.03	[.05]
Advantaged district			-.11	[-.17]	-.08	[-.12]	-.07	[-.10]	-.00	[-.00]

Attitudes				
Diversity (white)		.09 [.16]	.08 [.14]	.09 [.16]
Inequity		.15** [.23]	.14** [.21]	.10 [.16]
School prayer		-.00 [-.00]	.00 [.00]	.02 [.05]
Parent influence		-.04 [-.07]	-.05 [-.08]	-.05 [-.08]
School size		.02 [.03]	.01 [.02]	-.02 [-.02]
Public school ideology		-.10* [-.15]	-.09 [-.14]	-.08 [-.12]
Markets		.01 [.02]	.01 [.01]	-.00 [-.01]
Moral values		.03 [.10]	.03 [.10]	.02 [.05]
Performance				
Performance			-.09 [-.14]	-.03 [-.04]
Go private?				.66*** [.66]
Constant	2.69***	2.42***	2.41***	2.40***
N^b	(505)	(476)	(454)	(454)
Adjusted R^2	.04	.06	.15	.15

* Significant at .10 level.
** Significant at .05 level.
*** Significant at .01 level.

a. Ordinary least squares regressions estimated using weighted data. The dependent variable is the initial voucher support item, which is coded from 1 (strongly disagree) to 4 (strongly agree). Unstandardized coefficients reported. For each nondichotomous independent variable, the impact coefficient represents the estimated change in the dependent variable (measured in standard deviations) when the independent variable shifts by two standard deviations, holding all other variables constant; for each dichotomous variable, the impact coefficient represents the estimated change in the dependent variable (measured in standard deviations) when the independent variable shifts from 0 to 1, holding all other variables constant. Models control for the full range of background and context variables, not all of which are reported in the tables.

b. N is the unweighted number of respondents.

tend to put the greatest personal value on education and are the most aggressive in pursuing it for their kids—for example, by seeking out private schools or moving to areas with good public schools.

Because we can't perfectly control for social class or motivation, the effects of education can be expected to *combine* these two influences, which work in opposite directions. The estimated impacts are essentially the sum of the two and could be either positive or negative, depending on which influence wins out. By this logic, questions about going private are largely personal in nature, and may tap the motivational side (for parents), leading to net positive effects. Questions about whether vouchers would make good public policy are inherently much more social, and may evoke responses that are more explicitly class-based (for everyone), leading to net negative effects.

This is a reasonable argument, and it provides a basis—along with all the other evidence linking vouchers to the less advantaged—for thinking that the educational effects we observed in the last section's analysis are simply a reflection of social class. People who are lower in education express support for vouchers, as do people who are lower in income, minority, and from disadvantaged districts. And all these effects appear to be part of the same syndrome, rooted in class.

There is, however, a very different argument that needs to be considered. This one has to do with information and sophistication. People with less education are likely to be less knowledgeable about the issue, less capable of bringing relevant concerns to bear in evaluating it—and more susceptible, as a result, to influence by whatever cues might be contained within the survey. This doesn't mean they are going to see vouchers more positively than other respondents do. But it could mean that.

Vouchers may be one of those policies that tend to sound good on the surface, especially when couched in terms of parental choice. Were this true, the survey responses would still be telling us something valid about people's preferences. Americans value choice in virtually all aspects of their lives, and there is no reason to think schooling should be much different. But if less-educated people are giving responses that are more superficial than substantive, and if they are heavily swayed by what sounds good, then this—and not class interests—may account for their higher level of support for vouchers.

The meaning of the education effect, therefore, remains something of a mystery. And the main reason for the mystery is that all of our analysis to this point has focused on the substantive bases of public opinion—on things like social class, in other words—without considering the separate effects of information and sophistication. In the analysis that follows, we'll try to do something about that.

Information and the Structure of Thinking

The mystery surrounding the education effect is part of a larger puzzle. If political scientists are right, there are basic differences between people who are informed and people who aren't. (Here and elsewhere, I use *informed* as a shorthand label for people who are knowledgeable and sophisticated.) The two groups are likely to *think* about vouchers, and indeed about most public policies, in very different ways. The informed are likely to pay more attention to the national debate, to think in more ideological terms, and to be more familiar with arguments for and against. For these reasons, they are likely to forge a much stronger connection between political party and the voucher issue than the uninformed do. The same may well be true for religion and for the whole range of attitudes that stand to be relevant. It is the informed who are likely to *see* them as relevant, and to take them into account in fashioning their policy positions.

The real import of the information/sophistication factor, then, is not that it might produce a sounds-good effect, although this is one possibility. Its import is far more general: that it may tell us something about how people go about assessing the whole issue and, in particular, how (or whether) they can connect it to their underlying values, beliefs, and interests. Do the uninformed think about vouchers in an unstructured, superficial way compared to those who are informed? Is most of the population basically out to lunch, incapable of connecting the voucher issue to things that they care about?

In this section we will explore these more fundamental issues—and gain insight into the education effect along the way—by using our survey's information variable as a proxy. Ideally, we should have a measure of how much people really know about the issue (not just whether they have heard of it), as well as a measure of their general level of political knowledge or sophistication (which is usually obtained by asking a number of factual questions about politics). Because the measure we have to work with is so crude by comparison, we have to be careful about pushing it too far. Still, it is a reasonable proxy, and we should try to take advantage of it.

The methodology is straightforward. I simply take our usual modeling framework (from the earlier analysis) and add a full set of interaction terms that allow all variables to have different impacts for informed and uninformed respondents. This is the same as running separate analyses for the informed and the uninformed, except that it indicates whether the estimated impacts for the two groups—which are guaranteed to be at least slightly different by chance alone—are large enough to be statistically significant.

Such an analysis produces an avalanche of statistical results that is cumbersome to present. So to make things manageable, table 7-7 offers a very simplified summary. It indicates, for each model, whether the relevant variables have impacts that are significantly different for informed and uninformed respondents. When the effects are indeed different, it also indicates which group makes the stronger connection (as measured by the absolute value of its effect). The basic patterns are discussed below, along with some of the details (about the values of various coefficients) that could not easily be included in the table. Let's begin with public parents.

There is no evidence here that uninformed parents tend to be more positive toward vouchers and are simply responding to whatever sounds good. When being informed or uninformed has any impact, it does so by affecting the connection people are able to make between the things they care about—party, for instance, or religion—and their stand on vouchers. As a result, the impact of information on support for vouchers may be positive, or it may be negative, depending on how these other variables come into play. An informed Republican, for instance, will be more supportive of vouchers than an uninformed Republican, but for Democrats the impact of information is just the reverse: an informed Democrat will be less supportive of vouchers than an uninformed Democrat. These other variables are the vehicles through which the effects of information are transmitted. And once the transmitted effects are taken into account, the impact of information alone—a proxy for any sounds-good effect—is never significant.[30] (If anything, the actual coefficients suggest that it is the informed, not the uninformed, who may be a bit more positive toward vouchers.)

The estimated impact of education, moreover, remains much the same as before, even in the presence of full-blown controls for information: parents who are low in education are more supportive of vouchers. If the education effect were actually due to a lack of information or sophistication, then its impact would presumably have been reduced or eliminated here. The fact that this doesn't happen is consistent with the argument (although it doesn't prove it) that the education effect is largely rooted in the needs and interests of social class. This argument is also supported by the fact that all the class variables—education, income, and race—have impacts that are much the same for informed and uninformed parents.

Parents who are less advantaged appear to support vouchers for substantive reasons, not because they are uninformed or unsophisticated.

Class aside, the analysis reveals certain differences in the way informed and uninformed parents connect vouchers to considerations that matter to them. A few of these are rather difficult to explain and may just be quirks in the data. But the others are precisely the sorts of differences that political scientists would lead us to expect.

(1) While our prior analysis has not shown political party to be very important to the way Americans approach the voucher issue (and related matters), we get a dramatically different picture once information and sophistication are taken into account. Among informed parents, political party emerges as one of the most salient influences on support for vouchers. Among the uninformed, on the other hand, party has nothing to do with it. The informed are tied into elite-level politics. The uninformed are not.

(2) Informed parents make a clear connection between religion and support for vouchers, with significant effects for both Catholics and born-again Christians. The uninformed are less able to make the connection. For them, the effect of being Catholic is weaker by about two-thirds (although difference across groups is not quite significant), and there is no effect at all associated with being born-again.

(3) Among the informed, the attitude that most strongly influences support for vouchers is their view of markets, a rather abstract set of concerns. The uninformed respond to market ideas too, but with less than half the weight. Much the same is true for public school ideology: the informed put a good deal of emphasis on this normative commitment in deciding where they stand on vouchers, but the uninformed see almost no connection between the two.

(4) For both informed and uninformed parents, low assessments of public school performance give rise to support for vouchers. But the connection is weaker for the uninformed by about half (a difference that is not quite statistically significant).

In basic respects, then, political science expectations are on the money. There is simply *less structure* to the responses of the uninformed parents: they do not make some connections at all, and some of the connections they do make are weaker than those made by the informed. In our earlier analysis, we found a substantial degree of structure in the way Americans respond to the voucher issue, even when presented with an out-of-the-blue support item. But now we can see that certain aspects of this structure arise from a relatively small subset of informed respondents. The

Table 7-7. Support for Vouchers: The Role of Information and Sophistication[a]

	Public school parents					Nonparents			
Variable	Background model	Context model	Attitude model	Performance model 1	Performance model 2	Background model	Context model	Attitude model	Performance model
Background									
Education	*	*	*	*	*	*	*	*	*
Income	*	*	*	*	*	*	*	*	*
Catholic	*	*	*	*	*	I > U	I > U	I > U	I > U
Born-again	I > U	I > U	I > U	I > U	*	*	*	*	*
Black (north)	*	*	*	*	*	*	*	*	*
Black (south)	*	*	*	*	*	*	*	*	*
Hispanic	*	*	*	*	*	*	I > U	I > U	I > U
Age	*	*	*	*	*	*	*	*	*
Party identification	I > U	I > U	I > U	I > U	I > U	I > U	I > U	*	*
Low expectations	I > U	I > U	I > U	I > U	I > U	*	*	*	*
Context									
Residential mobility		*	*	*	*		*	*	*
Advantaged district		U > I	*	*	U > I		U > I	*	*

Attitudes				
Diversity (white)	*	*	*	*
Inequity	*	*	*	*
School prayer	*	*	*	*
Parent influence	*	*	I > U	I > U
School size	*	*	*	*
Public school ideology	I > U	I > U	I > U	I > U
Markets	I > U	I > U	*	*
Moral values	*	*	*	*
Performance				
Performance	*	*		
Go private?	*	*		*
Constant	*	*	I > U	I > U

*Indicates no significant difference.

a. Ordinary least squares regressions estimated using weighted data. The dependent variable is the initial voucher support item, which is coded from 1 (strongly disagree) to 4 (strongly agree). Models control for the full range of background and context variables, not all of which are reported in the table. Inequality indicates whether, for the variable in question, the estimated coefficients are significantly different for people who are informed (I) and people who are uninformed (U) and shows which is larger in absolute value.

most prominent examples are party and religion, the traditional bulwarks of the voucher movement. These are central to the way informed parents think about the issue—as we should expect, if their views are framed by the elite-level debate. But among the uninformed, who are not tuned in, these traditional sources of support are weaker.

These are important differences. But the essential point to be made about the bigger picture is that, all things considered, informed and uninformed parents are remarkably *similar* in the way they approach the voucher issue. Social class, remember, has much the same effects for both. As table 7-7's overview suggests, moreover, so does the one variable that is by far the most powerful determinant of parental support for vouchers: the interest in going private. And while public school ideology and belief in markets do have different effects for the informed and the uninformed, the effects of *all* the other attitudes—diversity, inequity, prayer, parent influence, school size, and moral values—are not significantly different across groups.

Overall, therefore, it appears that informed and uninformed parents are mostly responding to the same influences in the same ways. In some cases, the influences are weaker for the uninformed, as we would expect. But the uninformed are *not* out to lunch. Despite their unfamiliarity with the issue, they are thinking about the issue in a surprisingly coherent way and connecting it to concerns that matter to them.

The conclusions for nonparents are roughly the same. There are clear differences between the informed and the uninformed—on party, on religion, and on a few attitudes. But for the most part, the same basic variables seem to be shaping their approach to vouchers, and the influences are much the same. As with parents, then, the uninformed are not simply at a loss when it comes to linking their values, beliefs, and interests to a position on vouchers. They seem to do a pretty good job of it, on the whole.

We should also note that, with nonparents too, there is no evidence of a sounds-good effect among the uninformed. When we factor out the differential ways in which the informed and the uninformed respond to all the substantive variables, the impact of information alone is sometimes significant (in two models)—but it turns out that the uninformed actually tend to be less positive than the informed are, not more positive. As with parents, moreover, the education effect remains the same as before, and is unaffected by controls for information—which is additional evidence that the connection between low education and support for vouchers is largely due to class.

This said, there is a final contrast worth drawing as well, one that serves as a harbinger of things to come. The above analysis gives us one view of how respondents structure their thinking on the voucher issue. It puts the informed and the uninformed together in the same regressions and asks how they respond to particular variables. This tells us something about the pattern of influences on their thinking, and thus about whether their thinking is structured. But another way to measure structure is in terms of overall explanatory power: how much influence do all the variables, taken together, have on the way respondents think about the issue? Presumably, the more these factors can explain overall, the more respondents' support for vouchers is grounded in an underlying connection to their values, beliefs, and interests, and the more structured it is.

Suppose, then, that we carry out separate regression analyses for informed parents, uninformed parents, informed nonparents, and uninformed nonparents and see how successfully the whole set of variables can explain their support for vouchers. When we do this, the explained variance for each group, measured in terms of the regression R^2, is as follows: .20 for informed parents, .12 for uninformed parents, .22 for informed nonparents, and .09 for uninformed nonparents.[31]

All of these R^2s are lower than they might otherwise be, due to the high levels of measurement error that plague virtually all survey data. But assuming there is a core validity to these numbers, they point to two basic conclusions. One is that, for parents and nonparents alike, the informed are much more structured in their approach to vouchers than the uninformed are: in relative terms, the independent variables explain a good bit more of their behavior. The second is that, if we look over all four groups of respondents, it is the uninformed nonparents who have the least structure to their thinking on this issue.

These results make good sense and are a nice complement to the analysis we just carried out. Overall, it appears that the *kind* of structure that shapes popular thinking about vouchers—that is, the kinds of considerations that are relevant and how they come into play—is pretty much the same for informed and uninformed people. But the *strength* of that structure—how much it explains—is a good deal weaker for the uninformed, and this is especially true for the uninformed nonparents. Of all the respondents in our sample, then, it is the uninformed nonparents who seem to have the least grounding—and who, it is reasonable to suspect, are the least committed to their positions and the most susceptible to change.

Stability and Change

In most surveys that deal with the subject, people are asked an out-of-the-blue question on support for vouchers, with no prior information on the issue, and the survey moves on to other matters. Responses to that single question are presumed to represent public opinion.

To this point, we have been looking at our own survey's version of the same thing. People were asked an initial question about support for vouchers, with no prior discussion of the issue, and they gave responses. What we've found is that those responses are surprisingly meaningful, connecting to people's values, beliefs, and interests in ways that make sense. The connection is stronger for some people than for others. But in general, public opinion does seem to be telling us something, even when people come to the issue with little background.

Our survey, however, does not abandon the voucher issue once its out-of-the-blue question is asked. It goes on to explore the topic in some depth, often by raising issues salient in the national debate—and then asks respondents again, in an item worded identically to the first, whether they support vouchers as public policy. This technique adds a new dimension to our evidence on public opinion and gives us new leverage in trying to understand it.

What happens to support for vouchers the second time around? Do many people change their positions? And more fundamentally, *why* do they change? Is it essentially a random process with little rhyme or reason, as Converse would maintain? Is it a quasi-rational response to new considerations arising during the survey, as Zaller would argue? Or is it a more rational process still, in which people actually seem to be thinking the issue through and arriving at a more coherent view of things, as rationalist scholars might expect?

So far, there is little to suggest that Converse's pessimism is justified. People are not ciphers, and there is a good deal of structure to their thinking, even when they are uninformed. Their positions are shaped by a variety of considerations, so much so that even Zaller may be a bit on the pessimistic side. People may be engaging in more "real thinking" than he gives them credit for, and the rationalist scholars may be more on track (in this respect).

The Extent and Direction of Change

The responses to the second support item are set out in table 7-8, alongside the responses to the first item. They show that people became more

Table 7-8. *A Comparison of Initial and Follow-up Support for Vouchers*
Percent, unless otherwise indicated[a]

Position on vouchers	Total population	Non-parents	Public school parents	Private school parents	Inner-city parents
Initial Position					
Oppose	32	36	26	13	14
Support	60	57	66	81	77
Don't know	7	7	8	6	9
N[b]	(4,700)	(1,617)	(2,553)	(530)	(539)
Follow-up position					
Oppose	25	27	22	10	11
Support	68	65	71	84	81
Don't know	8	8	7	6	7
N[b]	(4,700)	(1,617)	(2,553)	(530)	(539)

a. Percentages are based on weighted data. They may not sum to 100 due to rounding.
b. N is the unweighted number of respondents.

favorable toward vouchers during the course of the survey. In the population as a whole, support increased from 60 percent to 68 percent. The positive shift took place across the board, for all the basic groups of respondents. Nonparents moved from 57 percent support to 65 percent, public parents from 66 percent to 71 percent, private parents from 81 percent to 84 percent, and inner-city parents from 77 percent to 81 percent.

Voucher advocates might be inclined to view this sort of groundswell as a sign that, when people become more familiar with vouchers, and when they get to think about the issue a bit, they become more sympathetic. This argument shouldn't be dismissed. Vouchers are an alien concept in American education, and some people may be unwilling to go along until they have had a chance to get used to the idea. After grappling with some forty questions on the matter, they may feel more comfortable with it and more positive. This can't explain, of course, why so many people are favorable toward vouchers (on this survey) from the very beginning, even when they are unfamiliar with the issue. But it could explain why some people shift at the margins and why the shift is uniformly positive.

Critics might offer another argument to explain the groundswell: that the survey is biased and induces people to give overly positive responses. This needs a bit of discussion. It is important to note, first, that the survey was designed with the explicit purpose of minimizing potential biases. Every effort was made to provide a balanced set of questions. On some items, respondents were presented with arguments both for and against vouchers on a particular issue, and they were asked to choose. When this was not possible, and they were asked to agree or disagree with one-sided statements, the survey contained equal numbers of positively and negatively worded items. Throughout, the aim was to probe the respondents' thinking and avoid pushing them in one direction or another.

Nonetheless, it is possible that positive forces are implicitly at work here, at least to some degree. Any survey is vulnerable to this sort of thing, and it has to be recognized. The Phi Delta Kappa polls are clearly about the public schools, and may subtly encourage people to be more negative toward vouchers than they otherwise would be. Similarly, the poll carried out by the National Catholic Education Association was clearly about private schools, and could have generated cues encouraging people to be more positive toward vouchers. Our own survey, by asking people to evaluate the public schools in various ways and then spending so much time exploring the ins and outs of vouchers, may also have given off signals that vouchers are somehow good, or that positive answers are somehow expected. Even when surveys are designed to be neutral, they may create a mood that isn't.

In the absence of further research, we cannot know the answer. It is important to recognize, however, that the meaning of *bias* is unclear in this context. In traditional measurement theory, a biased measure is one that systematically mismeasures the true value of a variable—for example, by being consistently too positive (relative to the truth) or too negative (relative to the truth). In the modern study of public opinion, however, many scholars believe that there *isn't* a simple, underlying truth when it comes to most public policy issues. If Zaller is right, most people could come down in favor of vouchers, or they could come down against them, depending on considerations that happen to be at the "top of the head" at the time—and these will vary from survey to survey, and within any given survey as well.

Even if we think that people have a bit more on the ball than Zaller claims, therefore, bias is not the crux of the issue here. What we want to know is not whether 60 percent or 68 percent is closer to the "real" level of voucher support within the American public, nor, for that matter, whether the "real" level might be closer to what other surveys say it is. What we want to know in each case is *why* people give the responses they do, and thus what sorts of considerations seem to be shaping the policy positions they take.

Who Changes Their Views?

Table 7-9 offers a first look at the dynamics of change. Seventeen percent of respondents changed their positions during the survey, 5 percent moving from support to opposition and 12 percent moving from opposition to support.[32] Presumably, the magnitude of change would have been much larger had we asked the second support item even a day later, not to mention a month or a year. Other studies (of other issues) have shown massive instability over long periods of time.[33] As it is, our respondents were asked the second support item about fifteen minutes after the first—and still, 17 percent changed their views.

Who is doing the changing? For obvious reasons, we should expect the uninformed to have less-developed views than the informed, and to be more susceptible to change as new information is presented. The evidence bears this out. For the public at large, 22 percent of the uninformed change their positions, compared to 11 percent of the informed.

The impact of being uninformed, however, is different for public parents than for nonparents. Among public parents, the uninformed are only slightly more likely than the informed to shift their positions, by 15 percent to 12 percent. At least in the aggregate, moreover, both groups are about twice as likely to shift from opposition to support as from support to opposition. Nonparents are a different story. Here, the uninformed are much more likely to change their positions than the informed are—fully 24 percent of the uninformed make a change, compared to just 10 percent of the informed. And when they do change, they are much more likely to move in a positive direction. Indeed, if we look at the table as a whole, we can see that the uninformed nonparents stand out from all other groups: they are far more likely to change their positions, and more likely as well to shift in a positive direction.

One way of making sense of these findings is simply to recognize (again) that parents have a much greater stake in the voucher issue than nonparents do. Because of this, it is reasonable to suggest that even when parents are uninformed, they find it easier to connect to the issue right from the start than nonparents do. By this rationale, being uninformed should have less impact for parents than it does for nonparents—and the uninformed nonparents are clearly the ones who should be the most susceptible to change. Of all groups, the uninformed nonparents have the least to work with: they are low in substantive connection, *and* they are low in initial background and political sophistication. Earlier, our analysis began to

Table 7-9. *Who Switches Sides?*
Percent, unless otherwise indicated[a]

Position on vouchers (Initial/Follow-up)[b]	Total population			Public school parents			Nonparents		
	Total	Uninformed	Informed	Total	Uninformed	Informed	Total	Uninformed	Informed
Support/Support	61	61	61	68	71	61	57	57	58
Support/Oppose	5	6	4	5	5	4	5	6	4
Oppose/Support	12	16	7	9	10	8	14	18	6
Oppose/Oppose	22	18	29	19	14	26	24	20	32
N[c]	(4,153)	(2,403)	(1,750)	(2,232)	(1,374)	(894)	(1,361)	(812)	(571)

a. Percentages are based on weighted data. They may not sum to 100 due to rounding.
b. Excludes people who answered "don't know" to either item.
c. N is the unweighted number of respondents.

document what this combination means in practice, showing that their thinking on the issue is less structured than for any other group. It makes sense that they now turn out to be the big shifters.

Why Do People Change Their Positions?

Because so much of the change comes from the uninformed, especially the uninformed nonparents, and because so much of it is in the same direction, it is tempting to conclude that change must be driven by superficial concerns, and that perhaps Converse is on the mark in arguing that change is essentially a random process (with bias), having little to do with the substance of the issue. As we will see, however, the evidence suggests otherwise.

If there are substantive reasons why people are changing their views, the obvious place to look is at the new considerations the survey introduces after the first support item and before the second. Clearly, these are the considerations most likely to be at the "top of the head" when the second support question is asked, and they are the prime candidates for explaining why people might change their minds.

Many of these items ask respondents to ponder the consequences that a voucher system might have for society. All address issues that are central to the national debate. Is competition good or bad for the public schools? Would vouchers aggravate segregation problems, or would they promote integration by giving minorities more choices? Would vouchers be dominated by the well-to-do, leaving the poor behind in inadequate schools, or would they work to benefit the poor by giving them valuable new options? Would vouchers increase the costs of education or help control them? And so on.

People may know little about some of these issues and have little factual basis for answering them. But whether they give insightful answers or not, the mere fact that they are asked to think about them and formulate responses means that they are more likely to recognize them as *relevant* to an assessment of vouchers, and to emerge with somewhat different views of whether vouchers would make good public policy.

If this is the case, then we would expect their responses on these items to tell us something about whether they are likely to switch sides. Consider the people who are initially opposed to vouchers. As a group, of course, they will tend to give rather negative responses to the items on social consequences. But some of them will give more positive responses than others will—and the former should be the ones likely to change sides. Similarly, people who are initially supportive of vouchers will tend to see the social consequences in a rather positive light; but within this group, those who see them more negatively should be the ones likely to switch to opposition. This is what we should expect, at any rate, if there is a substantive rationality to the process of change and if switching is not a random or frivolous thing.

The data are set out in the top portion of table 7-10. How people respond to the new considerations is quantified in a single index, which provides a summary measure of how positively or negatively each person views the social consequences of a voucher system. For purposes of presentation, the index is dichotomized here into high (more positive) and low (more negative). If issues matter, initial opponents should tend to switch sides when they have high social scores; initial supporters should tend to switch when their scores are low.

In order to interpret table 7-10 properly, it is important to recognize that the rate of shifting *must* be a lot greater among opponents than among supporters, given what we already know. Even if the aggregate level of public support on the second voucher item had been exactly the same as on the initial item, opponents would still shift their positions at about *twice* the rate of supporters. There is a simple mathematical reason for this: because supporters outnumber opponents on the initial support item by about 2 to 1 (when the "don't knows" are omitted), the positive and negative shifters can only balance one another out when opponents defect at twice the rate of supporters. And if we assume—to reflect the facts of our case—that aggregate support actually increases by 8 percent rather than remaining constant, it can be shown that opponents have to shift at almost *six times* the rate of supporters to make it happen.

The conclusion, then, is that there are different baselines at work for opponents and supporters, given the parameters we're starting with, and there will necessarily be an asymmetry built into the data. Empirically, however, the most interesting questions have to do with what happens *within* each group. Granted that a big proportion of opponents will be shifting their positions, and granted that a much smaller percentage of supporters will be doing so: how do we account for *which* opponents and supporters decide to make the change?

Now let's turn to the data—which are quite striking. Consider, for example, the results for uninformed public parents. Of those who are initially opposed to vouchers, but who score high on the social consequences index, a remarkable 63 percent change their position from opposition to support. For those who score low on the social index, and thus have social views congruent with their initial opposition, only 28 percent change from

Table 7-10. *The Impact of Social and Personal Considerations on Change in Support for Vouchers*
Percent[a]

	Uninformed		Informed	
Index	Initially oppose	Initially support	Initially oppose	Initially support
Social index—public school parents				
Low on social scale				
Follow-up oppose	72	15	81	15
Follow-up support	28	85	19	85
High on social scale				
Follow-up oppose	37	3	48	2
Follow-up support	63	97	52	98
Social index—nonparents				
Low on social scale				
Follow-up oppose	61	17	89	14
Follow-up support	39	83	11	86
High on social scale				
Follow-up oppose	33	5	55	2
Follow-up support	67	95	45	98
Personal index—public school parents				
Low on personal index				
Follow-up oppose	69	15	79	15
Follow-up support	31	85	21	85
High on personal index				
Follow-up oppose	31	2	63	2
Follow-up support	69	98	37	98
Personal interest—public school parents				
Not interested in using voucher				
Follow-up oppose	72	17	82	22
Follow-up support	28	83	18	78
Interested in using voucher				
Follow-up oppose	29	2	58	2
Follow-up support	71	98	42	98

a. Percentages are based on weighted data. They may not sum to 100 due to rounding.

opposition to support. This is a huge difference and clearly suggests that many parents are shifting their positions because they have come to think about vouchers in a different way. Differences of this magnitude are not possible among supporters, because the baseline is much lower: only 6 percent are shifting overall. Still, when judged by reference to this baseline, the new social considerations appear to have a big impact on them as well. For supporters with low scores on the social index, 15 percent switch to opposition. For those with high social scores, just 3 percent make the switch.

If we look across all four groups of respondents—parents and nonparents, informed and uninformed—it is clear that the inclination to switch sides is strongly connected to these new social considerations for all of them. It is also clear that the uninformed nonparents—who are the least grounded and the biggest switchers—are not outliers here. While there are surely other factors that explain why so many of them switch from opposition to support, social considerations seem to have a lot to do with it. Much of their switching, at least, is not random or frivolous, despite their lack of grounding.

Another kind of evidence is relevant as well. How people see the voucher issue may depend on how they see its consequences for society. But it may also be shaped by whatever value vouchers hold for them personally. This is most obviously true for parents, particularly those who want to use vouchers for their own children. If substance matters and if switching is a fairly rational process, then self-interest should help us explain why some parents change their positions.

It might seem that, unlike concerns about social consequences—which may often be new considerations for many people—this personal stake in the issue would be much more constant and firmly grounded throughout the survey. If so, self-interest could have a lot to do with the positions people take initially, but little to do with why they *change* them. We have to remember, though, that parents enter the survey unfamiliar with what vouchers might have to offer them. And as they think and learn about the issue, their notions of their own self-interest may evolve—and alter their views on policy.

The survey offers us two means of exploring the impact of self-interest on switching. The first is a battery of questions that measure the extent to which parents see vouchers as being valuable to them personally. Would vouchers enable them to seek out better schools for their kids? Give them more control over their children's educations? Make schools more responsive? And so on. By combining these items into a single indicator, we can arrive at a personal index that is comparable to the social index used above. The second measure is more straightforward: it is a question that asks parents directly whether they would consider using a voucher to send their children to private school.

The data are set out in the bottom portion of table 7-10. The results, again, are quite dramatic. Take, for instance, the uninformed parents who initially say they are opposed to vouchers. Of these parents, 69 percent who score high on the personal index (indicating that vouchers would be valuable to them) change their position to one of support later on, while just 31 percent of those who score low on the personal index do the same. Comparable figures emerge from the other measure. Of opponents who say they might use a voucher for their own children, 71 percent switch sides to become supporters, while the same is true for only 28 percent of those who express no interest in putting vouchers to use.

If we look at uninformed parents who start out being supportive of vouchers (and if we adjust for their different baseline), we find that self-interest has a strong influence for them as well. Those who score low on the personal index are much more likely to switch to opposition than those who score high (by 15 percent to 2 percent), and those with no desire to use a voucher are much more inclined to shift than those who do want to use one (by 17 percent to 2 percent).

A look at the rest of the table shows that, details aside, much the same is true for the informed. In general, therefore, whether we look at parents who are informed or uninformed, and regardless of which measure of personal stake we consider, switching behavior is strongly related to self-interest. Parents appear to change sides, at least in part, because they have a personal stake in the issue that prompts them to do so.

We needn't concern ourselves here with whether people's views on vouchers are primarily shaped by social concerns or primarily shaped by self-interest. Chapter 8 will explore this in more detail. The bottom line here is simply this: when people change their positions during the survey—or when they decide not to—they appear to be engaged in a rational process of decision that is strongly related to the substance of the issue. Whether that substance is social or personal, the evidence suggests there are good reasons for what they are doing.

"Final" Support for Vouchers

As a final step, let's take a closer look at where people ultimately come down on the voucher issue. If they are engaged in "real thinking," then their revised position—taken in light of more information and with the benefit of time to mull things over—should be more meaningful than the one adopted earlier, at first blush. Indeed, we already have reason to think that this second position *is* more fully in line with their underlying values, beliefs, and interests: for some percentage of people have changed their positions in the interim, and they seem to have done so because their initial positions did not square with important considerations they (now) consider relevant. This shifting should bring about a greater congruence of views and a more clearly defined structure.

But it remains a question how much "real thinking" is going on here. If Zaller is on target, the answer is: not much. In his view, people are simply responding to whatever considerations come to the "top of the head" and averaging over them in a mechanical way to determine whether they feel positively or negatively about vouchers. They are not developing a more integrated sense of the issue and are not really learning anything. Rationalist scholars would give people more credit. They would expect people to think about the issue and arrive at a perspective more strongly anchored in their own values, beliefs, and interests. If the rationalists are right, public opinion should be more meaningful at the end of the process than at the beginning.

As I said earlier, this delineation of theories is a bit too neat. It is not so easy to tell where Zaller's argument leaves off and those of the rationalist scholars pick up. Both camps agree that the shifters should respond to new considerations, and thus that the second support item should be a better reflection of what matters to them than the first item was. The two camps appear to differ, however, when it comes to the issue of structure—particularly as it applies to the more generic considerations that make up the framework of background, context, attitudes, and performance variables we have been employing throughout this book.

These measures are all based on items that were not part of the voucher section of the survey at all, and were not explicitly connected to the voucher issue by the survey itself. If respondents wanted to relate these prior considerations to their position on vouchers, they had to do it themselves. On the whole, the rationalists would expect them to do a better job of this than Zaller would. Our analysis showed that, on the initial support item, respondents were surprisingly effective at linking these things together. As we turn our attention to the second support item, the question is whether their thinking seems to be more structured, or different in some revealing way, than it was the first time through.

To investigate, let's take the second support item as the dependent variable and carry out exactly the same analysis we carried out earlier for the initial support item. When this is done, we get the results reported in table 7-11. By looking at the pattern of impacts across variables, we can get a sense of the new structure of thinking that seems to guide responses to the second support item. And by comparing this structure to the one for the initial support item (see table 7-4), we can get a sense for how the respondents' thinking seems to have changed and whether the structure seems to have evolved and improved.

As we can only expect, the two structures are quite similar in all basic respects—the roles of social class, the various attitudes, performance, and parental interest in going private are all much the same as before. Peeking through all the similarities, however, are some important differences that suggest people *have* been doing some new thinking, and have arrived at a more coherent view of how vouchers connect to the things that matter to them.

(1) On the initial support item, people did not make a consistent connection between religion and support for vouchers. Among public parents, being Catholic had a significant impact on voucher support, but being born-again did not. Among nonparents, this oddity was reversed: being Catholic was not a significant determinant of support, but being born-again was. Substantively, of course, there is no reason to expect this sort of thing. As table 7-11 shows, however, these oddities are eliminated the second time around, after people have had a chance to think about things. For parents and nonparents alike, responses to the second support item reveal that both the Catholic and born-again variables are significant influences on support for vouchers. People are better able to make the connection.

A more detailed analysis would show, moreover, that this "correction" is largely due to rational adjustments among the uninformed. Consider, for instance, the uninformed public parents. On the initial item, support for vouchers was 81 percent for Catholics and 67 percent for born-again Christians, compared to 70 percent for the baseline group of regular Protestants, which clearly suggests that the born-again Christians were somehow failing to make the connection. On the follow-up item, however, it is the born-again parents who have made the biggest adjustments. The new support figures are: 82 percent for Catholics, 79 percent for born-again Christians, and 73 percent for regular Protestants, which makes much more sense. Exactly the same sort of rational adjustment process occurs among uninformed nonparents, except for them it is the Catholics who do the adjusting—because the Catholics were the ones initially out of line. Support scores on the initial item were 62 percent for Catholics, 72 percent for born-again Christians, and 60 percent for regular Protestants. The "improved" support scores on the second item are: 79 percent for Catholics, 77 percent for born-again Christians, and 67 percent for regular Protestants. The uninformed seem to have learned something.

(2) When people expressed their support or opposition to vouchers the first time through, party had the traditional impact—Republicans tended

Table 7-11. *Follow-up Support for Vouchers:*
Public School Parents and Nonparents[a]

	Public school parents							
	Background model		Context model		Attitude model		Performance model 1	
Variable	Coeffi-cient	[Impact]	Coeffi-cient	[Impact]	Coeffi-cient	[Impact]	Coeffi-cient	[Impact]
Background								
Education	−.06***	[−.15]	−.05**	[−.12]	−.07***	[−.16]	−.07***	[−.18]
Income	−.04***	[−.15]	−.04***	[−.15]	−.03**	[−.12]	−.03**	[−.10]
Catholic	.15**	[.14]	.15**	[.14]	.14**	[.13]	.15**	[.14]
Born-again	.22**	[.20]	.20**	[.18]	.14	[.13]	.15*	[.14]
Black (north)	.26***	[.24]	.18**	[.16]	.15*	[.14]	.13	[.12]
Black (south)	.37***	[.34]	.35***	[.32]	.31***	[.28]	.33***	[.30]
Hispanic	.15**	[.14]	.06	[.05]	.02	[.02]	.03	[.03]
Age	−.05***	[−.18]	−.05***	[−.20]	−.05***	[−.19]	−.05***	[−.18]
Party identification	.01	[.05]	.01	[.05]	.02	[.06]	.01	[.05]
Low expectations	.00	[.00]	−.00	[−.01]	−.00	[−.01]	.00	[.01]
Context								
Residential mobility			.02	[.04]	.02	[.04]	.04*	[.07]
Advantaged district			−.06**	[−.11]	−.04	[−.06]	−.02	[−.03]
Attitudes								
Diversity (white)					.10***	[.15]	.10***	[.15]
Inequity					.17***	[.26]	.14***	[.22]
School prayer					.06***	[.12]	.05***	[.12]
Parent influence					.06**	[.09]	.04	[.07]
School size					.09***	[.14]	.08***	[.12]
Public school ideology					−.16***	[−.22]	−.14***	[−.20]
Markets					.21***	[.32]	.20***	[.30]
Moral values					.01	[.04]	.01	[.04]
Performance								
Performance							−.22***	[−.29]
Go private?								
Constant	3.28***		3.11***		2.67***		2.74***	
N[b]	(2,385)		(2,161)		(2,161)		(2,161)	
Adjusted R^2	.07		.07		.14		.16	

* Significant at .10 level.
** Significant at .05 level.
*** Significant at .01 level.
  a. Ordinary least squares regressions estimated using weighted data. The dependent variable is the follow-up voucher support item, which is coded from 1 (strongly disagree) to 4 (strongly agree). Unstandardized coefficients reported. For each nondichotomous independent variable, the impact coefficient represents the estimated change in the dependent variable (measured in standard deviations) when the independent variable shifts by two standard deviations, holding all other variables constant; for each dichotomous variable, the impact coefficient represents the estimated change in the dependent variable (measured in standard deviations) when the independent variable shifts from 0 to 1, holding all other variables constant. Models control for the full range of background and context variables, not all of which are reported in the tables.
  b. N is the unweighted number of respondents.

Parents (cont'd)		Nonparents							
Performance model 2		Background model		Context model		Attitude model		Performance model	
Coefficient	[Impact]	Coefficient	[Impact]	Coefficient	[Impact]	Coefficient	[Impact]	Coefficient	[Impact]
−.08***	[−.19]	−.04*	[−.10]	−.04*	[−.12]	−.04	[−.10]	−.04	[−.11]
−.02	[−.08]	−.00	[−.01]	.00	[.00]	.01	[.02]	.01	[.02]
.12**	[.11]	.22***	[.22]	.20**	[.18]	.13	[.12]	.13	[.12]
.08	[.07]	.30***	[.26]	.39***	[.35]	.30**	[.27]	.28**	[.25]
.10	[.09]	.41**	[.35]	.34**	[.31]	.24	[.22]	.20	[.18]
.32***	[.29]	.25**	[.23]	.24*	[.22]	.20	[.18]	.21	[.19]
−.03	[−.03]	.13	[.11]	−.26**	[−.24]	−.21	[−.19]	−.20	[−.18]
−.04***	[−.16]	−.07***	[−.44]	−.08***	[−.49]	−.07***	[−.45]	−.07***	[−.46]
.02	[.06]	.01	[.04]	.01	[.05]	.00	[.00]	−.00	[−.00]
−.00	[−.00]	.03*	[.09]	.03	[.07]	.03	[.08]	.04*	[.10]
.03	[.07]			.00	[.01]	.01	[.02]	.03	[.04]
−.03	[−.05]			−.08*	[−.11]	−.06	[−.08]	−.04	[−.05]
.11***	[.16]					.08**	[.12]	.09**	[.13]
.11***	[.17]					.17***	[.24]	.15***	[.21]
.05***	[.12]					.11***	[.24]	.10***	[.24]
.03	[.04]					.05	[.08]	.04	[.07]
.07**	[.10]					.03	[.05]	.03	[.04]
−.11***	[−.15]					−.17***	[−.23]	−.15***	[−.21]
.18***	[.27]					.20***	[.29]	.19***	[.27]
.00	[.01]					.01	[.03]	.01	[.03]
−.09***	[−.12]							−.16***	[−.20]
−.48***	[−.45]								
2.59***		3.11***		3.06***		2.53***		2.53***	
(2,072)		(1,458)		(1,317)		(1,317)		(1,317)	
.20		.08		.09		.15		.15	

to be more supportive—although we later found that this was true only among the informed. For them, party was a very strong influence, while for the uninformed it played no role at all. The results for the second support item may seem to suggest that party has mysteriously dropped out of the picture: as table 7-11 indicates, there is no longer any relationship between party and support for vouchers, whether we look at parents or nonparents. The answer to the mystery lies beneath the surface. A more detailed analysis would show that party continues to have the same strong influence as before among the informed, for parents and nonparents alike. But it would also show that things are now very different among the uninformed. Now they not only make a connection between party and vouchers, which they didn't do before, but they make a connection that is exactly the *opposite* of the one made by respondents who are informed. Among the uninformed, it is the Democrats who tend to be more supportive of vouchers, not the Republicans. This is why, in the population as a whole, party appears to be having zero effect—because it is having opposite effects among the informed and the uninformed.

It would be easy to write off this "wrong-way" shift among the uninformed as something irrational, or as a statistical oddity without meaning. But that would be a mistake. In the first place, it is a shift that turns up for both parents and nonparents, so it is probably not a fluke. In the second place, there is a substantive rationale for it that is quite persuasive. Traditionally, the elite battle lines put Republicans on the pro-voucher side and Democrats on the anti-voucher side, and informed citizens have had their views framed by this political lineup. But among the uninformed, there is essentially no framing. Moreover, the people who tend to support vouchers are those who are low in social class, minorities, from disadvantaged districts, and motivated by the inequities of the current system— characteristics associated with the Democratic party. Indeed, the main thrust of the modern voucher movement has been to promote constituencies and values normally associated with Democrats. Thus it only makes sense that, in the absence of framing effects, there could well be a tendency for Democrats to gravitate toward vouchers—which is precisely what happens among the uninformed. They seem to have learned something, in other words, during the course of the survey and arrived at a clearer sense of how to connect their partisanship to vouchers.

(3) In the earlier analysis, district context had the expected negative effect for public parents—the worse the district, the greater the support for vouchers—but no such effect showed up for nonparents. In all models, in fact, the effect was weakly positive. There is no good explanation for

this, and it flies in the face of all the other results we've been getting throughout the book. Ideally, it would be "corrected" if nonparents had a chance to think about things more fully. And as table 7-11 shows, this is precisely what happens. District context continues to have the expected negative impact among public parents—and for nonparents, the perverse results from the previous analysis are reversed, and the impact is now negative and significant, as it ought to be.

A more detailed analysis, moreover, would show that the big adjustment among nonparents comes from the uninformed. For this group the first time around, support for vouchers was 52 percent in the least advantaged districts, and 60 percent in the most advantaged districts: the opposite of what we would expect. The second time around, however, the support scores were 77 percent and 67 percent, respectively—reflecting a huge 25 percent jump in support within the least advantaged districts, compared to just 7 percent in the advantaged districts. Once again, therefore, a mysterious initial result has been "corrected" by what appears to be a rational adjustment among the uninformed.

(4) These are interesting cases that add up to a larger pattern. Perhaps the most compelling evidence, however, is contained in the findings on attitudes. The first time around, despite their lack of information, respondents did a surprisingly good job of connecting their attitudes to support for vouchers. But if respondents are actually thinking things over as they gain information, they should do an even better job the second time around—and in fact they do.

Consider the findings for public parents. A comparison of the attitude models in tables 7-11 and 7-4 shows that one attitude, the concern for moral values, becomes less relevant to the way parents think about the voucher issue. For every other attitude, however, the impact is greater the second time around than it was the first (as measured by the impact coefficients)—and *all* of these second-time impacts are statistically significant, even those associated with race and parental influence, which were not significant the first time through. The pattern is clear: in deciding where they stand on vouchers, parents are simply more responsive to these underlying issues than they were before, and better able to make the connection. Much the same is true for nonparents. Owing to their lesser stake in the voucher issue, their thinking was somewhat less structured than that of parents the first time through, and it remains less structured on the second item. Nonetheless, there are important commonalities in their patterns of effects—the declining role of moral values, the emerging influence of race—and nonparents too are clearly

Table 7-12. The Changing Influence of Attitudes on Voucher Support: Uninformed Public School Parents and Nonparents[a]

| | Public school parents | | | | Nonparents | | | |
| | Initial support | | Follow-up support | | Initial support | | Follow-up support | |
Variable	Coefficient	[Impact]	Coefficient	[Impact]	Coefficient	[Impact]	Coefficient	[Impact]
Attitudes								
Diversity (whites)	.04	[.05]	.13***	[.19]	.08	[.11]	.18***	[.26]
Inequity	.16***	[.24]	.20***	[.33]	.11*	[.14]	.25***	[.38]
School prayer	.03	[.06]	.03	[.05]	.06	[.11]	.08**	[.16]
Parent influence	.01	[.02]	.02	[.03]	.02	[.03]	-.03	[-.06]
School size	.05	[.08]	.08**	[.13]	.03	[.04]	.01	[.02]
Public school ideology	-.03	[-.05]	-.06*	[-.09]	-.01	[-.01]	-.14***	[-.21]
Markets	.14***	[.21]	.16***	[.25]	.24***	[.31]	.10**	[.15]
Moral value	.07*	[.10]	.01	[.02]	.08***	[.21]	-.02	[-.06]
Constant	2.56***	2.85***	2.46***	2.85***				
N[b]	(1,317)		(1,335)		(797)		(783)	
Adjusted R^2	.11		.13		.09		.15	

* Significant at .10 level.
** Significant at .05 level.
*** Significant at .01 level.

a. Ordinary least squares regressions estimated using weighted data. The dependent variable is either the initial or follow-up voucher support item, both of which are coded from 1 (strongly disagree) to 4 (strongly agree). Unstandardized coefficients reported. For each nondichotomous independent variable, the impact coefficient represents the estimated change in the dependent variable (measured in standard deviations) when the independent variable shifts by two standard deviations, holding all other variables constant; for each dichotomous variable, the impact coefficient represents the estimated change in the dependent variable (measured in standard deviations) when the independent variable shifts from 0 to 1, holding all other variables constant. Models control for the full range of background and context variables, not all of which are reported in the tables.

b. N is the unweighted number of respondents.

making stronger connections between key values and support for vouchers than they did before.

A more extensive analysis would show, not surprisingly, that these adjustments are largely driven by changes taking place among the uninformed. It is useful, therefore, to take a closer look at how the uninformed are now connecting their attitudes to their support for vouchers, and how this has evolved since their first attempt earlier in the survey. Table 7-12 sets out the relevant figures, which are taken from the corresponding attitude models.

What they show is quite revealing. Among uninformed nonparents—the group most open to new information and change—attitudes are now a much more potent force in determining where they stand on vouchers. The explained variance increases from .09 on the first support item to .15 on the second, which in relative terms is a substantial shift. The uninformed nonparents are simply better able to make connections. The changing nature of the *kinds* of connections they make, moreover, is an indication of how their priorities seem to have shifted during the survey. They put less emphasis than before on moral values and on markets—two key attitudes associated with the traditional wing of the voucher movement. They put a great deal more emphasis than before on racial diversity, inequity, and public school ideology, the first two of which are key attitudes associated with the modern wing of the movement. Indeed, the enhanced salience of these liberal social concerns is quite striking. The impact of racial diversity—indicating that those who *support* diversity are the ones who support vouchers—jumps from .11 on the first item to .24 on the second. And the impact of inequity—indicating that those who perceive the public system as inequitable are inclined to support vouchers—jumps from .14 on the first item to .38 on the second. These are huge increases, and strongly suggest that uninformed nonparents have emerged from the survey with a different view of what vouchers are about. In the context of voucher politics, they are thinking less like traditionalists and more like modernists. And there is simply more substance to their positions.

Uninformed parents are better grounded and less subject to shifting than uninformed nonparents are, so we should expect the new information to have less dramatic effects on them. Which is indeed the case. But still, the basic pattern is similar: the uniformed parents make a stronger connection between attitudes and voucher support the second time around, they put less emphasis than before on traditional considerations (moral values), and they put much more emphasis on the liberal social values of diversity and equity.

The fact that parents and nonparents have moved in similar directions, of course, does not suggest that this is somehow the right way to think about vouchers. The important point to take away from all this is a more neutral one: that the respondents' thinking seems to have evolved in a meaningful, systematic way during the survey. Having had a chance to mull things over and process new information, they seem to have arrived at a more coherent sense of the voucher issue and how it connects to their under-lying values, beliefs, and interests. Odd results from the earlier analysis have been "corrected." Connections have been strengthened. New values have come to the fore. There seems to be some "real thinking" going on here.

Conclusion

Virtually all surveys on the voucher issue rivet attention on just one num-ber: the percentage of Americans who express support for vouchers. In an intensely democratic society, this number is freighted with profound sig-nificance. If most Americans support vouchers, there are normative grounds for arguing that government ought to follow through, and there are prac-tical grounds for arguing that policymakers who value their jobs would be wise to respond. Little wonder, then, that voucher advocates want the magic polling numbers to be high and often latch onto the biggest num-bers available. And little wonder that critics want the magic numbers to be low, and often tout the smallest figures they can find.

These numbers don't mean very much. The percentage of people sup-porting vouchers will vary, sometimes greatly, with the wording of ques-tions and the broader content of the surveys—and this happens, in large measure, because people simply don't have definite views on the subject. As with most issues of public policy, people tend to be poorly informed, not especially interested, not very sophisticated in their thinking, and in-fluenced by whatever considerations come to the "top of the head" during the survey. Many could find themselves on either side of the issue, depend-ing on which considerations are evoked.

Our own survey shows that 60 percent of Americans initially express support for vouchers, and that 68 percent do so the second time through, after they have had a chance to think about things. On the surface, this would appear to be good news for the voucher movement. And perhaps it is. But the outcomes would have been different had the support items been worded differently and had the general content of the survey been differ-ent. And there can be no pretense that they are measuring the "true" level of public support anyway, for there isn't one to measure.

It would be wrong to conclude, though, that these support scores have nothing to tell us. They have useful information to convey, but most of it lies beneath the surface—in factors that explain why people respond as they do. This is what the current chapter has been about. Our challenge has been to determine how people connect the voucher issue to their own values, beliefs, and interests, and whether their expressions of support and opposition are thus meaningful reflections of what they care about.

The results paint a picture of the American public that is much rosier than one might expect, given the bashing citizens have taken over the years from political scientists. Although most people are unfamiliar with the voucher issue, they do a much better job of formulating their opinions than skeptics would lead us to expect. Our evidence suggests the following:

(1) There *is* a structure to the way the uninformed think about vouchers, and in basic respects (the main exception being political party) it is essentially the *same* structure that guides the thinking of the informed. The connections are just weaker on some counts.

(2) In evaluating vouchers, the uninformed are not simply responding mindlessly to what sounds good on the surface (at least not any more than the informed are).

(3) Although the uninformed are the big shifters, they often change their positions for good substantive reasons, just as the informed do.

(4) After being exposed to vouchers during the survey, the uninformed arrive at a stronger, more coherent structure for thinking about the issue. They seem to learn when given the opportunity and to express more meaningful opinions.

The purpose of this book is not to carry out finely grained tests that pit one theory of public opinion against another. Still, our analysis has been guided by some of these theories, and it sheds light on their relative merits. In the context of vouchers, it appears that Converse's minimalist view of the American public does not give people nearly enough credit, and that even Zaller's more charitable theory—which in most respects is quite consistent with our findings—sees people as less thoughtful and capable than they are. Even at the beginning of the survey, people do a surprisingly good job of linking the voucher issue to things that they care about. And as the survey progresses, their thinking seems to evolve, leading to opinions that are more meaningful still. In this respect, then, the rationalist scholars appear to be more on target. This doesn't mean that the masses are rocket scientists in disguise. It just means that their opinions are often thoughtful expressions of what matters to them.

Which brings us to the substance of the issue. When Americans take positions on the voucher issue, what *does* matter to them? The evidence points to several basic conclusions:

(1) For parents, an interest in going private is by far the most important determinant of their support for vouchers.

(2) Support for vouchers is especially strong among parents who are low in social class, minority, and from low-performing school districts: the same types of parents who are especially interested in going private. A similar pattern applies in weaker form to nonparents, who have less stake in the issue. It is clear that vouchers have a constituency among the less advantaged, and that the modern movement is cultivating a clientele that is very receptive indeed.

(3) The traditional wing of the movement also finds its reflection in public opinion. This is particularly true for religion, with both Catholics and born-again Christians especially supportive of vouchers. For party, however, the traditional connection—with Republicans more supportive than Democrats—only shows up among the informed, whose views are framed by the political battle lines of the national debate. Among the uninformed, party has no relevance to the voucher issue initially, but it becomes relevant during the course of the survey—and it is the Democrats among them who come to express greater sympathy for vouchers. This is a shift with substantive meaning, for the modern movement has special appeal to the disadvantaged and to people who put special weight on diversity and equity, and these are constituencies and values associated with the Democratic party. Without the traditional framing, to which the uninformed are oblivious, vouchers look very much like a Democratic issue.

(4) Support for vouchers is influenced by a whole range of attitudes, reflecting the specific concerns Americans have about their public schools. People tend to support vouchers when they think the public school system is inequitable and when they think diversity is an important social goal. They also tend to support vouchers when they believe in school prayer, when they want more influence for parents, when they prefer smaller schools to larger ones, and when they think competition and market-based incentives are conducive to school performance. They are less likely to support vouchers, on the other hand, when they believe in the public school system and are normatively committed to it.

(5) Overall satisfaction with public school performance (largely based on academics) is an important determinant of support for vouchers. But it plays a less prominent role here in the realm of public policy than it does in explaining why parents find private schools attractive options for their

children. A plausible reason is that, while parents see a direct connection between (low) performance and the personal value of going private, they are less convinced that vouchers will improve the public schools for everyone (via competition).

In most respects, the findings of this chapter bode well for the voucher movement and its political prospects. Vouchers appeal to broad constituencies: the American public is open to the idea, with no evidence of widespread resistance; public parents are attracted to private schools, and have a self-interested stake in vouchers; and the kinds of arguments that voucher advocates make—on issues ranging from equity to markets to school size—find a receptive audience. At the same time, vouchers also appeal to the more targeted constituencies that have propelled the movement's politics: they are popular among the less advantaged and among people who are concerned about diversity and social equity; they are also popular among Catholics, born-again Christians, and (informed) Republicans.

These combinations—constituencies that are general and constituencies that are specialized, constituencies that are modern and constituencies that are traditional—are potentially very powerful. They give the movement a lot to work with in mobilizing public support and in fashioning the kind of heterogeneous coalition necessary for real political progress.

Unavoidably, its efforts will be fraught with uncertainty. Most Americans do not have well-developed opinions, and, as the political battle generates new information, the contours of public opinion could change, possibly in ways adverse to the voucher movement. There are no guarantees. But even so, our analysis suggests that Americans are not mere ciphers whose views are totally up for grabs. There is a structure to their thinking about vouchers, a consistency to the way they connect their values, beliefs, and interests to the issue—and these elements should provide a fairly stable core to public opinion and lend a certain form and predictability to the larger political struggle.

8 *The Consequences of a Voucher System*

WHEN PEOPLE DECIDE whether vouchers would make good public policy, they are likely to base their judgment on some notion, however selective or poorly developed, of what the consequences would be if vouchers were adopted. There are two types of consequences for them to consider. One has to do with the effects of vouchers on society. The other has to do with the effects on them personally.

What these effects are, and whether they are good or bad, is largely what the national debate is about. Advocates see immense benefits for society: vouchers would improve the schools, promote social equity, give parents more influence, bring down education costs, and produce an education system that is more effective, productive, and just. Critics argue the opposite: vouchers would ruin the public schools, exacerbate social inequities, undermine parent interests, escalate costs, and create a system that is elitist and unfair.

Elite opinions are just as divided on the personal value of vouchers. As advocates see it, vouchers would allow parents to seek out better schools, to gain more control over their children's educations, and to make schools more responsive to their needs and concerns. Critics discount all this. Most parents would have a difficult time exercising choice to good advantage, and, were they to venture out into the private sector, would find discrimination and elitism shutting the doors they want to enter. Private schools, they argue, are really no better than public schools anyway, and children wouldn't learn more even if they were admitted.

Our survey asks Americans a variety of questions along both dimensions, the social and the personal, and in this chapter we'll take a look at their answers. This allows us to move beyond a simple analysis of support and opposition to explore what people think about a full range of substantive issues related to vouchers—and to determine what types of issues (and consequences) seem to matter most in explaining the positions they ultimately take on policy.

As part of this larger effort, we will be examining a question that is not only central to an understanding of vouchers, but has also been a matter of controversy among political scientists for decades. When Americans take a position on policy, are they mainly thinking about what is best for society, or are they mainly thinking about what is best for themselves? Are they approaching the issue as citizens or as consumers? We already know that self-interest has an important influence on parental support for vouchers. But we don't really know how important the social side of the ledger is and how the two compare. In this chapter, we'll find out—and gain new insight into the democratic character of the voucher issue.[1]

The Social Consequences of Vouchers

When we ask people about the social impacts of vouchers, we are moving (again) into uncertain waters. These issues are inherently complex, even for experts, and most Americans are thinking about them for the first time, with little information or background. They are not being asked to state a simple preference, but rather to evaluate objective conditions and cause-effect relationships in the real world—questions to which they literally do not know the answers. Perhaps even more than with the support items, then, their answers here will tend to be "top of the head" responses, sensitive to question wording and whatever considerations come to their minds at the time.

As we saw in the last chapter, however, there *is* important content in what people have to say, even when they are quite uninformed. And if we put their responses to careful use, we can learn something from them.

Race and Equity

When elites debate the social consequences of a voucher system, there is plenty of disagreement over whether vouchers will promote better schools or help kids to learn more. But the disagreement is especially bitter on matters of social equity and race. We already know that these issues have been central to the modern voucher movement, and we know what advocates and critics have to say on either side. What do the American people seem to think?

Let's begin by considering an item that asks respondents to choose between two arguments about the impact of vouchers on race: "(a) Vouchers would lead to racial and ethnic separation, because some groups would choose not to go to school with other groups, or (b) Vouchers would promote racial and ethnic balance, because minorities would have access to many more schools than they do now." The results are set out in table 8-1, and they are quite striking. They show that a large majority of the American public—60 percent to 25 percent—think that vouchers are likely to have *positive* effects on racial balance by giving minorities more opportunities. The figures are in roughly the same ballpark for all the subgroups we've distinguished here: nonparents, public parents, private parents, and inner-city parents. But it is the (mainly minority) parents from the inner city who are most optimistic (at 72 percent).

These results are consistent with the findings about race and class from previous chapters. The people who are most interested in private schools and vouchers are the less advantaged—and those who, whatever their class, are most concerned about social equity. So it shouldn't be surprising that people tend to associate vouchers with expanded choices for minorities and with positive consequences for racial balance. The basic pattern is the same.

A second item on race paints a somewhat different picture. This one asks respondents whether they agree or disagree with the following statement: "Private and parochial schools would discriminate against poor and minority kids." As table 8-1 shows, 49 percent of Americans disagree with this statement and thus give a response favorable to vouchers. But there is also a large minority, 43 percent, who suspect that disadvantaged kids would not have an equal shot at the private schools they want to attend. Taken at face value, this item points to a higher level of public concern than the first item did.

Now let's turn to issues of class-based inequalities. One approach is to ask respondents whether they think vouchers would be particularly valuable to children who are economically disadvantaged. The survey does so by asking whether they agree or disagree with the following statement: "Vouchers would be especially helpful to low-income kids, because their public schools tend to have the most problems." By a huge majority, 76 percent to 18 percent, Americans agree that low-income children would benefit from vouchers. As table 8-1 shows, oversized margins obtain for all subgroups. But support is highest among the inner-city poor, at 82

Table 8-1. *Vouchers' Effects on Diversity and Equity*
Percent, unless otherwise indicated[a]

Survey item	Total population	Non-parents	Public school parents	Private school parents	Inner-city parents
Effect of vouchers on racial balance					
Promote racial balance	60	58	64	70	72
Lead to racial separation	25	26	22	15	16
Don't know	15	16	14	15	11
Private schools would discriminate					
Agree	43	43	46	24	47
Disagree	49	48	46	73	44
Don't know	9	9	8	4	8
Vouchers help low-income children					
Agree	76	76	77	80	82
Disagree	18	18	18	16	14
Don't know	6	6	6	4	5
Wealthy would benefit, poor would be left behind					
Agree	41	42	40	30	35
Disagree	50	48	52	65	57
Don't know	10	11	8	6	8
Who benefits from vouchers? Current private school parents	24	26	19	22	16
Parents without choice now	65	62	71	72	75
Don't know	11	12	9	6	9
N[b]	(4,700)	(1,617)	(2,553)	(530)	(539)

a. Percentages are based on weighted data. They may not sum to 100 due to rounding.
b. N is the unweighted number of respondents.

percent. They *are* low income, and their take on the equity issue suggests that they see vouchers as a valuable response to their needs.

As with race, however, there are also signs of concern. These show up in a second item that deals directly with the class issue, asking respondents to agree or disagree with the following: "It will be the better-off families who use vouchers, leaving poor families in the public schools." By this measure, as table 8-1 indicates, the weight of public opinion again favors a positive view of vouchers: 50 percent don't expect a class bias in the types of families that benefit from vouchers, while 41 percent do. Here too, inner-city parents are far more positive (with 57 percent rejecting the bias argument) than the general public on this issue, and this is a fact of social significance: for they *are* poor, yet they do not suspect that the well-to-do are going to run away with the benefits and somehow leave them behind. Having said this, though, we still have to recognize that—by this measure, at least—a large segment of the public remains skeptical. Many expect a class bias that favors the economically advantaged.

Let's consider one more equity item. Critics commonly argue that vouchers would be an elitist windfall for private school parents, not a means of empowering parents who currently don't have choice. The survey gets at this by asking respondents to choose between the following arguments: "(a) Vouchers will mainly help those who already have children in private schools, or (b) Vouchers will give choices to those who do not have them now." Here are the results: 24 percent of Americans think vouchers would primarily benefit existing private parents, while 65 percent think they would expand choices for parents generally. In this case, most people appear to have very positive expectations about the impact of vouchers on social equity. But again, it is the inner-city poor (at 75 percent) who are most likely to believe that vouchers will have egalitarian effects.

Considered as a whole, these findings would seem to be good news for voucher advocates. We have to remember, however, that people might have responded differently to these issues had the questions been worded differently or presented in a different setting. Aside from our own survey, the study that probes popular attitudes about vouchers in greatest detail is Public Agenda's recent *On Thin Ice*.[2] This survey is useful in helping us gain perspective. We can learn something by comparing its results to our own and asking what both studies seem to be telling us about public opinion.

At one point in its survey, Public Agenda asks a series of agree-disagree items about the social consequences of vouchers, three of which have to do with race and equity. Let's take a look at them. The first argues, "There will be more segregation because many parents will send their kids to schools where there are students from similar backgrounds." Our own survey showed that 60 percent of Americans see vouchers as promoting racial balance. But the Public Agenda results are precisely the opposite: 65 percent agree that vouchers would cause greater segregation. Right away, then, we have reason to wonder what our own findings on racial balance—or theirs, for that matter—are really telling us.

The second Public Agenda item heightens the mystery. It asks respondents whether they think that "Parents and students who care most would take advantage of vouchers, and the cream of the crop would leave public schools." Results show that 64 percent of Americans agree, which suggests they think that vouchers would promote inequities. Our own survey asks a similar question, about whether better-off families would be the ones using vouchers, but we find that a much smaller segment of the public, 41 percent, sees it as a problem. Again, different findings.

Interestingly, things come back into alignment with the third Public Agenda item, which presents respondents with the following claim: "School vouchers will rescue many kids from failing public schools and give them a chance to fulfill their potential." This time, 64 percent of Americans see vouchers as having a very positive impact on social equity—a result consistent with most of our own findings.

What is going on here? Two factors probably contribute to the disconcerting pattern of results. The first is that these issues are truly complex, and most people may be quite uncertain how to answer them. As such, they may be especially sensitive to question wording and any other cues within the surveys, and thus capable of expressing very different opinions. The second is that, as all survey researchers are aware, there can be a positive bias to agree-disagree items, especially when respondents are poorly informed: they will sometimes seek to resolve their uncertainty (and perhaps try to please the interviewer) by simply agreeing with the statements posed to them. This is not always a problem, and survey designers have ways to reduce its severity.[3] But a positive response bias on the agree-disagree items may have affected the outcomes we're observing here—and if so, this could help us understand patterns that otherwise make little sense.

The Public Agenda items we've just discussed were part of a battery of nine agree-disagree items, all of which asked about the social consequences of vouchers. Of these items, two were worded such that a pro-voucher response called for an "agree," while seven were worded the other way around, so that a pro-voucher response called for a "disagree." The actual responses people give, of course, turn in part on the substantive content of each item. But if we put this aside, we can get a rough sense of any response bias by comparing the percentage of pro-voucher responses for the two types of items. If there *is* a positive response bias, people should be more inclined to give the pro-voucher response to the first type of item (where pro-voucher calls for an "agree") than for the second type of item (where pro-voucher calls for a "disagree").

The evidence suggests that this is what happens. Based on the full set of results reported by Public Agenda, 73 percent of Americans gave pro-voucher responses (on average) to its items of the first type, but just 37 percent gave pro-voucher responses to its items of the second type. This could be a fluke, of course, but it probably isn't. When Public Agenda characterizes public opinion on a particular issue, such as the connection between vouchers and racial segregation, how people respond seems to be heavily influenced by which way the question is worded. Our own survey is victim to the same problem. If we arrange our own agree-disagree items on the social consequences of vouchers into the same two categories (there are three items in the first and four in the second), the average incidence of pro-voucher responses is 75 percent for items of the first type, but 48 percent for items of the second type.

If this assessment is basically correct, the response bias goes a long way toward making sense of the survey evidence. Consider the racial issue. Our own study shows that people associate vouchers with racial balance, while Public Agenda shows that they associate vouchers with racial segregation. In this case, however, our results are not based on an agree-disagree item at all, but rather on a forced-choice format that gives people arguments on both sides. There is no reason to think that this format involves any bias, one way or the other. The Public Agenda finding, on the other hand, is based on an agree-disagree item of the second type, which, as we have seen, heavily discourages pro-voucher responses. In large measure, this seems to be why the two studies produce such different findings on race.

Now consider the Public Agenda equity items. Public Agenda reported one item (about the "creaming" problem) in which people thought vouchers would have negative effects on social equity, and another (about rescuing kids from failing schools) in which people thought vouchers would have positive effects. A good part of this differential probably doesn't have anything to do with substance at all. For the "creaming" issue was posed as an agree-disagree item of the second type, while the "rescuing kids" issue was posed as an agree-disagree item of the first type—and if there were a response bias at work, we would expect the former to produce more negative responses than the latter. Which is just what happens.

With this problem of response bias in mind, let's look back and reassess our own data on race and equity.

(1) Two of the items—one on racial balance, another on whether vouchers help private kids or extend choice to all—are based on the forced-choice format, and we have no reason to think they are biased. It is valuable to know, then, that the pro-voucher contingent is 60 percent on the first and 65 percent on the second. To the extent we can think of Americans as having meaningful opinions on these questions, both suggest they think vouchers will have positive social effects.

(2) The other items, however, raise questions. One asks whether vouchers would be especially helpful for low-income kids, and it evokes an especially high vote of confidence from the public, with 76 percent giving the pro-voucher response. But this is an agree-disagree item of the first type, and it probably inflates public support. The overall evidence suggests that people tend to be positive about the equity effects of vouchers, but not this positive.

(3) The other two social items that we've discussed—one on whether private schools would discriminate, the other on whether vouchers would favor better-off families—are problematic in the other direction. On the surface, both seem to signal areas of public concern, because in each case the incidence of pro-voucher responses is low—49 percent on the first, 50 percent on the second. But some of this is simply due to the way the questions are worded: they are agree-disagree items of the second type and thus are biased against pro-voucher responses. The best bet is that Americans are more positive on these counts.

All in all, the findings probably *are* pretty good news for the voucher movement. True, there are signs of suspicion and mixed views. And almost surely, the response bias is such a big factor here because people don't have firm, well-developed opinions—and could, under the right circumstances, turn against vouchers. But a balanced look at the evidence suggests that, at least for now, Americans are inclined to see vouchers in rather favorable terms and, in particular, to see them as having positive effects on racial balance and social equity.

Competition, Choice, and the Quality of Schools

While race and equity are volatile issues in American politics, perhaps the most fundamental ideas about the social impacts of vouchers have to do with the effects of competition and choice on the quality of schools. Among elites, the battle lines are firmly drawn, the arguments well developed. But what do ordinary Americans seem to think?

In the voucher section of our survey, the item that addresses this issue most directly is one that asks respondents to choose between two conflicting arguments about competition: "Under a voucher plan, public schools have to compete with private schools, because students can go where they want. Which is closer to your view? (a) Competition would be good for the public schools, because they would have to improve in order to keep students, or (b) Competition would hurt the public schools, because they would lose the resources they need to do a good job." This simplifies the

Table 8-2. *Competition, Choice, and the Quality of Schools*
Percent, unless otherwise indicated[a]

Survey item	Total population	Non-parents	Public school parents	Private school parents	Inner-city parents
Effects of competition					
Good for schools	56	54	58	70	58
Hurts schools	31	32	31	21	31
Don't know	13	14	11	10	11
Vouchers help get kids out of bad schools					
Agree	77	75	80	85	83
Disagree	16	17	15	11	11
Don't know	7	8	5	4	6
Parents would have enough information					
Agree	72	70	77	84	81
Disagree	21	23	17	12	14
Don't know	7	8	6	4	5
Parents don't understand children's needs					
Agree	57	58	56	56	67
Disagree	39	38	41	41	30
Don't know	4	4	3	2	3
N[b]	(4,700)	(1,617)	(2,553)	(530)	(539)

a. Percentages are based on weighted data. They may not sum to 100 due to rounding.
b. N is the unweighted number of respondents.

issue, of course, but it does present respondents with arguments on either side and presumably reduces the problem of response bias.

The results on this item, set out in table 8-2, are suggestive. When given a choice of arguments, 56 percent of Americans agree that competition would promote educational improvement, while 31 percent accept the critics' claim that it would harm the schools by draining off resources. This is an interesting result. It is not a hands-down victory for competition and points to a sizable minority of people who think vouchers would be bad for the public schools. Still, it suggests that, even when faced with the standard argument of opponents, most people believe competition would have positive effects. Its appeal, moreover, is widespread across all subgroups.[4]

For perspective, let's consider the Public Agenda study again. With regard to competition, its survey contains two items of special relevance. The first asks whether public school teachers and administrators "will try harder to do a good job if they see they are losing more and more kids to the private schools." By this measure, Americans appear to be almost evenly split on the issue—49 percent agree and 47 percent disagree—and less positively disposed toward competition than our own measure suggests. If a positive response bias is at work, moreover (which is unclear, as this item was not part of the battery of items discussed earlier), there is even less support for competition here than meets the eye. On the second item, however, the results look very different. This one gives people three options, to which they respond as follows: 57 percent say the public schools "would fight to get better and eventually improve in order to hold on to their students," 18 percent say the schools "would become steadily worse as they lose more money and more students," and 19 percent say the schools would change very little. Here, Americans present themselves as very positive indeed toward competition.

The differences across these two items attest to how sensitive the public's responses are to the precise wording of the questions. The explanation in this case may be that the first item personalizes the impact of competition (in terms of teachers and administrators) while the second describes it impersonally (in terms of schools). But we cannot know. If we look more broadly at all these items, though, both our own and Public Agenda's, two conclusions seem to be justified. One is that Americans tend to see competition as good for schools. The second is that their support for competition can drop off markedly, depending on how the issue is framed. Their positive inclinations probably do not run very deep.

The latter is reinforced by evidence from Public Agenda focus groups. In several cities around the country, participants discussed the pros and cons of vouchers, most of them considering the issue for the first time. And although they tended to be positive about the voucher idea and positive about competition, Public Agenda reports that "almost no one saw vouchers as something that would transform the local public schools."[5] The bottom line is that people seem to think competition is a good thing, but that they don't expect dramatic results from it.

In some measure, competition almost surely suffers as a political idea because the rationale behind it is abstract and theoretical, and its effects indirect. To economists, competition works by creating incentives for efficient behavior and by weeding out those who don't or can't behave efficiently. This logic is not so obvious to the average citizen, and the consequences it predicts are off in the future somewhere. These drawbacks do not apply, however, to a second basic way that vouchers use markets to shape society: namely, through the simple act of choice itself.

Even if competition did not work as advocates contend, and thus had no impact on school quality, vouchers would still allow parents to choose their kids' schools and take direct action on their own behalf. There is nothing theoretical about this aspect of markets. It is straightforward and easy to understand—and likely, one would suspect, to play a prominent role in the public's thinking.

Now let's return to our own survey and to an item that focuses on the direct effects of choice per se. This item presents respondents with a simple claim, "Vouchers would help parents get their kids out of bad schools and into better ones," and asks whether they agree or disagree. The responses are set out in table 8-2. By a huge majority, 77 percent to 16 percent, Americans agree that vouchers would be directly beneficial to parents and children in this crucial way. Opinions on this issue are overwhelmingly positive for all subgroups, but (private parents aside) the most enthusiastic responses come from inner-city parents—who, by any account, are the ones most likely to find themselves trapped in bad schools.

We need to be cautious about this item, because its wording could have produced a positive response bias. Support for the proposition may not be as high as our figures suggest. Two Public Agenda items provide a bit more nuance. The first asks whether, in the respondent's view, kids who are currently doing badly in public schools will improve their performance in private schools. The results show that 23 percent of Americans have "a lot of confidence" that these kids will improve, 40 percent have "some confidence," and 32 percent have "little or no confidence." When asked a similar question about low-income children in poor neighborhoods, 31 percent say most or all of these kids will improve, 45 percent say only some will, and 20 percent say only a few or none will.

In effect, both Public Agenda items are about the consequences of direct parental choice, just as ours was. Our question asks whether vouchers would allow parents to find better schools for their kids, which, it appears (even with a downward adjustment), most people agree will be the case— but the Public Agenda items ask what the benefits will be when children actually attend those schools. And the answers here are much more mixed. Most Americans express qualified optimism, but will not say with conviction that they expect most kids to be better off in private schools (and thus with vouchers).

Some of this may be due to the framing of the Public Agenda items, for they tend to set up the midrange responses as the only reasonable way to answer the questions. Their tepid findings, moreover, don't square with the widespread belief that private schools are better than public schools, which surely implies that Americans *do* think kids learn more in the private sector. Indeed, a recent Phi Delta Kappa poll shows just that. When people were asked whether children moving from public to private schools would have higher, lower, or similar academic achievement as a result, a full 65 percent indicated that they thought such kids would learn more.[6]

Nonetheless, the lesson here is that the apparent enthusiasm our own study has uncovered with regard to the benefits of parental choice is probably tempered by uncertainties that lie beneath the surface. People like the power of action that choice brings with it, and they believe that many (but not all) kids will be better off if they use a voucher to go private. But they don't think of choice as a silver bullet.

Finally, our survey also gets at a third dimension related to how choice and competition work (or don't) in the education marketplace. This one has to do with whether parents are up to the challenges of a choice system. Advocates think parents can make good choices for their kids. Critics think they can't and often portray parents as downright incompetent. To see what the general public thinks, our survey asks them to agree or disagree with the following statement: "Most parents would be able to get enough information to make good choices for their children." Here again, the vast majority of Americans give the pro-market response, with more than 72 percent seeing parents as capable decisionmakers. This positive view of parent capabilities is widespread across all subgroups. But it is especially high, interestingly enough, among the inner-city poor (at 81 percent)—the very parents regarded as least capable by critics.

These figures may be on the high side, because the item is probably subject to a positive response bias. Indeed, it is worth noting that, in an item asked much earlier in the survey, respondents were presented with the following agree-disagree item: "Most parents really don't understand the education needs of their children"—and only 39 percent gave the pro-parent response by disagreeing with it. In this case, they seem to be saying that parents are *not* capable of making good choices for their kids. Inner-city parents, moreover, rather than being the most optimistic about parents by this measure, are the most likely (at 67 percent) to say that parents aren't up to the task. This item, however, is also vulnerable to a positive response bias—which translates, in this case, into an excessive number of people who agree with the anti-parent wording of the question.

Given these ambiguities, the parent influence item that we have been using throughout the book may be helpful here. This question is not couched in agree-disagree format, but poses a forced choice between two reasonable alternatives: "(a) Parents should have more influence than they do now, or (b) Parents should trust the judgment of administrators and teachers, because they know more about education than parents do." As we saw in chapter 2, respondents come down heavily on the side of parents: 66 percent say parents should be granted more influence, while only 27 percent put their faith in professionals. There is no reason to suspect any response bias here.

What do Americans "really" think about parents, then? More than likely, there is simply an ambivalence to their views: they are inclined to see parents in a positive light, but they also have worries that lie just beneath the surface, and when prompted by the right framing, they can express opinions about parents that are rather negative.

Much the same is true of their thinking about markets more generally. There is a lot of variance to their views and a lot of uncertainty beneath the surface, but on the whole Americans come across as positive: they think competition is likely to improve the public schools, and they think choice is a direct means of getting kids out of bad schools and into better ones. They are not firmly committed to these beliefs. But they are inclined to sit on the voucher side of the fence.

Practical Issues

In politics, the two dimensions we've just considered—race and equity, competition and choice—are at the heart of the debate over the social consequences of vouchers. A number of other issues are often important to the debate as well, however. These are more practical and less associated with partisan intensity, but they could well be important concerns for many Americans.

Consider the simple issue of cost. When costs are discussed at the elite level, the arguments on either side are predictable. Critics argue that vouchers would lead to higher education costs (and higher taxes), because it would be expensive to dismantle the current system and put new structures in its place, and because the vouchers themselves would be expensive. Advocates argue that vouchers would help control costs because the money could come out of existing budgets, because schools would have incentives to operate more efficiently, and because more children would get educated in lower-cost private schools.

Objectively, there are no easy answers here. The true costs of a voucher system depend on exactly how it is designed and funded, and these details are rarely specified in public argument. Even if they were, the design details and their cost implications would probably be too complex for most people to fathom. Be this as it may, the cost issue is of concrete

Table 8-3. *Practical Concerns about Vouchers*
Percent, unless otherwise indicated[a]

Survey item	Total population	Non-parents	Public school parents	Private school parents	Inner-city parents
Vouchers' effect on cost of education					
Increase	47	47	46	39	39
No effect	15	14	17	18	21
Control	26	26	26	35	26
Don't know	12	13	12	8	14
Large-scale voucher plan too risky					
Agree	48	50	47	39	38
Disagree	42	40	45	55	55
Don't know	10	11	8	6	7
Worry that public school employees lose jobs					
Agree	39	39	38	31	37
Disagree	51	49	54	61	54
Don't know	11	12	8	8	8
N[b]	(4,700)	(1,617)	(2,553)	(530)	(539)

a. Percentages are based on weighted data. They may not sum to 100 due to rounding.
b. N is the unweighted number of respondents.

relevance to all taxpayers, and people are likely to have opinions on it, whatever the basis.

The survey asks the following simple question: "What effect do you think a voucher plan would have on the overall costs of education? Would it probably increase costs, help control costs, or have no effect on them?" The results, set out in table 8-3, show that the most popular perception by far—held by 47 percent of the American public—is that vouchers will increase the costs of education. Only 26 percent accept the notion that market-based reforms will help control education costs. And just 15 percent think there will be no effect on costs. For each of our subgroups— even for private parents and inner-city parents—the modal belief is that vouchers will be expensive, imposing costs beyond what it takes to run the current system.

This is bad news for voucher advocates, for the cost issue can only temper popular support for vouchers. People may be impressed with the possible benefits of a voucher system, but some and perhaps many of them may not be willing to pay what strikes them as a steep price.

Now let's look at a second practical issue: risk. Voucher advocates rarely talk about the risks involved in moving away from the traditional education system toward a new arrangement whose structure and operation are very different. In their eyes, vouchers would have the consequences they expect—for school quality, for social justice, for efficiency—and they see no reason why there would be any operational problems in shifting from the traditional system to a voucher system. Vouchers would work, and work as expected.

One doesn't have to be a staunch critic, however, to believe that there are risks involved in shifting wholesale from the traditional system to a voucher system. Nothing is guaranteed. Most everyone knows enough about government to know that a lot can go wrong when lofty ideas are put into practice, and that unintended consequences of all sorts are common. In addition, we must remember that people are fairly satisfied with the current system and are not desperate for change. When things are pretty good, the risks of change seem greater.

It makes sense, then, that many people might be leery of vouchers for reasons of risk: not because they don't support the idea or associate it with positive outcomes, but because they are afraid of what might go wrong and what they might have to give up—a reasonably satisfactory traditional system—if things don't work out as planned. The survey includes an item that tries to get at this. It asks respondents to agree or disagree with the following statement: "I worry that a large-scale voucher plan might be too risky and experimental to try out on our kids."

The results suggest that many people do seem to be concerned about the risks of moving toward a voucher system. In the public as a whole, 48 percent say they worry that vouchers might be too risky to implement as public policy, while 42 percent don't see this as a problem. Because this is an agree-disagree item, however, its wording may inflate the extent to which Americans are actually worried.

Again, Public Agenda provides us with some perspective. Two of its items are relevant here. One presents respondents with the following claim: "There would be chaos and confusion because there would be less control of who goes to what school"—with which 43 percent agree and 50 percent disagree. This item, like our own, is subject to a positive response bias and may overstate the public's concern. Even so, it reinforces the notion that risk is quite relevant for many people. The second item is especially helpful because it is not presented in agree-disagree format. It asks respondents whether they would want a voucher program established in their local area. Thirty-two percent say they would, 19 percent say they wouldn't, and 44 percent say "I would want a school voucher program in my area only if it first shows good results in other communities"—which is a pretty good indication that a sizable number of people, including many who are supportive of vouchers, are concerned about the risks and want some assurance that vouchers will actually work as advertised.

All things considered, then, attitudes toward risk may well be a factor in shaping the politics of vouchers. Despite the sympathy people have for vouchers, many are afraid that things may not work out as planned, and afraid of giving up what they have. This could dilute their enthusiasm for a reform that in basic respects they seem to like.

There is one final issue of a practical nature that needs to be discussed here: jobs. This is an issue that rarely gets talked about openly in politics. Nonetheless, elites are well aware of it, and behind the scenes it is clearly a major motivator for some of the participants. The fact is, the American school system is an enormous reservoir of jobs, perhaps the biggest in the country. These jobs are valuable to those who hold them: teachers, administrators, janitors, cafeteria workers, nurses, librarians, psychologists. They are also valuable to the public officials and administrators who get to fill the positions. Patronage is power.[7]

Millions of people have stakes in these jobs. And a voucher system puts many of them at risk: for when kids and resources move out of the public sector into private schools, public education will be smaller and leaner. Elites and job-holders, then, are threatened by vouchers and have reason to be opposed. Their friends, families, and allies may react the same way.

To get at this prospect, the survey asked respondents to agree or disagree with the following: "I worry that some people who work for the public school system might lose their jobs because of vouchers." By 51 percent to 39 percent, Americans disagree and indicate that they are not too concerned about the jobs issue. They are probably even less concerned than these figures suggest, moreover, as this item is likely subject to a positive response bias that inflates the level of agreement.

Nonetheless, a nontrivial minority *is* concerned about jobs, and this is politically important. At the current time, with people so uninformed about vouchers, there is little reason for many of them to connect vouchers to jobs—and to the job-holders they may care about. But as vouchers gain in power, and as opponents launch publicity campaigns to stop them, the jobs issue—and the very real effects on enormous numbers of current job-holders—may become much more salient.

To get a better sense of this issue's political potential, consider the following: our survey asks respondents whether they or anyone in their

Table 8-4. *Impact of Social Considerations on Support for Vouchers*[a]

Variable	Public school parents				Inner-city parents				Nonparents	
	No control for personal interest		Control for personal interest		No control for personal interest		Control for personal interest			
	Coefficient	[Impact]	Coefficient	[Impact]	Coefficient	[Impact]	Coefficient	[Impact]	Coefficient	[Impact]
Markets										
Competition good	.13***	[.22]	.10***	[.17]	.04	[.09]	.02	[.05]	.12***	[.21]
Out of bad schools	.16***	[.38]	.11***	[.25]	.17***	[.44]	.10***	[.26]	.12***	[.27]
Parent information	.03*	[.07]	.03**	[.07]	.03	[.08]	.02	[.06]	.08***	[.20]
Race and equity										
Racial balance	.15***	[.25]	.13***	[.22]	.01	[.02]	-.02	[-.03]	.13***	[.20]
Private discrimination[b]	-.01	[-.03]	-.00	[-.01]	-.05**	[-.19]	-.05**	[-.20]	.04**	[.12]
Help low-income	.12***	[.29]	.10***	[.25]	.07**	[.20]	.02	[.07]	.15***	[.36]
Benefit wealthy	-.01	[-.04]	-.02**	[-.07]	-.02	[-.08]	-.00	[-.02]	.01	[.04]
Benefit private kids[c]	-.07**	[-.10]	-.05**	[-.07]	-.05	[-.09]	-.03	[-.05]	-.15***	[-.25]
Practical considerations										
Cost	-.14***	[-.23]	-.12***	[-.18]	-.15***	[-.28]	-.11***	[-.22]	-.22***	[-.35]
Risk	-.14***	[-.42]	-.10***	[-.30]	-.08***	[-.30]	-.07***	[-.27]	-.13***	[-.37]
Lose jobs	-.01	[-.04]	-.02*	[-.06]	-.01	[-.04]	-.00	[-.02]	-.02	[-.04]
Constant	2.63***		1.87***		3.23***		2.61***		2.64***	
N[d]	(2,161)		(2,095)		(480)		(464)		(1,317)	
Adjusted R^2	.37		.47		.20		.29		.40	

* Significant at .10 level.
** Significant at .05 level.
*** Significant at .01 level.

a. Ordinary least squares regressions estimated using weighted data. The dependent variable is the follow-up voucher support item, which is coded from 1 (strongly disagree) to 4 (strongly agree). "Personal interest" is based on a survey item that measures an individual's interest in putting a voucher to personal use. Unstandardized coefficients reported. The impact coefficient represents the estimated change in the dependent variable (measured in standard deviations) when the independent variable shifts by two standard deviations, holding all other variables constant. Models control for the full range of background and context variables.

b. "Private discrimination" refers to the survey item that asks respondents whether private schools would discriminate against disadvantaged kids (see text).

c. "Benefit private kids" refers to the survey item that asks whether vouchers would benefit existing private school children exclusively or give choices to those who do not already have them (see text).

d. N is the unweighted number of respondents.

immediate family has ever worked for a public school district as a regular employee, and 33 percent of Americans answered affirmatively.[8] This is a stunning figure. For now, analysis (not presented here) suggests that people who have job-related connections to the schools do not worry about the loss of jobs more than other people do, nor are they more likely to oppose vouchers. But this will almost surely change as the politics of vouchers heats up in the years ahead.

Which Social Concerns Seem to Matter—and Which Don't?

So far, we have taken a look at where Americans stand on social issues. But we don't yet have much sense for how influential these issues are in shaping their stands on vouchers. Consider the problem of costs, for example. We know many Americans worry about the costs of vouchers, but that tells us nothing about whether a concern for costs affects their support for vouchers or whether costs are more important to them than equity, race, or parent capabilities. The question is: which social concerns (if any) seem to matter and which don't?

Here is the approach, which is purposely kept very simple.[9] The dependent variable is the second voucher support item, which was asked at the end of the voucher section, just after the social items.[10] The estimation is carried out separately, as usual, for public parents, nonparents, and inner-city parents. In these models, support for vouchers is regressed against the various social concerns, controlling for background and contextual factors. This makes for easy comparability across groups. Additional models are estimated for public parents and inner-city parents, however, to recognize that they also have a personal stake in the voucher issue (explored later on) whose influence needs to be taken into account if the impacts of social concerns are to be well estimated. These additional models are identical to the first set, except that they include a control for whether parents are interested in using vouchers for their own children.[11]

The results are set out in table 8-4. Here is a brief summary, based on the first set of models (without controls for parental interest in going private).

(1) If one factor stands out, it is the *risks* people associate with a voucher system. For public parents, risk has greater influence on support for vouchers than any other social concern. For nonparents, it is essentially in a three-way tie for the top spot. And for inner-city parents, it is essentially in a two-way tie for second. We know that most people take a positive position on vouchers, so the risks at this point are not high enough to scare them away. But this could change, and its salience may well be a key to the future politics of vouchers—for opponents could have their greatest

political impact, this finding suggests, by convincing Americans that vouchers are risky.

(2) After risk, public parents put greatest emphasis on the role of vouchers in getting kids out of bad schools. And significantly, this is the top concern of inner-city parents, far outdistancing any other factor. Note that, for both groups, the emphasis is on the direct effects of choice in empowering parents to take action on their own behalf. The effect of competition on school quality—a much less direct effect—is farther down the list and indeed is not really of any salience to parents in the inner city. It appears that, to the extent a belief in markets affects their support for vouchers—as we know it does, from chapter 7's analysis—Americans are thinking largely in terms of the direct benefits of choice rather than the indirect benefits of competition.

(3) Nonparents come across as much more concerned with practical issues: of their three top concerns, two are cost and risk. This is entirely in keeping with their more removed connection to the voucher issue, and speaks volumes about the kinds of appeals that might motivate them during a political campaign. Parents are especially concerned about kids. Nonparents are concerned about kids too, but they are at least as concerned about taxes.

(4) Both parents and nonparents, in calibrating their support for vouchers, attach special importance to whether vouchers will help low-income children. Thus social equity appears to be a major concern. They also care about racial balance, but for both groups a concern for diversity comes out lower in priority than a concern for equity does. This is the same pattern we have observed throughout the book: equity trumps diversity (as we have measured them).

(5) Some social concerns appear important on the surface, due to their provocative content, but in fact don't matter much in explaining where people come down on vouchers. One of these is parent capability, which is of modest relevance to nonparents and even less important to parents. This is another indication that parent-related issues (aside from choice per se), which are so central to the arguments of voucher advocates, are not central to the way ordinary people think about things. Also weak are three equity items: one on whether private school kids would benefit at the expense of others (although this is fairly important to nonparents), another on whether the wealthy would benefit and leave the poor in the public schools, and a third on whether private schools would discriminate against the poor. All of these seemed to provide signs of public suspicion

about the equity effects of vouchers, but they don't have much impact on the positions people take. And finally, there is the jobs issue, which for now is quite unimportant.

For public parents and inner-city parents, the additional models show how the estimated impacts of these social concerns are altered when we take account of the parental interest in going private. The estimates don't change much, and the patterns are basically the same as in the other models, which means that we can have greater confidence in the above results. But there is one shift of genuine interest: for inner-city parents especially, but also for parents generally, "getting kids out of bad schools" loses a portion of its original impact. It remains quite important for both. But its drop in impact suggests that some of the high parental concern for "getting kids out of bad schools" is actually a reflection of their *personal* interest in being able to use vouchers for that purpose rather than their concern that others in society be able to do so.

The Personal Consequences of Vouchers

Now let's take a more explicit look at the personal side of the equation. When Americans decide whether vouchers are worthy of their support, they may be thinking about society as a whole. But they may also be thinking about themselves and about how vouchers would directly affect their own lives.

Because nonparents don't have children in school, they don't have much of a personal stake in the voucher issue. Vouchers could affect property values, or lead to higher taxes, or in other ways affect them personally. But these effects are usually generated by broader social effects—related to the costs of education, for instance, or the demographic composition of kids attending local schools. For the most part, then, it seems likely that nonparents are primarily thinking in broader, social terms when they decide whether to support or oppose vouchers.

Parents are in a different situation. They are part of society too, and presumably no less responsible in wanting public policies that are good for everyone. Yet they also have children in school, and they have a personal stake in vouchers that nonparents just don't have. Their decision about whether to support vouchers, then, is made up of two components, one social and one personal—and the personal component may be quite influential in their thinking. Here, we will take a closer look at a number of factors that help explain why.

The Advantages of Choice

Questions exploring personal considerations are set out in a battery of agree-disagree items within the voucher section of the survey. Four of these items are especially important because they strike to the heart of the issue—asking, in different ways, what parents think the direct effects of choice would be on their own lives. Here is their wording:

(1) "A voucher would help me find better, safer schools for my kids."

(2) "A voucher would give me more control over my own children's education."

(3) "A voucher would make schools more responsive to parents like me, because they know we can leave if we aren't happy."

(4) "A voucher would help me find schools that teach better values."

If we take the figures in table 8-5 at face value, parents overwhelmingly believe that vouchers would work to their advantage in these respects. Sixty-three percent say vouchers would help them find better, safer schools for their kids. Seventy-four percent believe vouchers would give them more control over their kids' education. Seventy-five percent think vouchers would make the schools more responsive. And 68 percent say vouchers would help them find schools that teach better values. The numbers are even higher among parents in the inner city, especially on the connection between vouchers and finding better, safer schools.

These are impressive levels of support, and they are doubtless telling us something about the value Americans attach to choice. In a literal sense, people seem to view choice as empowering. It allows them to take direct action on their own behalf and to pursue opportunities not otherwise available to them. We have to recognize, however, that these figures may be inflated by a positive response bias. All four items are worded in such a way that an "agree" counts as a pro-voucher response, and all the results may be a bit on the high side. We would expect this bias to be less of a factor here than it was for the social items, because the personal items bear on issues much closer to home and easier for people to evaluate. Respondents are likely to have firmer ideas of their own and to be less susceptible to influence by external cues. Still, these figures may overstate parents' enthusiasm.

A fifth item on the personal value of choice puts things in a more sobering light. This item asks respondents to agree or disagree with the following: "The public schools in this area are good enough, so I wouldn't have much use for a voucher." Here we find that, despite the benefits they associate with choice, most public parents (by 53 percent to 41 percent) say

Table 8-5. *Personal Considerations: The Advantages of Choice*
Percent, unless otherwise indicated[a]

Survey item	Public school parents	Private school parents	Inner-city parents
Vouchers would help me find better, safer schools			
Agree	63	75	73
Disagree	30	19	21
Don't know	7	6	5
Vouchers would give me more control			
Agree	74	78	79
Disagree	22	17	17
Don't know	5	4	5
Vouchers make schools more responsive			
Agree	75	78	77
Disagree	18	16	14
Don't know	7	6	9
Vouchers would help me find schools that teach better values			
Agree	68	75	73
Disagree	25	19	20
Don't know	7	6	7
Local public schools good enough			
Agree	53	24	40
Disagree	41	69	54
Don't know	6	7	6
N[b]	(2,553)	(530)	(539)

a. Percentages are based on weighted data. They may not sum to 100 due to rounding.
b. N is the unweighted number of respondents.

that their public schools are good enough, and thus that they wouldn't have much use for vouchers. To some extent, this turn of affairs could be due to response bias. For while all the other items are worded such that an "agree" response is pro-voucher, this one is worded the other way around. So we can't simply assume that its more negative responses are due entirely to the substance of the issue.

Even if we adjust both sets of results to account for a modicum of bias, these findings nonetheless point to a theme consistent with the other findings in this book. As this last item attests, public parents are reasonably satisfied with their schools and are not desperate to leave them. They don't think of themselves as mired in an educational crisis. They do, however, want greater access to private schools, which they think are better (and safer). As the first set of items indicates, public parents see vouchers as giving them that access, and as offering a mechanism—choice—that gives them greater control of their children's educational lives. In their view, it seems, there is no real conflict between liking their public schools and seeing the benefits of vouchers. Vouchers are not a path to revolution. For most parents, they are simply a means of opening up new options.

Normative Concerns

We already know that many parents have a normative commitment to the public schools, a sympathy or attachment that has little to do with performance. This public school ideology is a blend of the social and the personal. It is an obligation to the larger community, and thus a social concern. But it is also an obligation that is personally felt, and that doesn't require a belief that vouchers would have bad effects on school quality, race, or equity.

The survey offers several measures of this ideology, perhaps the best of which is contained within the voucher section's battery of personal items. It asks respondents to agree or disagree with the following statement: "I believe in public education, and I wouldn't feel right putting my kids in private or parochial school." The results were discussed in chapter 3, but we will briefly review them here.

This is a strongly worded statement that, one would think, self-interested parents should flatly disavow. If going private were just a matter of deciding which schools are best, why would they feel badly? As the figures in table 8-6 indicate, however, there is much more to going private than a pragmatic judgment of school quality. For a large minority of public parents, some 43 percent of them, it seems to imply a violation of their commitment to public education. Indeed, even among the inner-city poor, who are stuck in the nation's worst schools, 39 percent express this same normative angst about going private.

While response bias may inflate the level of agreement somewhat, our prior analysis has shown that this phenomenon is important to the way Americans think about their schools—and about vouchers. In this section, it is a reminder that, when parents assess the personal value of vouchers, they are not necessarily thinking solely about their self-interest. They may also feel a personal sense of duty, obligation, and commitment to the current system; and to the extent they do, this affects the value they would get from using vouchers.

Practical Concerns

Even if parents are attracted to vouchers, there may be certain practical problems that stand in the way of their actually using them. The survey

Table 8-6. *Personal Considerations: Normative, Practical, and Supply Side*
Percent, unless otherwise indicated[a]

Survey item	Public school parents	Private school parents	Inner-city parents
Believe in public education and wouldn't feel right going private			
Agree	43	21	39
Disagree	49	73	54
Don't know	8	6	8
Only use voucher if transport provided			
Agree	44	22	52
Disagree	50	73	44
Don't know	6	4	4
Switching schools too disruptive			
Agree	40	27	32
Disagree	52	65	61
Don't know	8	8	7
Don't know enough about private schools			
Agree	49	21	50
Disagree	45	75	45
Don't know	6	4	5
Not enough private schools to choose from			
Agree	43	33	40
Disagree	44	60	50
Don't know	13	6	11
N[b]	(2,553)	(530)	(539)

a. Percentages are based on weighted data. They may not sum to 100 due to rounding.
b. N is the unweighted number of respondents.

asks about two possibilities. One deals with transportation problems, the other with the difficulty of moving children already in school.

The transportation issue is frequently mentioned in the elite-level debate over vouchers. Critics argue that, for people who don't have ready transportation—particularly the poor—choice will be more nominal than real, and that this is a major factor restricting the value of vouchers and skewing their benefits along class lines. Advocates counter that government is already busing most students anyway and could continue to do so under a voucher plan. Besides, people are resourceful and would find ways to get their kids to desirable private schools, even if government transportation were not provided.

The survey presents respondents with a simple agree-disagree item: "I could only use a voucher if transportation is provided." This is a strongly worded statement, yet even so some 44 percent of public parents agree with it, 52 percent in the inner city. Again, there may be a response bias here that inflates the level of positive responses. But still, the critics appear to be correct in arguing that transportation is an obstacle to choice for many parents.

The flip side, however, is that half of all public parents, and almost half of the poor, say they would take advantage of choice without any transportation assistance at all. And when we recognize that the government is already busing most children today and would presumably continue to do so, it is not clear that transportation problems would really turn out to be much of an obstacle, nor that people view them that way.

The second practical issue we've measured here has to do with parents' resistance to moving kids from their current schools and thus away from their friends and established activities. Even if the new schools are perceived to be better, there are clearly many personal costs associated with uprooting children from their familiar surroundings and putting them down somewhere else.

To explore this issue, the survey presents respondents with the following agree-disagree item: "My kids are already in school, and using a voucher to switch schools would be too disruptive." Most parents disagree, but a rather large minority, 40 percent, say that it would indeed create a problem that would make vouchers less desirable. Even in the inner city, where parents presumably have more reason to change schools, 32 percent say that moving their kids is too disruptive.

The level of concern here may be overstated a bit due to response bias. Nonetheless, we need to recognize that virtually all the children who would be immediately affected by vouchers *are* already in school—and this may serve as an inertial force that works against reform. Many people may see change as too disruptive to a status quo that is good enough.

The Supply Side: Private Schools

People like what vouchers can do for them, and for society. These aspects of public opinion constitute the demand side of the equation, which seems quite positive. But there is also a supply side that needs to be taken into account. As a practical matter, parents can benefit from vouchers only if there are desirable private schools in the local area for their kids to attend, schools that they know about and can choose.

The survey poses two supply-side questions. The first asks respondents to agree or disagree with the following: "Right now, I don't know enough about private or parochial schools to say whether I would be interested in them." As table 8-6 shows, 49 percent of public parents agree, as do 50 percent of parents in the inner city. Even if these figures are a bit inflated, they suggest that large numbers of public parents know little about their private options.

This shouldn't come as a big surprise. These are public parents, and, lacking a program that actually puts vouchers in their hands, the vast majority have no incentives to shop around for alternatives in the private sector. So it makes sense that, as things now stand, they are poorly informed about what is out there. They have the impression that private schools are good, but they don't actually know much about the specific private schools in their area.

The second survey item is about availability, asking respondents to agree or disagree with the following: "There aren't enough private schools to choose from." As table 8-6 shows, 43 percent of public parents and 40 percent of parents in the inner city agree. Although these figures too may be somewhat inflated, they suggest that many parents aren't aware of private options in their local area—and may be thinking that, were vouchers introduced, they wouldn't have the vast array of new choices that voucher advocates envision. In some geographic areas, especially rural communities, this is surely accurate. But it is also pretty much what we ought to expect from a population that has little knowledge about local private schools. Even if the schools were out there, many people wouldn't be aware of them and might easily believe that there are few schools to choose from.

Given this background, it is understandable that widely publicized surveys—by the Carnegie Foundation and Phi Delta Kappa—have argued that public parents are not interested in going private.[12] They ask public parents whether, given a choice, they would move their child into a different school, possibly a private one, and most parents say they would stay with their existing public school. Hence the conclusion that people really don't want to go private. But the phrasing of their survey items requires, in effect, that parents know enough about the private schools in the local area to have concluded that a specific private school is better than their current public school. The Carnegie item, for instance, begins by asking, "Is there some other school to which you would like to send your child?" Most parents haven't yet investigated private schools in a serious way and aren't in a position to know.

It is only after parents are granted the power of choice that they would have strong incentives to seek out information about private schools, and know enough to say that they would leave their current school for another. Indeed, at one point (outside the battery of personal items) our survey asks parents, "If you had a voucher, how much effort would you make to learn about the private and parochial schools in your area?" Sixty-one percent say they would devote a lot of effort to it, 19 percent say a little, and 15 percent say none. If this is even remotely accurate, the state of information and knowledge would change radically if choice became a reality. In the meantime, it is quite rational for people to stay relatively uninformed—and unable to say, therefore, that specific private schools are preferable to the schools their kids now attend.

In view of all this, how should the lack of parental knowledge about the supply of private schools affect support for vouchers? The simplest expectation is that parents would see fewer personal benefits to vouchers and be less enthusiastic about reform. But things may be a bit more complicated. Parents may not know much about specific private schools, but they do think that the private sector as a whole has very good schools to offer and that it would be beneficial to have greater access to these (unnamed, unknown) schools. Thus parents could well think about the supply side in abstract terms and see it very positively, despite their ignorance of specifics. If so, their lack of information about private supply may not undermine their support for vouchers at all. The analysis below will tell us more.

Which Personal Concerns Seem to Matter—and Which Don't?

Parents have opinions on all of these personal issues, but some are presumably more important than others in explaining their support for vouchers. To explore this, we could carry out the same kind of multivariate analysis that we pursued earlier for social consequences, showing how the various personal considerations affect support for vouchers. This, however, would hide what is surely their essential role. Their direct effect is not on support per se, but on whether parents want to *use* a voucher for their own children. It is the latter that really defines the parents' personal stake in the policy and directly affects their support. There is a simple causal chain at work: personal considerations affect the desire to use a voucher, and the desire to use a voucher affects support for the policy. If we want to understand the impact of personal considerations, then, it makes sense to focus on the first part of the chain.

Accordingly, the dependent variable in this section's analysis is the survey item (discussed in chapter 7) that asks parents whether they would use a voucher to send their children to private schools.[13] The explanatory variables consist of all the personal considerations discussed above (with the usual controls for background and context). The results, which are quite

Table 8-7. *Impact of Personal Considerations on Interest in Using Vouchers*[a]

Variable	Public school parents		Inner-city parents	
	Coefficient	[Impact]	Coefficient	[Impact]
Advantages of choice				
More control	.11***	[.25]	.15***	[.35]
Make schools more responsive	.03*	[.07]	.02	[.05]
Help find better, safer schools	.13***	[.34]	.12***	[.32]
Teach better values	.12***	[.29]	.15***	[.39]
Public schools good enough	−.14***	[−.40]	−.08**	[−.23]
Normative considerations				
Believe in public education	−.12***	[−.33]	−.10***	[−.31]
Practical considerations				
Transportation	.01	[.04]	.04	[.12]
Switching schools too disruptive	−.05***	[−.14]	−.08***	[−.22]
Supply side: private schools				
Don't know enough about private schools	−.02	[−.05]	−.03	[−.08]
Not enough private schools	.02	[.05]	.02	[.04]
Constant	2.26***		1.80***	
N[b]	(2,206)		(485)	
Adjusted R^2	.43		.38	

* Significant at .10 level.
** Significant at .05 level.
*** Significant at .01 level.

a. Ordinary least squares regressions estimated using weighted data. The dependent variable is an individual's personal interest in using a voucher, which varies from 1 (no, definitely) to 4 (yes, definitely). Unstandardized coefficients reported. The impact coefficient represents the estimated change in the dependent variable (measured in standard deviations) when the independent variable shifts by two standard deviations, holding all other variables constant. Models control for the full range of background and context variables.

b. N is the unweighted number of respondents.

similar for public parents and inner-city parents, are set out in table 8-7. They point to the following conclusions:[14]

(1) The major personal influences, aside from public school ideology, all have to do with the direct benefits of choice. When parents consider whether vouchers would be useful to them, they are especially concerned about how their public schools are performing (which is a measure how beneficial it would be to have choice), and with whether they think vouchers will allow them to find better, safer schools, give them greater control of their kids' educations, and enable them to find schools that teach better values.

(2) We already know from the prior analysis that public school ideology has an important influence on the desire to go private, and the findings here are consistent with that. People who are normatively committed

to the public schools are less inclined to want to use a voucher for their children. When grouped together, however, the impacts of the choice variables—which arise from self-interest—are far greater.

(3) The one choice variable that doesn't have much impact is the one that asks whether vouchers would make schools more responsive. This is yet another indication, consistent with the findings of previous chapters, that parents don't attach much weight to influencing the schools. Parent influence is a prime motivation for voucher advocates, but not for parents.

(4) The supply side has little impact on how parents see the desirability of vouchers. This is rather surprising, for on logical grounds there are reasons for expecting a connection. It only makes sense that parents who know the most about private schools, and are aware of having lots of private alternatives from which to choose, would be the most interested in going private. But the facts suggest otherwise. It appears that parents tend to think in the abstract—and very positively—about the private sector and do not condition their demand on having specific private schools they want their kids to attend.

(5) The two practical concerns—the need for transportation and the disruption of moving kids who are already in school—have little influence on whether parents find vouchers desirable. The transportation finding may reflect the same tendency to think abstractly about the possibilities of choice rather than concretely about specific situations. In practice, many parents could find transportation to be an obstacle, but for now it doesn't affect their thinking about the desirability of vouchers. The "already in school" factor is different. The analysis shows that it doesn't matter much— and it doesn't, as long as variables related to school quality are controlled. Were these quality variables omitted, however (and they shouldn't be, of course), the "already in school" factor would increase substantially in importance. This doesn't change our conclusions. But it does tell us something interesting. It is a signal that school quality probably has a lot to do with *why* people find moving their kids so disruptive—and suggests that the "already in school" factor, often taken (by critics) as evidence that parents are driven by nonacademic concerns, is in fact strongly influenced by academic quality. People see moving as disruptive when the public schools are good enough to make leaving problematic.

Comparing the Social and Personal Bases of Support

We are now in a position to address a fundamental issue. When parents decide whether to support or oppose vouchers, are they mainly concerned about what vouchers can do for them personally, or are they also—and perhaps even primarily—concerned about the effects of vouchers on society as a whole? What is the balance between the personal and the social?

Political scientists have something very interesting to say here. Viewed in larger perspective, this is a profound question whose relevance extends well beyond vouchers to all of public opinion and indeed to the nature and quality of democracy itself. Before the onset of most modern research, it was widely accepted (if lamented) that public opinion is largely driven by self-interest. Workers support redistribution and higher taxes, the wealthy support minimal government and low taxes; the whole thing seemed pretty obvious. Yet once scholars began to study self-interest in a systematic way, the evidence pointed in just the opposite direction.

One of the classic studies, for instance, was carried out by Donald Kinder and Roderick Kiewiet.[15] They showed that, when people make their voting decisions in national elections, they are heavily influenced by their broader assessments of economic conditions, and thus of how the economy is performing for everyone, and are hardly influenced at all by their own, personal economic situations (for example, whether they have recently been unemployed). Americans tend to approach public policy from a "sociotropic" standpoint, Kinder and Kiewiet argued, rather than from the standpoint of their own self-interest.

A raft of other studies reinforces this same basic conclusion across a range of policy areas. Often these studies have looked at whether the obvious beneficiaries of particular types of policies are more likely to support them than other citizens are, and the answer has consistently been no. In a recent review of the evidence, Kinder sums it up as follows:

> When faced with affirmative action, white and black Americans come to their views without calculating personal harms and benefits. The unemployed do not line up behind policies designed to alleviate distress. The medically indigent are no more likely to favor government health insurance than are the fully insured. . . . On such diverse matters as racial busing, . . . antidrinking ordinances, mandatory college examinations, housing policy, bilingual education, compliance with the laws, . . . gun control, and more, self-interest turns out to be quite unimportant.[16]

Today, this is a widely accepted view among researchers in the field. They do not rule out self-interest altogether as an influence on public opinion. They argue that, under certain conditions, it can play an important role—notably, when a policy has major effects on material interests and is the subject of intense political debate, media attention, and elite framing. An obvious example is California's Proposition 13, which proposed to (and ultimately did) set limits on property taxes and set off a political firestorm that led to self-interested voting among ordinary citizens.[17] But these are unusual circumstances. Under more normal conditions, the mainstream expectation is that self-interest should have little influence.

This body of research applies straightforwardly to the voucher issue. And the voucher issue, in turn, is well suited for testing out its main theoretical claim: for vouchers clearly have a personal impact on parents, and the circumstances surrounding the issue are well within the normal range. Indeed, vouchers are unfamiliar to most Americans, who seem largely untouched by media or elites on the subject. If political scientists are right, then, where Americans stand on the voucher issue should be determined mainly by their assessment of its consequences for society, and not by whether they want to use vouchers for their own benefit.

From chapter 7, we already have reason to believe that self-interest *does* have a major influence on support for vouchers. Parents have much greater personal stakes in the issue than nonparents do, and they are consistently more supportive of vouchers. Private parents and inner-city parents have more to gain from vouchers than regular public parents do, and they too are more supportive. The list could go on. The multivariate analysis confirms what these descriptive results suggest: when the key measure of parental self-interest—their interest in going private—is allowed to compete with a broad range of other factors, this self-interest variable turns out to be the single most powerful influence on their support for vouchers.

So far, then, our evidence is flatly inconsistent with political science expectations. Yet this is only part of the story. It is possible that, even if political scientists are wrong in discounting self-interest, they are correct in claiming that social concerns—taken as a whole, rather than as separate variables—are actually far more important. Our evidence from previous chapters does not point to a clear conclusion on this score. Its framework includes a potent measure of self-interest (the interest in going private), but no comparable measure that pulls together the main components of social concern.

The new survey items help us get a better sense of how the social and the personal both contribute to the way parents think about the voucher issue. We can't arrive at definitive answers, but we can take a few, very interesting steps forward. Here is the approach. The survey contains eleven different items that variously deal with the social consequences of vouchers, and, as we have seen, most of these demonstrate at least some rel-

Table 8-8. *Social and Personal Determinants of Voucher Support* [a]

| | Public school parents | | Inner-city parents | |
Variable	Coefficient	[Impact]	Coefficient	[Impact]
Social index[b]	.27***	[.82]	.15***	[.44]
Personal interest[c]	.30***	[.67]	.28***	[.71]
Constant	2.28***		2.68***	
N[d]	(2,095)		(464)	
Adjusted R^2	.46		.28	

* Significant at .10 level.
** Significant at .05 level.
*** Significant at .01 level.

a. Ordinary least squares regressions estimated using weighted data. The dependent variable is the follow-up voucher support item, which is coded from 1 (strongly disagree) to 4 (strongly agree). Unstandardized coefficients report. The impact coefficient represents the estimated change in the dependent variable (measured in standard deviations) when the independent variable shifts by two standard deviations, holding all other variables constant. Models control for the full range of background and context variables.

b. The social index is constructed through principal components factor analysis using all of the items in Table 8-4, except for the one on jobs and the one on benefiting the wealthy, both of which show little connection to support for vouchers.

c. "Personal interest" is based on the survey item that measures an individual's interest in putting a voucher to personal use.

d. N is the unweighted number of respondents.

evance to whether people are ultimately willing to support vouchers as public policy. If we construct an index of just the "relevant" social items, this index can be employed as a summary measure of social considerations. (See appendix A.) We could do the same with the survey's battery of personal items to create an index of parental self-interest, but we needn't do so. We already have a simpler, more direct measure of that: whether parents are interested in using a voucher to send their children to private schools.

The question is: what happens when these two key variables—one representing social concerns, the other representing self-interest—are pitted against one another in explaining support for vouchers? To see, we will use the same framework as in the prior sections.[18] The dependent variable is the second voucher support item, and controls are included for all the usual background and contextual variables.[19] Results are set out in table 8-8.

They can be appreciated from two angles. On the one hand, the impact coefficients for public parents suggest that social concerns—now that they are considered as a group—actually *do* seem to have more influence than self-interest in explaining support for vouchers. Any notion that parents are driven mainly by naked self-interest, then, clearly fails. Even though public parents have a direct personal stake in the voucher issue, and even though they could easily take policy positions based entirely on their own self-interest, they don't do so. They think about what is best for themselves, but they also put substantial weight on social concerns, and thus on the effects vouchers are likely to have for the larger society. They appear to be combining two roles: they are consumers, concerned about their own personal interests, and they are citizens, concerned about society as a whole.[20]

On the other hand, these same results also suggest that self-interest is far more important than political science would lead us to believe. True, social considerations carry great weight. But so does self-interest, to the point where it rivals the social side in explanatory power. If political science were right, social concerns should have dominated this competition for explanatory power—but they don't even come close to doing that.

We can learn more by looking across different types of parents. Consider, for instance, the results for inner-city parents, which are set out in table 8-8. If we use the ratio of the two impact coefficients as a simple metric, it is clear that inner-city parents (whose ratio of social to personal impacts is .62) are much less social in their approach to vouchers than public parents generally (with a ratio of 1.22), and thus much more inclined to evaluate vouchers in terms of their own self-interest.

What might account for this result? A plausible explanation is that a strong element of rationality is at work here and that, despite its dismissal by mainstream scholars, self-interest actually has a key role to play in explaining opinion differences across population groups. Without any activation by the media or political campaigns, and without much information of their own to guide them, parents simply make their own connection between the voucher issue and their personal needs—and those with the greatest needs make the strongest connection. The corollary is that social concerns may be something of a luxury: people can afford to be socially oriented toward vouchers when their own needs are not pressing and do not demand priority.

A simple extension of the analysis is helpful here. If this argument is basically correct, the relative importance of personal and social concerns should vary systematically with district context, which is an objective measure of personal need. And this is exactly what the evidence shows, in a pattern that is remarkably consistent. The results are set out in table 8-9, which reports the impact coefficients from regressions identical to those above but carried out separately for respondents in different types of districts. For parents in the least-advantaged districts, support for vouchers is far more heavily determined by self-interest than by social concerns

Table 8-9. *Impact of Social and Personal Considerations on Support for Vouchers*[a]

Variable	Social impact	Personal impact	Ratio (social/personal)
District advantage			
1 Least advantaged	.29	.46	.63
2	.29	.31	.94
3	.46	.31	1.48
4 Most advantaged	.54	.25	2.16
Performance			
1 Low	.30	.39	.76
2	.34	.40	.85
3	.44	.31	1.42
4 High	.47	.30	1.57
Income			
Low	.30	.34	.88
Middle	.41	.33	1.24
High	.51	.30	1.70

a. Impact coefficients, as defined in earlier tables, are reported from weighted ordinary least squares regressions in which the dependent variable is the follow-up voucher support item, and all the usual background and context variables are controlled.

(social ratio = .63). As district context improves, the relative role of self-interest declines, to the point where, in the most advantaged districts, social considerations are by far the dominant influence (social ratio = 2.16).

Exactly the same pattern obtains if we shift from an objective measure of personal need to a subjective measure: satisfaction with public school performance (see table 8-9 again). The parents who give their schools the lowest evaluations are the ones who put the heaviest emphasis on self-interest in taking a position on vouchers (social ratio = .76). But as parents give their schools better marks for performance, self-interest declines in importance, and social considerations become predominant (with a ratio of 1.57 at the highest performance level).

Finally, suppose we carry out separate regressions for respondents at different levels of family income, which is another basic measure of personal need. The results show the same pattern. As table 8-9 indicates, parents who are low in income are the most self-interested (social ratio = .88), those in the middle-income group are less self-interested (social ratio = 1.24), and those in the high-income group are less self-interested still (social ratio = 1.70).

All in all, then, this section's analysis is quite revealing. We knew coming in that self-interest is important to the way American parents approach

the voucher issue. We now know that social concerns are of major importance as well, and that the balance people strike between the personal and
the social seems to reflect a rational assessment of their personal needs.
The needier the parents are, and thus the more valuable a voucher might
be to them personally, the more their position on the voucher issue is determined by their self-interest. The parents who take a broader, social
view of the issue are the parents who need vouchers the least.[21]

Conclusion

When elites wrangle over vouchers, their claims almost always boil down
to claims about consequences: that vouchers would have good or bad
impacts on society as a whole, or good or bad impacts on the lives of
parents and children. Advocates see good impacts. Critics see bad impacts. This is what the national debate is largely about.

The current chapter has examined what the American people have to
say about the possible impacts of vouchers, and which side of the debate
they seem to favor. It has also given us a chance to get beyond their simple
expressions of support and opposition in order to gain a more finely grained
sense of their thinking. These tasks are hardly straightforward. Most Americans are poorly informed, and the issues here are truly complex, so the
views people express are likely to be tentative, dependent on question
wording, and open to change (and influence). We have to be careful about
drawing firm conclusions.

The evidence, however, is quite suggestive. For the most part, Americans seem to believe vouchers would have rather positive effects on society. Most think vouchers would provide healthy competition for the public
schools, that they would help kids get out of bad schools, that they would
enhance racial balance, and that they would benefit disadvantaged kids—
and these considerations carry real weight in their thinking, affecting their
support for vouchers.

There is also a downside, however. Large numbers of Americans worry
that vouchers are too risky and experimental, and many think they would
lead to higher costs (and taxes). Concerns about risk and cost, moreover,
clearly affect whether people are willing to endorse vouchers as public
policy. Indeed, across the population as a whole, risk appears to be the
single most powerful influence on where people stand on the issue.

On the social side, then, the news for the movement is largely favorable: people tend to agree with the arguments of voucher advocates and
discount the arguments of critics, and this bodes well for the movement's

political appeal. Yet the public is also concerned about the risks and costs associated with radical (or merely unfamiliar) change, and this is something opponents may be able to capitalize on. Opponents may not need to convince people that vouchers will lead to bad consequences. Their best tack may simply be to sow the seeds of doubt and uncertainty: a strategy made easier by the public's lack of information.

These social concerns and the political responses to them are especially relevant as they apply to nonparents—who, we have to remember, make up two-thirds of the electorate. Nonparents usually do not have a personal stake in the voucher issue and are likely to evaluate it primarily in social terms. Parents, on the other hand, *do* have a personal stake in vouchers, and where they stand on the issue can be expected to turn in part on their own self-interest. This is a simple fact that leaders have long counted on in plotting strategy and figuring their prospects for success. They are betting that parental self-interest will work to the movement's great advantage once the word about vouchers spreads.

The evidence on this score is quite positive. Most public parents seem to believe that choice puts valuable new powers in their hands: that it will give them greater control over their children's educations, that they will be able to seek out better, safer schools, that they will have access to schools with better values, and that schools will be more responsive to them. These, of course, are the movement's key political appeals to parents—and (responsiveness aside) they turn out be the most influential of all personal considerations in determining where parents stand on the voucher issue.

Although this personal side of the equation seems to auger well for the voucher movement, many political scientists would say it should be discounted. If mainstream research is any guide, we should expect that the social views of parents would dominate their thinking about vouchers, and that their self-interest in the issue—once forced to compete with social concerns for explanatory power—should prove quite unimportant. Whether political scientists are right about this is of more than academic interest. For the balance that parents strike between the social and the personal will determine how they evaluate the issue, and thus what needs to be done in politics—by advocates and opponents alike—to attract their support.

The analysis points to two very interesting findings. The first is that, if we look at public parents overall, the social and the personal seem to play roughly equal roles in explaining support for vouchers. As political scientists would expect, parents do put a great deal of weight on how vouchers would affect the larger society. Even though vouchers may affect them quite directly, and even though most indicate they would personally benefit were vouchers provided, they are not thinking just of themselves. They appear to judge vouchers from the standpoint of democratic citizens. Yet, in striking contrast to what political scientists would expect, public parents also put substantial weight on their own self-interest. As voucher leaders have always hoped and believed, self-interest actually has a very big influence on the way parents think about things—which is a clear political plus for the movement.

The second finding is that some parents are more inclined to emphasize self-interest, while some are more inclined to emphasize social concerns, and the balance between the personal and the social varies as a function of personal need. The public parents in greatest personal need—those from disadvantaged districts, for instance—are most likely to be self-interested in their approach to vouchers and to discount social concerns. Advantaged parents are far more inclined to think socially about vouchers and to downplay their own self-interest in the issue. All of this comes across as quite rational, given the situations in which people find themselves.

From a political standpoint, then, the analysis of this chapter suggests that the personal and the social are both of great relevance to the politics of vouchers and both, in most respects, are rather positive in what they imply for the movement's prospects. But they have intriguingly different roles to play. Because nonparents make up two-thirds of the electorate, and because parents are only motivated in part by self-interest, the social consequences of vouchers are likely to be the primary determinants of overall levels of political support—and elites on both sides will find that arguments about the broader social effects, and about the connection between vouchers and the public interest, will mainly determine their ability to win adherents to their sides.

Parents, however, do put substantial emphasis on their own self-interest, and the parents most likely to do so are the very parents who make up the prime constituency of the modern movement: those who are low in income and from disadvantaged districts. This not only gives the movement a bedrock of support (assuming the word gets out), but the flip side— namely, that more advantaged parents tend to be socially motivated— helps to ensure that, under the right conditions, many of the latter may be happy to support a modernist strategy even though their own self-interest takes a back seat. This asymmetry in the social and the personal across constituencies, therefore, is something the movement may well be able to use to its advantage.

9   *Regulating a Voucher System*

To ANYONE FAMILIAR with the voucher debate, there is something unsatisfying about asking people whether they support or oppose a "voucher system" or what the consequences of such a system might be. Because a voucher system is not a single thing, but a family of possibilities. All voucher systems involve government grants that assist parents in choosing private schools for their children. But beyond this common feature, they may have very different properties indeed, and very different consequences for children, schools, and society.

It is hardly surprising, then, that when vouchers are being debated at the elite level, the controversy is not just about vouchers per se, but also about the properties a voucher system ought to have if one were adopted. For example:

—Should parents be allowed to redeem vouchers at religious schools?

—Should private schools be subject to rules (regarding, say, curriculum or student testing) requiring that they meet certain public standards?

—Should private schools be allowed to set their own admissions requirements?

—Should parents be allowed to add their own money to the voucher when choosing private schools that cost more?

—Should vouchers be available to all children, or only to the children in greatest need?

The controversy is essentially about the kinds of *regulations* that should be adopted, if any, to create a system whose outcomes are socially desirable.

At the elite level, the classic argument of traditional voucher advocates has been for the fewest regulations possible and thus for something like a free market. This is the Milton Friedman solution.[1] Activists within the modern wing of the movement, on the other hand, are less taken with the automatic beneficence of markets. They are especially concerned with social equity and are much more inclined as a result to favor regulations, especially the limitation of vouchers to needy children. This is the regulated-markets approach, first proposed by Christopher Jencks and John Coons and Stephen Sugarman, that has taken center stage over the last decade.[2] And then, of course, there are the elite opponents of vouchers. Their first preference is for no voucher system at all. But when pressed to indicate what properties they prefer, they come down even more strongly on the side of regulation. In the eyes of opponents, the "best" voucher system would be small pilot programs for needy kids, religious schools would be excluded, and the remaining private schools would be heavily regulated—leaving government, rather than markets, firmly in control.[3]

Among elites, then, there is a political continuum at work. At one extreme are the free-market traditionalists (who are often libertarians), at the other are their staunchly pro-government opponents (who are mainly liberals), and in between are activists from the modern wing of the voucher movement (an ideologically mixed group), who favor low-income vouchers and equity-promoting regulations. Given this continuum, the movement's shift from free markets to a more regulated approach during the 1990s appears to have been quite rational politically, for it has broadened the appeal of vouchers, created a bigger and more powerful coalition, and enhanced the prospects for political success.

But all of this has taken place at the elite level. The question for us is: what do ordinary people think about the "details" of a voucher system, and what do their opinions suggest about the *kinds* of voucher systems that might gain the most support from the American public? Is the centrist move toward greater regulation and low-income vouchers, which has worked so well at the elite level, likely to attract support among ordinary people as well? In this chapter, we'll try to provide some answers.

Religion

Religion is a flash point of conflict in the national struggle over vouchers. On both sides, various motivations are at work. Some supporters are ardent believers in religious education, and for them a major goal of vouchers is to promote access to religious schools. But most supporters, especially in the modern wing of the movement, are not interested in religion per se. They believe that parent preferences deserve to be respected, and that the exclusion of religious schools would be an unwarranted restriction on choice.

Most supporters also see a key link between religion and competition. Because the vast majority of private schools are now religious, vouchers would give parents very few choices in the private sector if only nonreligious schools were allowed to participate. For the near future, many parents wanting to leave the public schools would find it impossible to do so. Desirable schools would quickly be filled, and less desirable schools in both sectors would continue to attract "support" even if performing poorly. As a result, there would be less competitive pressure on schools to perform, and the benefits of choice would be undermined.[4]

Voucher opponents are strident in wanting religious schools excluded. But here too there are mixed motives at work. Some, like the teachers unions, have a direct stake in preventing children and money from flowing into the private sector, and excluding religious schools from any voucher plan is an obvious means of eliminating most of the exit options. For other opponents, the antagonism to religious schools is more visceral: they simply don't like religion and don't want public money being used to promote it.

For still others, opposition to religious schools has little to do with antireligious fervor, but is based on beliefs about the "separation of church and state." These beliefs come in two separable components. The first involves a certain view of the proper role of religion in society, namely, that religion should be restricted to the private sphere and that government funding or support for religious institutions is improper. The second introduces a complementary but wholly different contention: that the inclusion of religious schools is actually illegal in our political system, prohibited by the Establishment Clause of the Constitution. While these two parts of the argument need not go together, voucher opponents almost always assert both.[5]

In the midst of all this sound and fury at the elite level, what do ordinary people have to say? The survey asks respondents which of the following statements is closer to their own view: "(a) Parents should only be able to use their vouchers at private schools that are not affiliated with a church or religion, or (b) Parents should be able to use their vouchers at both private and parochial schools." Their responses, set out in table 9-1, reveal a striking fact about the American public: virtually everyone agrees that religious schools ought to be included. Overall, 79 percent think parents

Table 9-1. *Should Religious Schools Be Included in a Voucher System?*
Percent, unless otherwise indicated[a]

Type of respondent	Should religious schools be included?			N[b]
	Yes	No	Don't know	
Total population	79	11	10	(4,700)
Nonparents	77	12	11	(1,617)
Public parents	83	9	10	(2,553)
Private school parents	84	10	6	(530)
Inner-city parents	80	12	8	(539)
Position on vouchers				
Support	85	10	5	(3,229)
Oppose	70	15	15	(1,134)
Political party (informed)				
Democrat	74	15	12	(779)
Republican	83	10	7	(649)
Religious affiliation				
Catholic	82	9	9	(1,292)
Protestant	78	11	11	(1,372)
Born-again	86	8	6	(342)
No religion	76	17	7	(346)

a. Percentages are based on weighted data. They may not sum to 100 due to rounding.
b. N is the unweighted number of respondents.

should be able to choose both religious and nonreligious schools with their vouchers, while only 11 percent think the choice should be restricted to nonreligious schools. Our survey, moreover, is not the only survey to show that Americans are so favorable toward religion on this score. A recent poll by Public Agenda asked a similar question and produced almost identical results, with 78 percent of Americans saying religious schools should be included in a voucher program.[6]

This high level of support for religious schools is uniform across the population: the figures are 77 percent for nonparents, 83 percent for public parents, 84 percent for private parents, and 80 percent for inner-city parents. It is noteworthy that public parents are just as positive toward religious schools as private parents are. The vast majority of private parents are actually sending their kids to religious schools, while none of the public parents are currently doing so—yet the two groups view the issue in virtually the same way. Americans simply take a favorable view of religion, almost regardless of their circumstances.

If we look hard, we can find differences across groups. Voucher supporters, as we might expect, are more open to religious-school participation than voucher opponents are, by 85 percent to 70 percent; but even the opponents give religion an overwhelming vote of approval. The story

is a similar one for political party. Among respondents who are informed—
and thus for whom party is likely to be most influential—Republicans are
more positive toward religious-school participation than Democrats are,
by 83 percent to 74 percent. But this is a far cry from the chasm that
separates the two parties at the elite level.

Much the same is true for groups that are otherwise quite different in
their stances toward religion. Born-again Christians (at 86 percent) and
Catholics (at 82 percent), the groups that presumably have the strongest
religious reasons for supporting vouchers, are only modestly more positive toward the inclusion of religious schools than regular Protestants are
(at 78 percent). And indeed, people who say they have *no* religion are
overwhelmingly positive too (at 76 percent).

Overall, then, what we find is a complete disjunction between what is
happening at the elite level and what is happening among the general
public. For ordinary Americans, the inclusion of religious schools is *not* a
controversial issue. Almost everyone wants to see religious schools included. It is only at the elite level that opposing camps go to battle over
this issue. And in this battle, the opponents of vouchers—led by Democrats, liberals, and representatives of the education community—are wholly
out of step with the American public. This in itself does not mean that, in
some philosophical or legal sense, their views are not "right." But their
views are clearly not shared by ordinary Americans, who not only disagree with them, but are virtually of one mind on the subject.

It is worth recalling that, in our earlier analysis, we found that the
public expressed a similar consensus on the question of voluntary prayer.
When asked whether "prayer should be allowed in the public schools if it
is voluntary," some 86 percent of Americans agreed, and this extraordinarily high level of agreement was maintained across nonparents, public
parents, private parents, and inner-city parents. The broader picture, then,
is that Americans are simply very supportive of religion in general. The
controversy at the elite level comes about not because Americans are themselves conflicted about the "separation of church and state," but because
one of the elite camps is taking a position that few in American society
agree with.

Accountability

A rule excluding religious schools is just one way that a voucher system
might be regulated. The more general question is whether the private
schools that do participate, whether religious or not, should be regulated
further—and if so, how heavily and in what ways.

These are not arcane issues of law or administration, but issues of real substance that go to the heart of the education process and indeed of democracy itself. Should participating private schools have to follow a government-specified curriculum? Should they be required to jettison their own admissions criteria and admit any student who applies? Should they have legal responsibilities to educate disadvantaged students? The answers to these and other regulatory issues clearly have a huge impact on the kind of voucher system that is created, how such a system will perform—and presumably, who will support and oppose it in politics.

From prior analysis, we know that Americans are open to ideas about choice, competition, and markets in education. This does not mean, however, that they buy into the laissez-faire philosophy that surrounds the traditional wing of the voucher movement, nor that there is any connection in their minds between support for market-based ideas and their attitudes toward regulation. They may see the two as quite independent. Indeed, we know that Americans are reasonably satisfied with the current system—and the current system is highly regulated. We also know that some of the issues that lead critics to call for tight regulations—equity, for instance—are important to the public, and could prompt in them a similar concern for protective rules. Indeed, regulation may for most people be an automatic response to virtually *any* social problem: when something is wrong, their natural impulse may be to say that the government should pass a law prohibiting bad behavior or requiring good behavior.

To see how Americans approach regulation, let's turn to the survey. In this section, we'll begin with a simple battery of items that asks respondents to agree or disagree with the following proposals for participating private schools:

(1) "They should be required to hire teachers that are certified by the state."

(2) "They should be required to follow certain curriculum requirements about what courses to offer and what their content must be."

(3) "They should be required to submit yearly financial statements and agree to public audits."

(4) "They should be required to give their students standardized tests, and publish average results for the school as a whole."

At the elite level, these accountability regulations would be controversial. Critics would heartily support them as the bare essentials of democratic control and would ask for more. Many activists in the modern wing of the voucher movement might agree, at least when it comes to limited forms of regulation. But traditional voucher leaders are openly hostile to regulation. In their view, the great advantages that private schools have to offer—quality, innovation, flexibility, programmatic diversity—are outgrowths of their freedom to fashion their own organizations, personnel, and academic missions as they see fit. To restrict this freedom would undermine the very educational strengths that vouchers are trying to encourage.[7]

What do ordinary Americans have to say? Their responses, set out in table 9-2, reveal a fact of enormous importance to the politics of vouchers: *the American public is overwhelmingly in favor of regulation.* The degree of support is phenomenally high across all four items: 88 percent for teacher certification requirements, 80 percent for curriculum requirements, 83 percent for financial reporting and auditing requirements, and 86 percent for student testing. In each case, moreover, the great majority of responses are in the "strongly agree" category. This enthusiasm for regulation is remarkably uniform and cuts across groups and classes—including private parents, who appear quite willing to see the autonomy of their own schools compromised in the interests of public accountability.

In the population at large, there is no difference between voucher supporters and voucher opponents on this issue. Virtually everyone sees the issue the same way. Only with regard to political party do there appear to be any differences to speak of—informed Republicans are less supportive of accountability regulations than informed Democrats are (except, interestingly, on the requirement of student testing). But the real finding here, pretty obviously, is that even informed Republicans, who we might expect to be big dissenters, are almost totally in favor of holding private schools accountable to public authority.

We should be aware that, because these survey items are part of a battery of agree-disagree items, and because an "agree" answer is pro-regulation, there could be a positive response bias at work here. If there is, however, it probably is not very large. A recent survey by Phi Delta Kappa, for example, asked respondents about the same issue in the following way: "Do you think private or church-related schools that accept government tuition payments should be accountable to the state in the way public schools are accountable?" Seventy-seven percent of Americans answered favorably: an overwhelming vote of approval for government regulation.[8]

In the previous section, where we looked at opinions on religious school participation, it became clear that the critics of vouchers are way out of line with the American public. In the case of regulation, however, the shoe is on the other foot. Accountability regulation is exceedingly popular, and it is the traditional voucher leaders who are on the wrong side of the issue

Table 9-2. *Support for Accountability Regulation*
Percent, unless otherwise indicated[a]

Type of respondent	Teachers should be certified by state					N[b]
	Strongly agree	Weakly agree	Weakly disagree	Strongly disagree	Don't know	
Total population	73	15	4	5	4	(4,700)
Nonparents	72	15	4	5	4	(1,617)
Public school parents	76	13	4	4	3	(2,553)
Private school parents	67	14	5	12	3	(530)
Inner-city parents	75	14	4	4	4	(539)
Position on vouchers						
Support	74	15	4	5	1	(3,229)
Oppose	75	13	4	5	3	(1,134)
Political party (informed)						
Democrat	75	13	4	4	5	(779)
Republican	64	16	6	12	3	(649)

	Private schools should follow curriculum requirements					
	Strongly agree	Weakly agree	Weakly disagree	Strongly disagree	Don't know	
Total population	59	21	6	10	4	(4,700)
Nonparents	58	22	6	10	5	(1,617)
Public parents	62	22	6	7	4	(2,553)
Private parents	54	17	6	20	3	(530)
Inner-city parents	65	19	5	6	5	(539)
Position on vouchers						
Support	60	21	7	10	2	(3,229)
Oppose	59	22	5	10	4	(1,134)
Political party (informed)						
Democrat	60	21	8	8	3	(779)
Republican	46	20	11	20	3	(649)

if they want to attract political support. It is true that many Americans look favorably on competition and choice. But they do not think good outcomes will emerge automatically through the unfettered operation of the market. They think the government needs to play a role.

Fairness and Social Equity

When government regulates, it can do more than hold schools account-able for meeting certain standards. It can also try to promote fairness and social equity.

Type of respondent	Private schools should be subject to financial audits					N^b
	Strongly agree	Weakly agree	Weakly disagree	Strongly disagree	Don't know	
Total population	63	20	6	6	5	(4,700)
Nonparents	63	20	6	6	5	(1,617)
Public school parents	65	19	5	6	5	(2,553)
Private school parents	60	20	8	10	3	(530)
Inner-city parents	63	18	6	7	6	(539)
Position on vouchers						
Support	64	21	6	7	2	(3,229)
Oppose	64	19	5	6	5	(1,134)
Political party (informed)						
Democrat	63	20	6	6	5	(779)
Republican	59	18	10	9	4	(649)

	Private schools should be required to give standardized tests and publish results					
	Strongly agree	Weakly agree	Weakly disagree	Strongly disagree	Don't know	
Total population	65	21	5	5	4	(4,700)
Nonparents	64	21	5	5	4	(1,617)
Public school parents	66	21	5	4	5	(2,553)
Private school parents	68	17	6	7	3	(530)
Inner-city parents	68	18	5	3	6	(539)
Position on vouchers						
Support	67	22	4	5	2	(3,229)
Oppose	64	19	7	6	4	(1,134)
Political party (informed)						
Democrat	63	22	7	4	4	(779)
Republican	65	20	5	7	2	(649)

a. Percentages are based on weighted data. They may not sum to 100 due to rounding.
b. N is the unweighted number of respondents.

Critics, of course, think that choice and markets are inherently unfair, particularly to the less advantaged, and use this to argue for a better regulated (and funded) public system.[9] Within the modern wing of the voucher movement, many supporters share the critics' social concerns—they just take it to a different conclusion. They agree that American society is fraught with inequities that can distort the operation of school choice, and that there are corresponding dangers to relying on free markets. But they also believe that, with the right regulations, choice and competition can greatly benefit poor and minority families and liberate them from a public school system that is not serving their interests.[10]

Not all voucher supporters think this way, though. The dissenters are the traditionalists, many of them libertarians, who not only oppose regulation per se, but also take a jaundiced view of redistribution and thus of programs tilted toward the disadvantaged. Their ideal is a universal voucher system that treats all children alike and, in free-market fashion, grants parents and private schools total autonomy to make their own decisions. Choice and competition will work best if left alone, they believe, and will automatically work with special power for the disadvantaged, who are in greatest need of what choice has to offer.

As we explore where the American public seems to stand on these issues, it is useful to start with regulations that have nothing explicitly to do with class or race or redistribution, but are simply intended to ensure that all children have an equal shot at getting into the private schools of their choice. The obvious focus here is on student admissions. As things currently stand, private schools make their own decisions about which students to admit and which to turn away, using virtually any criteria they want. Should they be allowed to continue doing so under a voucher system?

The survey asks respondents to choose between the following two ways of setting up a voucher system: "(a) Private and parochial schools should be allowed to make their own decisions about which students to admit, based on their own standards, or (b) Private and parochial schools should be required to admit all students who apply, as long as there is room." The results are set out in table 9-3, and they are again striking. While the regulation proposed here would mean a radical reversal of traditional practice, the overwhelming majority of Americans favor it. Sixty-one percent think participating private schools should be required to admit all students who apply, while just 29 percent think private schools should be able to continue selecting students according to their own standards.

For parents, support for "regulated fairness" may have something to do with their self-interest in seeing that their own children have a good chance of getting into the private schools of their choice. If such concerns were at work, we would expect public parents to be more supportive of fairness rules than nonparents are, and this is in fact the case. Sixty-seven percent of parents favor such rules, versus 59 percent of nonparents. Similarly, it is the inner-city poor who have greatest reason to fear being treated unfairly, and they are the most in favor of regulation (at 72 percent). Private parents, who have already succeeded in getting their kids into private schools, have the least to fear and are the least supportive of regulation (at 52 percent).

While these differences may arise from self-interest (a topic we'll pursue later on), what is most impressive about these results is that they are so uniformly high across groups—which suggests that, when it comes to fairness, self-interest seems to take a back seat to social values that are widely shared. Americans have an egalitarian streak, and they want an education system that offers opportunities fairly to all kids, even if it means government restrictions on the freedom of private schools. How else to explain that nonparents, who have no direct stake in school admissions, express strong support for fairness regulations—and that private parents, who don't really need such rules and who have reason to resist outside encroachment on their own schools, nonetheless support regulation by a reasonably wide margin (52 percent to 40 percent)?

Another survey item also speaks to the issue of whether the government should regulate private school admissions under a voucher system. This one blends considerations of fairness with considerations of religion. It asks respondents whether they agree with the following statement: "Parochial schools should be required to admit children of all religions on an equal basis."

We might think that many Americans would be cross-pressured on this issue. On the one hand, they want fairness for the nation's children and are very much in favor of regulation. On the other hand, they are very sympathetic toward religious schools and could well want the rights of these schools respected. As table 9-3 indicates, however, there is actually no contest between these competing concerns. Fairness wins, hands-down. Americans are virtually unanimous in saying that religious schools should be required to admit students of all religions on an equal basis. Support for such a regulation is a lofty 82 percent among the population as a whole, and it remains at this extraordinary level for all the groups we consider here—including private parents, most of whom have their kids in religious schools. (Because this is an agree-disagree item, it could be a little on the high side. But the results for the previous, forced-choice item on student admissions suggest that it is probably not far off the mark.)

Now let's consider another regulatory issue that, like the ones above, has nothing explicitly to do with class, race, or redistribution and applies to all families in the same way. This one deals with whether parents should be able to add their own money onto the voucher in order to choose a school with a higher tuition. The idea behind prohibiting parent add-ons is that, without such a restriction, parents with higher incomes would have access to more and better schools. Eliminating add-ons would level the playing field. Within the modern wing of the voucher movement, this

Table 9-3. *Support for Regulations that Promote Fairness and Equity*
Percent, unless otherwise indicated[a]

| Type of respondent | How should private schools admit students? | | | |
	Admit all applicants	Own decision	Don't know	N[b]
Total population	61	29	10	(4,700)
Nonparents	59	30	10	(1,617)
Public school parents	67	24	8	(2,553)
Private school parents	52	40	8	(530)
Inner-city parents	72	20	9	(539)
Position on vouchers				
Support	65	30	6	(3,229)
Oppose	58	31	11	(1,134)
Political party (informed)				
Democrat	62	29	9	(779)
Republican	45	48	6	(649)

| | Parochial schools should admit students of all religions | | | | |
	Strongly agree	Weakly agree	Weakly disagree	Strongly disagree	Don't know
Total population	62	20	6	8	5	(4,700)
Nonparents	62	20	6	7	5	(1,617)
Public school parents	63	19	5	8	5	(2,553)
Private school parents	55	21	7	13	3	(530)
Inner-city parents	67	18	3	6	6	(539)
Position on vouchers					
Support	65	20	5	7	3	(3,229)
Oppose	58	19	8	10	5	(1,134)
Political party (informed)					
Democrat	64	19	6	7	5	(779)
Republican	52	20	8	17	3	(649)

| | Families should not be allowed to supplement vouchers with own funds | | |
	Agree	Disagree	Don't know
Total population	38	50	12	(4,700)
Nonparents	39	48	13	(1,617)
Public school parents	37	52	11	(2,553)
Private school parents	17	76	7	(530)
Inner-city parents	35	52	13	(539)
Position on vouchers			
Support	37	57	7	(3,229)
Oppose	41	39	19	(1,134)
Political party (informed)			
Democrat	38	49	13	(779)
Republican	27	65	8	(649)

Type of respondent	Families earning more than $100,000 should not be eligible for vouchers			
	Agree	Disagree	Don't know	N[b]
Total population	66	25	9	(4,700)
Nonparents	67	24	10	(1,617)
Public school parents	67	25	8	(2,553)
Private school parents	59	34	7	(530)
Inner-city parents	69	19	12	(539)
Position on vouchers				
Support	67	27	6	(3,229)
Oppose	68	22	9	(1,134)
Political party (informed)				
Democrat	65	26	9	(779)
Republican	49	43	7	(649)

	Spaces at private schools should be set aside for low-income families					
	Strongly agree	Weakly agree	Weakly disagree	Strongly disagree	Don't know	
Total population	50	25	9	10	6	(4,700)
Nonparents	49	25	10	10	6	(1,617)
Public school parents	53	25	8	9	6	(2,553)
Private school parents	48	23	8	15	5	(530)
Inner-city parents	64	21	3	4	7	(539)
Position on vouchers						
Support	54	25	8	9	3	(3,229)
Oppose	43	24	12	15	6	(1,134)
Political party (informed)						
Democrat	49	26	8	10	7	(779)
Republican	32	25	17	20	5	(649)

a. Percentages are based on weighted data. They may not sum to 100 due to rounding.
b. N is the unweighted number of respondents.

kind of restriction has a measure of sympathy. But not among traditional-ists, who want to give parents as many options as possible, and who argue that, by prohibiting add-ons, designers will heavily constrain the numbers and types of schools that emerge in the private sector—for only schools with sufficiently low tuition (and thus fewer programs, lower-paid teach-ers, and so on) will be able to accept vouchers.

Most Americans are not aware of all the fine points, of course, but the survey tries to offer some perspective by presenting them with simple ar-guments on both sides. The item is worded as follows: "A voucher may not cover the entire cost of tuition at some schools. Which is closer to your view? (a) Parents should be allowed to add their own money onto the voucher, because this would give them access to more schools, or (b) Parents should not be allowed to add onto the voucher, because this would give wealthier families an unfair advantage"

The results are set out in table 9-3. They show that Americans are *not* in favor of this kind of regulation. Overall, only 38 percent think parent add-ons should be restricted as a means of promoting social equity. Private parents, who can already afford their private schools as things now stand, are the least sympathetic, at 17 percent. But it is telling that the inner-city poor, supposedly the chief beneficiaries of such a restriction, also express very low levels of support (at 35 percent) and, like public parents generally, seem more interested in expanding their own options than in accepting rules that limit what they can do (or appear to).

Why do Americans reject the regulation of parent add-ons while being so enthusiastic about regulating the admissions process and imposing accountability standards? Part of the answer may be that the regulation of parent add-ons is a regulation of *parents*, while the others are regulations of *private schools*. The regulation of parents may strike many as an unnecessary restriction on individual choice, especially given that most American parents would probably be capable of adding some amount onto the voucher if they really needed to. The regulation of private schools, on the other hand, may not strike them as restricting parent choice at all, but rather as protecting parents—and the public generally—from whatever discriminatory decisions these organizations might make.

This conjecture is reasonable, but it leaves an important question unanswered. If Americans accept parent add-ons, does this mean that their approach to regulation is not much affected by considerations of social class (or race)? The analysis of previous chapters indicates that class *is* important to the way Americans think about the voucher issue, and the same concerns should presumably extend to regulation. We know, moreover, that Americans are highly supportive of regulations that guarantee fairness in admissions, and this too could well be rooted in class-based concerns for equity. In the case of parent add-ons, the lack of enthusiasm for regulation may mean that class has taken a back seat to freedom of choice, which is clearly highly valued. But it needn't mean that class is somehow irrelevant.

Two additional survey items suggest that class is indeed a major force in their thinking and that, the add-ons issue notwithstanding, Americans are quite enthusiastic about regulations that promote equity. The first asks respondents, "If a voucher plan were adopted, do you think parents who make more than $100,000 should be eligible for vouchers?" The idea behind such a rule, of course, is that relatively affluent parents already have the resources to send their children to the schools of their choice, whether public or private, and do not need government assistance. Vouchers should go to people who need them, and, at minimum, this should exclude people at the upper end of the income distribution.

Critics, of course, would agree with this restriction, as would many in the modern wing of the voucher movement. Traditional voucher supporters would generally be opposed. This is not because they favor the rich, as critics claim, but because they strongly believe that a choice system should be universal—that it should constitute a genuine education system for the nation, or for a state or community, and not a benefit limited to some segment of the population.

For most Americans, this kind of regulation does not restrict freedom of choice in any way, because only a small portion of families make more than $100,000 per year (as of 1995). The question is: are Americans willing to restrict access to vouchers on purely class grounds, so that some classes are treated differently from others? The answer is a resounding yes. As table 9-3 shows, 66 percent of Americans think that the more affluent members of society should not qualify for vouchers. Parents and nonparents alike are highly supportive of such a rule. But so are private parents—who, stereotypes aside, are not typically very affluent themselves and are happy to see the affluent excluded.

The second survey item asks respondents to consider a dramatic, potentially far-reaching regulatory mechanism for promoting social equity. The idea, championed by Coons and Sugarman, is that private schools that participate in a voucher system should be required to set aside a certain percentage of their new admissions every year for low-income children. Coons and Sugarman are themselves great believers in markets and vouchers. But they argue that a low-income set-aside is necessary to ensure that the neediest children have genuine access to all schools in the private sector.[11]

This kind of thinking is paradigmatic of the modern wing of the movement. But among traditional voucher supporters, the set-aside meets with passionate opposition. They see it as another unwarranted government intrusion on the private schools—and an unnecessary one, because the natural operation of choice and competition, combined with the great attraction of vouchers for the poor, ensures that low-income families will be heavily represented in private schools. They also see low-income set-asides

as a governmental policy of "preferences"—a variant of affirmative action—to which they are strongly opposed on principle.

How do Americans come down on this controversial issue of social
equity? The survey presents respondents with the following agree-disagree
item about participating private schools: "To promote equal access, these
schools should be required to set aside a certain percentage of their new
spaces every year for low-income children." The responses, summarized
in table 9-3, show that the public is quite positive toward this kind of
regulation. Overall, 75 percent of Americans support the low-income set-
aside, while only 19 percent are opposed. As we might expect, support is
higher for inner-city parents (at 85 percent) than for public parents generally (at 78 percent). But it is high across all groups, parents and nonparents
alike, and about half say they are "strongly" in favor. Even private parents are enthusiastic, and once again willing to see their own schools restricted by new social regulations.

There may be a positive response bias at work here, because the set-
aside item is part of a battery of agree-disagree items. But given the high
support Americans express for the regulation of admissions and the exclusion of the wealthy, both of which were measured in other ways, it seems
probable that these scores for the set-aside are meaningful and that they
are tapping much the same set of concerns and aspirations.

On the whole, then, Americans are quite supportive of equity-promoting
regulations, remarkably so in light of how controversial these proposals
are at the elite level. What variation there is, on the other hand, does
reflect a basic reality of elite politics: that regulation is an issue dividing
Democrats and Republicans. As table 9-3 shows, informed Democrats are
consistently more likely to support equity-promoting regulations than informed Republicans are. They are more inclined to say private schools
should have to admit all children who apply (62 percent of Democrats say
so, versus 45 percent of Republicans), that religious schools should have
to admit children of all religions (by 83 percent to 72 percent), that parents should be prohibited from adding on to their vouchers (by 38 percent
to 27 percent), that high-income families should be excluded from a voucher
program (by 65 percent to 49 percent), and that private schools should be
required to set aside seats for low-income kids (by 75 percent to 57 percent).

It is tempting to think that similar differences must apply to supporters
and opponents of vouchers, and that supporters, such as Republicans, are
the ones resisting the regulation of private schools (to the extent anyone
is). But on reflection, we shouldn't expect this to be so. For voucher supporters are a mixed group, weighted toward people who are low in in-

come, concerned about inequity, and supportive of diversity—people who might want *more,* rather than less, regulation. And while Republicans tend to be supportive of vouchers, most voucher supporters are in fact not Republicans, and many embrace Democratic values.

As the figures in table 9-3 suggest, even though voucher leaders are known for resisting regulation, supporters within the general population simply do not feel that way, and indeed are often more sympathetic toward regulation than voucher opponents are. Supporters, for instance, are more inclined than opponents to say that private schools (including religious schools) should accept all children who apply, and that private schools should set aside some of their seats for low-income children. And they are just as inclined as opponents to say that wealthy families should be excluded from voucher programs. Only when it comes to parent add-ons are supporters less inclined to regulate. But this, it seems likely, is because they want to ensure that parents have as much choice as possible, not because they don't like regulation.

As with accountability regulation, then, traditional voucher leaders appear to have staked out a distinctly unpopular position on these issues. They are out of step with the American public, which views equity-promoting regulation with great favor. They are out of step with their own supporters, who are often more in favor of regulation than opponents are. They are even out of step with informed Republicans, who, although more receptive to the traditionalist argument than other groups, are nowhere close to the anti-regulation end of the continuum. The traditionalists are basically out there by themselves.

A Closer Look at Support for Regulation

Now let's try to understand why people take the positions they do on issues of regulation. Because support for accountability regulation is high across the board, the focus here will be on the equity-promoting regulations, which offer more variation to study and explain, and which highlight the kinds of social concerns that, in one form or another, have been at the heart of the modern voucher movement.

The basic question here is whether people are able to connect these regulatory issues to their underlying values, beliefs, and interests. If they make a connection, and thus if there is a measure of coherence to their thinking on regulation—as there was, to a surprising degree, to their thinking on the voucher concept in general—this should tell us something about how regulation and vouchers come together as political issues. In particular, it should tell us what types of people would be attracted to the movement, and what types would be alienated, if the movement continues to shift away from free markets toward greater regulation.

What should we expect to find? We already know that, as is true throughout American politics, informed Democrats are more sympathetic toward regulation than informed Republicans are. What is especially interesting about the equity-promoting regulations we have been discussing here, however, is their relation to social class. For among the broader public, it is class rather than party that best captures the way people respond to vouchers. If opinion on regulatory issues is going to shape the politics of vouchers, it is likely to be because both are connected to social class.

As I hinted earlier, these connections to social class may well create a big problem for traditionalists. We know that people who are low in social class are especially positive toward private schools and vouchers. But it is reasonable to suspect that these same people will turn out to be especially positive toward regulation. For the regulations are clearly intended to level the playing field and ensure that less advantaged children gain equal access. The upshot, then, is that the constituency that best reflects the modern wing of the voucher movement is likely to be highly supportive of vouchers *and* highly supportive of regulation: a combination that flies in the face of traditional thinking on the issue and, if documented by the data, stands to have major consequences for the future direction of the movement.

The same sort of reasoning applies to other factors associated with social disadvantage. For example, it makes sense to expect that blacks and Hispanics would be especially supportive of regulation (compared to whites), even with social class controlled, because they want to guard against racial discrimination. More generally, people who see the public school system as inequitable, and people who believe in diversity—whatever their class or race—should be supporters of regulation as well.

Beyond class and race, people may have other reasons for favoring regulation. One is simply the risk factor. As we saw in chapter 8, many people are worried about the uncertainties associated with vouchers; indeed, it is a concern for risk, more than any other social consideration, that determines whether people are willing to support vouchers as public policy. This same concern for risk, one would think, ought to lead people to support regulation.

Another basic factor is public school ideology. People who are normatively committed to the current public system are likely to believe that the

best way to promote its ideals—common schooling, for instance—is precisely the way the current system actually attempts to do so: by regulation. To these people, regulations probably seem good and necessary. They
would presumably want the same for a voucher system.

And then, of course, there are attitudes toward markets. We can't expect Americans to be social theorists, and they may not make a clear connection between markets and regulation. But this is surely a connection
that elites make, and ordinary people may do the same. If they do, the
more they think that competition is good for schools and that market-
based incentives promote effectiveness, the less enthusiastic they should
be about regulation

Last but not least, we have to recognize the role of self-interest. When
people say they are for or against parent add-ons, or any of the other
equity-promoting regulations—regulations that in each case clearly work
to the advantage of some families and social groups and to the disadvantage of others—are their positions driven by a self-interested concern for
how they would personally be affected by the regulations? Or are they
primarily thinking about what would be best for others and for society
more generally?

There is no definitive way to answer this, because most of the factors
we've discussed could cut both ways. Low-income parents, for instance,
could support regulation because they personally benefit from it. But they
could also support regulation because they believe it helps all families who
are disadvantaged, and because they think programs that promote equity
are good for society generally—in which case self-interest may have nothing to do with it.

We do, however, have means of gaining leverage on this question. In
the first place, some of the factors we're dealing with seem largely social
in nature, rather than personal, and we can explore their impact. Specifically, attitudes toward equity and diversity—especially in an analysis that
controls for social class and other possible sources of self-interest—probably represent social concerns. The same can be said for public school
ideology and perceptions of risk. If our data analysis shows that these
factors are important influences on the way people think about regulation, this would be evidence that social concerns are at work.

A second means of leverage is that nonparents have little or no personal stake in these kinds of regulations. Regulations have direct effects
on parents and children, but any effects on nonparents would usually be
experienced indirectly, through the broader effects on society. Thus, if it
turns out that some factors we might associate with self-interest—class

and race, in particular—influence the way nonparents approach regulation, this would suggest that these variables are also (and perhaps the only) carriers of social concerns and not simply reflections of self-interest.

We will have learned something if we can show that social concerns have an important bearing on the way people approach regulation. But political scientists would find this unsurprising. If the research literature is correct, it is normal for Americans to emphasize social concerns in taking positions on these issues and to put little weight on self-interest. As we discussed in chapter 8, the intriguing research question is not whether social concerns play a role in the public's thinking, but whether *self-interest* does.[12]

Fortunately, a third means of leverage allows us to carry out a direct test of the self-interest theory. We know that parents stand to be personally affected by the voucher issue. But we also know that some parents are interested in using a voucher, while other parents are not—which means that the former have a much greater personal stake in the issue than the latter do. If self-interest has an influence on the way parents think about regulation, then the "personal use" factor should help us discover it.

The impact of self-interest could take various forms. But to keep things simple, our focus here will be on a very basic one that, if documented in the data, would prove quite revealing. Here is the logic. Perhaps the most basic expectation, going into a study of regulation, is that parents who are lower in income are likely to be more supportive of equity-promoting regulation than parents who are higher in income. If self-interest is important to their thinking, however, the strength of this relationship should depend on whether they intend to use a voucher. A low-income parent would see regulation as personally beneficial, and a high-income parent would see regulation as personally costly, but only if they intended to use a voucher. If they had no intention of using one, there would be no personal component to their calculations, and parents at different income levels would have no reason to see regulation in different terms. Any differences would likely be due to social concerns, not to self-interest. If self-interest is operating, then, we should find that income has a bigger impact for parents who want to use a voucher than for parents who don't.

We have now set out a number of expectations about why people might support or oppose regulation. What do the data have to tell us? To see, let's take as our dependent variable a summary index that incorporates all five of the equity-related survey items discussed in the previous section. The higher the score on this index, the more pro-regulation the respondent. The task of the analysis is to determine whether the various influences we've just covered—from income to risk to public school ideology to the personal use factor—help to explain the way people think about regulation.

The findings are set out in table 9-4 and presented in three columns. The first and second present regression results for nonparents and parents, respectively. Because the same variables are included in each, they offer a useful comparison of the two groups. The third column introduces the personal use factor into the parents' model, along with a term that interacts personal use with income. This allows for a test of the self-interest theory.

For starters, these results suggest that Americans *are* able to connect the regulation issue to their values, beliefs, and interests in ways that make eminently good sense. This is especially true of parents, for whom virtually every one of the factors we've discussed turns out to be influential. Aside from party, the most prominent of these is income: parents who are low in income are much more likely to favor regulation than parents who are high in income. In general, parents make a clear connection between their social class and the kinds of rules they think are desirable.

Political party is as powerful an influence (among the informed) as income is, with informed Democrats much more pro-regulation than informed Republicans. But most parents, we have to remember, are uninformed—and with all other variables controlled, the estimated impact of party for them is near zero. As far as the population of parents as a whole is concerned, then, income is the variable with the most generalized and consequential impact.

While income stands out, other influences clearly enter into parents' thinking as well. Parents tend to support regulation when they think the public system is inequitable, when they believe in diversity, when they embrace the public school ideology, when they worry about risk, and when they are only weak believers in markets. In each case, the direction of the effect is precisely what we should expect if American parents (or at least many of them) are capable of thinking about the issue in a reasonable way—and if regulation is associated in their minds with the same sorts of concerns that, at the elite level, are associated with the liberal coalition.

The only variable that fails to register is race. Blacks and Hispanics are no more likely to favor regulation than whites are, once class and other factors are controlled. This is surprising, because racial discrimination is a standard rationale for regulation, and our data show that parents who support diversity are indeed inclined to regulate. If there is an explanation for this, it may simply be that blacks and Hispanics are quite positive in their views about the racial consequences of vouchers

Table 9-4. *The Determinants of Support for Equity Regulation*[a]

Variable	Nonparents (social model)		Public school parents (social model)		Public school parents (self-interest model)	
	Coefficient	[Impact]	Coefficient	[Impact]	Coefficient	[Impact]
Black (north)	-.01	[-.02]	.01	[.02]	.03	[.06]
Black (south)	-.14	[-.22]	.01	[.02]	.01	[.02]
Hispanic	.01	[.01]	-.02	[-.04]	-.02	[-.04]
Voucher support	.03*	[.09]	-.05***	[-.17]	-.03**	[-.11]
Personal interest					.06***	[b]
Personal interest*income					-.02***	[b, c]
Income	-.05***	[-.33]	-.06***	[-.40]	-.01	
Risk	.02	[.07]	.02**	[.09]	.03**	[.11]
Inequity	.01	[.03]	.03***	[.09]	.03***	[.09]
Diversity (whites)	.06***	[.16]	.09***	[.25]	.10***	[.28]
Party (informed)	-.05***	[-.34]	-.06***	[-.43]	-.05***	[-.36]
Party (uninformed)	-.01	[-.06]	-.01	[-.06]	-.00	[-.03]
Public school ideology	.12***	[.29]	.06***	[.16]	.06***	[.16]
Markets	-.02	[-.05]	-.03*	[-.08]	-.03*	[-.07]
Constant	.28*		.36***		.15	
N[d]	(1,231)		(2,030)		(1,979)	
Adjusted R^2	.19		.19		.19	

* Significant at .10 level.
** Significant at .05 level.
*** Significant at .01 level.

a. The dependent variable is an index of equity regulation, constructed as the mean of all the standardized measures reported in table 9-3. Ordinary least squares regressions estimated using weighted data. Unstandardized coefficients reported. For each nondichotomous independent variable, the impact coefficient represents the estimated change in the dependent variable (measured in standard deviations) when the independent variable shifts by two standard deviations, holding all other variables constant; for each dichotomous variable, the impact coefficient represents the estimated change in the dependent variable (measured in standard deviations) when the independent variable shifts from 0 to 1, holding all other variables constant. Model controls for the full range of background and district variables.

b. *Impact of Income*: For individuals who are definitely interested in using a voucher, a two–standard deviation decline in income changes their support for equity regulation by .59; for individuals who are probably interested in using a voucher, it is .46; for individuals who are probably not interested in using a voucher, it is .33; and for people who definitely are not interested in using a voucher, it is .2.

c. *Impact of Personal interest*: For individuals earning less than $20,000 per year in income, a two–standard deviation increase in personal interest changes their support for equity regulation by .16 (where the dependent variable is measured in standard deviation units as well); for people earning between $21,000 and $30,000, the change in support is .08; for people earning between $31,000 and $40,000, it is .00; for people earning between $41,000 and $50,000, it is -.08; for people earning between $51,000 and $60,000, it is -.16; for people earning between $61,000 and $75,000, it is -.24; for people earning between $75,000 and $100,000, it is -.32; and for people earning more than $100,000, it is -.4.

d. N is the unweighted number of respondents.

(chapter 8) and do not see discrimination as a major problem where vouchers are concerned.

In chapter 7's analysis of support for vouchers, we found that parents think more coherently about the subject than nonparents do. The same is true for regulation—which, again, is probably because nonparents have less stake in the issue. Nonetheless, despite some gaps (most notably, that inequity has no effect at all, which makes little sense), the overall pattern of results is similar to what we find for parents: with income, party, diversity, and public school ideology having the expected effects, and the respondent's race once again proving unimportant.

Now let's turn to the findings on self-interest. To begin with, the first two models suggest that social concerns have a lot to do with the way Americans think about regulation. This is evident in the kinds of values and beliefs that are being brought to bear. It is also evident in the major role that income plays for nonparents—which, given their low personal stake in the issue, suggests that their class-based response is driven by broader concerns: a desire to help needy children, for instance, or to ensure fairness. If this is true for nonparents, it stands to reason that at least some of the class-based response of parents is probably based on social concerns as well, and not on simple self-interest.

Still, the intriguing question, given the background of political science research, is whether self-interest also has an important role to play here. And the evidence shows quite strongly that it does. The results, set out in the third model of table 9-4, may be a bit difficult for some readers to interpret, because the impacts of the key variables here—income and the personal use factor—cannot be read off directly from their estimated coefficients. Their impacts are interconnected and have to be computed. To clarify matters, this is done in the notes below the table.

As expected, the impact of income on parental attitudes toward regulation depends heavily on whether parents have a direct stake in the issue, and thus on whether they want to put a voucher to personal use. For parents who say they are definitely not interested in using a voucher, a drop in income from high to low leads to an increase in support for equity-promoting regulation of .20 (standard deviations). For parents who say they definitely *do* want to use a voucher, on the other hand, the same drop in income produces an increase in support for regulation of .59. One implication is that social class does matter to parents even when they have little or no personal stake in the issue—which is consistent with the results for nonparents, and presumably a reflection of social concerns. But another implication is that social class plays a *greater* role in parents' thinking as their personal stake in the issue grows: the more self-interested they are, the more class-oriented their approach to regulation. Judging by the impact coefficients, social class has three times the influence for parents who are self-interested than it does for parents who aren't. Self-interest clearly matters.[13]

Overall, then, this section's analysis provides a nice complement to what we've learned in the prior sections. There, evidence showed that the level of support for regulation is quite high among Americans generally, even among those who are voucher supporters—which suggests that traditional voucher leaders are isolated and out of step, and that a shift away from free markets is politically wise. Here, we have been able to gain a more refined sense of the types of people that favor and oppose regulation—and this allows us to see how a shift toward regulation might affect the attractiveness of vouchers to particular social groups.

If one conclusion deserves to be emphasized, it is simply this. The people who are the hallmark of the modern wing of the voucher movement— people who are low in income, who view the current system as inequitable, and who support diversity—are also the most supportive of regulation. Their attachment to regulation, moreover, is underpinned by self-interest, and is likely to be an enduring fact of life within the politics of vouchers.

Given the roots of the voucher movement in traditional, conservative thinking, and given the predominance of conservative leaders at the elite level, this is a fact of revolutionary potential. A movement that seeks to attract and hold this constituency will be under pressure to move toward greater regulation—and to promote an agenda very different from what many traditionalists envision or are comfortable with.

Low-Income Vouchers

So far, our attention has centered on a universal voucher system—one that would extend vouchers to all parents (or virtually all)—and what the rules for such a system should be. This leaves a key question unanswered. What do Americans think about universalism itself?

The modern voucher movement has become a force in American politics by championing programs that are *not* universal, but targeted solely at needy children. Its major political successes (as of this writing)—in Milwaukee, Cleveland, and the state of Florida—all involve programs of this sort. In addition, more than forty voucher programs have been set up in recent years by private foundations, all of which restrict vouchers to low-income children.[14]

At the elite level, targeted programs have clearly made it easier for advocates to build winning coalitions and attract funding. But as the voucher issue grows in national salience, both sides are competing aggressively for public support—and the movement's future success will increasingly depend on what ordinary Americans think. Do they like the idea of limiting vouchers to the kids in greatest need? Or do they favor programs that are broadly based?

Vouchers for the Inner-City Poor

As background, let's begin with an item that appears early in the survey, before the concept of vouchers is even introduced. It asks respondents whether they would support or oppose the following proposal for education reform: "In inner-city areas where public schools are performing badly, the government should put some of its education funds into scholarships for low-income children, so that they might attend private or parochial schools instead."

Responses to this item must be interpreted with care, in part because it uses the term *scholarship* rather than *voucher*, and in part because it asks people for a judgment on inner-city voucher programs before they have been able to think about the voucher concept and its possible uses, problems, and consequences. Still, this question captures the essence of what an inner-city voucher program actually does: it provides financial assistance to poor children, enabling them to leave troubled public schools and seek out private alternatives.

Note that, when the issue is framed in this way, Americans are not asked to choose between a targeted voucher plan and a universal voucher plan. If they were, they would be faced with a trade-off: to favor targeting would be to say that only needy kids should get vouchers and all other kids should be excluded. As the question is worded, however, it says nothing about whether these other children might eventually have access to vouchers too, through programs adopted at some future time. It simply asks whether, right now, a program for the inner-city poor would seem a good incremental move—and even people who are strongly in favor of universalism might easily agree. There is no conflict between the two approaches.

The responses to this item are set out in table 9-5. What they show, most generally, is that Americans look quite favorably on programs that

Table 9-5. *Support for Scholarships for Inner-City Children*
Percent, unless otherwise indicated[a]

	Support inner-city vouchers?			
Type of respondent	Yes	No	Don't know	N[b]
Total population	61	32	7	(4,700)
Nonparents	60	33	7	(1,617)
Public school parents	64	30	6	(2,553)
Private school parents	65	31	5	(530)
Inner-city parents	77	17	6	(539)
Position on vouchers				
Support	71	24	5	(3,229)
Oppose	38	55	7	(1,134)
Political party (informed)				
Democrat	57	35	9	(779)
Republican	52	42	6	(649)

a. Percentages are based on weighted data. They may not sum to 100 due to rounding.
b. N is the unweighted number of respondents.

would provide inner-city children with publicly funded scholarships to attend private schools. The margin of support is roughly 2 to 1, and its level is much the same for nonparents (60 percent), public parents (64 percent), and private parents (65 percent). As we might expect, given their personal stake in the issue, inner-city parents are the group most in favor of publicly funded scholarships, with 77 percent expressing support for such a program.

The table also shows that support for inner-city scholarship programs is strongly related to support for vouchers generally, even though the scholarship item was asked before the voucher section of the survey, and indeed was separated from the final support question (used here) by more than forty intervening items. Of people who support vouchers, 71 percent express support for inner-city scholarship programs. And of people who oppose vouchers, 38 percent think these inner-city programs are good ideas.

Assuming there is a certain substance and consistency to people's responses—which the analysis of this and previous chapters seems to support—the last figure is worth appreciating from a different angle. Voucher opponents are not totally opposed to vouchers: more than a third of them are open to the idea of voucher programs for the inner-city poor. This is an indication that, as a political proposal, targeted voucher plans can indeed attract support from the other side. Another indication can be found in the figures on political party: even though these programs involve vouchers, informed Democrats are more likely to support them than informed Republicans are. Indeed, inner-city scholarship programs win by a 22 percent margin among Democrats (57 percent versus 35 percent), but by a margin of only 10 percent among Republicans (52 percent versus 42 percent).

Targeted Programs versus Universalism: Where to Start?

Targeted programs have been at the forefront of the voucher movement, but this is not because most voucher leaders prefer them. Traditional leaders, of course, are strong believers in universalism; and the more libertarian not only favor universalism over targeting, but go so far as to argue that targeting is undesirable. Milton Friedman, for example, is quite explicit in saying that he supports targeted programs only for strategic reasons, and that on the merits "programs for the poor are poor programs."[15] This is an extreme view that, so far as I can tell, is not widely shared among those who play leading roles in the movement. Still, most voucher advocates would like to see the nation move toward a universal system (or something close to it) over the long haul. There are, however, important figures in the modern wing of the movement—Polly Williams, among others—who only favor voucher programs that are targeted at the disadvantaged. Their fear is that, if programs are broadened, needy children will not be as well served.[16]

Ordinary Americans look quite favorably on inner-city scholarship programs. But this says nothing about where they stand on universalism. People may express support for programs for needy children, yet think that a broadly based system would be far preferable. Or they may be attracted by the equity or low-risk aspects of targeted programs and be opposed to universalism. Whatever their views may be, these views are likely to shape their orientation to the voucher issue and the sides they choose when real proposals are offered them in politics.

Several survey items are helpful here, each of them looking at the tradeoff between targeted programs and universalism in somewhat different ways. The first reads as follows: "There are many ways to design a voucher program. Which is closer to your view? (a) In order to promote the greatest reform and include the most children, vouchers should be made available to all children in the state, or (b) Because a voucher plan would be such a big change, it is better to start with a smaller plan that is limited to children whose educational needs are the greatest."

This item forces people to choose between a universal system and a targeted system. But it does not ask them which of the two they would ultimately prefer. This is a question about the short run, and about which

Table 9-6. *Where Should Reform Start: With All Children or with Needy Children?*
Percent, unless otherwise indicated[a]

| | Where should reform start? | | | |
| | All children | Limited to needy children | Don't know | N[b] |
Type of respondent				
Total population	40	48	13	(4,700)
Nonparents	38	48	14	(1,617)
Public school parents	41	48	11	(2,553)
Private school parents	57	36	7	(530)
Inner-city parents	39	50	11	(539)
Position on vouchers				
Strongly support	48	48	5	(1,856)
Weakly support	43	51	6	(1,373)
Weakly oppose	35	48	16	(424)
Strongly oppose	25	45	30	(710)
Political party (informed)				
Democrat	37	47	17	(779)
Republican	50	40	10	(649)

a. Percentages are based on weighted data. They may not sum to 100 due to rounding.
b. N is the unweighted number of respondents.

approach is the more attractive way of starting the reform process. Universalism is presented as a thoroughgoing reform that brings vouchers to all children right away. The targeted plan is described not simply as a program limited to needy children, but also as a "smaller plan" that offers an incremental approach to change.

The results are set out in table 9-6. Thirteen percent of respondents do not answer this question, and these missing responses are anything but random (see below). So we have to be careful here. But of the people who do give a response, more would rather see a limited voucher plan—at least to begin with—than a major reform that extends vouchers to all children right away. The plurality in favor of the targeted approach is 48 percent to 40 percent (which translates into a 55 percent to 45 percent majority if the missing cases are omitted from the calculations).

Private parents depart from the mainstream on this, supporting universalism by 57 percent to 36 percent. This only makes sense, because most would not qualify for vouchers under a targeted plan. Private parents aside, however, public opinion seems quite uniform on this issue. The targeted approach is not a runaway winner, but it consistently tops universalism as a short-term strategy of reform, winning by 48 percent to 38 percent among nonparents, by 48 percent to 41 percent among public parents, and by 50 percent to 39 percent among inner-city parents.

If we look at how voucher supporters and voucher opponents tend to view these competing approaches to reform, we can see immediately why the earlier results were plagued by so many missing responses: a large percentage of voucher opponents do not answer this item. The chief reason, presumably, is not that they are undecided, but that they object to choosing among two types of voucher systems when their real preference is for no voucher system at all. Of those who strongly oppose vouchers, 30 percent fail to answer this item, and of those who are weakly opposed, 16 percent fail to answer it. By contrast, only 5 percent of voucher supporters don't give an answer, which is about average for most items on the survey.

Missing values aside, what would we expect from supporters and opponents on this issue? The obvious expectation is that, even if supporters and opponents were equally concerned with helping needy children, opponents would be more inclined than supporters to choose targeted plans over universalism, because targeted plans limit the scope and spread of vouchers. The findings indicate as much. Not counting the missing cases, almost two-thirds of strong voucher opponents say they prefer a targeted system to a universal system, while about half of strong voucher supporters have the same preference. The differential would be still greater if we assume that the vast majority of the opponents who refused to answer this item would have chosen the targeting option, which is reasonable. Thus the figures throughout table 9-6 probably understate the popularity of targeting as a short-term approach to reform. Were there no missing cases, it would beat universalism by a wider margin than it already does.

It is worth emphasizing, moreover, that this sympathy for targeting as a short-term approach to reform is prevalent even among voucher *supporters*. One might expect them to heavily favor an immediate shift toward universalism—as the traditional leadership clearly does—but in fact they are fairly evenly split between universalism and targeting. At this point, we can't say why this is so (although we'll soon learn more). It could be that many voucher supporters have a genuine preference for programs that focus on needy children and have no desire for universalism. It could also be that they do favor universalism, but see an immediate shift as overly risky and regard targeted programs as a sensible way of moving incrementally toward a more broadly based system. In either event, the public constituency for vouchers comes across as rather moderate in its approach to education reform.

Targeted Programs versus Universalism:
What Is the Ultimate Goal?

To know where the movement is headed and what its prospects are for mobilizing public support, we have to know what Americans want over the long run. Granted, most think that targeting vouchers at needy kids is the most reasonable place to start, assuming a voucher system were to be adopted at all. But this embrace of targeting may often be rooted in concerns about risk and does not tell us where they would like to see these reforms go over time. What, then, is their basic preference? Do they think vouchers should stop with the disadvantaged? Or are they universalists at heart, believing that, if vouchers are made available to the disadvantaged, they should eventually be extended to the broader population of kids as well?

The survey does not allow us to measure these preferences with precision, but it does include an item that is quite helpful. This item asks respondents to give a preference ordering among the three basic alternatives at issue here. It reads as follows: "I'm now going to list three different approaches to vouchers. Please put them in order for me, from the one you like best to the one you like least. (a) A voucher plan for all children in the state. (b) A voucher plan for low-income children. (c) No voucher plan at all."

Note that this item, unlike the one we considered earlier (which also appears much earlier in the survey), does not frame the voucher issue in terms of the greater risks of universalism, nor in terms of the prudence of starting with smaller, more limited programs. These considerations are not mentioned at all. It is framed in terms of how much respondents *like* each system and simply asks them to indicate which approach they prefer.

If we restrict our attention to the comparison between universalism and the low-income approach, the basic results are set out in table 9-7. They are quite striking, especially in light of the earlier finding that most Americans prefer the incremental, targeted programs to start out the process of reform. When prudential considerations are put aside and respondents are simply asked what type of system they would prefer, the winner is universalism. And by a wide margin.

For the population as a whole, 58 percent favor universalism, 30 percent favor the low-income approach, and 12 percent are undecided. Private parents are the most enthusiastic about a system that includes all children, an obvious reflection of their personal stake in the matter. Sixty-eight percent of them support universalism, as against just 22 percent for

Table 9-7. *Basic Preferences: Universalism or Targeting?*
Percent, unless otherwise indicated[a]

	Basic preference			
Type of respondent	Universal voucher plan	Low-income voucher plan	Don't know	N^b
Total population	58	30	12	(4,700)
Nonparents	56	31	13	(1,617)
Public school parents	61	29	10	(2,553)
Private school parents	68	22	10	(530)
Inner-city parents	53	35	12	(539)
Position on vouchers				
Support	63	28	9	(3,229)
Oppose	50	40	10	(1,134)
Political party (informed)				
Democrat	51	34	15	(779)
Republican	70	20	11	(649)

a. Percentages are based on weighted data. They may not sum to 100 due to rounding.
b. N is the unweighted number of respondents.

the low-income approach. But support for universalism is high across all
the remaining groups as well: the comparable figures are 56 percent to 31
percent for nonparents, 61 percent to 29 percent for public parents, and
53 percent to 35 percent for the inner-city poor.

A recent study by Public Agenda shows much the same thing: when
presented with a choice between programs for all children and programs
for low-income children, Americans chose universalism by 72 percent to
22 percent.[17]

Support for universalism even runs high among the opponents of vouchers. People who truly oppose vouchers would presumably want no voucher
system at all, and one would think that a targeted approach, which limits
the scope of vouchers, would be far superior in their eyes to a system that
gives vouchers to all kids. But as the table shows, this is not the case.
Opponents may not like vouchers, and they may believe (as the earlier
evidence shows) that targeting—and thus a limited, incremental approach
to reform—is a far better place to *start* if vouchers are to be adopted. But
in terms of their basic preferences, they are surprisingly sympathetic to
universalism, which they favor by 50 percent to 40 percent over the low-
income option.

This is an important indication that opposition among ordinary people
takes a very different form than it does among elites. At the elite level,
opponents are dedicated to stopping vouchers entirely and, failing that, to

limiting their scope. For them, universalism is the worst possible outcome, to be prevented at all costs. But opponents within the general public do not see it that way. They seem to think that, if such a system were adopted—against their wishes—the goal (over the long run) is not to limit it at every turn, but rather to ensure that it is the *kind* of system that conforms to their own values, beliefs, and interests, which is often a universal system. This may be because they want a system that is fair and equitable for everyone and not permanently restricted to special groups. But it may also be because voucher opponents tend to be more advantaged than supporters are—higher in income, from better districts, less likely to be minority—and some may see themselves and their communities as having a stake in universalism.

We can get additional insight into the popularity of universalism by taking a look at table 9-8, which cross-tabulates this section's basic preference item with the earlier item on short-term approaches to reform. What it shows, most important, is that much of the enthusiasm for targeting as a way of starting the reform process actually comes from people whose basic preference is for universalism—and who seem, therefore, to view targeting as a prudent, low-risk way to moving toward a broader system. Among those who favor targeting as a short-term approach, 56 percent are universalists.[18]

In the earlier analysis, one of the most interesting findings was that voucher supporters were almost evenly split between an immediate shift to universalism and the option of starting (and perhaps ending) with the targeting approach. Now we can see that, for the most part, the attraction of targeting is due to its pragmatic appeal—for underneath it all, most (59 percent) of the voucher supporters who embrace the short-term targeting strategy would ultimately prefer universalism. Indeed, even among voucher opponents, a surprising 46 percent of those who express an interest in starting out with targeting are actually universalists in what they ultimately prefer.[19]

If we put all the evidence together, a coherent picture emerges. Americans look very favorably on vouchers for needy children, both because such programs are socially valuable in their own right (as the scholarships item showed), and because they represent a sensible, low-risk way to initiate an incremental process of reform. But most Americans are universalists at heart. They think the best voucher plan is one that is open—eventually—to the broader population of kids, and that targeted plans are reasonable ways to get there.

Table 9-8. *Universalism versus Targeting: The Connection between Short-Term Preferences and Basic Preferences*
Percent, unless otherwise indicated[a]

	Basic preference		
Where should reform start?	*Universal voucher plan*	*Low-income voucher plan*	N[b]
Total population			
All children	78	22	(1,792)
Limited program	56	44	(2,020)
Nonparents			
All children	76	24	(535)
Limited program	55	45	(693)
Public school parents			
All children	79	21	(982)
Limited program	59	41	(1,133)
Private school parents			
All children	86	14	(268)
Limited program	62	38	(180)
Inner-city parents			
All children	68	32	(195)
Limited program	54	46	(258)
Voucher supporters			
All children	80	20	(1,416)
Limited program	59	41	(1,433)
Voucher opponents			
All children	69	31	(305)
Limited program	46	54	(483)
Informed Republicans			
All children	92	8	(318)
Limited program	64	36	(223)
Informed Democrats			
All children	80	20	(277)
Limited program	47	53	(319)

a. Percentages are based on weighted data. They may not sum to 100 due to rounding.
b. N is the unweighted number of respondents.

A Closer Look at Targeting vs. Universalism

The choice between targeting and universalism is actually a choice about how to regulate a voucher system. In an earlier section, we looked at regulations—dealing with private school admissions, for example, or parent add-ons—that promote equity *within* a universalistic system. Here the focus is simply on a more extreme form of equity-promoting regulation:

one that does away with universalism itself (at least in the short run) and restricts access to needy children.

It makes sense that people would think about this issue in much the same way that they think about equity-promoting regulations in general. Most obviously, the values, beliefs, and interests that prompt people to embrace the targeting approach, rather than universalism, should be those associated with the liberal coalition—low social class, concerns about inequity, support for diversity, belief in the public school ideology, a jaundiced view of markets. Targeting is also more likely to be favored by people who worry about the risks of a voucher system—and, of course, by people who are simply opposed to vouchers.

What about self-interest? Political scientists would expect it to play little or no role in shaping how people think about this issue, but they have been wrong before and may well be wrong again. If self-interest does have a role to play, what should it be? The answer is that it should find a somewhat different expression on this issue than it does for the other equity-promoting regulations. The reason is worth taking seriously, because it highlights a nonobvious connection between incentives and policy that may be politically important.

Consider first how self-interest works in a universal system. When everyone qualifies for a voucher, equity-promoting regulations are essentially just rules that try to level the playing field by favoring the less advantaged. Parents who don't want to use a voucher are unaffected by such rules, and (social concerns aside) there should be little connection between their incomes and their position on regulation. The more interested parents are in using vouchers, on the other hand, the more they are personally affected by equity regulations, and the stronger the connection should be between their incomes and their policy positions: parents who are low in income should favor equity-promoting rules, and enthusiasm for such rules should turn to opposition as income rises. The empirical evidence shows that this is what happens.

Things are provocatively different when the issue is universalism itself. It is still true that, to the extent parents want to use a voucher, there should be a connection between their incomes and their policy positions: low-income parents should be more inclined to favor targeting (and less inclined to favor universalism) than higher-income parents. The explanation, however, is not what it appears. The obvious explanation is that low-income parents have a stake in targeted programs, whereas higher-income parents have a stake in universal programs, and this accounts for the difference. Yet the first part of this explanation is false. The reason is that, regardless of whether a targeted or a universal program is adopted, *low-income parents get the benefits anyway*. Because this is so, they should be indifferent between the two (other things, like social concerns, being equal). It is the *higher*-income parents who have a real stake in which alternative gets chosen, because *only* under a universal system are they allowed to participate.

When it comes to the choice between targeted programs and universalism, then, we should expect self-interest to work entirely in favor of universalism. This does not mean that low-income parents literally don't care about targeted programs. They have strong incentives to support such programs when the alternative is no voucher program at all. But when the alternative is a universal voucher program, they have no self-interested reason for choosing one over the other, whereas parents who are higher in income have a clear interest in universalism. The real incentives on this issue are concentrated in the parents who are more advantaged.[20]

We now have a clear set of expectations with regard to both social concerns and self-interest. What do the data have to tell us? The results are set out in table 9-9 and follow the same format as the earlier analysis of equity-promoting regulation (table 9-4). Here, probit analysis is carried out separately for the two items in question. The short-term item compares all-at-once universalism (coded 0) to an incremental targeting approach (coded 1), while the other asks about basic preferences between universalism (coded 0) and low-income vouchers (coded 1). In each case, we estimate two social models, one for parents and one for nonparents, that make no attempt to get at the self-interest issue (and are thus identical in form for the two groups). We then estimate a third model that introduces new variables into the parent equation in order to test for the impact of self-interest.[21]

The results show that there is a definite structure to public opinion. People appear to connect universalism and targeting to their own values, beliefs, and interests in ways that make good sense. As is common in statistical analysis, there are some minor glitches, but these are probably not worth paying attention to. The key finding is the pattern itself, which is the pattern we ought to expect. Judging from the social models, it is the people who have liberal traits—who are lower in income, Democratic (if informed), concerned about inequity, supportive of diversity, endorse the public school ideology, and disinclined to believe in markets—who tend to favor targeted programs over universalism. The same is true of people who see vouchers as risky, and of people who are simply opposed to having any voucher program at all. With some exceptions (which are in the

Table 9-9. *Choosing between Targeting and Universalism*[a]

| | Where to start | | | | | | Basic preferences | | | | | |
| | Nonparents (social model) | | Public school parents (social model) | | Public school parents (self-interest model) | | Nonparents (social model) | | Public school parents (social model) | | Public school parents (self-interest model) | |
Variable	Coefficient	[Impact]	Coefficient	[Impact]	Coefficient	[Impact]	Coefficient	[Impact]	Coefficient	[Impact]	Coefficient	[Impact]
Black (north)	.17	[6.76]	.04	[1.44]	.02	[0.63]	-.02	[-0.83]	.02	[0.70]	.03	[1.09]
Black (south)	-.26	[-10.15]	.26	[10.21]	.26*	[9.99]	-.13	[-4.40]	-.00	[-.00]	.01	[0.41]
Hispanic	-.18	[-6.98]	-.12	[-4.78]	-.14	[-5.66]	.38**	[14.55]	.20*	[7.23]	.19	[7.01]
Voucher support	-.07*	[-5.96]	-.10***	[-8.15]	-.07*	[-5.64]	-.23***	[-18.13]	-.26***	[-18.61]	-.21***	[-15.16]
Personal interest					-.11***	b					-.16***	c
Personal interest*low income					.14**	b,d					.19***	c,e
Low income			.12*	[4.76]	-.27	d	-.06*	[-7.96]	.22**	[7.69]	-.31*	e
Income	-.08***	[-11.46]	.09***	[7.39]	.08***	[6.87]	-.02	[-1.50]	.10***	[7.04]	.08***	[6.18]
Risk	.08**	[6.12]	.08**	[5.17]	.10***	[6.29]	.16***	[8.58]	.16**	[9.06]	.15***	[8.58]
Inequity	.16***	[9.20]	.03	[1.98]	.05	[3.14]	.29***	[16.49]	.09*	[4.87]	.09*	[4.78]
Diversity (whites)	.10	[6.14]	-.05*	[-7.60]	-.03	[-5.63]	-.05	[-7.74]	-.06*	[-8.21]	-.06*	[-7.43]
Party (informed)	-.06*	[-8.84]	.03	[3.85]	.04	[5.21]	-.00	[-.32]	-.06***	[-7.32]	-.05**	[-6.47]
Party (uninformed)	.04	[5.35]			.08*	[4.73]	.08	[4.17]	.04	[2.12]	.03	[1.43]
Public school ideology	.15***	[9.24]	.08**	[4.93]								

Markets	-.05	[-3.14]	-.12***	[-7.11]	-.10***	[-6.46]	-.00	[-.00]	-.09**	[-5.16]	-.07*	[-4.08]
Constant	.66*		-.28		-.11		.94**		.69**		-.09
N[f]	(1,099)		(1,864)		(1,823)		(1,124)		(1,878)		(1,838)
Pseudo R^2	.06		.05		.05		.13		.08		.09

* Significant at .10 level.
** Significant at .05 level.
*** Significant at .01 level.

a. The dependent variable in the "Where to start" equations is the short-term item set out in table 9-6. The dependent variable in the "Basic preferences" equations is the basic preference item set out in table 9-8. For both dependent variables, universalism equals 0 and targeting equals 1. Probits estimated using weighted data. Unstandardized coefficients reported. The impact coefficient is the change in estimated probability as the independent variable shifts from one standard deviation below its mean to one standard deviation above its mean (for nondichotomous variables) or from 0 to 1 (for dichotomous variables), holding all other variables constant at their means.

b. *Impact of personal interest, "Where to start" model:* When personal interest in using a voucher increases by two standard deviations, the probability of favoring targeting over universalism changes by 2.51 for low-income parents and by –10.24 for high-income parents.

c. *Impact of personal interest, "Basic preferences" model:* When personal interest in using a voucher increases by two standard deviations, the probability of favoring targeting over universalism changes by 2.82 for low-income parents and by –12.26 for high-income parents.

d. *Impact of low income, "Where to start" model:* When income shifts from high to low, the probability of favoring targeting over universalism changes by 11.24 for parents who are definitely interested in using a voucher, by 5.75 for parents who are probably interested in using a voucher, by –.23 for parents who are probably not interested in using a voucher, and by –5.23 for parents who are definitely not interested in using a voucher.

e. *Impact of low income, "Basic preferences" model:* When income shifts from high to low, the probability of favoring targeting over universalism changes by 15.35 for parents who are definitely interested in using a voucher, by 9.34 for parents who are probably interested in using a voucher, by 2.79 for parents who are probably not interested in using a voucher, and by –4.20 for parents who are definitely not interested in using a voucher.

f. N is the unweighted number of respondents.

right directions, but insignificant), these results hold for both parents and nonparents and for both survey items.

As the results for income show, there is a clear class dimension to this issue. The lower their income, the more inclined people are to support targeting. The higher their income, the more inclined they are to support universalism. Some of this connection between income and regulation is surely due to social concerns, because even nonparents, who have little or no self-interest in the matter, are responding on a class basis. The impacts of other variables that are largely social in nature—inequity, diversity, public school ideology—only reinforce the notion that social concerns are centrally at work here.

But self-interest also has an important role to play. Indeed, when new variables are introduced to test for the impact of self-interest, the results are pretty much as we ought to expect. Consider, for instance, the summary figures for the "basic preference" item, which are described below table 9-9. They show two things. The first is that income has a much bigger impact on how parents evaluate regulations when they have a personal stake in the issue. Among those who are definitely interested in using vouchers, low-income parents are 15 percent more likely to favor targeting than higher-income parents are. The impact of being low-income declines for those less interested in actually putting vouchers to personal use.[22]

From this result, we know that low-income parents and higher-income parents see regulation very differently when they have personal stakes in the issue. But this is only part of the story. For as we discussed earlier, low-income parents should actually be indifferent between targeting and universalism (on self-interest grounds alone)—and the reason for the differential across income groups should be that the higher-income parents have a self-interested preference for universalism. The action should be coming from the higher-income parents, not from the low-income parents.

The rest of the findings suggest that this is what is going on. Suppose we look just at parents in the higher-income group and ask: what difference does it make whether they have a personal stake in the voucher issue?[23] The answer (for the basic preferences item) is that those who have a personal stake are 12 percent more likely to favor universalism than those who don't have a personal stake. If we now take a separate look at the low-income parents, those with a personal stake in the issue are just 3 percent more likely to favor the targeting approach than those without a personal stake. The action, in other words, is coming almost entirely from the higher-income parents. The low-income parents are largely indifferent—as they should be, because they get the benefits regardless of which approach is chosen. (The results for the other survey item lead to the same conclusions.)

The political implications are intriguing. On the one hand, targeting is attractive on social grounds to people whose values and characteristics are associated with the liberal coalition—and many low-income parents fall into this category. When voucher leaders move to the center by proposing programs for needy children, then, they are likely to pick up liberal (and low-income) support. As they do so, however, the self-interest of parents actually works against them, at least for a while: for the low income parents who would seem to benefit from targeting would actually be just as happy (on self-interest grounds alone) with universalism, while the higher-income parents have self-interested grounds for resisting.[24]

This is a fascinating political dynamic, but it may not pose a real problem. For as the movement goes to the center, some higher-income parents may be attracted by the possibility that targeted programs are just the beginning of a process that will ultimately bring vouchers to everyone. Others may be attracted to targeting on social grounds alone. Even in the short run, then, some may resist—but some may follow. And in the long run, as leaders seek to expand from targeting to more universalistic programs (which seems a likely scenario), the self-interest of higher-income parents could work to the movement's advantage and provide it with extra support down the home stretch.

Public School Choice

A system of school choice can take many different forms, depending on exactly what regulations are built into the design. When vouchers are involved, the biggest issues have to do with which children and private schools are allowed to participate and what rules they must follow once in the program. In the grander scheme of things, however, a choice system needn't involve vouchers at all. Families can be allowed to choose, but their choices can be restricted to schools within the public system. This too is simply a matter of regulation.

At the elite level, public school choice is not nearly as controversial as vouchers. Almost all voucher advocates support it. They just think that, as a stand-alone reform, it doesn't go far enough: it doesn't give parents enough choices, it doesn't provide enough competition for schools, and it involves too much regulation and political control. They see it as a limited but useful step toward what they really want: a voucher system.

Voucher opponents are divided on the issue. Some see the merits of choice and competition but want to ensure that kids and resources remain in the public sector. For them, public school choice is just what the doctor ordered. It means they can be against vouchers but in favor of choice and competition. This is a compromise many Democrats find appealing these days.

Many in the liberal coalition, however, do not buy the advantages of markets and see choice among public schools as disruptive and problematic. They are opposed to it and want to keep it limited. Yet even among these groups, which include the teachers unions, there are growing numbers who now say (for public consumption) that they "support" public school choice. Sometimes they even agree to new legislation. This kind of support, when it happens, is usually strategic. The purpose is to show that they are flexible on the choice issue—and to engineer limited forms of choice that, by satisfying enough people, will stop the move toward vouchers.[25]

What do ordinary Americans think about public school choice? Our survey focuses on the voucher issue and does not provide much information on this score. It does, however, contain two items that are helpful in giving us a sense of where people stand and why, and we can learn something by taking a look at them.

Respondents are asked about two very general approaches to public school choice. In practice, these reforms can be adopted either separately or in combination. One allows parents to choose among the public schools within their own districts, the other allows them to choose public schools located in other districts. The first is the most direct way of introducing choice and competition to the public sector and is likely to affect by far the greater number of parents. The second is most relevant to parents who are willing to send their kids to schools rather far from their homes, and who are capable of providing the necessary transportation; but it is also a way of expanding the choice set for anyone who is dissatisfied and, in particular, of making desirable schools available to children who might otherwise be trapped in low-performing districts.

On the survey, respondents are asked about these alternatives before vouchers are even mentioned. In introducing them, the interviewer says, "Now I want you to consider some education reforms that are being discussed these days. Please tell me whether you would support or oppose each of the following proposals for reform." Here is the wording of the items:

(1) "Within a school district, parents should be allowed to choose the public school their children will attend rather than having the district assign them to a school."

(2) "If the public schools outside their own district have space, parents should be allowed to choose one of those schools for their children to attend."

These items do not explore the pros and cons of the issue, and responses might have been different had more information been provided. Still, most people are likely to be familiar with the way the public school system operates, to have some knowledge of their own district as well as surrounding districts, and thus to have a substantive basis for deciding whether more parental choice would be a good thing. Their responses should be telling us something meaningful.

Descriptive results are set out in table 9-10. They suggest that Americans are quite sympathetic to both forms of public school choice. This dovetails with the results of other studies—for example, those carried out annually by Phi Delta Kappa—which have consistently shown high levels of support.

For the population as a whole, 69 percent favor intradistrict choice, compared to just 26 percent opposed, and the positive scores are even higher for interdistrict choice, with 75 percent in favor and 21 percent opposed. Across groups, the patterns are the same as those we have found for vouchers: public parents are more supportive of public school choice than nonparents are, and inner-city parents are even more supportive than public parents generally. As with vouchers, then, public school choice seems to have a special attraction to those who are most affected by it and most in need of new opportunities.

Note that more Americans express support for public school choice than express support for vouchers. (Recall from chapter 7 that support for vouchers on the initial voucher item was 60 percent.) This is what we ought to expect, simply because public school choice is a more moderate version of choice-based reform. In principle, almost everyone who supports vouchers should also support public school choice, even though it may not be their first preference. And a reasonable number of the people who oppose vouchers should support it as well.

If we look at how voucher supporters and opponents respond to these items, this is pretty much what we find. Voucher supporters are overwhelmingly in favor of public school choice. Seventy-six percent express support for intradistrict choice, with just 20 percent opposed. And 81 percent support interdistrict choice, with 16 percent opposed. Voucher opponents are less disposed toward choice in general and have already indicated their opposition to a radical version of it; but when presented with the idea of choice among public schools alone, *most* voucher

Table 9-10. *Support for Public School Choice*

Percent, unless otherwise indicated[a]

Type of respondent	Choice of public schools within the district			N^b
	Support	*Oppose*	*Don't know*	
Total population	69	26	5	(4,700)
Nonparents	66	29	5	(1,617)
Public school parents	74	21	5	(2,553)
Private school parents	82	15	3	(530)
Inner-city parents	84	14	2	(539)
Position on vouchers				
Support	76	20	3	(3,127)
Oppose	52	43	5	(1,083)
Political party (informed)				
Democrat	72	24	4	(751)
Republican	64	31	5	(621)

	Choice of public schools outside the district			
	Yes	*No*	*Don't know*	
Total population	75	21	4	(4,700)
Nonparents	72	24	5	(1,617)
Public school parents	81	16	3	(2,553)
Private school parents	86	12	2	(530)
Inner-city parents	88	9	3	(539)
Position on vouchers				
Support	81	16	3	(3,142)
Oppose	58	38	3	(1,107)
Political party (informed)				
Democrat	74	21	5	(750)
Republican	69	29	2	(639)

a. Percentages are based on weighted data. They may not sum to 100 due to rounding.
b. N is the unweighted number of respondents.

opponents see it as an attractive reform proposal. Fifty-two percent favor intradistrict choice, with 43 percent opposed, and 58 percent favor interdistrict choice, with 38 percent opposed. The result is an extraordinarily high level of support among the population as a whole. As with most policy issues, moderation is a winner.

We cannot launch into a detailed analysis of public school choice at this point and don't have the data to do so anyway. But because this is our only opportunity to look at the subject, it is useful to carry out an analysis using the same framework we used for the voucher issue. What types of people seem to be supporting public school choice, why do they do so, and how does all this compare to what we know about vouchers?

Tables 9-11 and 9-12 set out the results, which are based on regressions in which the dependent variable is a simple sum of the two public school choice items we've been looking at here. Its values range from 0 (opposition to both) to 2 (support for both).[26] Details aside, several findings seem to warrant emphasis:

(1) Like vouchers, public school choice tends to be attractive to the less advantaged. There is no connection with parental income. But the racial effects, especially for parents, are strong and significant: blacks and Hispanics are much more likely to favor choice than whites are. Also, support for choice is higher among people who come from less-advantaged districts—and again, this is especially true for parents.

(2) As we ought to expect, religion tends to be rather unimportant in explaining support for public school choice. But there are a few findings to suggest that, if religion has any effect at all, the connection tends to be positive, as it is with vouchers. The effect for born-again Christians is positive and statistically significant for nonparents (sometimes) and positive and insignificant for parents. Support for voluntary prayer has a significant influence for public parents but not for nonparents or the inner-city poor. These could be flukes. But they could also be an indication that religious groups tend to be looking for alternatives to the regular public schools, and are hoping that they might be able to find better moral climates (and the like) if they had more to choose from, even if restricted to secular schools.

(3) There is some indication (among informed nonparents) that public school choice may have a special attraction to Democrats. The aggregate statistics in table 9-10 suggest the same thing. This is consistent with the notion that, once the aspects of choice associated with conservatism (such as free markets) are factored out and choice is offered in a more targeted and regulated way, it resonates with the kind of values that are more likely to be held by liberals and Democrats.

(4) The attitude models reinforce this conclusion. They show that many of the attitudes that shape support for vouchers also shape support for public school choice, and the direction of their effects is the same. Two dimensions stand out. Among public parents, the most influential concerns are inequity and diversity: parents who think the current system is inequitable are more likely to endorse public school choice, as are those who believe in diversity. Among nonparents, a belief in diversity is far and

Table 9-11. *Support for Public School Choice:*
Public School Parents and Nonparents[a]

	Public school parents					
	Background model		Context model		Attitude model	
Variable	Coefficient	[Impact]	Coefficient	[Impact]	Coefficient	[Impact]
Background						
Education	−.02	[−.06]	.00	[.01]	−.00	[−.01]
Income	−.00	[−.01]	.01	[.05]	.01	[.08]
Catholic	−.05	[−.07]	−.05	[.08]	−.04	[−.06]
Born-again	.08	[.12]	.08	[.12]	.06	[.09]
Black (north)	.23***	[.35]	.08	[.12]	.06	[.09]
Black (south)	.25***	[.36]	.21***	[.31]	.19***	[.28]
Hispanic	.13***	[.20]	.03	[−.05]	.00	[.00]
Age	−.01**	[−.09]	−.02**	[−.10]	−.01	[−.07]
Party identification (informed)	.00	[.00]	.00	[.00]	.01	[.06]
Party identification (uninformed)	−.02	[−.11]	−.01	[−.06]	−.01	[−.06]
Low expectations	−.01	[−.05]	−.01	[−.04]	−.00	[−.02]
Context						
Residential mobility			−.01	[−.04]	−.01	[−.05]
Advantaged district			−.09***	[−.25]	−.08***	[−.22]
Attitudes						
Diversity (whites)					.08***	[.19]
Inequity					.10***	[.23]
School prayer					.05***	[.16]
Parent influence					.07***	[.16]
School size					.02	[.04]
Public school ideology					−.01	[−.03]
Markets					.05***	[.12]
Moral values					−.00	[−.01]
Performance						
Performance						
Constant	1.68***		1.57***		1.22***	
N[b]	(2,406)		(2,176)		(2,176)	
Adjusted R^2	.04		.04		.11	

* Significant at .10 level.
** Significant at .05 level.
*** Significant at .01 level.

a. The dependent variable measures support for public school choice and is coded from 0 (strongly oppose) to 2 (strongly support). "Performance" is the index of absolute public school performance (which excludes comparisons to private schools) that was used in chapter 4's analyses. Ordinary least squares regressions estimated using weighted data. Unstandardized coefficients reported. For each nondichotomous independent variable, the impact coefficient represents the estimated change in the dependent variable (measured in standard deviations) when the independent variable shifts by two standard deviations, holding all other variables constant; for each dichotomous variable, the impact coefficient represents the estimated change in the dependent variable (measured in standard deviations) when the independent variable shifts from 0 to 1, holding all other variables constant. Models control for the full range of background and context variables, not all of which are reported in the tables.

b. N is the unweighted number of respondents.

| Parents (cont'd) | | Nonparents | | | | | | | |
| Performance model | | Background model | | Context model | | Attitude model | | Performance model | |
Coefficient	[Impact]	Coefficient	[Impact]	Coefficient	[Impact]	Coefficient	[Impact]	Coefficient	[Impact]
−.01	[−.02]	.03*	[.11]	.02	[.09]	.03	[.10]	.03	[.10]
.01	[.08]	−.03**	[−.14]	−.02	[−.09]	−.02	[−.08]	−.02	[−.08]
−.03	[−.04]	.02	[−.03]	.01	[.01]	−.02	[−.03]	−.02	[−.03]
.06	[.09]	.12	[.16]	.20**	[.26]	.15*	[.19]	.14	[.18]
.06	[.09]	.24**	[.31]	.25**	[.32]	.21*	[.27]	.21	[.27]
.20***	[.30]	.04	[.05]	.01	[.01]	−.00	[−.00]	.00	[.00]
.01	[.02]	−.08	[−.10]	−.15	[−.19]	−.10	[−.13]	−.11	[−.14]
−.01	[−.06]	−.03***	[−.26]	−.03***	[−.30]	−.02***	[−.20]	−.02***	[−.20]
.01	[.06]	−.04**	[−.20]	−.04**	[−.20]	−.05***	[−.28]	−.05***	[−.28]
−.01	[−.06]	−.00	[−.00]	.00	[.00]	.00	[.00]	−.00	[−.00]
−.00	[−.00]	−.00	[−.01]	.00	[.01]	.01	[.03]	.01	[.04]
−.01	[−.02]			.01	[.03]	.01	[.01]	.01	[.03]
−.07***	[−.19]			−.07**	[−.14]	−.06**	[−.13]	−.05*	[−.11]
.08***	[.19]					.15***	[.31]	.15***	[.31]
.09***	[.22]					.04	[.08]	.04	[.07]
.05***	[.17]					.02	[.08]	.03	[.08]
.06***	[.15]					.07***	[.18]	.07***	[.17]
.01	[.03]					.01	[.01]	.00	[.01]
−.01	[−.02]					−.05*	[−.11]	−.05*	[−.10]
.05***	[.11]					.12***	[.24]	.12***	[.24]
−.00	[−.00]					−.00	[−.01]	−.00	[−.01]
−.07***	[−.17]							−.05*	[−.10]
1.23***		1.68***		1.61***		1.41***		1.41***	
(2,176)		(1,475)		(1,331)		(1,331)		(1,331)	
.12		.04		.05		.08		.09	

Table 9-12. *Support for Public School Choice: Inner-City Parents*[a]

Variable	Background model		Context model		Attitude model		Performance model	
	Coefficient	[Impact]	Coefficient	[Impact]	Coefficient	[Impact]	Coefficient	[Impact]
Background								
Education	-.01	[-.02]	.00	[.00]	-.01	[-.02]	-.01	[-.03]
Income	-.01	[-.02]	-.01	[-.01]	.00	[.01]	.01	[.02]
Catholic	.05	[.09]	.07	[.13]	.08	[.15]	.09	[.17]
Born-again	.13	[.25]	.13	[.25]	.14	[.26]	.13	[.25]
Black (north)	.16**	[.30]	.14*	[.26]	.16*	[.30]	.16*	[.30]
Black (south)	.41***	[.77]	.36***	[.68]	.35***	[.66]	.35***	[.66]
Hispanic	.21***	[.40]	.17**	[.32]	.15*	[.28]	.15*	[.28]
Age	.01	[.06]	.01	[.07]	.01	[.09]	.01	[.10]
Party identification (informed)	-.00	[-.00]	-.03	[-.19]	-.02	[-.13]	-.02	[-.13]
Party identification (uninformed)	-.02	[-.13]	-.01	[-.06]	-.01	[-.06]	-.01	[-.06]
Low expectations	.01	[.08]	.02	[.13]	.03*	[.18]	.03**	[.20]
Context								
Residential mobility			-.02	[-.08]	-.02	[-.08]	-.02	[-.07]
Advantaged district			-.06*	[-.18]	-.05	[-.15]	-.05	[-.14]

Attitudes				
Diversity (white)			-.01 [-.02]	-.01 [.02]
Inequity			.11*** [.32]	.11*** [.30]
School prayer			.02 [.11]	.03 [.12]
Parent influence			.07** [.20]	.07** [.20]
School size			-.04 [-.11]	-.04 [-.13]
Public school ideology			-.00 [-.01]	.00 [.01]
Markets			.03 [.10]	.03 [.09]
Moral values			-.01 [-.04]	-.01 [-.03]
Performance				
Performance				-.04 [-.14]
Constant	1.53***	1.39***	1.21***	1.21***
N[b]	(523)	(493)	(493)	(493)
Adjusted R^2	.03	.04	.06	.07

* Significant at .10 level.
** Significant at .05 level.
*** Significant at .01 level.

a. The dependent variable measures support for public school performance (which excludes comparisons to private schools) that was used in chapter 4's analyses. Ordinary least squares regressions estimated using weighted data. Unstandardized coefficients reported. For each nondichotomous independent variable, the impact coefficient represents the estimated change in the dependent variable when the independent variable shifts by two standard deviations, holding all other variables constant; for each dichotomous variable, the impact coefficient represents the estimated change in the dependent variable (measured in standard deviations) when the independent variable shifts from 0 to 1, holding all other variables constant. Models control for the full range of background and context variables, not all of which are reported in the tables.

b. N is the unweighted number of respondents.

away the most important influence. And among inner-city parents, it is inequity that matters most. As with vouchers, then, choice in the public sector seems to be viewed as a way of promoting equity and racial balance.

(5) Performance has somewhat less impact on support for public school choice than it does on support for vouchers, presumably because people see fewer performance differences among their local public schools than they do between public and private schools. Still, performance has a significant influence—again, especially for parents—and in the same direction as with vouchers: the lower the assessments of public school performance, the greater the support for choice.

While we don't have much data to work with here, public school choice comes across very much as we might expect. As a moderate version of choice-based reform, it naturally attracts more positive responses than vouchers do. And when we look beneath the surface, the influences that help us understand what types of people are especially inclined to support it, and why, are essentially the *same* forces that seem to be driving the modern centrist wing of the voucher movement. Whether we look at centrist approaches to vouchers or at public school choice, the people favoring choice over the status quo tend to be minority, from low-quality districts, to see the current system as inequitable, to support diversity, and to put significant weight on their own (relatively low) assessments of public school performance. The pattern of results is more consistent in the case of vouchers, both in these respects and in regard to the full range of variables. But public school choice is clearly a phenomenon that lies along the same basic continuum, and is attractive to many of the same constituencies.

Conclusion

When Americans are asked whether they support or oppose vouchers, their answers tell us something about how they react to the general concept. But this only takes us so far. Voucher systems come in different forms, and people can be expected to have very different reactions—and make very different choices in politics—depending on what type of system is being considered.

The question, in the final analysis, is how Americans think a voucher system should be *regulated*. Should the rules permit religious schools to participate, or should the rules exclude them? Should private schools be forced to follow certain rules in the interests of accountability, and perhaps fairness and social equity as well, or should they be allowed to chart their own course as they see fit? Should the rules make vouchers available to all children, or should the rules limit vouchers to children who are disadvantaged?

At the elite level, these sorts of regulatory issues are bound up with the struggle between free markets and government control. For traditional voucher leaders, the aim is to transform the American education system through choice and competition, with as few regulations as possible. For voucher opponents, regulations are a way of ensuring equity and accountability, protecting against problems—and drastically limiting the scope of vouchers. Both sides are well aware that their aims are better realized if public opinion is on their side. The national debate, accordingly, is not just about whether vouchers are good or bad public policy, but about what a voucher system should actually look like and whom it should serve.

The American people, it is fair to say, do not think of vouchers in terms of free markets versus government control. They react to the specifics of each issue, dealing with each one separately and on its own merits. In this chapter, we have explored their opinions in some depth. Here is a brief summary of where they appear to stand.

On religion, Americans overwhelmingly take the side of traditional voucher leaders: the vast majority think religious schools should be allowed to participate in a voucher system. It is clear that voucher opponents, and liberal elites generally, are way out of step with the American public on this issue and that, by taking a strict stand on "separation of church and state," they are taking a stand that is highly unpopular.

When it comes to regulations for accountability and equity, on the other hand, traditional voucher leaders are out of step. By huge majorities, Americans think private schools should be subject to basic regulations—for curriculum, teacher qualifications, financial audits, student testing—that hold them accountable for quality and proper management. They also believe in the need for basic regulations—on private school admissions, for example—to ensure that all children, especially those who are disadvantaged, have equal access. Americans, then, clearly do *not* believe in free markets. Not even remotely. They find private schools very attractive, and they like the idea of choice and new opportunities. But they believe that basic, governmentally imposed protections are necessary if the marketplace is to work as they want.

As we saw earlier with the concept of vouchers, the way Americans approach these regulatory issues is not frivolous or thoughtless. There is a structure to their responses, a connection to their underlying values and beliefs. And to their self-interest. While regulation for accountability and equity is quite popular across all social groups—even informed

Republicans—it is especially popular among people who are less advantaged, who are concerned about equity and diversity, who are informed Democrats, who support the public school ideology, and who worry about the risks of vouchers. In political terms, regulation for equity and accountability is especially attractive to people with liberal values, and to constituencies that are the hallmark of the modern wing of the voucher movement.

Aside from the religion issue, the traditionalists' great strength with the American public is that the vast majority of people are universalists and believe that a voucher system should be broadly based, at least eventually. As I argue in the next chapter, this is likely to be a factor of real political significance. Yet a closer look at public opinion also shows that Americans tend to be concerned about the risks of vouchers, and that most—even among voucher supporters—are inclined to favor an approach that *starts* with smaller programs limited to needy children and perhaps expands outward from there, in incremental fashion. Sizable majorities, moreover, seem to be quite comfortable with voucher programs that are set up exclusively for the poor (as the inner-city scholarship item demonstrates).

When we carry out a more detailed analysis of how people come down on the question of targeting versus universalism, their responses again prove to be meaningful reflections of their values and beliefs—and their self-interest. The structure of support for targeting is much the same as the structure of support for regulation more generally: it is the people with liberal characteristics and those who are socially less advantaged who are most in favor of targeting.

Compared to universalism, targeting is a moderate form of choice. But there is a still more moderate approach that, along with targeting, has played an important role in the politics of vouchers. This one rules out vouchers entirely and gives parents choices that are limited to public schools alone. Because public school choice involves a much smaller change from the status quo than vouchers, it ought to be acceptable to larger numbers of people. And this is in fact the case: Americans are overwhelmingly in favor of having more choices within the public school system. Not surprisingly, the kinds of people who favor a shift toward greater public school choice are much the same as the ones who favor a shift toward vouchers: they are minority, from less-advantaged districts, see the current system as inequitable, support diversity, and have (relatively) low assessments of public school performance. In important respects, at least, vouchers and public school choice appear to lie along the same continuum and appeal to many of the same constituencies.

Voucher leaders are happy to promote public school choice, of course—but they want more. This chapter suggests that, to maximize their chances of getting it, they need to propose the kinds of voucher programs that centrist constituencies can support. This means they should start with programs for needy kids, put the emphasis on equity and diversity, and encourage a process of incremental change. It also means they should get away from free markets and accept an integral role for government regulation in the design of voucher programs that can promise to be accountable, fair, and equitable. Traditionalists may chafe at these ideas. But the modern wing of the movement is firmly committed to putting them into practice—and the path it has chosen appears far better suited to political success than the one traditionalists would prefer.

10 Public Opinion, Politics, and the Future

In the policymaking process, elites carry far more weight than ordinary citizens do. But elections ensure that the various groups of elites must compete with one another for power, and that they are much better able to achieve their policy objectives when they have important constituencies on their side. Because this is so, their political struggles over policy tend to generate a larger struggle for public support. Ordinary citizens usually have little knowledge about the details of policy, and they rarely get involved. But what they think does matter. It affects the strengths of the contending sides, it affects who wins and who loses, and it ultimately finds its reflection (if imperfectly) in the content of public policy.[1]

As a general matter, then, when we learn about public opinion we are not simply learning about where the American public stands on important policy issues. We are learning about the foundations of democratic politics, about the forces that animate and guide the competition among elites, and about where politics and policy are likely to be headed in future years.

So it is with public opinion on vouchers. This book is largely an effort to clarify and extend our knowledge of where the American people stand on the voucher issue, and how their thinking reflects the deeper values, beliefs, and interests that matter to them. The survey data speak directly to these sorts of questions, and each chapter contributes a piece of the bigger picture—beginning with an examination of how Americans view the public schools, moving on to a study of why some parents want to go private, and then addressing the voucher issue directly and in depth: exploring who gets informed about it, who supports and opposes the idea, how people assess its consequences, and what kind of system they are inclined to favor.

We have covered a lot of ground here and learned quite a bit about where people stand on vouchers and why. But the real value of this kind of analysis is that it has much broader implications. For in telling us about public opinion, it conveys important information about politics and policy. This has been apparent throughout the book. In chapter after chapter, the determinants of public opinion have been rooted in social class, in attitudes toward inequity, in religion, in party, in information, in perspectives on regulation, and in a number of other factors that are clearly bound up with politics and affect the prospects and strategies of the main elite combatants in predictable ways.

In this final chapter, I want to begin with a brief overview of our analysis of public opinion in an effort to bring together the most basic findings. But my primary purpose is to train the spotlight more directly on politics. If the analysis of this book is essentially correct about the key features of public opinion, what does it mean for the future politics of vouchers—and for the future of American education?

Public Opinion on Vouchers: An Overview

The place to start is with a simple point that couldn't be more profound in its importance for politics: Americans like the public school system. While they may not be ecstatic about its performance, most are reasonably satisfied with what they are getting overall, particularly on academics. And this is especially true of public school parents, whose experiences with their own schools are generally pretty good. For the voucher movement, then, the problem is obvious but fundamental: it must attract support from a public that is actually quite sympathetic to the existing system.

The political dilemma is more insidious than this suggests, because sympathy for the public schools is nurtured by certain features that, for all intents and purposes, are built into the system.

—Many parents who are dissatisfied with the public schools, and who are sufficiently motivated and have the money, can pay to go private— which drains off an important pool of malcontents and raises the average level of satisfaction within the public system.

—Similarly, the more motivated and advantaged parents can choose to live in neighborhoods or districts with good public schools (and stay out of areas with bad public schools), which again has the effect of raising average levels of satisfaction, especially among the types of people who are most inclined to complain if displeased.

—Many Americans embrace what I have called the public school ideology: they feel a normative attachment to the public school system, a belief in its ideals and a concern for its well-being, that leads them to support the system even when it is performing poorly.

—Last but not least, there is a troubling phenomenon that disproportionately affects the most disadvantaged members of American society. People who are low in education and expectations, many of them located in low-performing districts, are more satisfied with their schools than we would otherwise expect them to be, and they are less likely to complain; yet these are the constituents the modern voucher movement is most intent on mobilizing.

For all these reasons, the voucher movement is fighting an uphill battle against satisfaction with the current system. People like it, they believe in it, and there are forces at work that continually bolster and safeguard its public support, even when the system is not doing its job very well.

Were this the whole story, the prognosis for vouchers would be gloomy. But the rest of the story is far more positive. To begin with, it is of enormous importance that most people think private schools are superior to public schools. On an absolute scale, they are reasonably satisfied with what they are currently getting from the public sector. But they think there are more attractive options in the private sector. They are *relatively* dissatisfied with public school performance—they think they can do better. This is one of the keys to understanding how a "satisfied" population might be enlisted to support vouchers.

In addition, while Americans give the public schools fairly high marks overall, they are *not* very satisfied when it comes to specific aspects of policy and performance. They think the public schools are inequitable, providing low-income and minority kids with lesser-quality educations. They think voluntary prayer should be allowed in the classroom. They think parents should have more influence. They think schools should be smaller. And many are inclined to believe that market-like incentives would make schools more productive. All of these issues—along with the perceived superiority of private schools—are at the heart of the voucher movement's critique of the public school system, and the basis of its political appeals. There *is* a constituency for this critique.

Throughout this book, an underlying question has been whether we can attribute genuine substance to the opinions people express. The evidence is quite positive in this respect. With regard to performance, it suggests there is a rational core to the way many Americans go about evaluating the schools, a structure to their thinking that makes sense. When Americans evaluate school performance, the major influences on their thinking arise from the objective context: from their direct experiences with schools, from how advantaged the district is, and from residential mobility (the choice of context). More concretely, the people who are especially dissatisfied—despite the perverse effects of education and expectations— are those who are low in income, African-American, from low-performing districts, do not exercise residential choice, and have lower-quality experiences with their children's schools. This is what we should expect if people are responding in sensible ways to their objective settings. Perceptions of inequity, moreover, turn out to have an important bearing on the public's satisfaction with the schools—and these concerns are particularly strong among low-income parents in the inner city. This too makes sense and is an early sign, repeated in chapter after chapter, that the equity issue is central to the way Americans think about their education system, and is potentially a very powerful appeal of the voucher movement as it seeks to attract support.

Whatever attracts people to vouchers, one thing is clear: if the movement is to succeed, many parents must be interested in going private. The evidence suggests that the demand for private schools is strong indeed. Most parents in the public sector indicate that, if money were not a problem, they would consider sending their kids private. There is a very large constituency, then, for what the voucher movement is offering. It is not a constituency that is intensely disaffected and scrambling to leave the public schools, although for some groups in some niches of the system this is surely true. For the most part, it is a constituency interested in better alternatives.

The concern of critics is that, were choice expanded and "interested" families allowed to leave the public schools, the social biases of the existing system would be worsened, producing more inequity, more segregation, more religious separation. There are good logical reasons, however, for expecting the opposite. Existing biases are largely due to the fact that choice is costly, which guarantees that the socially advantaged have special access to private schools. When the costs of choice are dramatically reduced, the less advantaged are granted access too, and an expansion of choice should promote moderation.

The evidence suggests as much. The current private system is indeed a source of social bias, although less so than common stereotypes imply. The parents who currently go private are (among other things) higher in education and income and more likely to be Catholic or born-again than existing public parents are. The public parents interested in going private, on the other hand, not only tend to be lower in income, more often minority, and more likely to live in low-performing school districts than current private parents, but they are also less advantaged in these respects than the public parents who *don't* want to go private.

If we simulate the systemwide effects of an expansion of choice, the results point to a considerable moderation of the social biases that currently distinguish the public and private sectors. Indeed, under reasonable assumptions, the new private sector would actually be more ethnically diverse than the new public system. Of the original social biases, only religion remains largely unchanged (although this bias too is slightly reduced). The fact is, religion is viewed quite sympathetically by the broad population of Americans, not just by private school parents; and when public parents are given the chance to go private, these same values come into play.

Bias and moderation aside, the deeper question is: what motivates parents to go private? Here too, as with assessments of performance, a corollary issue is whether parents seem to be thinking in a rational, coherent way about their options, and whether their opinions are really telling us something of substance. The evidence, again, is quite positive. The first point to be made is that, contrary to the disparaging view of parents that is standard fare among the critics of choice, *parents put primary emphasis on school performance* in deciding whether to go private. This is far and away the number-one influence on parental thinking. The same is also true for the inner-city poor, whom voucher critics portray as incapable of making responsible decisions.

More generally, there appears to be a distinctive structure to parents' thinking, as indicated by the influence of a full range of attitudes. Parents are more interested in going private when they think the public school system is inequitable, when they support school prayer, when they want more influence and smaller schools, when they are concerned about the teaching of moral values, and when they believe in markets. They are less likely to want to go private when they embrace the public school ideology. All these concerns (except the latter) are fundamental appeals of the voucher movement, and their salience among parents suggests a receptive audience.

One of these dimensions stands out. Performance evaluations aside, a concern about social inequity is the single most important attitude affecting the desire of parents to go private. The salience of the inequity issue, moreover, is especially strong for low-income parents, who are most likely to suffer from the system's unequal outcomes. This reinforces the conclusion that private schools are especially attractive to families who are less advantaged, and that their response arises from a recognition that they are less well served by the existing system than other families are.

The attitudinal dimension that has the weakest impact is race. This may be due to limitations in the survey's measures, and more research is surely warranted. But this result, if on the mark, is of great political relevance: for critics are convinced that vouchers will unleash the basest of racial motivations and lead to greater segregation, yet there is no evidence that this is actually a problem among the general population of public school parents. Parents who oppose diversity are no more interested in going private than those who support diversity. There *is* evidence, on the other hand, that racial motivation may be a factor among inner-city whites. In this context, the critics may be quite right, and those who advocate and design voucher programs need to be on alert.

When we learn about who wants to go private or about how people evaluate the public schools, we gain important background for understanding the voucher issue. Public opinion on vouchers, one would think, ought to be shaped by these things. The connection, however, is not so automatic. We have to recognize that, when people are asked to take a position on vouchers, they are no longer being asked about something that is intrinsically close to home, as the attractiveness of private schools is or as the performance of the public schools is. They are being asked about a public policy issue that is much more complicated, abstract, and remote from their lives, and that they probably haven't thought much about. Indeed, precisely because it *is* a public policy issue, they have little incentive to get informed about it in the first place—for policy issues are decided through a democratic process in which any given individual's impact is minimal and investments in information are rarely justified.

There is no reason to think that vouchers are any different from other public policy issues in this respect. And the evidence indicates as much: some two-thirds of Americans say they have not heard about vouchers. This in itself creates a major challenge for the movement. People can't be mobilized if they don't know the issue exists. It would help if people who stand to benefit most from vouchers—public parents who want to go private, for example—were especially inclined to get informed, and thus if the social transmission of information at least ensures that latent supporters are more likely to get informed than latent opponents. But this is not the case. With slight exceptions, the people who might seem to have incentives to find out about vouchers are *not* better informed than other citizens are. On the voucher issue, the people who get informed are the same types of people—"generalists"—who tend to know about public policy issues in general: people who are higher in social class and older. Needless to say, this is not the movement's prime constituency.

When the issues shift from matters that are close to home to matters of public policy, then, the movement is faced with serious information problems. Most people are uninformed. Incentives don't work. And the people who do get informed tend to be generalists who have no necessary stake in the issue and are not its prime constituents. The movement must overcome these challenges if it is to mobilize support for its cause. And it won't be easy, because there is a rationality at work that makes the information problems enduring and difficult to change.

If one question stands out from all the others in this analysis of public opinion, it is the apparently simple one of where the American public stands on the voucher issue. Yet pervasive information problems ensure that this cannot be a simple question at all. If most of the public is uninformed, the obvious danger is that the opinions they express will be meaningless, and not connected in coherent ways to their underlying values, beliefs, and interests. The movement's apparent supporters, to judge from the polls, may not really be supporters at all, but rather people who happen to give meaningless positive responses to survey items they don't really understand. And similarly for the apparent opponents, whose negative responses may be just as empty. Under the circumstances, can we say that Americans actually *have* opinions on the voucher issue, and that these opinions have genuine consequences for politics?

Our evidence suggests that the answer is yes. The responses people give are not random or cavalier, but seem to be thoughtful reflections of their values, beliefs, and interests. There appears to be some "real thinking" going on. Even among the uninformed, there is a sensible structure to the way they approach the issue—and their thinking becomes more structured as the survey progresses, and they are able to learn a bit more about what vouchers are and what sorts of controversies and social concerns are relevant. This does not mean that the positions people express are well thought out, nor that they couldn't be changed markedly by new information (or propaganda). But it does suggest that, at least for many people, there is genuine substance to their opinions.

Among parents, support for vouchers is most heavily influenced by the desire to go private, a very rational basis for support indeed. More generally, vouchers are especially attractive to parents who are low in social class, minority, and from low-performing school districts: the core constituency of the modern wing of the voucher movement. Vouchers are also attractive to parents who are Catholic or born-again and (among the informed) Republican: constituents of the traditional wing of the movement. Similar patterns obtain for nonparents as well. The basic structure of the elite-level voucher movement is reflected in the structure of public opinion.

Support for vouchers is also influenced by a whole range of attitudes. Americans are more inclined to support vouchers when they believe the public system is inequitable, when they support diversity, when they want more parent influence, when they prefer smaller schools, when they support voluntary prayer, when they are concerned about the teaching of moral values, and when they believe in market incentives. Here again, there appears to be a constituency for what the movement advocates and believes. The downside is that Americans are less likely to support vouchers when they embrace the public school ideology—a normative attachment that is widespread. This is a prime constituency for the opposition.

A few of the specifics deserve to be highlighted. One is that inequity again proves to be especially important to the way Americans think about vouchers. It is one of the top attitudinal influences on their support, especially among low-income parents (among the inner-city poor, it is *the* most influential attitude)—and it becomes even more salient as the survey progresses and respondents get more familiar with the issue. A related result is that diversity, which has little to do with assessments of performance or going private, and which initially has little to do with support for vouchers, *becomes* important as the survey progresses and respondents gain familiarity with the voucher issue. And it is the people who *support* racial diversity who turn out to be especially favorable toward vouchers, not the reverse, as critics would contend. Both of these results reinforce the connection between vouchers and the socially disadvantaged, which is at the heart of the modern movement.

The results on political party do much the same. At the elite level, of course, the traditional leadership is Republican; and among the informed segment of the American public, it is the Republicans who are most likely to support vouchers. This only makes sense, since they are likely to be paying attention to the national debate and know the partisan terms in which it is often framed. But among the uninformed (and far more numerous) segment of the population, the results are different: it is the Democrats who are more likely to support vouchers. This too makes good sense, because vouchers are especially attractive to people who are low in education and income, and who put weight on equity and diversity—and these tend to be Democratic constituencies. Absent the framing effects of national politics, the voucher issue very easily translates into a liberal or Democratic issue.

Finally, it is worth noting that school performance, the dominant influence on the desire of parents to go private, is also quite important in explaining support for vouchers—but its impact is more moderate. A reasonable conjecture is that this happens because support for vouchers is much more heavily influenced by *social* concerns than going private is. While parents who give low marks to school performance may see going private as a solution to their personal problem, it does not follow that they would see vouchers as a solution to the larger social problem, and thus that they would support vouchers as public policy for everyone. Given the values involved, as well as the scope of the problem, there is good reason to believe that the connection between performance and going private should be stronger than the connection between performance and support for vouchers. And it is. Still, performance is a major determinant of how people see the voucher issue and a factor of great relevance for politics.

Overall, these findings are good news for the voucher movement. They do not mean, of course, that people will somehow be easy to reach or mobilize, because information problems set up barriers between the movement and its potential constituents. Nonetheless, it is important to know that there *do* appear to be lots of potential constituents out there. Despite the fact that people are largely uninformed about the issue, they have sensible opinions that reflect their underlying values, beliefs, and interests; they seem to be very open to the idea of vouchers; and they are inclined to respond favorably to the movement's appeals. This is especially true of people who are less advantaged and who share liberal concerns for equity and diversity—the very people the movement is most actively trying to recruit.

Exploring support and opposition is one way to understand how Americans see the voucher issue. But we can learn a good deal more by considering the range of consequences they think vouchers might have, both for society in general and for themselves personally. This adds substance and detail to the simple positions they take on the issue, and gives us a deeper sense of their thinking. In the final analysis, moreover, an assessment of whether vouchers would have good or bad *effects*—on school performance, on equity, on race, on families—is what the elite-level voucher debate is really about, and absolutely central to the politics of the issue.

With Americans so uninformed about vouchers, it is prudent to regard their assessments of consequences with caution. For they literally do not know what the consequences are. They are offering guesses that are sensitive to question wording, and that could well change with new information—particularly if they were faced with the intense propaganda of a political campaign. As things stand, however, Americans seem to think vouchers will have positive effects on society, at least for the most part. They think vouchers will help improve the schools, promote social equity, and enhance racial balance. These findings are consistent with the prior analysis, based on quite different survey items, which shows that these same considerations are important influences on their support for vouchers.

To the extent Americans express concern about the social effects of vouchers, two factors stand out: risk (especially) and cost. Both are particularly salient to nonparents, who make up most of the electorate. Indeed, if there is one danger sign here that voucher leaders need most to recognize and the opponents can most build upon, it is the nearly universal concern for risk—which suggests, as do other data in this analysis, that Americans are most likely to be comfortable with a strategy of incremental change.

Just as, on balance, Americans tend to think vouchers will benefit society, so they also tend to think vouchers will benefit them personally. Here the key group is obviously parents. America's public school parents see choice as personally empowering: giving them more control over their kids' educations and allowing them to find better, safer schools. They are not, however, entirely unconflicted on the subject. Many parents think their public schools are "good enough." Many embrace the public school ideology and say they "wouldn't feel right" if they went private. Still, the fact is that most parents express an interest in putting vouchers to personal use, and as they balance these sorts of conflicting considerations, it is the direct benefits they associate with choice—better schools, more control—that prompt many to see vouchers in positive terms.

This juxtaposition of the social and the personal raises a question that is fundamental to the politics of the issue. What sort of balance do America's parents strike between the public interest and their own self-interest when they decide whether vouchers are worthy of their support? Are they thinking mainly about what is best for society, or are they thinking about what is best for themselves? The answer has a lot to say about the kinds of appeals that will hit home with them as elites struggle for their support.

The results are quite interesting. For the broad population of public parents, the social and personal influences on support for vouchers turn out to be almost equally balanced. Parents put a great deal of weight on

both. They are consumers, supporting or opposing vouchers on the basis
of the personal benefits they expect to receive. And they are citizens, supporting or opposing vouchers on the basis of how they think society as a
whole will be affected. Not all parents are alike, however—for it turns out
that the balance they strike is a direct function of personal need: parents
who are low in income and from low-performing districts are the most
likely to emphasize the personal benefits of vouchers, while those who are
more advantaged and more satisfied with their schools tend to emphasize
the broader social consequences. In effect, the voucher issue is evaluated in
social terms by those who can "afford" to think socially, and it is evaluated
in self-interest terms by those who can't and who need change the most.

Politically, the lesson for the voucher movement seems clear. Appeals
based on parent self-interest will tend to work well among inner-city and
low-income groups of parents—groups that are crucial to the early stages
of the movement's success. But among other groups—the more fortunate
parents, along with the much larger population of nonparents—social
appeals are likely to have more clout. This means that, in the end, the
movement can only succeed in its larger mission if it convinces Americans
that vouchers are in the public interest.

All of these findings, taken together, tell us a great deal about how
Americans see the voucher issue. But an important level of detail is still
lacking. The fact is, a voucher system is not a single thing, but a family of
possibilities, and any two voucher systems can be very different from one
another depending on what properties they have. One may include religious schools, the other only secular schools. One may be regulated to
promote accountability and social equity, the other may have no rules to
speak of. One may be universal, the other targeted at low-income kids. To
know what Americans think about vouchers, then, we need to know where
they stand on the various properties that make any given voucher system
what it is and that determine what its social and personal consequences
will be. Where they come down on these design issues, moreover, is of
great political significance, for it tells voucher leaders what kinds of proposals they need to make in order to maximize their public support.

Here is what Americans seem to want. To begin with, they overwhelmingly believe that, if a voucher system were adopted, religious schools
should be included. This is a contentious issue among elites, with voucher
opponents and their liberal allies arguing vehemently that religion can
have no place in a publicly funded system of education. But the opponents
are totally out of step with the public on this issue, and voucher leaders
very much in the mainstream.

Their roles are reversed when it comes to regulation. Traditional voucher leaders are strongly opposed to regulation, but the American public is strongly in favor of it. By massive majorities, they support rules to hold private schools accountable for quality education—through curriculum and teacher-qualification requirements, for example. They support regulations to promote social equity by requiring private schools to admit all applicants, say, or to set aside slots for low-income kids. The numbers spell trouble for traditional voucher leaders unless they are willing to compromise their principles. Free-market voucher proposals are likely to garner substantially less political support than proposals built around basic regulations for accountability and equity.

In considering whether voucher programs should be universal or targeted, the public's approach is more nuanced. Most Americans are universalists at heart: they think that if a voucher system were adopted, virtually all children should qualify—at least eventually. But they are also quite sympathetic to the idea of special programs for children in need (scholarships for the inner-city poor, for example), and they are risk-averse about the prospect of moving too quickly to a full-blown universal system. Most seem to think it would make more sense to approach reform incrementally, beginning with smaller programs for needy children and moving over time to a more inclusive system. These nuanced views may be a blessing in disguise for the modern voucher movement. For they suggest that proposals for targeted programs are likely to be attractive to a broad audience, including many people whose underlying preference is for universalism.

The bottom line is that, if voucher leaders want to maximize their public support, they need to endorse policy proposals that appeal to centrist constituencies. This means, among other things, that they need to pursue programs targeted at disadvantaged children (at least in the short run), and to put explicit emphasis on equity and diversity—as the modern wing of the movement has indeed been doing. They need to get away from free markets and embrace a regulated approach to vouchers that recognizes the public's concern for accountability, fairness, and equity. And as they do these things, they need to resist the impulse to attack the public school system, and instead promote voucher programs that are designed to improve and contribute to the existing system rather than destroy or privatize it.

Elites and Public Opinion

When we study public opinion, we are studying basic features of the political landscape that elites on both sides of the issue are forced to recognize and deal with. Traditional voucher leaders must recognize that the libertarian vision does not sell and that the bigger numbers are nearer the center. More generally, it matters enormously for both elite camps that Americans are fairly satisfied with the public schools, normatively attached to the system, and concerned about the risks of major change. It is also important that so many Americans think private schools are superior to public schools, that so many are positively inclined toward vouchers, and that vouchers have special appeal to the less advantaged.

These are just some of the basic contours of public opinion on the voucher issue. And they, along with many others discussed above, provide a *structure* for elite behavior, a structure that constrains and channels what elites need to do in order to win—shaping their proposals, their arguments, their appeals, their mobilization strategies. This structuring role of public opinion helps us understand the politics of vouchers and lends a measure of predictability to it.

We have to recognize, however, that public opinion doesn't just play a structuring role. It also *gets* structured—and by the very same elites who are presumably so responsive to it. This is unavoidable. The reality is that most Americans are uninformed about the voucher issue, more ambivalent than committed to their views, and likely to shift in the presence of new information. Elites are well aware of this and inevitably see it as an opportunity to swing public opinion over to their side.

Elites can shape public opinion in two basic ways. First, by taking positions on issues and spreading the word, they can provide cues to constituencies that identify with their goals and trust them to provide guidance on policy issues. Many Catholics may look to the Church, many blacks to civil rights groups, many teachers to their unions. And large numbers of Americans identify with a political party and may take their cues from high-profile Democrats and Republicans.

The cue-giving role of elites can help citizens deal with the complexities of public policy and make choices consistent with their own values, beliefs, and interests. To be sure, the availability of elite cues doesn't always enhance democracy. Some people are too poorly informed to recognize them. And even when people do recognize them, elites may sometimes take positions that are not in the best interests of their constituents. Still, elite cue-giving can clearly function to make public opinion more meaningful and effective.[2]

There is a second dimension to elite influence that is not nearly so pretty. At its most positive, it involves elite efforts to educate the public by providing accurate, balanced information on the issue in question—a good thing, of course, if that were the whole of it. But in the world of power politics, the competing sides are often driven to be Machiavellian in their use of information, "educating" the public by means of one-sided claims and arguments whose purpose is simply to win converts, not to promote balance or truth. The danger is that public opinion will simply shift in the direction of whichever side spends the most money in the propaganda wars, or has the hardest-hitting sound bites, or is the most powerful. If this occurs, victory goes not to the elite group that best represents the public, but to the group that best manipulates it. And public opinion, supposedly the driving force of democratic politics, becomes a passive reflection of whatever elites want it to be.[3]

In this book, we have explored public opinion on the voucher issue in great depth. But there is little point in studying public opinion if it actually has no independent influence on politics or its outcomes. The question, then, is quite fundamental: to what extent is public opinion an enduring, substantively meaningful force that can structure and guide the politics of vouchers—and to what extent is it a formless mass that elites can manipulate at will? The answer turns on several basic factors.

First, while it is true that uninformed individuals can easily be influenced by new information, the systematic manipulation of public opinion on a grand scale is very difficult and expensive, and neither elite camp can afford to pursue this strategy (in a serious, sustained way) in the normal course of affairs. On rare occasions—notably, when the voucher issue is subject to direct popular vote through the initiative process—both sides may spend big money on massive public relations campaigns. And these campaigns may have considerable influence on public opinion, at least in the short term. But during normal politics, when vouchers are being actively considered by state legislatures—which is the usual way that new public policies are formally adopted (or formally rejected)—elite groups simply do not have the wherewithal to carry this off.[4]

Second, even though the voucher issue has been hotly contested in recent years, and even though elites on both sides have tried to get their messages out, public opinion does not seem to have changed very much. One reason, as noted, is that the elites are usually ineffective at influencing public opinion. But another reason, essentially the other side of the same coin, is that most people are probably not paying attention. Vouchers may pierce their consciousness during rare, high-profile campaigns (if then), but the rest of the time people are not interested or involved, and so are insulated from much of the elite battle and its propaganda. Research suggests that this sort of insulation is fairly common. As David Sears and

Richard Whitney observe, "The problem for most political propagandists is not that they fail to reach their enemies but that they fail to reach anyone at all."[5]

Third, our own data show that, despite the public's lack of information, there is substance to the way people think about vouchers; indeed, even when they shift their positions, they are often shifting in response to newly raised substantive concerns that are important to them. The voucher issue, moreover, is ultimately about education, schools, and children, which are things most everyone knows about and can relate to. A big media campaign could easily push them to one side or the other, at least temporarily. But underneath it all, there is a certain core to people's thinking that is not so easily manipulated and, once the short-term forces die down, will continue to shape their views over the long haul. Parents whose children are stuck in bad schools, or who think the public school system is inequitable, will continue to have good reason to support vouchers. People who ardently embrace the public school ideology will continue to have good reason to oppose them.

The conclusion is that, outside of rare, expensive campaigns, elites cannot expect to influence mass public opinion in a major way. They usually have to take public opinion pretty much as it is and respond to it—or maneuver within its constraints—as rationally and effectively as they can.

Initiative Campaigns

As this discussion implies, the role and impact of public opinion depend on the political context in which the elite struggle is waged. Most commonly, policy issues are pursued through the legislative process, and in this context elites have incentives to pay attention to public opinion and cannot count on molding it in their own image. Less commonly, policy issues are fought out in initiative campaigns, with citizens voting on the issues directly. In this very different context, elites tend to unleash high-powered political campaigns that can drastically change public opinion (if temporarily). Here, what passes for public opinion may simply be a manufactured product of elite power, not a democratic determinant of it.

These two contexts, and the differences between them, have a lot to tell us about the politics of vouchers and where it is headed. The contexts themselves, in fact, are choices that voucher leaders can make in trying to promote their cause. Leaders can invest their resources in the legislative process, in initiative campaigns, or both. But whatever they do, they are choosing a distinctive brand of politics—and a distinctive role for public opinion—that is likely to affect their prospects for winning.

In this section, we'll take a closer look at initiative campaigns to see how the movement has fared and, more generally, what it can expect from this context of direct democracy.

A Story of Defeat: California's Proposition 174

In the recent history of the voucher movement, two events are most symbolic of its politics. The first is the 1990 adoption of the Milwaukee voucher program. This was the movement's breakthrough victory, in which a new coalition of conservatives and the urban poor won a targeted voucher program for disadvantaged kids in the inner city—and did so by bringing pressure on the state legislature through the normal politics of policy-making. The victory wasn't easy. But normal politics, combined with a centrist political appeal, ultimately led to success.

The second symbolic event is the 1993 initiative on California's Proposition 174. This was not a victory for vouchers, but a horrendous defeat. The citizens of California voted by an overwhelming margin, 70 percent to 30 percent, not to adopt a constitutional amendment that would have created a voucher system in their state. The story of Proposition 174 is not nearly as well known as the Milwaukee story, but its lessons are important indeed. Here is what happened.[6]

As the nation entered the 1990s, school choice was on the rise, and voucher leaders were feeling a rush of optimism. There was no agreement, however, on the best way to proceed. The breakthrough in Milwaukee created a new wing of the movement focused on bringing vouchers to inner-city kids. But traditionalists had more ambitious aims. They wanted voucher systems built around free markets and universalism—and they believed the American people would move in this direction if given a chance to vote on it.

With Proposition 174, the traditionalists acted on this belief. In 1991 Californians were extremely dissatisfied with their public schools, and traditional voucher leaders saw this as their opportunity to pull off a revolution in the most populous state in the nation. Polls revealed that the voucher concept was in fact quite popular among Californians. In the prevailing climate of intense dissatisfaction, leaders felt they could win.

Although the legislature was heavily influenced by the California Teachers Association (CTA), the initiative process allowed voucher activists to craft their own proposal exactly as they wanted it, and then—if they could collect more than half a million signatures of registered voters—put it directly on the state ballot. The legislature could not stop them from doing this. Nor could the teachers union. The people would simply get to vote.

The first stage was to write the actual initiative and thus to fashion the specific *kind* of voucher system that the Californians would be voting on. Most of the key architects were traditionalists, among them Milton Friedman, who was the guiding spirit of the enterprise. But John Coons and Stephen Sugarman were also actively involved, arguing strongly for a voucher system tilted toward the disadvantaged with basic regulations for accountability and equity.

The traditionalists, however, ultimately designed the initiative on their own terms.[7] Coons and Sugarman abandoned the effort entirely and refused to participate in the coming campaign. Proposition 174 would embody the libertarian vision of what a voucher system ought to look like. Details aside, it provided for a new system of choice based on free markets: all California children would qualify for a voucher of about $2,600 (equal to half of the prevailing per-child expenditure within the public school system), and private schools would be subject to virtually no new regulations.[8]

With the proposition thus written, money was raised (largely from libertarian sources) to get the necessary signatures, and, despite an unprecedented campaign by the CTA to block the signature-gathering drive, the proposition was eventually qualified for the ballot. Because of state requirements beyond the group's control, the vote was scheduled for a special election during November of 1993.

As the campaign approached, polls showed that the proposition was popular and in the lead. But signs of trouble came early on, as advocates tried to line up influential elites throughout the state—public officials, members of the media, business leaders, community leaders, representatives of minorities—to support their cause. This appeal was entirely unsuccessful, and for an obvious reason: most elites were not libertarians by any stretch of the imagination, and simply did not think free markets should be applied wholesale to remake the education system. The common inclination was to worry that a free-market approach might hurt the public school system, that it might work against children who are less advantaged, that the money might be put to unproductive or frivolous (or worse) use by totally autonomous private schools, and that the new costs (arising mainly because existing private school students, previously free to the state, would now get vouchers and cost the state money) could bust the state education budget. They saw it as ill conceived and extremely risky.

In the end, the proposition attracted elite support from libertarians and leaders of the religious right—and from *no* other groups. It was even opposed by Republican governor Pete Wilson, who endorsed vouchers in principle (and later proposed his own program for kids in failing schools) but was concerned about its impact on the budget. Going into the campaign, then, the movement was unable to point to respected groups of elites that might lend legitimacy to its cause. And largely for this reason, it was unable to raise money. It raised small amounts from libertarian contributors and even less from groups on the religious right—about $4 million in total, including the money used early on to gather signatures. But no other groups contributed.

The teachers union, meantime, was in great shape. In waging its campaign, it could point to the support of virtually every elite group in the state and had the solid backing of the media. It was flush with money and eager to spend it in crushing the opposition. Before the dust had settled at the end of the campaign, the union had amassed a war chest of more than $16 million.

The campaign itself was no contest. The CTA launched a well-designed, multimillion dollar media blitz that reached all corners of the state and recited its anti–Proposition 174 messages over and over again. It also relied on an army of volunteers, mainly teachers, to make phone calls, ring doorbells, discuss the issue with parents, and get out the vote. Proponents had a much smaller group of activists and little money to conduct their own media operation. As a result, virtually all the information generated by the campaign was one-sided. And Californians, not surprisingly, began to move away from their early support for Proposition 174. By August, a Field Poll showed that the initiative had already fallen behind, by 46 percent to 36 percent, and by October the gap had grown to a formidable 60 percent to 24 percent. On election day, the results simply confirmed what everyone already knew.

In an important sense, the CTA took an uninformed public and (temporarily) molded its thinking. But despite the union's success in winning people over, there was an underlying integrity to public opinion that was not destroyed. Indeed, it seems clear that the CTA's main strategy was to reinforce latent values and concerns that were *already* inherent in the public's thinking and that simply needed to be amplified.

Near the end of the campaign, for instance, a poll carried out by PACE, a respected policy organization housed at UC Berkeley and Stanford University, found that Californians still—despite all the pummeling—agreed with the basic idea behind Proposition 174, with 56 percent in favor and

39 percent against. But they expressed two major concerns. First, they worried about the well-being of the public schools. Second, they worried about the problems that might arise if private schools were not held accountable through basic regulations.

While a skeptic might argue that these ideas were planted in voters' heads by the CTA, our own analysis suggests otherwise. Americans like the public schools and want the best for them. They believe strongly in the need for regulation to ensure accountability. And most generally, they are concerned about the *risks* that go along with a major policy change. Californians doubtless came into the campaign with exactly these sorts of latent views, and, until the information explosion, had not clearly linked them to the specific features of Proposition 174. The CTA did that for them, for these were the very concerns—the public's own concerns—that the CTA played to during the campaign.

The CTA was not the only powerful actor making these arguments. Californians were hearing them from other elites too, including influential media organizations well known for their moderate or even conservative views and that would normally be sympathetic to choice-based reforms. The *Los Angeles Times*, for instance, led off one of its editorials with the byline "Even voucher fans shouldn't want this one to pass," and went on (using the PACE poll as a springboard) to express its concerns about the lack of regulation, the threat to the state's education budget, and the risks of such a monumental shift in statewide policy. It concluded by saying, "No one in California, or in the rest of the nation, has any experience with educational change on such a massive scale. Proposition 174 is, for California's children, simply a leap too far into a very uncertain future."[9]

The *Long Beach Press Telegram*, obviously quite sympathetic, put it this way:

> Unfortunately, Proposition 174 is too great a gamble for California. . . . Voucher supporters ought to work on a scaled-down proposal, perhaps one that starts by offering vouchers to low-income inner-city families. Then later, say in about five years or so, open it up to everyone. That way both public and private systems would have sufficient time to adjust to the plan before it would become a statewide policy. California schools need some competition, and they need significant reform. Regretfully, this initiative is not the solution. The Press-Telegram recommends a "No" vote on Proposition 174.[10]

In the aftermath of their crushing defeat, Proposition 174's leaders put the blame on the one-sidedness of the campaign, and thus on their lack of money. Their own supporters in the business community had "wimped out," making it impossible for them to launch an effective media campaign of their own, and the union had simply blown them out with an unanswered propaganda barrage.[11] If the voucher side had just been able to match the union's resources, its leaders argued, the initiative would have passed.

Explaining Defeat: The Perverse Politics of Initiative Campaigns

Why did Proposition 174 go down to defeat? On the surface, its leaders might seem to be right about the key role of money. For reasons I will discuss below, however, the connection between money and political outcomes is not nearly as direct as voucher leaders portray it. Had they somehow been able to raise a lot more money for their cause, they almost certainly would have lost anyway.

Given the themes of this book, it is tempting to suggest that the real problem was the libertarian content of Proposition 174 itself. Traditionalists wrote an initiative promoting their own preferences, but few people in California shared those preferences. Had they instead moved to the political center, opting for a voucher system that was small and low-risk, regulated to promote accountability and equity, and targeted at children in need, they might have attracted far higher levels of public (and elite) support—and they might have won the election.

Yet something about this scenario is not right either. It implicitly assumes a world of normal politics, in which elites adapt and respond to public opinion. Initiative campaigns, however, are very different. They represent a world of direct democracy and high-intensity media in which public opinion, rather than driving behavior, is being molded by it. Because this is so, initiatives have a political logic all their own, and any effort to explain their outcomes must recognize as much.

There is now a fair amount of research on initiative campaigns generally (for all types of issues), and these studies yield several findings that are quite revealing.[12] One is that, while initiatives are usually put on the ballot after initial polling has shown them to be quite popular, they typically decline in popularity during the campaign—and often lose once the votes are in. As one expert (writing in 1984) summarizes it, "The typical pattern of change in voting intentions on propositions moves from widespread support—often by as much as two to one—early in the campaign to one-sided rejection on election day, often by the same margin."[13] Lopsided losses are not always the case. Indeed, propositions have improved their track record in recent years, and 50 percent were actually approved by voters during the 1990s. But even when propositions ultimately win, they usually do so only after losing a good bit of their initial advantage in public support.

Why would this be? The reason is well known to professionals who run initiative campaigns, as well as to researchers. Voters are poorly informed about most propositions, and their initial positions are not firmly held. During the campaign, they are barraged by conflicting claims, often presented in the most inflammatory and extreme language and with little regard for the truth. For many citizens, the effect of all this propaganda is to create uncertainty and fear about the possible effects of a change in public policy—and their response, even if they were inclined to support change at the outset, is to fall back on the security of the status quo. The guiding rule of thumb for voters in initiative campaigns is: when in doubt, vote no.

Opponents are well aware of this. And although they typically start out behind in the polls, they have a huge advantage during the course of the campaign. To win converts, they don't have to convince people that a proposal would make bad public policy. They simply need to create doubt and uncertainty. On some issues, of course—taxes, the death penalty, immigration, term limits, gambling, assisted suicide—voters come to the campaign with fairly high levels of familiarity and well-developed views of their own. When this happens, opponents may not have much to work with, and they may lose to a good campaign by proponents. But many issues aren't like this. They are unfamiliar to the broader public, deal with substantive matters that are inherently rather complex, and have social consequences that can be disputed. Under these conditions, opponents can have a field day: raising questions, promoting confusion, generating uncertainty. With enough money to get the word out, this is a winning formula.

Which brings us back to money. Because opponents have by far the easier job in an initiative campaign, it makes sense that a dollar spent by opponents should often have a much more powerful impact than a dollar spent by proponents. And this is what research has shown.[14] Generally speaking, opponents can often defeat initiatives even if they are far outspent by proponents. And if they actually spend more than the proponents do, they are virtually assured of winning. These generalizations may not hold when the issues are simple, familiar, and already matters of firm opinion. But otherwise they do. As one veteran of California initiative campaigns summarizes it, "Big money can defeat an initiative, but big money cannot pass one"[15]

If the broader research literature is any guide, then, there can be little mystery why Proposition 174 was so soundly defeated. Vouchers are unfamiliar to most voters, fairly complex in application, and may have an array of social consequences—for school quality, for the funding and ideals of the public school system, for social equity and racial balance, for the level of taxes, for democratic accountability in government, and more— that cannot be mapped out with total confidence. There are enormous opportunities here for a strong opponent to generate doubt and uncertainty. And the teachers unions are about as powerful and well financed as opponents get. The fact of the matter is, Proposition 174 never really had a chance, given the structure of the situation. It was poorly funded and poorly designed. But even if it hadn't been, the teachers unions would have defeated it.

As a general matter, then, the defeat of vouchers in initiative campaigns is not what it seems to be on the surface: a simple expression of public opinion in which voters thoughtfully consider and then reject the idea. Indeed, it says more about the perversity of initiative campaigns than it does about public opinion. Elites are clearly manipulating the vote. Opponents have huge advantages. The deck is securely stacked from the outset.

Even so, it is important to recognize that the teachers unions are not manufacturing opposition out of nothing. Californians, and American more generally, are on both sides of the fence at once when it comes to vouchers. They are open to the idea, they think private schools are superior to public schools, and they believe it makes sense to give new opportunities to children who need them. Yet they also have genuine attachments to the public school system and its social and democratic ideals, as well as concerns about costs—and it is precisely because they *do* care about these things that they are especially vulnerable to union claims about the frightening risks of vouchers. The unions are manipulating public opinion. But they are doing it by strategically playing upon values and concerns that people actually do hold.

Additional Evidence: The Election of 2000

Aside from Proposition 174, there have been a number of other initiatives promoting vouchers or tuition tax credits over the last decade. All these initiatives have failed, and by huge margins. Here is the postmortem:[16]
—Oregon, 1990, tax credits defeated two-to-one.
—Colorado, 1992, vouchers defeated 67 percent to 33 percent.
—Washington state, 1996, vouchers defeated 66 percent to 34 percent.
—Colorado, 1998, tax credits defeated 59 percent to 41 percent.

—California, 2000, vouchers defeated 71 percent to 29 percent.

—Michigan, 2000, vouchers defeated 69 percent to 31 percent.

The details are different from case to case. But the broad-brush political dynamics are very much the same. Although the issue was initially popular, proponents found themselves up against a powerful teachers union, and the union created enough doubt among voters to undermine the issue's initial popularity and bring about its defeat.

There are no surprises here, but the campaigns waged during the 2000 election—one in California, the other in Michigan—are particularly instructive. Each offers important new evidence that helps nail down the argument.

The California campaign provides a wonderful test of whether big spending by proponents can bring about a victory for vouchers.[17] The idea to put vouchers on the ballot—again—was the brainchild of Silicon Valley venture capitalist Timothy Draper, who, having made a fortune financing high-tech businesses, turned his sights to California education. The initiative itself was essentially a free-market proposal, offering a $4,000 voucher to all kids and imposing almost no rules to ensure accountability or equity—very much like Proposition 174. The difference was in the money: Proposition 174 was vastly outspent by the unions, but Draper pledged to spend whatever it might take to overcome the union advantage, and to win.

Despite Proposition 174's drubbing just seven years earlier, the Draper initiative started out ahead in the polls—attesting to the short-term effects that these campaigns have on the public's thinking. Outside the perversities of media campaigns, people were basically positive toward vouchers, and the polls showed it. The libertarian content of the initiative, however, was once again a very negative feature as far as the state's elite groups were concerned. All of them opposed it. Even conservative, business, and religious groups refused to get on board. So Draper was forced to go it alone. Virtually all of the money would come out of his own pocket.

During the course of the campaign, Draper and the teachers union engaged in an arms race, matching one another dollar for dollar. Draper orchestrated spending of more than $30 million—by far the most money, by many orders of magnitude, ever spent on behalf of a voucher initiative. Opponents spent roughly the same amount, 99 percent of it from organized labor, mainly the California Teachers Association.[18]

The impact on the California electorate was exactly what the research literature would lead us to expect. Despite Draper's extravagant spending, which guaranteed that proponents could fight the union on equal terms, the polling numbers began to fall as soon as the union began its media campaign—hammering away at how vouchers would hurt the public schools and how voucher schools would be unaccountable—and the initiative went down to defeat by the same humbling margin as Proposition 174, 71 percent to 29 percent. Draper's $30 million made no difference whatever. The adage is worth repeating: "Big money can defeat an initiative, but big money cannot pass one."

Now consider the experience of the Michigan voucher initiative.[19] This campaign is uniquely important in the evidence it generates because it is the *only* one in which the voucher side proposed a smaller, less risky program targeted at disadvantaged children. Specifically, it proposed making vouchers (of about $3,300) available to children living within the state's worst-performing districts, defined as districts where one-third or more of the students fail to graduate from high school. The question is: did this move to the center—which in normal political contexts is the rational strategy for maximizing public (and elite) support—actually lead to a more favorable outcome?

The Michigan initiative was spearheaded by Dick DeVos, president of Amway Corporation, and his wife Betty, the former chair of the Michigan Republican Party, but they were not alone in raising resources and prosecuting the campaign. In stark contrast to the libertarian ventures in California and elsewhere, the centrist nature of the proposal attracted support from important elites—most notably the Catholic Church, the Michigan Chamber of Commerce, and black ministers. This was the first time, really, that voucher leaders in any state had succeeded in putting together a serious elite-level coalition to give legitimacy and clout to an initiative campaign.

There were also major problems. Michigan's Republican governor, John Engler, refused to support the voucher effort—because, according to insiders, he feared it would stimulate a high turnout among voters inclined to vote Democrat, and that this would threaten Republican candidates on the state ticket. Other Republican leaders, including Senator Spencer Abraham, also came out in opposition. Thus the state Republican Party organization was of little help. Meanwhile, the NAACP and other mainline civil rights groups launched an aggressive effort to get black ministers and other leaders in the minority community to abandon the initiative. And teachers, administrators, and local school boards unabashedly used the public school system and public money to get their anti-voucher message out to parents.

Still, the voucher side had a lot going for it. The Catholic Church fought hard for the initiative, sending out three separate letters in support of it to more than 500,000 Catholic homes, and regularly arguing its virtues (as an issue of social justice) during Sunday services. The coalition, moreover, was quite successful at raising money. In fact, it was able to *far outspend* the union-led opposition—the only time that this has happened during a voucher campaign. The proponents raised about $13 million—almost $5 million of it from the DeVos family, another $2 million from the Catholic Church—while opponents raised about $6 million, almost all of it from the Michigan Education Association.[20]

Thus, while political alignments were hardly ideal, things looked a lot better for this voucher initiative than they had looked for any other—due, almost surely, to its focus on disadvantaged kids. Even so, none of this seemed to make much difference in the context of initiative politics. Opponents poured their resources into a high-powered media campaign whose basic theme was that vouchers would take millions of dollars away from the public schools, undermine their quality, and require an increase in taxes. They also argued that private schools would be unaccountable and would discriminate against kids on the basis of race and special needs. This was enough to do the job. Despite a massive, even better-financed media campaign on the pro side, the opponents' stridently negative messages succeeded—as always—in creating doubt and uncertainty. The voucher proposal had come into the election season with a big lead in the polls, but as soon as the teachers union began its advertising blitz, the polling numbers began to turn, and within a week or two the initiative was down by two-to-one. The final result: a 69 percent to 31 percent defeat for vouchers—virtually the same stomping Tim Draper had received in California, and that all the other voucher or tax credit initiatives had received in the past.

It is possible, of course, that future experiences with initiative campaigns will be different somehow. But at this point, the evidence seems clear and consistent, both on initiative campaigns in general and on voucher campaigns in particular. The elections in California and Michigan seal the case. When an issue like vouchers—popular, but unfamiliar and rather complicated—is faced with a strong opponent, the opponent has an overwhelming advantage. Money doesn't correct the imbalance. Nor does the otherwise rational strategy of going to the center. For the voucher movement, initiatives are probably no-win propositions.

In the wake of Election 2000, the unions wasted little time in explaining to the nation what their victories meant. The president of the National Education Association, Robert Chase, announced that the resounding defeat of the Michigan and California initiatives proved that Americans were strongly opposed to vouchers. The 2000 election, he said, marked the "death knell" of the voucher movement.[21] This kind of spin is standard fare in politics, but there is little substance to it. The voucher movement is hardly about to die. And because initiative campaigns are contexts in which public opinion is manipulated rather than simply expressed, the defeat of voucher proposals says little (at least directly) about what Americans really think about the issue. More than anything else, the outcome of Election 2000 is simply a reflection of the distinctive logic of initiative politics. And the power of opponents to get their way.

What Lies Ahead for Vouchers?

Voucher leaders face better odds when they pursue their goals through the usual, less direct mechanisms of American democracy, and thus through what I have called normal politics. Here, public opinion cannot readily be molded by one side or the other. It is largely an independent force that supporters and opponents must adapt to and use in making their cases to policymakers—and that policymakers, particularly legislators, are keenly concerned about as they make decisions about policy.

What should we expect from normal politics? The place to begin is by recognizing that all the elements that drive its dynamics—from the basic contours of public opinion to the goals, interests, and resources of elites—are contained within a larger system of democratic institutions, and this system shapes and constrains the course of political action. So far, we have talked a good deal about public opinion and a good deal about elites. But we haven't talked much about the system. The system, however, is really the key to much of what happens in the policy process.

The most fundamental property of the American democratic system is that it is built around separation of powers, and contains a variety of checks and balances fully intended by the founders to make it difficult to enact new laws. Fearing that the majority might tyrannize over the minority, they designed a system that puts obstacles in the majority's way and that gives numerical minorities lots of opportunities to block laws they do not like. Since the early years of the Republic, these veto points have proliferated and have gone well beyond what the Constitution requires. What is true at the national level is also true of the states, where much of the action on education reform takes place.

For a bill to become law at the national level, for instance, it must find its way out of subcommittees and full committees in both the House and Senate, and survive a gauntlet that includes filibusters, holds, and other

procedures that numerical minorities can use to derail measures they disagree with. If a bill somehow gets past all these veto points, it must then
be approved in some form by the floors of both chambers, go through a
conference committee of the two houses, and come back to be ratified
(now in identical form) on the chamber floors again. Assuming it survives
all this (although, even if it does, its content may bear little resemblance to
the original), it must go to the president, who has the right to veto it. If the
president rejects the bill, his veto can only be overridden with a two-thirds
vote of each house—which is extraordinarily difficult and historically has
happened in only 7 percent of all presidential vetoes.[22] If the bill does
become law, it may be overturned later by the courts, which may decide
that it is unconstitutional or interpret its provisions in unwanted ways.
Much the same institutional minefield is present at the state level.

This review of high school civics may sound overly familiar, but the
implications are profound. Because of all the veto points built into the
American system, the institutional deck is heavily stacked in favor of the
status quo. Groups that want to enact a new policy can only do so by
successfully overcoming *all* the hurdles that stand in their way, while opponents need only win *one* of these battles in order to prevent the policy
from being adopted. In a system of checks and balances, then, the opponents have a built-in advantage. They can win by merely blocking, and
blocking is relatively easy.

Thus, even in normal politics, the battle over vouchers is by no means
an equal fight. Even if the two sides were perfectly balanced in resources,
organization, and manpower, the American institutional system would
ensure that the opponents of vouchers would be able to block most of the
voucher proposals that come along. From the standpoint of the voucher
movement, this simple fact would be problem enough. But the reality is
more sobering still, for the two sides are not evenly balanced in the en-
dowments they bring into the battle. The opponents are far more powerful coming in—and they are able to use their greater power within a system
that is mightily stacked in their favor to begin with.

Despite all this, vouchers still have a much better chance of success in
normal politics than they do in initiative campaigns. The basic facts suggest as much. As we have seen, vouchers (and tax credits) have consistently suffered massive defeats in initiative elections, and the broader
research suggests that such defeats are virtually unavoidable. Meantime,
the voucher movement has managed to win victories through normal politics in Wisconsin, Ohio, and Florida, and it has come close to victory in

several other states. To put it simply, the movement has a far better track record when it opts for the conventional route to policymaking.

There is also a second, more general reason why this route appears more promising. In initiative politics, the presence of a powerful opponent essentially means that the voucher side will lose. But in normal politics, the voucher movement does not need to be more powerful than its opponents, in some overall sense, in order to realize a measure of political progress. The reason is that there are some 15,000 school districts, hundreds of cities, fifty states, and the national government, and all of them are political arenas in which the voucher issue can be fought out. Because the movement itself is fragmented and decentralized, it is guaranteed to generate a great many battles in the years ahead. For awhile, almost all of these battles will be lost. But with so much action taking place in arenas all over the country, and with the movement taking advantage of windows of opportunity—legislatures controlled by Republicans, districts known to have dismal performance, new leaders emerging to represent urban parents—the law of large numbers ensures that it *will* win some of these battles, even if the probability of victory is small overall.

Under normal politics, therefore, the movement can be expected to make progress. And once new programs are set up—irony of ironies—it can then use the status quo biases of the American institutional system to protect its creations: by blocking opponents' legislative attempts to overturn them.[23]

Voucher Elites: Going to the Center

Another interesting asymmetry arising from the American system of checks and balances is that, in order to move their cause ahead, voucher leaders have a much greater need for public support than their opponents do. Opponents only need to block, which they can achieve with numerical minorities. But voucher leaders need to enact new laws, and thus to amass enough political support to overcome all the obstacles in their path, which typically calls for super-majorities. This requirement gives them strong incentives to fashion proposals that meet with as much public (and elite) approval as possible—and thus strong incentives to go to the political center.

During the early years of the voucher movement, the free-market ideas of Milton Friedman were countered by Christopher Jencks, and by John Coons and Stephen Sugarman, who argued for regulated voucher plans tilted toward disadvantaged children.[24] For a long time, this debate was largely academic. But that came to an end with the victory in Milwaukee, which showed for the first time that vouchers could be *politically* potent when targeted solely at kids who need help the most. This approach had strong support from the urban poor and their local leaders. It attracted an unorthodox but powerful coalition of conservative and urban elites. And it succeeded in overcoming the formidable power of the teachers unions and their allies. With the example of Milwaukee before them, activists in cities and states around the nation began pushing aggressively for low-income voucher programs, and the early vision of Jencks, Coons, and Sugarman came to be the dominant force in the movement's dramatic growth.

In effect, then, the modern voucher movement—without plan or coordination—*has* been going to the center, and the centrist approach has worked remarkably well in view of the odds. More than any single factor, this explains why the movement has gathered so much political steam and represents such a threat to the establishment. There is every reason to believe that, in the years ahead, most voucher leaders will continue to endorse centrist solutions and hew to a middle path.

In more substantive terms, the targeted approach is well adapted to the basic features of public opinion, taking advantage of the movement's strengths while compensating for its weaknesses. Among other things:

—Americans like the public school system, are not overly concerned about its performance problems, and are sensitive to the risks and costs a voucher plan might pose. Because a targeted plan only applies to the neediest kids in the most troubled school districts, it clearly minimizes the risks and costs, and leaves the rest of the public system and its families unaffected (at least directly).

—Americans do not believe in totally free markets, which they suspect will lead to problems of accountability and equity. They think choice and competition can be good for education, but they want to see protections and limitations built in to ensure things don't go wrong. A targeted program fits the bill.

—Americans want education reform to proceed in incremental steps and are not inclined toward revolution. A targeted program is inherently limited in scope and, by focusing on the neediest children and schools, is a sensible way to start an incremental process of change.

—The people who would qualify for these programs, poor and minority parents in low-performing districts, are precisely the people who have the greatest objective need for new educational opportunities, and who have expressed the strongest support for vouchers. They are an extremely receptive constituency.

—The rest of the population is not averse to limited voucher programs simply because it has no direct stake in them. On the contrary, Americans are quite supportive of voucher programs targeted at the poor and, in evaluating the voucher idea more generally, place heavy emphasis on social concerns, especially social equity. Overall, the public interest is more important than self-interest in determining how Americans approach the voucher issue—and targeted programs, which clearly aim to address serious social problems, can readily be understood and embraced on public-interest grounds.

When the movement goes to the center, then, it enhances its public appeal and creates a favorable democratic base for advancing its cause. Yet voucher leaders cannot expect to win pitched battles with the teachers unions by making centrist proposals and counting on "the people" to rise up in revolt. The fact is that, outside of certain urban areas, Americans are not *demanding* vouchers, whether for themselves or as solutions to pressing social problems. They are positively inclined, especially when the proposals are moderate. But they are poorly informed, their views are not well thought out, and, when pushed, they can see merit in the other side of the argument. They are more ambivalent than committed.

Even in the inner city, where support for vouchers is clearly the strongest, it would be wrong to think that most parents are demanding such a reform. These parents are the most likely to be poorly informed. And, because they tend to have low expectations, they are more inclined to be satisfied with their troubled schools than objective conditions would seem to suggest. Parent uprisings have occurred—in Milwaukee, in Cleveland, in Jersey City, and a few other places. But this is not the norm. The norm is that, even in cities with abysmal schools, and even when parents are quite supportive of vouchers, there is little overt demand. The support is there, but it is latent.

From a political standpoint, then, perhaps the best way to think about public opinion on the voucher issue is that it is *permissive*. It allows voucher leaders to claim that most Americans are on their side, particularly those who are in greatest need of new educational opportunities, and to link this public support to their central arguments about improving school performance and promoting social equity. This, in turn, provides a democratic foundation for getting policymakers to move on vouchers. Policymakers who are otherwise sympathetic may see public opinion as giving them a green light to take action (which they probably would not do were opinion stacked on the other side). Policymakers who are uncommitted, or perhaps even opposed, may also have constituency-based incentives to go along—as their actions would tend to meet with favorable responses in their districts and be easily justified.

Yet the permissive nature of public opinion on this issue does not force policymakers to act. Moreover, it also gives policymakers an out, should they choose—as most Democrats currently do—to oppose whatever voucher proposals come down the pike. For while public opinion is basically positive, there is enough ambivalence to allow opponents to justify their opposition in terms that constituents can understand and accept—notably that vouchers might hurt the public schools. As things now stand, it is not clear that most Democrats who oppose vouchers are actually paying a political price for doing so.

Both elite camps would like to transform public opinion by convincing Americans to be firmly on their side. As noted earlier, the obvious way to go about this—through media campaigns—is overly expensive and unlikely to create a meaningful body of opinion that can be sustained over time. In this respect, both camps are on an equal footing. But in other respects, the voucher side actually has some key advantages, unmatched by its opponents, that may serve to firm up the public's inclination to see vouchers in a favorable light, and to create a measure of genuine demand in future years.

These advantages arise because, as voucher programs are actually put in place and become increasingly common, Americans touched by these reforms will grow more familiar with vouchers through their own experiences, as well as the experiences of their friends, neighbors, and relatives. In the process, ideas and arguments on the topic will cease to be purely intellectual matters. Many people will be able to see with their own eyes, and hear with their own ears, what vouchers and parental choice actually mean in the practice of everyday life. They will come to know something on the topic, and ambivalence will give way to a firmer sense of where they stand and why.

In principle, of course, the public's growing experience with choice could backfire for the voucher movement, because the experiences could be bad ones. The result could be a firmer sense of opposition, not a firmer sense of support. But the evidence suggests otherwise. Academic researchers squabble endlessly about whether vouchers succeed in promoting student achievement, just as they squabble about most everything else. Yet the evidence is very clear, based on quite a few studies, that the direct experiences of the parents and kids involved in voucher programs are very positive ones. They tend to be much more satisfied with their chosen schools, for instance, than with the schools they left, and more satisfied than the parents who remain in the regular public schools.[25] It seems quite likely, then, that the spread of voucher programs—and experience—will have a favorable effect on public opinion and firm it up over time.

Experience should prove consequential for another reason as well. In politics, the opponents' most effective argument has long been that vouchers would hurt the public schools. But this argument may well lose much of its value in communities that actually have voucher programs in operation. The best example is Milwaukee. This city has had a voucher system for the past ten years, and there is no evidence that its public schools are somehow suffering. Indeed, the design of the program (together with subsequent legislation) has protected the financial resources of the public schools, and, if anything, the long moribund district has shown signs of trying to improve and innovate in order to meet the competition.[26] Meantime, the people of Milwaukee have not responded to the teachers union's negative claims in anything like the way voters in California and Michigan did. For unlike these other voters, they could formulate their judgments on the basis of experience, and their experience with vouchers simply did not jibe with predictions of disaster. Polls show that the voucher program is quite popular among Milwaukee residents generally.[27] And in recent school board elections, voucher supporters organized to take on the teachers union directly, and they succeeded in sweeping three union-backed board members out of office and gaining control of the board.[28] Doubt and uncertainty about vouchers, which work so well for the unions in contexts where vouchers are untried, do not have the same effect in contexts where vouchers are a familiar, functioning part of everyday life.

In their quest to shape public opinion, then, voucher leaders have a certain advantage over their adversaries. They needn't rely on abstract argument to make their case, as union leaders essentially must. They can bolster their public support by bringing vouchers down from the clouds, putting them in the hands of parents and kids, and generating community-wide familiarity and experience with the issue. The question is: how can they actually do this?

The obvious answer is: by being politically successful in the first place. The more successful voucher leaders are at winning new voucher programs, the more they can generate familiarity and experience and bolster public support for their cause. But this is not much of an answer. For the whole point of seeking out higher levels of public support is to enhance the political power of the movement so that it *can* win new programs.

Making political victory a precondition puts the cart before the horse. The real challenge is to find some way of putting voucher programs in place *without* political victory, and then using the resulting familiarity, experience, and public support to make political victory possible.

The movement has hit upon a way of doing this: by pouring money and effort into private voucher programs. These are programs funded by private donations that offer vouchers to low-income kids in inner-city areas. At this writing, there are some 60,000 children using private vouchers in seventy-nine programs throughout the country (with 1.2 million on the wait lists), and the numbers will doubtless grow in future years.[29] The great advantage of these programs is that they can be set up outside the political system, and thus cannot be blocked by opponents.

By unilaterally setting up these programs, the movement is not simply informing its constituents about vouchers through abstract arguments. It is putting vouchers directly into their hands, and giving thousands of urban families concrete, everyday experience with vouchers in their own lives. Only a small percentage of inner-city families may participate. But these families, who tend to be the most dissatisfied, essentially serve as a vanguard for the rest. They are enthusiastic about these programs, and they can be expected to tell their friends and neighbors, who in turn will tell others. The word will increasingly get out—and, over time, should tend to firm up support for vouchers, give it a more substantive foundation, raise expectations among inner-city parents (who will be hearing that there are better alternatives out there, and ways to get them), and deepen their frustration with the current public schools. In the process, these programs will increasingly attract the attention of local elites, from black ministers to editorial writers to city council members, who will see real families in their communities putting vouchers to use and praising their advantages.

An important by-product is that the movement can use these private voucher programs as a source of *research-based evidence*—particularly important to elites—that vouchers are working for disadvantaged kids. Evidence has always been a political problem for the movement. Opponents have long done everything they can to prevent any sort of (public) voucher program from being adopted and thus, inevitably, to prevent any evidence from being collected about whether these programs actually work. They have then used this to their political advantage by arguing (to policymakers, for example) that voucher programs shouldn't be adopted *because* there is no evidence such programs work. Voucher leaders, as a result, have long been trapped in a Catch-22. It has been hard to win programs with no evidence. But it has been impossible to get evidence without programs.

Private vouchers are an answer to this conundrum as well. They allow leaders to create voucher programs that opponents cannot block, and then to see to it that these programs are studied. For voucher leaders, this is a gamble of sorts, as there is no guarantee that the studies will come out positively, much less with results so compelling that opponents cannot dispute them. So far, the early evidence on student achievement is positive but not compelling.[30] In other respects, however, the evidence is glowing: demonstrating that there is a strong demand for vouchers among the disadvantaged, that voucher parents are much more satisfied with their new private schools, and that private schools are happy to have them.[31] Assuming the gamble continues to go well, these sorts of studies will increasingly give the movement a factual basis for making their case to elites, and for shifting their arguments from abstract claims to practical outcomes.

In the meantime, the mere fact that lots of these programs exist, and that many thousands of poor children go to school through the use of vouchers, day after day, year after year, will help to make vouchers a more familiar part of the American educational landscape for many people in those communities—who are likely to recognize, in the process, that the programs operate in an orderly, manageable fashion, that kids do get educated, that the poor get much-needed assistance, and that the nightmare scenarios described by critics do not seem to be coming true. When the reality of vouchers begins to sink in, the risks associated with them should tend to recede, and more people should find themselves comfortable with the idea.

For all these reasons (and more), private programs contribute to the movement's prospects for success, helping build a foundation of public support. The gradual accumulation of government-financed voucher programs—first in Milwaukee, then (five years later) in Cleveland, then (four years after that) in Florida—obviously contributes to this same foundation. But these early political victories are difficult to win and slow in coming. The option of creating private programs makes it possible for voucher leaders to build their *own* foundation, outside of politics, and put it to political use in their effort to quicken the pace and broaden the scope of governmental action.

If their strategy pays off, government programs will soon begin to shoulder most of the responsibility for raising funds, distributing vouchers to needy families, and cultivating public support. Private programs—inherently small and limited—are a way to get the ball rolling.

Voucher Elites: A Movement in Transition

Going to the center and championing the cause of disadvantaged kids has clear political advantages and, over the long haul, is likely to yield results. In the short term, however, it also spawns an interesting problem for the movement—a believability problem—that acts as a drag on its political effectiveness.

Because the voucher movement is so closely associated with conservatism, many liberal and moderate elites that need to be swayed to the voucher side simply do not believe that its dedication to disadvantaged kids is real. They see targeted voucher plans as a conservative ploy, a way of using the poor to achieve the traditionalists' long-run goals of free markets and universalism, and not as a genuine effort to help poor kids. Similar suspicions arise from *within* the voucher movement, among representatives of the urban poor—who see vouchers as a way of empowering their own constituents, but do not want to be used, and do not want programs for needy children to serve as a springboard for broader free-market programs that might leave the needy behind again.[32]

These suspicions do not arise out of thin air. In politics generally, Republicans and conservatives usually oppose the liberal coalition when it comes to programs for the poor, so their motives in supporting vouchers for disadvantaged children tend to be questioned. It is also clear that many traditionalists, including Friedman, support targeted programs solely for their strategic value in moving toward a broader system, and not because they are valuable in themselves. Recall Friedman's unblinking claim that "programs for the poor are poor programs."[33]

Yet the stereotype does not apply to all conservatives and is often misleading. For within the voucher movement, especially as it has developed over the last decade, there are many conservatives who strongly believe in markets but who also believe, quite genuinely, that programs for the poor are socially desirable in themselves. A good symbol of this kind of conservative is Clint Bolick, the attorney who has represented the voucher movement in most of its key court cases. He is a market conservative but a true advocate for equity and the socially disadvantaged.[34] This is a combination that is increasingly common in modern American politics, and is not confined to the voucher movement.

In all likelihood, the voucher movement's believability problem will diminish over time. In part, this is simply because targeted programs for needy children, once set up, speak for themselves and generate their own activists. But the more interesting reason, and a profoundly consequential one for the politics of vouchers, is that the voucher movement itself is being transformed.

The traditionalists have essentially created something they can no longer control. As the movement gains momentum by going to the center, it attracts new recruits who tend to be lower in income, minority, liberal in their attitudes toward equity and race, and sympathetic toward the public schools. It also attracts new elites, often liberal and Democrat, who are eager to lead them and in tune with their thinking. The very rationality of the centrist solution, then, generates a powerful process of growth and attraction that is changing the movement from the inside and transforming both its membership and its leadership—away from traditionalism.

For now, the movement is still in transition. Traditional leaders continue to play pivotal roles, and they are hoping that low-income programs will lead over the long run to universal voucher systems and free markets. They are quite dependent, however, on their alliance with the urban poor, without whom they cannot be successful. Meantime, the representatives of the urban poor are not entirely comfortable with the alliance and do not trust its future direction. But as long as their usual liberal allies refuse to join them, they remain dependent on traditionalists for political support. The coalition is bound together by mutual dependence.

As time goes on, this will change. The political dynamics make it almost certain that the centrist component will grow in size and political strength, become less dependent on the traditionalists, and create a very different kind of movement. But to appreciate this more fully, and to see where it is likely to lead, we need to take a look at developments within the opposing coalition.

Opposition Elites: Strategies of Defense

Voucher supporters have incentives to go to the center. For many voucher opponents, the strategic situation is similar but viewed from the other end of the political continuum. They are more likely to make winning proposals, and less likely to be saddled with outcomes they detest, if they seek out higher levels of public support toward the center—where they would be within shouting distance of voucher leaders, who are approaching the center from the other end. Given the incentives on both sides, there is reason to expect an eclectic coalition around a compromise, centrist solution. Other things being equal.

Other things, however, are not equal. These incentives do operate among the opposition, but not as forcefully as one might think. Two factors loom large in explaining why. The first is that the American system is not based on majority rule, but is built to favor those who are defending the status quo. Its multiple veto points give opponents ample opportunity to block, even if their positions are wholly out of step with public opinion and their own constituents. Most of the time, they needn't go to the center—and make big policy sacrifices in the process—in order to win. This dilutes their incentives to take more moderate stands. Second, the most powerful opponents of vouchers are the teachers unions, and for them vouchers are a survival issue and not a matter for compromise. They are unalterably opposed to *all* voucher programs, including even small pilot programs for the neediest children in the most troubled school districts, and they are unlikely to move very far from this polar position.

For these reasons, the opponents of vouchers cannot be expected to mirror the behavior of their counterparts by rushing to the center. Rather than respond to public opinion, as voucher leaders have incentives to do, they are more inclined to stand their ground, block change through whatever institutional means they can, and bolster their public support by trying to convince the American people that vouchers would make bad public policy.

Our survey suggests that opponents have some promising raw materials to work with. Americans have genuine affection for the public schools and, despite their attraction to choice, are likely to reject ideas they see as threatening to the current system—which, of course, is the central theme of the opponents' argument. Americans are also sensitive to the risks and costs associated with vouchers, and have a shaky basis for evaluating the actual consequences that a voucher system would produce. Opponents can cultivate these and other concerns by raising doubt about what would really happen if vouchers were adopted.

As I suggested earlier, a nationwide strategy to shape public opinion is very difficult to pull off and unlikely to work. But Democrats and other opponent allies can clearly use these raw materials, which reflect the ambivalence of current opinion, to justify their unwillingness to go along with vouchers; and these justifications will often resonate with enough constituents enough of the time to get them by. Meantime, they can simply follow a strategy of blocking whatever proposals come up.

Even for opponents, however, there remain incentives for making at least some moves toward the political center. To make no compromises, and to offer no response to the widespread popularity of school choice, is to force a political face-off between the status quo and targeted voucher plans. And when these are the *only* alternatives on the table, opponents could find vouchers more and more difficult to block—as many policymakers in the middle, eager not to alienate their constituents, seek to embrace some brand of choice-based reform.

But what compromises to make, what alternatives to offer? There is really only one solution that is acceptable to the entire spectrum of voucher opponents, including groups like the teachers unions that have no intention of supporting any form of voucher program. That solution is *public school choice*—and especially, in more recent years, charter schools, which come closest (in principle) to offering the basics of a market-like system within the public sector.[35]

Over the last decade, public school choice has become the liberal coalition's way of participating in the choice movement, and of showing that its members are not simply in the business of blocking every version of school choice. While some of the earliest public school choice programs were established by liberal reformers, and while there is now genuine enthusiasm for such programs among some in the liberal coalition—Bill Clinton and Al Gore, for instance, are strong proponents of charter schools—the fact is that liberals on the whole were resistant even to public school choice in the early going and had to be pushed into it through political pressure from conservatives and parents.

There is nothing too surprising about this. For reasons of ideology and constituency, liberals have traditionally been proponents of government programs and top-down provision of government services. They have been unimpressed with the purported advantages of markets and convinced of their negative consequences for equity. This legacy remains a big part of liberal thinking and ensures that, even today, many in the coalition are not truly committed to public school choice. Much of their support is strategic.

This is clearly the case for the teachers unions, as well as for other groups within the education establishment. Choice and competition, even when entirely limited to public schools, are threatening to their basic interests. An influx of new charter schools, for example, would attract children away from the regular public schools, reduce the latter's current levels of funding and employment, put new pressures on teachers and administrators, and create a new population of public school teachers that may be nonunion and difficult to organize. So, while the unions now say (sometimes) that they support charters and other forms of public school choice, this is a strategic embrace of reforms they actually oppose. It is their way of edging toward the center, trying to find a middle way that will satisfy enough Americans and policymakers—and stop vouchers.

Americans are sympathetic toward the public school system, and the idea of public school choice is very popular with them. These are powerful foundations on which the liberal coalition can build a defense against vouchers. And since that is essentially the game they are playing—a defensive game, in which the real goal is to block—public school choice may be just enough of a move toward the center to prevent vouchers from making any more progress.

But this seems unlikely. One problem is that, however enthusiastic some liberals might be about creating true choice and competition within the public sector, there is much liberal resistance to reforms that are designed to make them work to best advantage. The unions, in particular, have a strong interest in supporting public school choice as a matter of strategy and then sabotaging the actual reforms by demanding designs that offer little choice, little competition, and little threat to the existing system. Among other things, they push for low ceilings on the number of charter schools allowed by law, for teachers in charters to be covered by the existing collective bargaining contract, for requiring charters to get the approval of their districts before they can begin operating, and for denying charters money for start-up and building costs. In most states with charter bills, as a result, there are not enough charter schools to offer real competition for the regular public schools, and they are burdened by many restrictions.[36]

Charters and other forms of public school choice have a broad spectrum of political support, including the enthusiastic support of conservative groups. So there are forces pushing for much more expansive systems of choice and competition within public education than the unions and their allies are comfortable with. Moreover, it may well be that, once the genie is out of the bottle and new constituencies emerge to protect and promote the new reforms, politics will produce systems that are genuine attempts to use what choice and competition have to offer. In the near term, however, the liberal coalition itself is providing more symbol than substance, and the unions are dedicated to using their preeminent power to see that this continues. Even in the longer term, charters and other public schools of choice are constrained to operate in a political environment in which the drive to control their behavior and stifle competition is strong. Public school choice, as a result, tends to be limited in what it can offer as a policy alternative, and its adoption may not reduce the support for vouchers very much.

In fact, it may not reduce the support for vouchers at all, and may even increase it. For it is reasonable to suggest that, were public school choice to spread, Americans would come to think of choice as a familiar, normal, and even necessary part of their education system—and this would encourage them to see vouchers as a closely related form of choice that is just a short step away, and not threatening or fraught with risk. It is difficult to argue that, once public school choice is adopted, Americans will somehow draw the line. It is more likely that as the school system as a whole becomes more thoroughly built around choice and competition, and as this way of thinking and behaving becomes the norm, attitudes and beliefs will adapt—and so will views toward vouchers.

There are good reasons, then, for suspecting that the liberal compromise of promoting public school choice will not prove to be an effective defense against vouchers. When all is said and done, however, there is another reason that is perhaps even more consequential: *the strongest support for vouchers comes from the liberals' own constituents*, particularly parents who are disadvantaged, minority, and from low-performing urban school districts. These parents like charter schools, but they are also highly interested in voucher programs that would allow them to go private—and there is no reason to think they will be satisfied with a reform that prevents them from gaining entrance to the private sector. Liberal elites may oppose vouchers and see public school choice as a way of doing that. But many of them also have constituency-based incentives to abandon their own strategy, and, as we will see, this has far-reaching implications for the future stability of the liberal coalition.

Opposing Elites: Defection in the Ranks

For the teachers unions, the disconnect with liberal constituencies is not a compelling reason to move further toward the center. These constituencies are not, after all, the unions' real constituencies anyway. The unions are concerned about teachers and about the interests, resources, and power of their own organizations. To protect these things, the unions need to defeat vouchers, and this keeps them from moderating their position. But there are other important groups in the liberal coalition, particularly those that represent disadvantaged populations, that have very different incentives—and that *will*, under the right circumstances, follow their own constituents by moving to the center. Two are especially critical to the future politics of the issue: civil rights groups and Democratic politicians.

From the beginning, the major civil rights groups have been against vouchers. The NAACP, in particular, has played a prominent role in the opposing coalition.[37] Most of the civil rights leadership has been around long enough to have participated in the pivotal years of their movement's struggle against segregation, racism, and inequality, and they have emerged from these years with a firm set of convictions. They believe in an active government, and in public institutions generally—including the public schools—because it is through government that they have been able to make progress. They do not believe in markets, because they think the private sector has failed to provide their constituents with good jobs and incomes, has discriminated against them, and has used the high-sounding principle of "choice" to allow whites to segregate themselves from minorities. The idea that the education system might work better for its constituents by moving away from government and toward a greater reliance on choice, therefore, goes against their most basic beliefs. In the words of NAACP president Kweisi Mfume, "vouchers don't educate, they segregate."[38]

Yet the NAACP's constituents don't see it this way. Not only do they support vouchers, they are the strongest supporters of vouchers in the entire country. This presents the NAACP, as well as the other civil rights groups on the anti-voucher side, with a serious political problem. By opposing vouchers, they are not responding to the people they claim to represent, and indeed are often in the painful position of having to engage in pitched battles *against* low-income minority parents. This disconnect with their constituents, moreover, has begun to create conflict and dissatisfaction within their own organizations, as some of the activists in local chapters—who are arguably closer to constituents, and who are often younger than the top leaders and indeed from another generation entirely—are much more open to vouchers and pressing for official changes in organizational policy.[39]

So far, NAACP leaders are holding the line. They have been listening to the other side and allowing a measure of internal debate, but they are still (at this writing) firm in their opposition. In fact, they have recently taken the offensive, launching a campaign (via town meetings and the like) to "educate" their constituents about the error of their ways—which, in effect, is an effort to close the gap between leaders and constituents by getting *constituents* to move to the leaders' official position, rather than having leaders do the moving.[40] This kind of strategy, however, is likely to fail. Disadvantaged parents have long been mired in our nation's worst schools, have been denied access to new opportunities available to others, and are simply responding to programs that would directly and immediately give them more control over their own lives and their children's educations. They have good reasons, firmly rooted in their own reality, for seeing vouchers as valuable and desirable, and this is something the civil rights groups cannot change.

The only way for the civil rights leadership to come into alignment with their own constituents is for the *leadership* to abandon its opposition to vouchers and switch sides. The best prediction is that, in the years ahead, this is what will happen. The current crop of leaders may be unwilling to do it, because their own views on government and markets, hardened decades ago, cause them to resist. But the younger activists—who are coming up through the ranks and who will someday assume leadership roles themselves—have had very different formative experiences and are much more pragmatic about what choice can do for their constituents. It may take awhile for this younger generation to move fully into positions of power. But as they do, the civil rights groups will move to the center (if they haven't already).

Even for the younger generation, making the switch will not be easy. Perhaps the main obstacle, aside from the anti-choice legacy of their own movement, is that urban public school systems have increasingly come under the political control of minorities and are a major source of jobs and upward mobility. There will be pressure, then, for reasons that have nothing to do with the education of children, for minority leaders to continue opposing vouchers as a way of protecting the jobs, patronage, and power that come from controlling the public schools.[41] It would be naive to underestimate the strength of these influences. They can only slow the movement of the civil rights groups to the center. Nonetheless, civil rights groups have always put tremendous emphasis on securing quality education for disadvantaged children, and have always seen education as the single most important foundation of an equitable society. Their leaders are likely, over the long haul, to put education ahead of parochial pressures.

A sign of things to come is the recent emergence of the Black Alliance for Educational Options (BAEO).[42] Led by Howard Fuller, former superintendent of the Milwaukee public schools and a forceful voucher advocate, the BAEO brings together a nationwide group of African American influentials and activists dedicated to the empowerment of black families through educational choice. This new organization has already launched an advertising campaign in black-owned newspapers and radio and television stations in Washington, D.C., is beginning to establish local chapters, and is fast on its way to challenging the mainline civil rights organizations on matters of education policy. Their claim: that the civil rights groups are out of step with the black constituency. This is another major reason for the civil rights groups to make a move. They now have competition on the choice issue, and their competitor is going to exploit and publicize the constituency-disconnect unless the civil rights groups can do something about it.

If the civil rights groups do switch sides over time, as seems reasonable to expect, the politics of vouchers will be dramatically changed. In a very real sense, these groups hold the balance of power. Their coalition with the teachers unions has been crucial to the latter's ability to block almost all voucher programs that have been proposed thus far. But without the civil rights groups on their side—indeed, with the civil rights groups on the *other* side, pushing for the adoption of targeted voucher programs— the unions will largely be isolated and far less capable of blocking change.

The civil rights groups will not be the only ones to abandon the unions by going to the center. The most visible sign of things to come is that certain high-profile liberals have begun to peel off and announce their support for targeted voucher plans. In recent years, the liberal converts include the *New Republic*, the *Washington Post*, former labor secretary Robert Reich, civil rights activist Andrew Young, and former secretary of health and human services Joseph Califano.[43] It is clear from what these converts have had to say—and they have said it very publicly—that their support for vouchers arises out of their liberal principles and concerns. They don't rave about the wonders of the market. Most see vouchers as experimental and carrying no guarantee of success. But they also see them as a sensible means of providing much-needed assistance to disadvantaged children, and of challenging and trying to improve a status quo that in many urban areas is demonstrably inequitable and resistant to change.

There is some evidence, then, that the opponents of vouchers are begin- ning to lose the intellectual and moral arguments within their own coali- tion. In addition, the teachers unions are beginning to lose their credibility as proponents of liberal principles. Increasingly, they are coming under public criticism from prominent liberals who, themselves dedicated to se- rious reform of public education, see the unions' unwavering defense of the status quo as a self-interested exercise in power that undermines rea- sonable, well-intentioned efforts to improve the system and help those in greatest need. Consider the strong language of the *New Republic,* which, in an editorial endorsing vouchers, observed, "The response of the teach- ers' unions to vouchers is to defend endlessly the principle of public schools—when, by their implacable opposition to virtually every effort to hold the public schools accountable, they themselves ensure that many of those schools make a mockery of the ideals upon which they were founded."[44] The *Washington Post*, in a recent editorial, sounded a similar theme: "The national teachers unions want to be seen as defenders of public education and advocates of reform. But when you move beyond rhetoric, you find them too often simply defending the status quo, even when that status quo means inferior education for too many children."[45]

Intellectual arguments and public-interest criticisms are not enough to convince most Democratic officeholders to turn against the unions. There are a few, of course, who do support vouchers. Of these, the best known is Senator Joseph Lieberman, who was the Democratic nominee for vice president in the 2000 election (and who stifled any mention of his support for vouchers during the campaign). Exceptions aside, however, the unions have always been able to rely on Democrats to cast the votes necessary to prevent voucher programs from becoming law. And there is little mystery why. Because of the tremendous clout they wield in national, state, and local elections, and their presence in virtually every electoral district in the country, the teachers unions have emerged over the last few decades as the most powerful interest group behind the Democratic party—and there are few Democrats willing to buck them on an issue as threatening to union interests as vouchers.[46]

Still, it appears this era of lock-step Democratic compliance cannot last much longer. For many Democrats, just as for many activists in the civil rights movement, opposition to targeted voucher programs has put them in an uncomfortable position: their own constituents are often disadvantaged and strong supporters of vouchers. At the mass level, vouchers could very easily be a Democratic issue, but Democratic politicians have not been able to treat it that way. Were it not for the unions, many Democrats, especially those representing inner-city areas, would simply line up with their own constituents. This is their most basic electoral incentive and the one they would respond to in the absence of interest-group power.

Eventually, the growing cracks in the liberal coalition are likely to loosen the unions' grip, freeing many of these Democrats to go with their constituencies. As prominent liberals switch sides, and as more join them over time, Democrats who want to support vouchers can at least justify their moves by pointing to actors and arguments that liberals respect. But more important by far—because it is really power and reelection that counts in their political calculations—the Democrats will be free to move once the civil rights groups have begun to make the switch themselves. This is the shift that will change the balance of interest-group power, and with it the incentives of Democratic politicians to vote their constituencies. Not all will break away from the unions. But with new (and liberal) power now arrayed on the other side—with their constituencies—more and more Democrats will find that they can attract enough political support to make the pro-voucher position a net winner. Increasingly, the unions will be left alone, out on the extreme.

These changes won't occur overnight, nor will the nation soon be caught up in a proliferation of voucher programs. It could take many years before a new generation takes charge of the civil rights groups and moves them toward the center. It could take just as long for the Democrats to move in significant numbers. And while all of this is happening—and for many years beyond—our system of checks and balances ensures that the teachers unions will be able to block many reform efforts and limit the number of new programs. The progress of vouchers will be very slow and very difficult. But the best bet is that progress will occur—and that, decades from now, vouchers will come to be an integral part of American education.

The Evolution of a New Education System

If the progress of vouchers takes the course I've suggested, the movement itself will be dramatically affected. Even now, its centrist approach is attracting new recruits who are less advantaged and more liberal and Democratic than its traditional clientele. But once the civil rights groups move from opposition to support, and as growing numbers of Democratic politicians shift over as well, the movement will be radically transformed.

At least for awhile, the groups in the center—the original centrist supporters of vouchers, along with the civil rights groups—will hold the balance of power. When it comes to the kinds of targeted programs they are interested in promoting, they will essentially be able to write their own ticket, almost regardless of what the traditionalists might want. *They* will play the major roles in shaping the design and adoption of voucher programs, because their support will mean the difference between winning and losing. Vouchers will multiply in urban areas, but on terms set by the civil rights groups and their centrist allies.

Looked at myopically, the traditionalists may seem destined to become victims of their own success. Unable to win on their own, they have coalesced with representatives of the urban poor, whose aims are quite different from theirs. As part of this coalition, traditionalists have supported vouchers for needy kids, hoping that incremental progress will lead to universalism and free markets. But once programs for the disadvantaged are achieved, representatives of the urban poor may turn around and *oppose* traditionalist efforts to expand the programs and achieve their ultimate objectives. Having already gotten what they want, and possessed of enough support to maintain their own programs, the centrists would no longer be dependent on the traditionalists and could choose not to promote the conservative cause.

This is more than simple speculation. It is already happening, as some black leaders within the movement—most notably, Polly Williams and Howard Fuller—have made it clear they do not support large-scale voucher systems for middle-class kids.[47] And once the civil rights groups enter the picture in the years ahead, there is even more reason to think that centrist leaders will be inclined to resist, with potentially great political power, an effort by traditionalists to achieve their larger aims.

Still, the traditionalists have an advantage they can trade upon as the game is actually played out over time: most Americans believe that vouchers (if adopted) should eventually be made available to virtually all children. They see low-income programs as a pragmatic, low-risk, and socially equitable place to start the process of reform, but not necessarily as an end point. These beliefs, moreover, are not confined to affluent parents in the suburbs. Even people who are disadvantaged and in troubled school districts—the centrists' own constituents—tend to favor universalism.

Civil rights groups and other centrists may refuse to go along anyway, fearing that their constituents would ultimately lose out. And if they were dedicated to such a position, they could probably succeed in using their power (together with that of the unions) to block major expansions. But as time goes on, they may not choose to do this. State or local experimentation with universal plans, for example, may convince them that expansion works out fine for the disadvantaged. More generally, the underlying attraction of universalism to most Americans (assuming this continues) should tend to be a unifying force, giving centrists less reason to obstruct and providing political support for policymakers who seek to move ahead— a support that could grow over time as vouchers become a more normal part of the educational landscape, and as more Americans become familiar with them in their own lives.

Given the centrists' very potent blocking power, there is no telling how far the expansion of vouchers will go. Most likely, some states and localities (those where the centrists are politically weak) will move toward broader plans, while other areas (where the centrists are politically strong) will stick solely to targeted plans. At the very least, the traditionalists would seem to have some basis for optimism as they seek to expand coverage beyond the disadvantaged and the inner cities.

They are likely to meet with disappointment, however, in their goal of promoting free markets. The brute fact is that regulation is popular with the American people. Every indication is that they will not support an expansion of vouchers unless the new systems are built around rules for accountability and equity. These rules can be very simple and few in number and needn't bury the schools in bureaucracy. But the acceptance of some form of regulation is a compromise traditionalists cannot avoid making if they want to succeed in extending vouchers to a broader population of kids.

There is another major advantage to such a compromise on regulation. The main reason centrists and civil rights groups tend to resist an expansion of vouchers to middle-class kids is not that they want to stop others from using vouchers. Rather, they fear that their own constituencies will suffer in the process: that advantaged parents will make greater use of vouchers, that private schools will give them priority in admissions, and that disadvantaged parents will have fewer and lower-quality opportunities by comparison. The centrists and civil rights groups need concrete assurances that this won't happen, and the way to give them such assurances—aside from not expanding the programs at all—is for traditionalists to go along with equity-promoting rules that are specifically designed to protect the disadvantaged and promote their interests within a larger system. There is strong reason for them to do that.

The most reasonable prediction, then, is that vouchers will indeed take root in American education—but that the programs will be regulated to ensure democratic accountability and promote social equity. They will turn out to be very different, as a result, from the free-market ideal that most traditionalists have long had in mind. In effect, the emerging education system will be very much a mixture of government and markets, just as the national economy is. Like the economy, it will give a central role to choice and competition. But it will also surround them with basic regulations that constrain how choice and competition work—and point them in directions consistent with important social values.

Finally, the public schools will not disappear or somehow be destroyed in the process. This is another respect—the hoped-for privatization of American education—in which the traditionalists will fall well short of their objectives. The fact is, aside from a small contingent of libertarians, no one in this country *wants* to privatize the education system. Americans like their public schools, and a great many parents (probably most) will continue to stay in the public sector even after vouchers are available to them. The reformers and policymakers who actually design the voucher programs, moreover, will be moderates who see vouchers as an integral part of the existing system—as a new dimension to it, rather than an alternative—and they will favor designs that help the public schools to adapt, improve, and ultimately prosper.

As time goes by, the public sector will grow smaller than it is now and be subject to competition from the private sector. But there is a big constituency for public schools: a constituency of parents who want to send their kids there, and a broader political constituency firmly dedicated to its well-being. The coming of vouchers will not put an end to that.

What Will the Supreme Court Do?

This scenario of future developments is based on an assessment of politics and public opinion that leaves a critical factor out of the equation. Sometime after this book is published, the Supreme Court will hand down a decision on whether voucher systems, by including religious schools, violate the Establishment Clause of the Constitution. In more conventional language, the Court will decide whether vouchers for religious schools violate the separation of church and state.

Whatever the Court ultimately does, the nature of its role in this issue needs to be appreciated. In the American system of checks and balances, the Court can sometimes make decisions forcing changes that other political institutions (such as Congress) refuse to make on their own—as it did, for instance, in promoting desegregation through *Brown* v. *Board of Education*. But it can also serve as a major veto point, making decisions that block changes that other institutions *have* made. On the voucher issue, it is this second role—the blocking role—that is coming into play (at least potentially). Voucher supporters have managed to get their programs adopted in the face of great political odds, overcoming hurdle after hurdle in the legislative process. What they want is to be left alone. They do not want to be in court. It is the opponents who, having lost the legislative battles and wanting to stop the spread of vouchers more generally, need to find some way of blocking. The courts give them opportunities for doing that.

The legal battle in the courts is essentially just an extension of the political battle. Lawyers and elites on both sides offer elaborate rationales to justify their positions, pointing to legal precedent, principles of constitutional interpretation, important social values, and the findings of social science. Both sides present their cases as though an objective understanding of the Constitution would surely support their positions. Both are well aware, however, that the law does not really provide objective answers, and that there is plenty of room for interpretation and disagreement about what the law "requires."

The Constitution itself says nothing about vouchers. What it says is that Congress "shall make no law respecting an establishment of religion"—which might be interpreted (with ingenuity) in any number of ways. To voucher supporters, the meaning seems plain enough. It rules out any attempt by the government to establish a state church or to favor one religion over another. But it does not mean that religious schools cannot participate in well-designed voucher programs (which, for example, would treat all religions equally, and public and private schools equally). In voucher programs, after all, the government is simply providing financial support to parents for purposes of education; and it is the parents, not the government, who then decide whether their kids will go to a public or private school, to a religious or nonreligious school, and what the religion will be. How, they argue, can this constitute a governmental establishment of religion? The opponents have no difficulty, however, generating lots of reasons they find compelling. For them, public money is still finding its way into church coffers, no matter who is making the decisions. Children are still getting an education with religious content that is funded by public money. And the government is clearly getting "entangled" with religion to an extent unintended by the founders.[48]

It might be tempting to think that, when judges are presented with arguments on both sides, they can be expected to arrive at some sort of impartial assessment of what the law ought to require. But "impartial" has little meaning when choices must be made among conflicting values, and when the law itself is elastic. Judges, moreover, do not come to their jobs as blank slates. They arrive with active backgrounds in politics, with their own ideologies and political preferences, and with judicial philosophies that orient their approach to the law. Because this is so, it is only reasonable to expect that judges will come to the voucher issue—and most other social issues that are important and controversial (the death penalty, abortion, civil rights)—with certain views of their own, and that these views will ultimately shape their decisions about what the law "requires." Indeed, there is a substantial body of political research to show that judicial decisions *are* heavily influenced by the philosophies and preferences of the judges themselves, and that judges often act strategically (for example, in forming coalitions with their colleagues) to see their own views embodied in law.[49]

When the voucher issue winds up in court, therefore, any given outcome is likely to turn less on what the Constitution "really says" than on precisely which judge or set of judges hears the case. Some judges, especially conservative ones, will be predisposed to say that well-designed voucher programs do not violate the separation of church and state. Other judges, especially liberal ones, will be predisposed to say they do and to strike the programs down.

In the short run, this kind of judicial diversity works well for the teachers unions and their allies. Court cases begin at the lower levels, whether in the federal system or the various state systems, and work their way up; and because there are so many lower court judges with varying political preferences, opponents will usually be able to find at least some friendly judges who are inclined to say vouchers are unconstitutional. This gives them plenty of opportunities to create new obstacles and to stop particular programs (if temporarily) from moving forward.

In principle, many of these obstacles can be swept away as cases are appealed to higher courts and a more coherent body of law is developed. This is especially true if the Supreme Court ultimately rules in favor of vouchers and settles things at the federal level. But whether this happens or not depends, just as it does at lower levels, on *who the judges are.* When a voucher case ultimately makes its way up to the Supreme Court, and the highest court in the land issues a decision, the content of the decision will turn almost entirely on the composition of the Court at that moment in time.

At this writing, the Supreme Court's decision is difficult to predict. The Court is rather evenly split, with many of its votes on important issues, including some related to church-and-state, determined by 5-4 conservative majorities. A first decision on vouchers is likely to be made during the next year or two and, if the current justices remain on the Court, there is a reasonable (but hardly certain) chance the majority would find that, at least when certain conditions are met, voucher systems can include religious schools without violating the separation of church and state. If this does happen, the Court could still shy away from setting a clear and broad precedent, opting instead for a narrow decision that ensures still more court battles in the years ahead. They could also strike down the voucher program in question, objecting to one or two specific features—but recognizing that better-designed programs (without these features) would be constitutional. This too would continue the legal battles. A scenario of all-out victory for the voucher movement, therefore, is just one of several possibilities. It seems unlikely, though, that the present Court would arrive at a sweeping decision that simply puts an end to voucher systems with religious schools under any and all conditions.

It is unclear how long the present Court will remain intact, as several justices have announced an interest in retiring. If the composition of the

Court changes before a decision on vouchers is made, these changes could easily alter the balance of power on the voucher issue and literally determine the outcome. Election 2000 may well prove to have been the pivotal event. With George W. Bush assuming the presidency, the voucher movement would appear to be in good shape, as Bush seems intent on solidifying the Court's conservative majority and is himself a voucher supporter. But nothing is guaranteed. Appointees have been known to surprise the presidents who appoint them—and with a single surprise, Bush could find himself facing a liberal Court, or a moderately conservative Court unable to muster a majority for vouchers.

Whatever the Supreme Court ultimately decides, the consequences for the movement are huge. While it might seem that the separation of church and state issue is mainly of importance for legal or philosophical reasons, it has practical implications that strongly determine how much progress the movement can make in the near future. The reason, very simply, is that the vast majority of private schools *are* religious under the current system, enrolling about 85 percent of all private school children.[50] This means that a voucher system that includes religious schools could immediately offer many children a range of new opportunities, but that a system legally restricted to nonsectarian schools could not, for supply would be quite limited and there would be *nowhere for most kids to go.*[51]

If the Court decides in favor of religious schools, the political prognosis I've developed in this chapter is unaffected, and the movement's prospects for incremental progress would appear bright. But if the Court comes down against religious schools, the world would be a somewhat different place. Newly established voucher systems would have to start out much smaller, and the numbers could increase over time only as the supply of nonsectarian schools increases. Obviously, this would present new problems for the voucher movement. Supporters might succeed in getting voucher systems adopted, but the scope and impact of their programs would be more limited, and would grow in smaller steps, than if the much larger population of religious schools were available from the outset. In addition, there is now a popular demand for religious education and its correlates—discipline, order, structure, a good moral climate—that helps fuel the demand for vouchers, and it is possible that political support might decline or be less enthusiastic if religious schools were completely unavailable.

Still, the greatest force behind vouchers is socioeconomic: less-advantaged families in low-performing districts want new options for their kids. This is deeply rooted, of profound political importance, and will not change. In addition, the ingenuity and dynamism of the supply side response should not be underestimated. Not only will vouchers (assuming they are large enough) call forth a supply of new private schools, but many religious schools will find "nonreligious" modes of participating that could well pass muster with the Court—for example, by removing explicit religious teachings from the classroom, or by setting up nonprofit organizations separate from the religious ones. Even in a nonsectarian world, the supply of schools—and the size of voucher programs—could therefore be much larger than the current private system would seem to indicate, and it could happen much faster.

The best bet is that a negative decision by the Supreme Court, should it happen, *will* slow the spread of vouchers. It could also lead, in the end, to an equilibrium in which the private sector attracts a somewhat smaller share of public school students than it otherwise would. It will not really change the fundamentals, however. And it will not secure the status quo against the political forces for change, which are substantial. Instead of twenty or thirty years, the thorough integration of vouchers into the American education system could take forty or fifty years. Or longer. But the result, in either event, is likely to be very much the same: a mixed system of government and markets that relies much more heavily on choice, competition, and private schools than the system we have today.

A Final Comment

Predicting the future is not for the faint of heart. And it is probably not for social scientists either, if they know what's good for them. Nonetheless, this book's analysis of public opinion, when combined with a perspective on American politics and institutions, does provide a basis for drawing inferences about the developments that lie ahead, and for concluding that vouchers are likely to take hold in the American education system. These inferences may someday be proven wrong. But they are reasonable given the available information, and I would be surprised if things work out very differently.

I do not, however, want to end the book by roaming too far afield. What I'd like to do, rather, is step back a bit and offer a few observations on what kind of analysis this has been and how I hope it will be interpreted.

Throughout this book, I have tried to build an analysis that is true to the facts in their particulars, but that adds up to a coherent perspective on the public opinion and politics of vouchers. I have tried to make sense of an inherently complicated situation and to give it meaning and direction.

As anyone who has ever dealt with survey data knows, this is not so straight-forward. The data never cover all the ground one would like; they are inevitably plagued by measurement and sampling error; and they are always messy, generating at least some findings that don't seem to fit. All this is par for the course. The challenge is to avoid being disabled by it and to use the evidence to best advantage. Done right, the enterprise is fundamentally scientific. But the science inevitably involves a great deal of judgment (and slippage). The analysis I've developed here is my best judgment, based on a systematic look at the evidence on public opinion, and based on a broader knowledge of American politics and institutions. My hope is that it will take us a few steps toward a better understanding of the voucher issue and its future role in American education.

I don't pretend to be making some sort of definitive statement. In the grander scheme of things, this analysis is part of an ongoing process of discovery in which many people are involved. Social science is a collective effort. A book like this presents and analyzes data, introduces new ideas, makes arguments, and offers a certain perspective on how the world works. But if it is at all successful, it also helps to get other researchers interested in the topic—prompting them to test out claims they disagree with, to explore ideas that may not have struck them before, to deepen and expand upon the arguments, to introduce competing arguments of their own, and thus to carry out their own research. The more enduring contribution of this analysis, then, may have less to do with its specific findings and arguments than with the work that follows from it—work that, over time, may add far more to our understanding than a single book does.

I can only emphasize that the larger aim of all this is to *understand* what is going on. The voucher issue is hotly political, and any new book on the topic is automatically regarded as a political act, especially by those (on both sides of the debate) who happen to disagree with its conclusions. The same is true for many other topics in the study of education. Empirical findings are dismissed as fabrications. Theoretical arguments are branded as ideology. With politics as it is, and education researchers caught up in it, the collective process of social science tends to get derailed. This is unfortunate and detracts from the important quest to understand how the education system works. What the field of education needs, beyond all else, is a true social science.

This book is an exercise in social science, and my best attempt to explore and come to grips with a difficult topic. There are any number of claims I make along the way that could ruffle some feathers, because they may seem to reflect poorly on particular groups (like the teachers unions), or because they tell certain people (including some of my libertarian friends and colleagues) what they don't want to hear. It is my job, however, to construct the best, most defensible analysis I know how to construct and to let the chips fall where they may. My hope is that others, especially those who disagree, will now respond with studies of their own, and that together we can move ahead. The point of research is to help figure out how the world works. This book is one effort, in one small corner of the world, to do that.

Appendix A

THE PURPOSE OF this appendix is to give readers some basic information about the survey itself, and then to describe how the main variables in the statistical analysis are actually measured. Readers who want more detailed information are invited to contact me, and I will be happy to provide it.

The Survey

During the mid-1990s, I was involved in a project with John Chubb on equity and school choice, and we felt that a public opinion survey would be a fitting complement to the other work we were doing. It was to be one component of the project. In the process of designing it, we came to realize that a broader analysis of public opinion on vouchers and choice would be a useful contribution, and we moved toward a more expansive questionnaire than we first envisioned. Our objective at the time was to present a rather general overview of opinion, and our thinking was not specifically oriented by all the political and theoretical issues that I will be trying to address in this book.

In hindsight, not surprisingly, there are certain questions I now wish had been asked, and other questions I wish had not been bothered with. Nonetheless, the survey that resulted is still extraordinarily useful for present purposes and well worth exploiting. It is probably the most comprehensive data set yet collected on how the American public views the voucher

398

issue, and it provides a wealth of information that can help shed light on most of the interesting issues that need to be addressed.

The survey was designed with the aid of an advisory committee, which we set up to evaluate the proposed questions and ensure that the content was appropriately balanced and unlikely to bias respondents in one way or another. This committee consisted of Douglas Rivers (Department of Political Science, Stanford University), James Guthrie (School of Education, Vanderbilt University), Michael Kirst (Graduate School of Education, Stanford University), and Paul Peterson (Department of Government, Harvard University). Early versions of the questionnaire were passed through this committee, adjustments were made in light of their comments, and the final version met with their approval.

To carry out the survey, we chose Fairbank, Maslin, Maullin and Associates, a commercial polling organization of reputation and experience. It was also known over the years for its work on behalf of Democratic political candidates; this was a consideration because, as voucher supporters ourselves, we wanted to eliminate any hint that the data were somehow the product of conservative or Republican or otherwise pro-voucher sympathies. Fairbank, Maslin, Maullin assumed all operational responsibilities for designing the sample, carrying out the interviews, coding the data, and providing the relevant statistical weights.

The survey was carried out through telephone interviews (using random digit dialing) in the early summer of 1995. The sample consists of 4,700 adults, a total that includes oversamples of 1,200 parents with school-age children and 1,000 parents from inner-city areas. With statistical weighting, this sample of 4,700 yields a nationally representative cross-section of the American adult population. The oversamples, when considered separately, allow for a more confident and detailed examination of two especially important subpopulations—public school parents generally and public school parents who are low in income and from the inner city— that would otherwise not be numerous enough in a national cross section to allow for much analysis. (The inner-city sample is discussed in more detail in the next section.)

Most of the data, of course, come from the survey itself. But because the survey asked respondents to supply their zip codes, this allowed for the collection of two kinds of contextual data. First, it was possible to tie each respondent to a school district, and, with the help of the U.S. Department of Education's *Common Core of Data,* to add information about the school systems and demographics of those local contexts. Second, by arrangement with SchoolMatch (a for-profit organization that provides educational information to parents who are relocating), it was possible to get test score data on these contexts and thus to obtain objective measures of how well their schools are performing. In these ways, individual respondents could be anchored to specific educational and social contexts, enabling an analysis of how (or whether) those contexts affect their opinions on schools and vouchers.

The Inner-City Sample

The inner-city component deserves some discussion. There are two difficulties here. One is that the "inner city" is not a precise location that can readily be measured. The other is that the inner-city poor are themselves difficult to locate and include in a survey (as the Census Bureau discovers, despite its sophisticated methods, every ten years). I could not eliminate these problems, of course, but simply tried to arrive at a reasonable sample for analysis using the following approach.

The inner-city oversample was drawn from the fifty largest metropolitan areas, proportionate to their populations, with inner-city areas identified through zip codes (and Fairbank, Maslin, Maullin making the necessary judgments). This oversample, however, naturally yielded many parents who were not poor or who did not send their kids to public school. For the analysis of this book, then, I singled out just those inner-city parents who do have kids in the public schools and whose incomes were below $30,000 per year. Of the 1,000 parents in the inner-city oversample, 453 fit these criteria. To this group, I added another 86 low-income, inner-city, public school parents who showed up as part of the larger cross section (including the parent oversample). Throughout the book, then, my separate treatments of the inner-city poor are based on this constructed sample of 539 parents (453 plus 86).

This sample should be regarded with caution, because it cannot be offered with confidence as a cross section of the inner-city poor. It is my best crack at it, though, and any survey of the inner-city poor is likely to involve a measure of slippage. I can think of no reason, moreover, to expect any particular type of bias.

Variables

In the course of this book, many variables are put to use in the statistical analysis. In this section, I will list the main ones and indicate how they have been measured. I am omitting those that are used merely for control purposes, as well as certain dependent variables that are defined in the text and tables of each chapter.

Before getting to the list of variables, I should first note how missing values are handled. On almost all survey items, a small percentage of people either refuse to answer or (more often) say they don't know. For descriptive tables, which simply give breakdowns on individual variables or cross-tabulate one variable against another, this is not a problem. The small number of missing values can simply be omitted. But if the analysis in question takes a large number of variables into account at once, as all of this book's multivariate analyses do (usually there are more than thirty variables), then many respondents will have missing values on perhaps one or two of these variables—and a big portion of the sample can wind up being tossed out if cases with missing values are excluded. If this rule were followed, we would lose a lot of important information and have less statistical confidence in the results.

To avoid this problem, I have chosen—for the multivariate analyses alone—to code most variables in such a way that their missing values can be included in the analysis. In a few cases—education and income (see below)—I have used predictor variables to come up with estimates for the missing values. But most of the time, I have simply assigned missing values a "middle" score on the variables in question. For example, for variables originally measured on a 4-point scale—strongly disagree, weakly disagree, weakly agree, strongly agree—I have moved to a 5-point scale, with missing values assigned the middle score of 3 (between weakly disagree and weakly agree). For most people who give "don't know" responses, this would seem to make good sense on substantive grounds. It is not a panacea, however, and obviously introduces some measurement error. As a result, correlations and regression coefficients (and significance levels) will tend to be smaller than they would be in the absence of such error. The alternative, however, is to carry out the multivariate analyses with drastically fewer cases, and this, in my view, is even less desirable.

Here is the list of variables used in the book's analyses, along with brief discussions of how they are coded.

(1) Education—Measures the respondent's education level. A 6-category ordinal variable, with 1 representing less than a 9th-grade education and 6 representing graduate or professional education beyond the college degree. For multivariate analyses, missing values are replaced by estimates, in which income, religion, age, district context, and other variables are used to predict a respondent's education level.

(2) Income—Measures total family income. An 8-category ordinal variable, with 1 representing an annual income below $20,000 and 8 representing an annual income above $100,000. For multivariate analyses, missing values are estimated using the same procedure as described above for education.

(3) Religion—Catholics and born-again Christians are represented by dummy variables, which are 1 when the trait is present and 0 otherwise.

(4) Race—Northern blacks, southern blacks, and Hispanics are represented by 0-1 dummies. All blacks outside the South (defined to include all the usual border states) are defined as being in the North.

(5) Age—Measured as a 10-category ordinal variable. It begins with 1 for 18–24 year olds, and increases by increments of 1 for each 5-year cohort after that, until it reaches a value of 10 for those who are 65 and older.

(6) Party identification—Takes on the following values: 1 for strong Democrats, 2 for weak Democrats, 3 for independents who lean Democrat, 4 for independents, 5 for independents who lean Republican, 6 for weak Republicans, and 7 for strong Republicans. For multivariate analyses, missing values are coded 4.

(7) Low expectations—Measured by an agree-disagree item that states, "The government provides us with free schools, so we should try to be satisfied with them." Ranges from 1 to 5, with 5 indicating strong agreement and missing values coded 3.

(8) District context—An average of two separate (and standardized) measures. The first is an index that measures how socially advantaged a district is on the basis of its demographics. This index is constructed by means of a principle components factor analysis on the following district characteristics: median income, median income divided by median rent, percent of adults with less than a high school education, percent of adults with a college education, percent of owner-occupied dwellings, percent of adults on public assistance, percent of at-risk kids, percent of students who are white, percent of funding that comes from the federal government. (All data were obtained from the *Common Core of Data*.) The second component is the district's test scores (which were obtained from SchoolMatch). These are normalized scores, varying from 0 to 100, based on high-school test results.

(9) Residential Mobility—Measured by a survey item that asks respondents, "Did you move into your neighborhood at least in part because of the quality of the public schools?" Responses were coded 0 if school quality was not a reason, 1 if it was one of many reasons, 2 if it was an impor-

tant reason, and 3 if it was the most important reason. For multivariate analyses, missing cases were coded 0, because people who say they "don't know" if education was an important reason for their choice of residence probably didn't put much weight on it.

(10) Diversity—Measured as an index that averages (after standardization) the responses to two survey items. One is an item on common schooling that asks respondents to choose between the following statements: "Public schools are an important means of building a common culture, so more effort should be made to put children of different backgrounds into the same schools," and "It is best for children to attend public schools near their homes and families, even if this means children of different backgrounds may not get to attend school together." The other is an item that asks, "In some cities, children are bused to schools outside their neighborhoods in order to promote racial balance. Do you support or oppose such a policy?" Both items are coded 0 if anti-diversity, 2 if pro-diversity, with missing values assigned a 1.

In the multivariate analysis, the impact of the diversity index is estimated separately for white and nonwhite respondents. Thus two diversity terms are actually included in each analysis. To keep things as simple and focused as possible, however, only the results for white respondents are presented in the tables, because these are the ones we are really interested in. We want to know whether whites who "oppose" (score lowest on) diversity are the ones most likely to go private.

(11) Inequity—Measured as an index that averages (after standardization) three survey items. The first two come from a general battery that asks respondents to indicate, on a scale from 1 to 10, the quality of education various groups of children are getting from the public schools: children from upper-income families, middle-income families, and lower-income families, and children who are white, black, or Hispanic. The first measure of inequity gives respondents a 1 if their scores indicate that they think middle-income kids are getting a better education than lower-income kids, and a 0 otherwise. The second measure gives respondents a 1 if their scores indicate they think white kids are getting a better education than black kids, and a 0 otherwise. The third inequity measure derives from the following statement that respondents were asked to agree or disagree with: "Families with low incomes often have little choice but to send their children to schools that are not very good." This last item is coded from 1 to 5, with 1 indicating strong disagreement, 5 indicating strong agreement, and 3 assigned to missing values. For the first two items, missing values were coded 0, because respondents were not willing or able

to make any distinctions between how whites and minorities —or children of different classes—are educated.

(12) School Prayer—Measured in terms of a single survey item, which asks respondents to agree or disagree with the following statement: "Prayer should be allowed in public schools if it is voluntary." Scores range from 1 to 5, with 1 indicating strong disagreement, 5 indicating strong agreement, and 3 assigned to missing values.

(13) Parent Influence—Measured in terms of a single survey item, which asks respondents to choose between the following options: "Parents should have more influence over the schools than they do now," and "Parents should trust the judgment of administrators and teachers, because they know more about education than parents do." Coded 2 and 0, respectively, with 1 reserved for missing values.

(14) School size—Measured in terms of a single survey item, which asks respondents to choose between the following options: "Small schools are better, because they provide students with more attention and a greater sense of belonging," and "Large schools are better, because they provide students with more variety, resources, and activities." Coded 2 and 0, respectively, with 1 reserved for missing values.

(15) Public School Ideology—Measured as an average (after standardization) of two survey items, both of which ask respondents to agree or disagree with certain statements. The first statement is: "The public schools deserve our support, even if they are performing poorly." The second is: "The more children attend public schools, rather than private or parochial schools, the better it is for American society." Both are scored from 1 to 5, with 1 indicating strong disagreement, 5 indicating strong agreement, and 3 assigned to missing values.

(16) Markets—Measured as an average of two survey items, both in agree-disagree format. The first statement is: "To give our schools strong incentives to improve, we need a system that rewards good schools and punishes bad ones." The second is: "Competition and consumer choice make business firms more effective and cost-conscious, and they would help do the same for schools." Both are scored from 1 to 5, with 1 indicating strong disagreement, 5 indicating strong agreement, and 3 assigned to missing values.

(17) Moral Values—The basic measure comes from a survey item that asks respondents to rate the public schools, on a scale from 1 to 10, in terms of their performance along five dimensions: academic performance, safety, discipline, moral values, and individual attention. The score on the moral values scale is a first-cut measure of how people think the schools

are doing on this dimension. The problem with using this measure on its own, however, is that it captures a concern about performance generally—because anyone who is critical of public school performance will tend to give the schools low scores on all dimensions, including moral values. The scores on moral values, then, are not just a reflection of what parents think about the moral values problem. To correct for this, the moral values score is regressed against all the other performance items in this battery (academics, safety, discipline, individual attention), and the residual is taken as a "purged" measure. The negative of this residual represents their concern that the public schools are not doing a good job on this dimension.

(18) Performance—This is an index based on five different survey items. The first asks whether the public schools in the respondent's districts are doing well, need minor changes, or need major changes. The second presents respondents with an agree-disagree item: "In our community, we are very proud of our public schools." The third asks respondents to rate their local public schools on a scale from 1 to 10. The fourth does the same, but asks them to offer specific ratings for several different dimensions—of which the ones for academic quality and individual attention (standardized and averaged together) were used in this performance index. The fifth asks respondents how the local public schools compare to private schools along the same dimensions; the comparison focusing on academic quality was used here.

Two separate performance indexes are used in the analysis. In chapter 4, which is solely about how people evaluate the public schools, the performance index combines the first four measures discussed above by averaging them into an index of public school performance. Because there is no explicit comparison to private schools, this is essentially an index of "absolute" performance evaluations. Subsequent analysis shows, however, that "relative" assessments of public school performance—how well people think the public schools are doing relative to private schools—actually do a (somewhat) better job of explaining respondents' orientations to choice and vouchers than their absolute assessments do.

For this reason, a second performance index was constructed—and used in chapter 5 and the remaining chapters—to give balanced representation to both the absolute and relative aspects of performance. This index is simply an average of the first index (made up of the first four items) and the fifth item, discussed above, that asks respondents to compare public and private schools on academic grounds. Had the first, absolute measure of public performance been used throughout the book, the results would have been quite similar, and performance would still have emerged as the dominant factor by far. But its impact and explanatory power would have been slightly lower than we obtained for the second index.

Missing values were handled as follows. With the first index, all four components were standardized, and people were given a score equal to the average of all nonmissing components. With the second index, the item in question asks respondents to say whether private schools are better, about the same, or worse than public schools. These are coded 3, 2, and 1, respectively, with missing values given a 2.

(19) Desire to Go Private—Based on the survey item that asks, "If you could afford it, would you be interested in sending your children to a private or parochial school?" Coded 1 if respondent answers yes, 0 if no.

(20) Informed—Based on survey item that asks, "Have you heard anything about the use of vouchers in education?" Yes = 1, No = 0. Missing values are assigned a 0.

(21) All of the independent variables measuring social considerations, as set out in table 8-4, are measured in the same basic way and consistent with the descriptions of their values set out in tables 8-1 through 8-3. In each case, the most anti-voucher response is given a score of 1, the next, more positive response a 2, and so on. All the agree-disagree items (except the one asking whether the wealthy would benefit and the poor would be left behind) actually run from strongly disagree to weakly disagree to weakly agree to strongly agree. For all variables, missing values are given middle values. On a four-point agree-disagree item, for example, the variable is scored from 1 to 5, with missing values coded 3.

(22) The same procedure is followed for the personal considerations in table 8-7. All the agree-disagree items are four-point scales that have been scored from 1 to 5, with missing values set equal to 3. The anti-voucher end of the scale begins with 1.

(23) Personal Interest—Based on the survey item that asks, "Would you consider using a voucher to put your children in a private or parochial school?" Scores range from 1 (definitely not) to 5 (definitely yes), with don't knows scored at 3.

(24) Risk—In the analysis of chapter 8, risk is simply measured by the survey item, discussed in the text, which asks respondents to agree or disagree with the following: "I worry that a large-scale voucher plan might be too risky and experimental to try out on our kids." In chapter 9, where risk serves as an independent variable in explaining support for equity regulation and low-income vouchers, it is measured a bit differently. In this analysis, it is important to make sure that risk is not capturing simple

opposition to vouchers per se. To make sure, the previous risk variable (a five-point scale, with missing values given a middle score) is regressed against support for vouchers (ditto), and the residuals are taken as the new risk variable, purged of the influence of voucher support.

(25) Low Income—A dummy variable that is 1 if respondents have family income below $30,000 per year, 0 otherwise, with missing values categorized as either 1 or 0 depending on the estimates given by predictor variables (see above).

Appendix B

THIS IS A BRIEF addendum to chapter 3, which attempts to explain why satisfaction with the public schools is higher and more uniform than we might expect. In any analysis, it is important to tell a consistent story in which all the parts fit together into a coherent whole. I have tried to do that in chapter 3, but there are a few loose ends that can't be resolved with the data at hand. The best I can do is to be clear about what they are, speculate as to their causes, and hope they can be resolved through future research.

Two issues stand out as somewhat perplexing. Both arise when we try to connect the last component of the analysis, about education and expectations, to some of the variables discussed earlier.

(1) As we have just seen, people who are poorly educated and have low expectations are more likely than others to be satisfied with their local public schools. Exactly the same relationships ought to obtain, one would think, if we shift the focus down one level to the direct experiences parents have with their children's schools.

In part, the data bear this out. A multivariate analysis shows that parents with low expectations are more satisfied with their own kids' schools than parents with higher expectations. But education appears to have no effect on satisfaction one way or the other (whether or not expectations are controlled). This is not entirely out of keeping with the earlier line of reasoning, since the argument there clearly suggests that expectations are the more proximate influence. But it does raise questions as to how robust the previous section's argument is and suggests we need to be careful in generalizing it.

What might explain the discrepant finding for direct experience? There are three possibilities. One is that imperfect measures are causing it. The measure for expectations is very rough. And our five indicators of direct experience capture only a small part of what is surely relevant to parents' satisfaction with their kids' schools. Given these sources of slippage, which are pretty standard for surveys, inconsistent results of the sort we get here are normal and not sufficient grounds for rejecting a very reasonable argument. The second possibility is that the kinds of positive biases I discussed earlier—which arise because educated people are likely to seek out the better schools in any district, and to be treated better within them—apply most forcefully to the direct experience analysis, and our inability to control for these biases could well account for why education doesn't have the expected negative effect. The third possibility is that, for many parents, there may actually be something conceptually different about evaluating the local school system as a whole, as compared to evaluating the schools their kids attend. The latter are experienced directly through personal contact, while the system is more of an abstraction and may call for a kind of thinking more strongly shaped by parent education.

All of these are plausible and may capture part of the truth. But my best guess is that, if we had excellent measures of all the relevant variables, the findings for direct experience would look very similar to the findings for the local school system. The basic argument, I think, is correct: people who have poor educations and low expectations are more likely than others to be happy with their schools—whether they are evaluating their own kids' schools or the local system as a whole.

(2) The second discrepancy arises when we try to connect these factors to the phenomenon of residential mobility. It only makes sense to think that, once income is controlled, parents with poor educations and low expectations should be less inclined to engage in residential choice. Again, the data bear this out only partially. Here, residential mobility is strongly determined by parent education—but not by expectations. Parents with low expectations are no less likely to exercise residential choice than parents without low expectations.

This result is so flatly inconsistent with both theory and common sense that I have to believe it is simply due to measurement problems and, in particular, to the rather primitive way that the expectations variable is measured. A better measure would almost surely reveal a clear connection between expectations and residential choice.

There may be other problems at work too. For instance, there may be a reciprocal connection between residential mobility and expectations that our models don't capture (and can't, with the available data). For just as expectations ought to affect residential mobility, so residential mobility may lead to an adjustment of expectations. But I suspect that the basic problem here is simply that the survey item does not do a great job of measuring expectations.

In the absence of new research, these issues cannot be resolved. What we do know, however, is that the earlier findings on class, expectations, and satisfaction with the local schools seem quite strong and consistent— and provocative for what they imply about larger issues of politics and social equity. It is true that not all pieces of the puzzle fit together in the simple, straightforward way we might hope. This raises some healthy doubts, and we need to be careful drawing firm inferences. But it is also the kind of untidiness we have to expect from survey research, where loose ends often seem to be the norm rather than the exception.

Notes

Introduction

1. See, for example, Milton Friedman, *Capitalism and Freedom* (University of Chicago Press, 1962); John E. Coons and Stephen D. Sugarman, *Education by Choice: The Case for Family Control* (University of California Press, 1978); John E. Chubb and Terry M. Moe, *Politics, Markets, and America's Schools* (Brookings, 1990); John E. Coons and Stephen D. Sugarman, *Scholarships for Children* (Institute of Governmental Studies Press, 1992); Myron Lieberman, *Public Education: An Autopsy* (Harvard University Press, 1993); and Andrew J. Coulson, *Market Education: The Unknown History* (Transaction Publishers, 1999).

2. See, for example, Amy Stuart Wells, *Time to Choose: America at the Crossroads of School Choice Policy* (Hill & Wang, 1993); Peter W. Cookson Jr., *School Choice: The Struggle for the Soul of American Education* (Yale University Press, 1994); Kevin B. Smith and Kenneth J. Meier, *The Case against School Choice: Politics, Markets, and Fools* (M. E. Sharpe, 1995); and Bruce Fuller and Richard F. Elmore, eds., *Who Chooses? Who Loses? Culture, Institutions, and the Unequal Effects of School Choice* (Teachers College Press, 1996).

3. The most exhaustive study of the teachers unions as organizations and political actors can be found in Myron Lieberman, *The Teacher Unions: How the NEA and AFT Sabotage Reform and Hold Students, Parents, Teachers, and Taxpayers Hostage to Bureauacracy* (Free Press, 1997). See also Lieberman, *Public Education;* and Tom Loveless, ed., *Conflicting Missions? Teachers Unions and Educational Reform* (Brookings, 2000). For a more optimistic appraisal of the role unions might play in education, see Charles T. Kerchner and Julia E. Koppich, *A Union of Professionals: Labor Relations and Educational Reform* (Teachers College Press, 1993); and Charles T. Kerchner, Julia E. Koppich, and Joseph G. Weeres, *United Mind Workers: Unions and Teaching in the Knowledge Society* (Jossey-Bass, 1997).

4. On the partisan and religious bases of the voucher movement, see, for example, Cookson, *School Choice*.

5. See John F. Witte, *The Market Approach to Education: An Analysis of America's First Voucher Program* (Princeton University Press, 2000); Daniel McGroarty, *Break These Chains: The Battle for School Choice* (Forum, 1996); and Terry M. Moe, "Private Vouchers," in *Private Vouchers*, edited by Terry M. Moe, pp. 1–40 (Hoover Institution Press, 1995).

6. On the origins and development of the private voucher movement, see Moe, "Private Vouchers." The most recent figures on programs and students were obtained directly from CEO America. For more information on private vouchers, see the organization's website, www.childrenfirstamerica.org (February 2001).

7. The survey is described in appendix A.

8. Of these, the most extensive and enlightening is a 1999 study by Public Agenda *(On Thin Ice: How Advocates and Opponents Could Misread the Public's Views on Vouchers and Charter Schools)*, which will be discussed at various points in the analysis that follows. There is also a good bit of information on vouchers in the annual polls conducted by Gallup for the *Phi Delta Kappan*. Some of these, too, will be discussed (and specifically cited) later on.

Chapter 1

1. See, for example, Frederick M. Wirt and Michael W. Kirst, *The Political Dynamics of American Education* (McCutchan, 1997); and John E. Chubb and Terry M. Moe, *Politics, Markets, and America's Schools* (Brookings, 1990), esp. chap. 2.

2. See, for example, Paul E. Peterson and Bryan C. Hassel, eds., *Learning from School Choice* (Brookings, 1998); and Bruce Fuller and Richard F. Elmore, eds., *Who Chooses? Who Loses? Culture, Institutions, and the Unequal Effects of School Choice* (Teachers College Press, 1996).

3. For studies of the kinds of values and principles that underlie American public opinion, see Herbert McClosky and John Zaller, *The American Ethos: Public Attitudes toward Capitalism and Democracy* (Harvard University Press, 1984); Sidney Verba and Gary R. Orren, *Equality in America: The View from the Top* (Harvard University Press, 1985); J. R. Pole, *The Pursuit of Equality in American History*, rev. ed. (University of California Press, 1993); and Jennifer L. Hochschild, *What's Fair? American Beliefs about Distributive Justice* (Harvard University Press, 1981).

4. See Martha Derthick and Paul Quirk, *The Politics of Deregulation* (Brookings, 1985); and John W. Kingdon, *Agendas, Alternatives, and Public Policies* (Little, Brown, 1984).

5. Milton Friedman, "The Role of Government in Education," in *Economics and the Public Interest*, edited by Robert A. Solo, pp. 123–44 (Rutgers University Press, 1955).

6. On this era, see, for example, James L. Sundquist, *Politics and Policy: The Eisenhower, Kennedy, and Johnson Years* (Brookings, 1968).

7. For discussions of education and its reform during this period, see, for example, Diane Ravitch, *The Troubled Crusade: American Education, 1945–1980* (Basic Books, 1983).

8. 347 U.S. 483 (1954).

9. On the aftermath of the *Brown* decision, the battle to integrate the schools, and its connection to choice, see Gary Orfield's *The Reconstruction of Southern Education: The Schools and the 1964 Civil Rights Act* (Wiley, 1969), and his *Must We Bus? Segregated Schools and National Policy* (Brookings, 1978).

10. For a discussion of alternative schools during this era, see Amy Stuart Wells, *Time to Choose: America at the Crossroads of School Choice Policy* (Hill & Wang, 1993); and Terrence E. Deal and Robert R. Nolan, eds. *Alternative Schools: Ideologies, Realities, Guidelines* (Nelson-Hall, 1978).

11. On magnet schools and their connection to both choice and integration, see the discussions in Jeffrey R. Henig, *Rethinking School Choice: Limits of the Market Metaphor* (Princeton University Press, 1994), and Wells, *Time to Choose*. See also Rolf K. Blank, Roger E. Levine, and Lauri Steel, "After Fifteen Years: Magnet Schools in Urban Education," in Fuller and Ellmore, *Who Chooses? Who Loses?* pp. 154–72.

12. Jencks presented his ideas at length in his proposal for the OEO (*Education Vouchers: A Report on Financing Education by Payments to Parents* [Cambridge, Mass.: Center for the Study of Public Policy, 1970]), and also in a more widely read article in the *New Republic* ("Giving Parents Money to Pay for Schooling: Education Vouchers," July 4, 1970, pp. 19–21).

13. Oddly, the Alum Rock program continued to be regarded as "voucher experiment," whose evidence was relevant for evaluating the effectiveness of vouchers. Perhaps the best-known discussion of this "experiment" is David K. Cohen and Eleanor Farrar, *Power to the Parents? The Story of Educational Vouchers* (Washington: Education Policy Institute, 1977). See also James A. Mecklenberg and Richard W. Hostrop, *Education Vouchers: From Theory to Alum Rock* (Homewood, Ill.: ETC Publications 1972).

14. For their early arguments for regulated vouchers—which appear to have influenced Jencks's own ideas on the subject—see John E. Coons, William H. Clune III, and Stephen D. Sugarman, "Educational Opportunity: A Workable Constitutional Test for State Financial Structure," *California Law Review*, vol. 57, no. 2 (April 1969), pp. 305–421; John E. Coons, William H. Clune III, and Stephen D. Sugarman, *Private Wealth and Public Education* (Harvard University Press, 1970); and John E. Coons and Stephen D. Sugarman, *The Family Choice in Education Act: A Model State System for Vouchers* (Berkeley: Institute of Governmental Studies, 1971).

15. 487 P.2d 1241 (Cal. 1971).

16. John E. Coons and Stephen D. Sugarman, *Education by Choice: The Case for Family Control* (University of California Press, 1978).

17. For an in-depth analysis of the Coons-Sugarman initiative and its political failure, see James S. Catterall, "The Politics of Education Vouchers," Ph.D. dissertation, Stanford University, School of Education (1982).

18. See, for example, Center for Education Research and Innovation, *School: A Matter of Choice* (Organization for Economic Cooperation and Development, 1994); and Andrew J. Coulson, *Market Education: The Unknown History* (Transaction, 1999).

19. See, for example, the discussions of the Reagan administration's involvement in the voucher issue in Wells, *Time to Choose;* and Henig, *Rethinking School Choice.*

20. National Commission on Excellence in Education, *A Nation at Risk: The Imperative for Educational Reform* (Washington: Government Printing Office, 1983).

21. For discussions and appraisals of the waves of school reforms that followed *A Nation at Risk*, see, for example, William A. Firestone, Susan H. Fuhrman, and Michael W. Kirst, *The Progress of Reform: An Appraisal of State Education Initiatives*, Rutgers University, Center for Policy Research in Education, Research Report Series RR-014 (1989); and Marshall S. Smith and Jennifer O'Day, "Systemic School Reform," in *The Politics of Curriculum and Testing: The 1990 Yearbook of the Politics of Education Association*, edited by Susan H. Fuhrman and Batty Malen, pp. 233–67 (Falmer Press, 1991).

22. See, for example, Myron Lieberman, *Public Education: An Autopsy* (Harvard University Press, 1993).

23. On the resources and power of teachers unions and the profound ways they shape the policies, organization, and performance of the public schools, see Myron Lieberman, *The Teacher Unions: How the NEA and AFT Sabotage, Reform and Hold Students, Parents, Teachers, and Taxpayers Hostage to Bureaucracy* (Free Press, 1997).

24. This is apparent to anyone who follows new accounts of the politics of vouchers. For a discussion of the various elements of the liberal coalition and their activities in opposing the Milwaukee voucher experiment, see Daniel McGroarty, *Break These Chains: The Battle for School Choice* (Forum, 1996).

25. These are all familiar arguments in the politics of vouchers and can readily be found in NEA and AFT publications on the subject. They are more systematically presented and justified in the work of academic critics of vouchers, among them, Wells, *Time to Choose*; Peter W. Cookson Jr., *School Choice: The Struggle for the Soul of American Education* (Yale University Press, 1994); Kevin B. Smith and Kenneth J. Meier, *The Case against School Choice: Politics, Markets, and Fools* (M. E. Sharpe, 1995); and Henry J. Levin, "The Theory of Choice Applied to Schools," in *Choice and Control in American Education*, vol. 1: *The Theory of Choice and Control in American Education*, edited by William H. Clune III and John F. Witte, pp. 247–84 (Falmer Press, 1990).

26. See Milton Friedman, *Capitalism and Freedom* (University of Chicago Press, 1962); and Milton and Rose Friedman, *Free to Choose: A Personal Statement* (Harcourt Brace Jovanovich, 1980).

27. See Jencks, *Education Vouchers*; Jencks, "Giving Parents Money"; Coons and Sugarman, *Education by Choice*; Coons and Sugarman, *Scholarships for Children* (Berkeley: Institute for Governmental Studies, 1992); Chubb and Moe, *Politics, Markets, and America's Schools*; and Diane Ravitch, "Somebody's Children: Educational Opportunity for *All* American Children" in *New Schools for a New Century: The Redesign of Urban Education*, edited by Diane Ravitch and Joseph P. Viteretti, pp. 251–73 (Yale University Press, 1997).

28. The theoretical literature I am referring to here is variously called the new economics of organization, the new institutional economics, or simply the new institutionalism. For overviews of some of this literature, see Dennis C. Mueller, ed., *Perspectives on Public Choice: A Handbook* (Cambridge University Press, 1997). It represented the cutting-edge theory of political institutions at the time

we wrote *Politics, Markets, and America's Schools,* and at this writing (in early 2001), it is still the cutting-edge theory and growing even more influential (and more elaborate and better developed) with time. For prior work Chubb and I had done in this emerging tradition, see John E. Chubb, "The Political Economy of Federalism," *American Political Science Review,* vol. 79 (December 1985), pp. 994–1015; Terry M. Moe, "The New Economics of Organization," *American Journal of Political Science,* vol. 28 (November 1984), pp. 739–77; Moe, "The Politics of Bureaucratic Structure," in *Can the Government Govern?* edited by John E. Chubb and Paul E. Peterson, pp. 267–329 (Brookings, 1989); and Moe, "The Politics of Structural Choice: Toward a Theory of Public Administration," in *Organization Theory: From Chester Barnard to the Present and Beyond,* edited by Oliver E. Williamson, pp. 116–53 (Oxford University Press, 1990).

29. See, for example, the critique of our book by Valerie E. Lee and Anthony S. Bryk ("Science or Policy Argument? A Review of the Quantitative Evidence in Chubb and Moe's *Politics, Markets, and America's Schools*") and our response ("The Forest and the Trees: A Response to Our Critics") in *School Choice: Examining the Evidence,* edited by Edith Rasell and Richard Rothstein, pp. 185–208 and 219–39, respectively (Washington: Economic Policy Institute, 1993).

30. See, for example, the historical perspective on the choice issue offered by Jeffrey R. Henig in *Rethinking School Choice,* chaps. 3–7.

31. For background on the politics and design characteristics of the Milwaukee voucher program, see John F. Witte, *The Market Approach to Education: An Analysis of America's First Voucher Program* (Princeton University Press, 2000); Robert C. Bulman and David L. Kirp, "The Shifting Politics of School Choice," in *School Choice and Social Controversy: Politics, Policy, and Law,* edited by Stephen D. Sugarman and Frank R. Kemerer, pp. 36–67 (Brookings, 1999); Jim Carl, "Unusual Allies: Elite and Grass-Roots Origins of Parental Choice in Milwaukee, *Teachers College Record,* vol. 98, no. 2 (1996), pp. 266–85; Daniel McGroarty, "School Choice Slandered," *Public Interest,* no. 117 (Fall 1994), pp. 94–111; McGroarty, *Break These Chains;* Paul E. Peterson, "Are Big City Schools Holding Their Own?" in *Seeds of Crisis: Public Schooling in Milwaukee since 1920,* edited by John L. Rury and Frank A. Cassell, pp. 269–301 (University of Wisconsin Press, 1993); James L. Baughman, *Impact of School Desegregation in Milwaukee Public Schools on Quality of Education for Minorities: Fifteen Years Later* (Wisconsin Advisory Commission to the U.S. Commission on Civil Rights, 1992).

32. I first discussed the emergence of this new politics of education in "Private Vouchers," in *Private Vouchers,* edited by Terry M. Moe, pp. 1–40 (Hoover Institution Press, 1995). See also Carl, " Unusual Allies."

33. For critical assessments of urban education, see Jonathan Kozol, *Savage Inequalities: Children in America's Schools* (Crown, 1991); Peterson, "Are Big City Schools Holding Their Own?"; and Wilbur Rich, *Black Mayors and School Politics: The Failure of Reform in Detroit, Gary, and Newark* (Garland, 1996).

34. For discussions of the appeal of vouchers to low-income and minority populations, see, for example, Siobahn Gorman, "Desperate Measures," *National Journal,* December 18, 1999, p. 3598; and Jeff Archer, "Black Parents at Heart of Tug of War, *Education Week,* June 24, 1998, p. 1.

35. For a discussion of conflicts within the voucher coalition in Milwaukee, see Witte, *The Market Approach to Education*. See also Bulman and Kirp, "The Shifting Politics of School Choice."

36. See Henig, *Rethinking School Choice*, esp. pp. 90–93, for a discussion of the G.I. Bill for Children and, more generally, of how the Bush administration handled the voucher issue.

37. See "Clinton Vetoes D.C. Voucher Bill," *Education Week*, May 27, 1998, p. 22.

38. For a discussion of state-level battles on school choice, see Nina Shokraii Rees, *School Choice 2000: What's Happening in the States* (Heritage Foundation, 2000).

39. For a recent overview of some of these developments, see Bulman and Kirp, "The Shifting Politics of School Choice."

40. See Witte, *The Market Approach to Education*; also Drew Lindsay, "Wisconsin, Ohio Back Vouchers for Religious Schools," *Education Week*, July 12, 1995, p. 1.

41. See Jay P. Greene, William G. Howell, and Paul E. Peterson, "Lessons from the Cleveland Scholarship Program," in *Learning from School Choice*, edited by Paul E. Peterson and Bryan C. Hassel, pp. 357–92 (Brookings, 1998); and Lindsay, "Wisconsin, Ohio Back Vouchers."

42. See Jessica L. Sandham, "Florida OKs First Statewide Voucher Plan, " *Education Week*, May 5, 1999, p. 1.

43. For an overview of the private voucher movement, see Moe, *Private Vouchers*. On the Children's Scholarship Fund, see Anemona Hartocollis, "Private School Choice Plan Draws a Million Aid-Seekers," *New York Times*, April 21, 1999.

44. As of February 2001, the Milwaukee program has been upheld by the Wisconsin Supreme Court (*Jackson v. Benson*, no. 97-0270 [Wis. S. Ct., decided June 10, 1998], reversing 213 Wis.2d 1, 570 N.W.2d 407 [Ct. App. 1997]), and, because the U.S. Supreme Court refused to hear the case (*Jackson v. Benson*, no. 98-376, November 9, 1998), has been indirectly granted legal legitimacy—until the Supreme Court does finally take a voucher case and make a decision. See Mark Walsh, "Court Allows Vouchers in Milwaukee," *Education Week*, June 17, 1998, pp. 1, 16. This will probably come with the Cleveland case, which is now working its way through the courts. The Court of Appeals for the Sixth Circuit recently affirmed the order of a federal district judge that struck down the program as a violation of the separation of church and state; an appeal to the U.S. Supreme Court is all but certain (*Simmons-Harris v. Zelman*, nos. 00-3055, 00-3060, 00-3063 [6th Cir., December 12, 2000], affirming 72 F. Supp. 2d 834 [N. D. Ohio, 1999]). See Darcia Harris Bowman, "Appeals Court Rejects Cleveland Voucher Program," *Education Week*, December 13, 2000, p. 1. In the meantime, a Florida state court judge, in March 2000, struck down the Florida program, not on the basis of separation of church and state (which is the central issue in the other cases), but on his interpretation of the state's constitutional duty to provide a public education system for its citizens (Final Order and Judgment, *Bush v. Holmes*, CV 99-3370 (Fla. Cir. Ct., Leon County, March 14, 2000). The order was subsequently reversed on appeal (*Bush v. Holmes*, nos. 1D00-1121 and 1D00-1150 [Fla. Dist. Ct. App., 1st Dist., October 3, 2000]), but that reversal, of

course, is also being appealed. See Jessica L. Sandham, "Voucher Plan Struck Down in Florida Court," *Education Week,* March 22, 2000, p. 1; and Mark Walsh, "Fla. Court Overturns Ruling Against Voucher Programs," *Education Week,* October 11, 2000, p. 1.

45. On public school choice generally, see Timothy W. Young and Evans Clinchy, *Choice in Public Education* (Teachers College Press, 1992). For a wide-ranging analysis of its effects, see Mark Schneider, Paul Teske, and Melissa Marschall, *Choosing Schools: Consumer Choice and the Quality of American Schools* (Princeton University Press, 2000).

46. The figures on the number of charter schools and students come from the Center for Education Reform. See their website, www.edreform.com (February 2001). The most comprehensive treatment of charter schools to date is Chester E. Finn Jr., Bruno V. Manno, and Gregg Vanourek, *Charter Schools in Action: Renewing Public Education* (Princeton University Press, 2000). See also Louann A. Bierlein, "The Charter School Movement," in Ravitch and Viteritti, *New Schools for a New Century,* pp. 37–60.

47. For discussions of the politics surrounding charter schools, and how unions and other political actors approach the issue, see Finn, Manno, and Vanourek, *Charter Schools in Action,* esp. pp. 169–219.

48. The official evaluator of the Milwaukee program was John Witte, who (with coauthors) issued several annual reports on its performance, beginning in 1991, which were generally positive about the satisfaction of parents but argued that children using vouchers did not actually learn more than those in the public schools. His findings are summarized in his recent book, *The Market Approach to Education: An Analysis of America's First Voucher Program* (Princeton University Press, 2000). Most other studies of voucher programs, both public and private, have been carried out by a team of researchers led by Paul Peterson. Their conclusions have generally shown that voucher children do learn more than their public school counterparts. See, for example, William G. Howell and others, "Test-Score Effects of School Vouchers in Dayton, Ohio, New York City, and Washington, D.C.: Evidence from Randomized Field Trials," paper presented at the annual meeting of the American Political Science Association, Washington, D.C., August 31–September 3, 2000; Jay P. Greene, Paul E. Peterson, and Jiangtao Du, "School Choice in Milwaukee: A Randomized Experiment," and Greene, Howell, and Peterson, "Lessons from the Cleveland Scholarship Program," in Peterson and Hassel, *Learning from School Choice,* pp. 335–56 and 357–92, respectively; and Paul E. Peterson, David E. Myers, William G. Howell, and Daniel P. Mayer, "The Effects of School Choice in New York City," in *Earning and Learning: How Schools Matter,* edited by Susan B. Mayer and Paul E. Peterson, pp. 317–39 (Brookings and Russell Sage Foundation, 1999). For additional studies by other researchers, see Kim K. Metcalf and others, "A Comparative Evaluation of the Cleveland Scholarship and Tutoring Grant Program: Year One: 1996–97," School of Education, Smith Research Center, Indiana University, Bloomington (March 16, 1998); and Cecilia Elena Rouse, "Private School Vouchers and Student Achievement: An Evaluation of the Milwaukee Parental Choice Program," *Quarterly Journal of Economics,* vol. 113 (May 1998), pp. 553–602.

Chapter 2

1. Over the years, there have been numerous assessments of school performance. For recent overviews, see Eric A. Hanushek, *Making Schools Work: Improving Performance and Controlling Costs* (Brookings, 1994); and Herbert J.
Wahlberg, "Achievement in American Schools," in *A Primer on America's Schools,*
edited by Terry M. Moe (Hoover Institution Press, 2001).

2. Probably the most comprehensive effort to make this argument is that of
David C. Berliner and Bruce J. Biddle, *The Manufactured Crisis: Myths, Fraud,
and the Attack on America's Public Schools* (Addison-Wesley, 1995). Gerald Bracey
has also been aggressive over the years in contending, through numerous articles
on the subject, that the schools are doing much better than generally perceived.
See, for example, his "Are U.S. Students Behind?" *American Prospect,* no. 37
(March–April 1998), pp. 64–70.

3. George H. Gallup, "The Sixteenth Annual Gallup Poll of the Public's Attitudes toward the Public Schools," *Phi Delta Kappan,* vol. 66 (September 1984),
pp. 23–47.

4. Stanley M. Elam, "The Twenty-second Annual Gallup Poll of the Public's
Attitudes toward the Public Schools," *Phi Delta Kappan,* vol. 72 (September 1990),
pp. 41–55.

5. Lowell C. Rose and Alec M. Gallup, "The Thirty-second Annual Phi Delta
Kappa/Gallup Poll of the Public's Attitudes toward the Public Schools," *Phi Delta
Kappan,* vol. 82 (September 2000), pp. 41–58.

6. All the 2000 data are taken from Rose and Gallup, "Thirty-second Annual
Poll," p. 43.

7. See Lowell C. Rose, Alec M. Gallup, and Stanley M. Elam, "The Twenty-
ninth Annual Phi Delta Kappa/Gallup Poll of the Public's Attitudes toward the
Public Schools," *Phi Delta Kappan,* vol. 79 (September 1997), pp. 41–56 (p. 47).

8. Ibid., p. 47.

9. See appendix A for the exact construction of the index. (A separate analysis for each measure would lead to very similar results in each case.) The results
presented in table 2-3 are based on models that incorporate a full range of background and contextual variables, as discussed in chapter 4. To keep things simple,
their coefficients are not included in the table.

10. A few points about the impact coefficients. (1) Some readers may expect to
see the usual beta-weights used here, which are based on shifts of just one standard deviation in the independent variables. But there is no single way to compute
impacts, and the one chosen here seems more useful to me. In the first place, a
shift of two standard deviations better represents a shift from low to high, which
seems a more meaningful change to examine. In the second place, this approach
offers a better way of making comparisons that involve dummy (dichotomous)
variables. Dummy variables—which do not arise in this section's analysis but play
an important role in the chapters to come (for example, in measuring the impacts
of religion and race)—cannot conveniently be thought of in standard deviation
terms. Their impacts are properly judged in terms of their total shift: a person is
either Catholic or not, for example. If we want to get a sense of the relative influence that the different variables are having, then, it seems better to compare the

impacts of these all-or-nothing shifts in the dummy variables to the impacts of shifts of two standard deviations in the other independent variables, rather than the impacts of shifts of one standard deviation. (2) In ordinary least squares regression, it doesn't matter whether the shift is symmetric about the mean, just that the total shift is two standard deviations. In subsequent chapters, however, we will sometimes be using probit analysis, and with probit it does matter exactly what the starting and ending values are for the shift.

11. See Stephen P. Broughman, and Lenore Colaciello, *Private School Universe Survey, 1997–98* (Washington: National Center for Education Statistics, 1999).

12. See Public Agenda, *On Thin Ice: How Advocates and Opponents Could Misread the Public's View on Vouchers and Charter Schools* (New York, 1999), pp. 17–18.

13. Here and elsewhere, the survey items are worded with reference to "private and parochial" schools rather than simply "private" schools (since some people might think the latter refers only to the proportionately small number of elite college prep schools in the private sector). *Parochial* is defined for respondents as including all religiously affiliated schools, not just Catholic schools.

14. Recent research suggests that private schools may in fact do a better job of socializing children to democratic norms. See, for example, Jay P. Greene, "Civic Values in Public and Private Schools," in *Learning from School Choice,* edited by Paul E. Peterson and Bryan C. Hassel, pp. 83–106 (Brookings, 1998); Patrick J. Wolf and others, "Private Schooling and Political Tolerance: Evidence from College Students in Texas," PEPG Working Paper 00-14, Cambridge, Mass., Program for Educational Policy and Governance, Harvard University (February 2000); and David E. Campbell, "Making Democratic Education Work: Schools, Social Capital, and Civic Education," paper presented at the Conference on Charter Schools, Vouchers, and Public Education, Harvard University, March 9–10, 2000.

15. Public Agenda, *Assignment Incomplete: The Unfinished Business of Education Reform* (New York, 1995).

16. See, for example, Paul M. Sniderman and Thomas Piazza, *The Scar of Race* (Belknap Press of Harvard University Press, 1993).

17. On the role of religion in American public education, see, for example, Charles L. Glenn, *The Ambiguous Embrace: Government and Faith-Based Schools and Social Agencies* (Princeton University Press, 2000); and Joseph P. Viteritti, *Choosing Equality: School Choice, the Constitution, and Civil Society* (Brookings, 1999), chaps. 4–6.

18. See the discussion of parent influence in John E. Chubb and Terry M. Moe, *Politics, Markets, and America's Schools* (Brookings, 1990), pp. 147–49, 163–64, 170–79.

19. On the structure of the current system, see Roald F. Campbell and others, *The Organization and Control of American Schools,* 4th ed. (C. E. Merriam, 1980). On the need for less bureaucratic, more personal, more flexible, and more nurturing schools—which often translates into smaller schools—see, for example, Anthony S. Bryk, Valerie E. Lee, and Peter B. Holland, *Catholic Schools and the Common Good* (Harvard University Press, 1993).

20. Public Agenda, *Assignment Incomplete,* p. 11.

Chapter 3

1. An alternative way to try to measure district quality is to take test scores as the key indicator, purge these scores of the influence of socioeconomic characteristics (by regressing the former against the latter), and use the residualized test scores. But this measure simply doesn't work out (in this data set). The idea is a good one, but in practice the more conventional index I've chosen proves to be more highly correlated with all the variables we would expect district quality to be correlated with.

2. See, for example, Jonathan Kozol, *Savage Inequalities: Children in America's Schools* (Crown, 1991).

3. See Mark Schneider, Paul Teske, and Melissa Marschall, *Choosing Schools: Consumer Choice and the Quality of American Schools* (Princeton University Press, 2000).

4. The index is created by standardizing all indicators and averaging them (after reverse-coding certain items), so that, in each case, a high number represents a positive experience.

5. For simplicity, I assume here that other things are equal. I should note, however, that the conventional argument among defenders of public schools is that residential and private-school choice, by depriving low-performing districts of their most motivated parents, actually makes the public schools in these districts *worse*. This may or may not be true (the research literature is of little help). But if it is, it suggests that the selection effects of choice should lead to lower satisfaction, not higher satisfaction, as objective conditions deteriorate, which is counter to the phenomenon we are trying to account for here.

6. Some readers may regard the term *ideology* as a pejorative one, but I certainly don't mean it that way. It is the best, most accurate way I can think of to describe the constellation of values that I am talking about here and is simply a convenient short hand.

7. In addition to the points noted here, we have to recognize that public school ideology may have a reciprocal connection to satisfaction: while people who embrace the ideology should tend to be more satisfied with their public schools, it may also be the case that people who are satisfied with their public schools are more likely to develop the ideology. In our data, there is not much indication that this is so. As noted in the text: in a multivariate analysis, district context and residential mobility are only weakly related to who embraces the ideology, while it is people who are low in education and income, rather than the reverse, who seem to have it. Even if there were such a reciprocal connection, moreover, it would not mean that this ideology is somehow less important a phenomenon for us to understand. It would mean, however, that our empirical results might yield an inflated correlation between ideology and satisfaction, which would tend to mislead us into thinking that the causal path from ideology to satisfaction is stronger than it actually is. To the extent that this is so, we cannot correct for it, given the limits of our data. The best we can do is be aware of the possibility.

8. For a comprehensive overview of the research literature, see Donald R. Kinder, "Opinion and Action in the Realm of Politics," in *The Handbook of Social Psychology*, 4th ed., edited by Daniel T. Gilbert, Susan T. Fiske, and Gardner Lindzey, vol. 2, pp. 778–867 (McGraw-Hill, 1998).

9. The same is true, to a somewhat lesser extent, in the other types of districts as well, with the possible exception of the most advantaged districts, where satisfaction runs high among everyone. (This could well be due, however, to the effects of other variables that are not controlled here.)

Chapter 4

1. I have to apologize to public opinion scholars for the way I use *attitudes* in this book. Although in the literature it is a technical term whose definition and use are subjects of careful thought and debate, I essentially use it as a term of convenience here, to refer to various attitudes, values, and beliefs that may play a role in people's thinking.

2. In this chapter and throughout the book, I do my best to make an inherently complicated analysis as simple as possible and to produce the most revealing analysis I can within the limits of the data. Inevitably, some methodological issues are not addressed with the kind of sophistication that some readers might want to see. The most important of these issues, in my view, is that some of the independent variables may be endogenous, at least to some extent. Public school ideology, most notably, may be a cause of satisfaction with the public schools, but it may also be caused by satisfaction, for parents with high evaluations of their schools may be the ones most likely to develop the ideology in the first place. As noted in the previous chapter, there is no strong evidence to believe this is so. Still, it is certainly plausible. And if there is a reciprocal connection of this sort, our method of analysis here—which assumes the causation is one way—will overstate the strength of the relationship. For reasons I will discuss at other points in this chapter, similar problems may arise for a few other variables. (The same is true in other chapters, where the dependent variables are different.) Ideally, these problems could be dealt with through two-step procedures in which the variables in question could be separately modeled and instruments used in the main equation. From a purely mechanical standpoint, this is an easy thing to do. Doing it well, however, requires that we have data on variables that are not in the main (satisfaction) equation, but are correlated with public school ideology and uncorrelated with the error term: data that we simply do not have. In this situation, which is actually quite a common one, it is best to stay with the more basic methods and simply urge caution in interpreting the results. If the data don't justify or support them, techniques that appear more sophisticated can easily lead to more problems than they solve.

3. They are: other nonwhite race (whites being the excluded category), other religion (regular Protestants being the excluded category), gender, urban-rural setting, child in high school, public school teacher, attended private school as a child, family member a school district employee, number of children in family, and region (measured as a set of dummy variables).

4. They are: revenue per student, degree of local control, geographic size of the district, percentage of students in small schools, and (for parents) whether the district offers parents any choice of public schools.

5. As noted in chapter 2, a given impact coefficient indicates how much the dependent variable changes (in standard deviation units) when the independent variable shifts by two standard deviations—which, roughly, represents a shift from low value to a high value.

6. Ideally, good estimates for the impact of residential mobility on satisfaction would require treating it as endogenous, for just as residential mobility can bring about greater satisfaction, so expectations of greater satisfaction are the reasons for (causes of) residential mobility. Looked at pragmatically, this is not such a worry here, because all we really want to know is whether there is a positive connection between the two. Modeling the relationship as we do, though, there is a nonobvious source of (possible) bias that we might want to keep in mind. Residential mobility and satisfaction have common causes—motivation and expectations—that (inevitably) are not perfectly measured in the main equation and thus are part of the error term. The connection between these omitted causes and residential mobility is likely to be positive, but their connection to satisfaction is likely to be negative (because people who are highly motivated and have high expectations are likely to be less satisfied with any given school, other things being equal). This could produce a negative bias, leading to an estimated association between residential mobility and satisfaction that is smaller than it should be. The positive estimate that our model gives us, therefore, may be conservative.

7. It is possible that the estimates for low expectations are affected somewhat by reciprocal causality. People with low expectations should (if we are right) have higher satisfaction with the schools, but it may be that their expectations are in turn shaped by their actual levels of satisfaction. If so, people who are trapped in low-performing schools should develop lower expectations, and people in high-performing schools should have their expectations raised. To the extent this is the case, however, the model we estimate in this chapter would tend to *underestimate* the relationship we expect to find, in which low expectations cause high satisfaction. It would provide conservative estimates of the true effect. The fact that these estimates are actually quite strong and positive, then, suggests that we can be reasonably confident that such a relationship exists.

8. This conclusion seems entirely justified, but we have to remember that the magnitudes of these estimates may have been affected somewhat by endogeneity problems that we couldn't correct for. Public school ideology, as discussed in an earlier note, may have had its impact inflated a bit by its (possible) reciprocal connection to satisfaction. The same could be true, at least to some extent, for the private school effect: dissatisfaction probably does cause parents to go private, but it may also be the case that some parents become dissatisfied (or more dissatisfied) because they go private—developing a "we-they" attitude, associating with other disaffected parents, being influenced by private-school-generated information, and so on. Again, these are possibilities we don't have the data to test, and they may not be very important. But we need to be aware of them.

9. In the current chapter, its impact is especially impressive given that the impacts of both public school ideology and parent influence, the other two attitudes in the top tier, may be somewhat inflated by reciprocal causation.

10. Even so, it is worth noting that the regression coefficient of income (which in this case is restricted to a shift from the lowest to the second lowest income category) is actually larger than we found for public parents generally (although it is not statistically significant, and its impact coefficient is smaller—likely because income can only take on two values), and that the regression coefficient of district context is roughly in the same ballpark of what we found for the other parents (although, again, it is not statistically significant).

Chapter 5

1. See Milton Friedman, *Capitalism and Freedom* (University of Chicago Press, 1962); Milton Friedman and Rose Friedman, *Free to Choose: A Personal Statement* (Harcourt Brace Jovanovich, 1980); John E. Chubb and Terry M. Moe, *Politics, Markets, and America's Schools* (Brookings, 1990); John E. Coons and Stephen D. Sugarman, *Education by Choice: The Case for Family Control* (University of California Press, 1978); Coons and Sugarman, *Scholarships for Children* (Institute for Governmental Studies Press, 1992); Myron Lieberman, *Privatization and Educational Choice* (St. Martin's Press, 1989).

2. See Amy Stuart Wells, *Time to Choose: America at the Crossroads of School Choice Policy* (Hill & Wang, 1993); Peter W. Cookson Jr., *School Choice: The Struggle for the Soul of American Education* (Yale University Press, 1994), and "Redesigning the Financing of American Education to Raise Productivity: The Case for a Just Voucher," chapter 7 of *Privatizing Education and Educational Choice: Concepts, Plans, and Experiences,* edited by Simon Hakim, Paul Seidenstat, and Gary W. Bowman (Praeger, 1994); Kevin B. Smith and Kenneth J. Meier, *The Case against School Choice: Politics, Markets, and Fools* (M. E. Sharpe, 1995); Carnegie Foundation for the Advancement of Teaching, *School Choice: A Special Report* (Princeton, N.J., 1992).

3. Perhaps the best figures on private school tuition nationwide are collected by the National Center for Education Statistics' School and Staffing Survey. Its most recent data show that in 1993–94 average tuition was $1,572 for a Catholic elementary school and $3,699 for a Catholic high school; tuitions were only slightly higher for other types of religious schools. They were more than twice as high for nonsectarian schools—but the great majority of children in the private sector attend schools that are religiously affiliated. See U.S. Department of Education, *Private Schools in the United States: A Statistical Profile, 1993–94* (Washington: National Center for Education Statistics, 1997), table 1-5.

4. See James E. Long and Eugenia F. Toma, "The Determinants of Private School Attendance, 1970–80," *Review of Economics and Statistics,* vol. 70 (May 1988), pp. 351–57; R. Hamilton Lankford and James H. Wykoff, "Primary and Secondary School Choice among Public and Religious Alternatives," *Economics of Education Review,* vol. 11 (December 1992), pp. 317–37; R. H. Lankford, E. S. Lee, and J. H. Wykoff, "An Analysis of Elementary and Secondary School Choice," *Journal of Urban Economics,* vol. 38 (September 1995), pp. 236–51; Richard J. Buddin, Joseph J. Cordes, and Sheila Nataraj Kirby, "School Choice in California: Who Chooses Private Schools?" *Journal of Urban Economics,* vol. 44 (July 1998), pp. 110–34.

5. See U.S. Department of Education, *Private Elementary and Secondary Education: A Final Report to Congress from the Secretary of Education* (Government Printing Office, 1983); Lankford and Wykoff, "Primary and Secondary School Choice"; Buddin, Cordes, and Kirby, "School Choice in California." For a contrary argument, see Smith and Meier, *The Case against School Choice.*

6. See, for example, Long and Toma, "The Determinants of Private School Attendance."

7. See Charles T. Clotfelter, "School Desegregation, 'Tipping,' and Private School Enrollment," *Journal of Human Resources,* vol. 11 (Winter 1976), pp. 28–50.

8. See Lankford, Lee, and Wykoff, "An Analysis of Elementary and Secondary School Choice."

9. See Lankford and Wykoff "Primary and Secondary School Choice"; Buddin, Cordes, and Kirby, "School Choice in California."

10. See, for example, Stephen Plank and others, "Effects of Choice in Education," chapter 4 of *School Choice: Examining the Evidence*, edited by Edith Rasell and Richard Rothstein (Washington: Economic Policy Institute, 1993); Valerie Lee, Robert Croninger, and Julia Smith, "Equity and Choice in Detroit," in *Who Chooses? Who Loses? Culture, Institutions, and the Unequal Effects of School Choice*, edited by Bruce Fuller and Richard F. Elmore, pp. 70–91 (Teachers College Press, 1996).

11. See John F. Witte, *The Market Approach to Education* (Princeton University Press, 2000); Jay P. Greene, William G. Howell, and Paul E. Peterson, "Lessons from the Cleveland Scholarship Program," in *Learning from School Choice*, edited by Paul E. Peterson and Bryan C. Hassel, pp. 357–92 (Brookings, 1998).

12. See, for example, Carnegie Foundation for the Advancement of Teaching, *School Choice.*

13. See Witte, *The Market Approach to Education.*

14. See Green, Howell, and Peterson, "Lessons from the Cleveland Scholarship Program"; Janet R. Beales and Maureen Wahl, "Private Vouchers in Milwaukee: The PAVE Program," in *Private Vouchers*, edited by Terry M. Moe, pp. 41–73 (Hoover Institution Press, 1995); Valerie Martinez, Kenneth Godwin, and Frank R. Kemerer, "Private Vouchers in San Antonio: The CEO Program," in Moe, *Private Vouchers*, pp. 74–99; and Michael Heise, Kenneth D. Colburn Jr., and Joseph F. Lamberti, "Private Vouchers in Indianapolis: The Golden Rule Program," in Moe, *Private Vouchers*, pp. 100–19.

15. See Chester E. Finn Jr., Bruno V. Manno, and Gregg Vanourek, *Charter Schools in Action: Renewing Public Education* (Princeton University Press, 2000); and Mark Schneider, Paul Teske, and Melissa Marschall, *Choosing Schools: Consumer Choice and the Quality of American Schools* (Princeton University Press, 2000).

16. See Greene, Howell, and Peterson, "Lessons from the Cleveland Scholarship Program"; Heise, Colburn, and Lamberti, "Private Vouchers in Indianapolis"; Schneider, Teske, and Marschall, *Choosing Schools*; but compare David J. Weinschrott and Sally B. Kilgore, "Comparing Public Choice and Private Voucher Programs in San Antonio," in Peterson and Hassel, *Learning from School Choice*, pp. 307–34.

17. See Jeffrey Henig, *Rethinking School Choice: Limits of the Market Metaphor* (Princeton University Press, 1994).

18. See U.S. Department of Education, *Private Schools in the United States.*

19. See Public Agenda, *On Thin Ice: How Advocates and Opponents Could Misread the Public's View on Vouchers and Charter Schools* (New York, 1999). Both our own survey and the Public Agenda survey ask respondents whether they would be *interested* in going private if money were not a problem, and both show that most parents respond positively. Critics of choice, however, often cite studies—for example, by the Carnegie Foundation for the Advancement of Teaching

(see *School Choice: A Special Report*) and Phi Delta Kappa (see Lowell C. Rose, Alec M. Gallup, and Stanley M. Elam, "The Twenty-ninth Annual Phi Delta Kappa/ Gallup Poll of the Public's Attitudes toward the Public Schools," *Phi Delta Kappan*, vol. 79 [September 1997], pp. 41–56)—that appear to show the opposite: that the vast majority of public parents would prefer to stay with their children's current schools rather than switch to private schools. The reason for the discrepant findings is that the latter studies are essentially asking a different kind of question, requiring that parents know about a specific private school they would prefer to send their kids to. See the discussion of these studies in chapter 8.

20. In this section, data for private parents refer to parents who only have children in private schools. This helps to heighten the contrast with public parents. It also avoids certain ambiguities that might arise if we included parents who have children in both sectors.

21. Two points. First, for each of the nondichotomous independent variables, the impact coefficient is calculated by holding all other variables constant at their means, and noting the effect on the probability of going private when the variable in question is allowed to vary from one standard deviation below its mean to one standard deviation above. If the independent variable is dichotomous, the shift in probability is calculated as the independent variable shifts from 0 to 1. Second, given that we are trying to explain the desire to go private, this chapter's analysis includes a new contextual variable that represents the available supply of private schools. Conventional sources provide data on the percentage of students who go private within each district, and that is the proxy employed here. We are not directly concerned with its impact on parental choice and won't be discussing it. But it needs to be included, in principle, for purposes of control. Doing so, I should note, could raise an endogeneity problem, because many of the same factors that explain why individuals want to go private would also explain the supply of private schools. This is especially true, of course, for models of who goes private under the current system, but it could also be true for models that are trying to explain which public parents want to go private. As I explained earlier (note 19 above), there are technical solutions for these problems, typically involving two-step procedures and instrumental variables, but our own data set makes this difficult to do very well. Rather than do a questionable job, it seems preferable to simply include the supply variable and see how it performs. Results show that, while it is significant in all equations, its presence or absence has little effect on the other coefficients

22. Technically sophisticated readers might be thinking that the appropriate way to model this would be to recognize that how variables affect the probability of going private should turn on the income constraint, and that a more complicated modeling strategy should be followed here. I have tried out a few options, none of which indicated that this path was likely to prove fruitful (with these data), and concluded that the best approach under the circumstances was to keep things as simple as possible. I leave it to others to use more involved techniques and to collect the data necessary for them to work.

23. From this new comparison, we also get a different perspective on the general relevance of attitudes to the phenomenon of going private. In the initial

analysis (table 5-5), which compares current private parents to all current public parents, the attitude model suggests that only three attitudes have a significant impact—and in addition, that the magnitude of their impacts is much smaller (by about half) than that of social characteristics like income, education, religion, and race. When we take the swing parents out of the picture, however, attitudes turn out to be far more important to the explanation. More attitudes are statistically significant, as we've seen. But as a more detailed presentation of results (an elaboration of table 5-6) would show, their impacts are also bigger relative to the various social characteristics. Moreover, attitudes now add more explanatory power to the model, as judged by the bigger boost they give to the pseudo R^2 (in moving from the background and context models to the attitude model). Thus attitudes actually have greater relevance to the phenomenon of going private than the initial analysis can reveal. Their underlying influence is simply hidden, because the swing parents tend to think a lot like current private parents.

24. Were the latter included in a model with performance, however, its direct impact would be reduced—for inequity operates, to some extent, through performance (as chapter 4's analysis suggests).

25. In anticipation of this adjustment, and to promote comparability, the adjusted measure was actually used in the previous section's analysis (table 5-5) of why current private parents go private. Had we stayed with chapter 4's definition of *performance* in that section, its impact would have been slightly smaller (as we should expect, if the new measure is actually more appropriate), but it would still have proven far more powerful than any other variable in the model. The same is true in this section's analysis.

26. The model does indicate, however, that residential mobility is associated with an interest in going private. Choice advocates would expect this relationship to be negative: people who don't exercise residential mobility ought to be the most eager to go private. But if residential mobility is to some degree a proxy for motivation, as education is, then perhaps this finding is just telling us that the more motivated parents are the ones most interested in choice.

27. Some readers may note that the impact of inequity here is 17 percent and may be tempted to wonder why this is the "same" as the impact inequity had for parents generally in the last section's analysis. But one has to be careful comparing across equations. The analysis of this section, which applies only to low-income inner-city parents, has a baseline of 70 percent who are interested in going private, while the prior section's analysis of all public parents had a baseline of just 55 percent. The more the baseline diverges from 50 percent, and especially as it approaches the extremes, the more difficult it will be for variables to have large effects (since the probability can never be more than 1 or less than 0). Thus the 17 percent impact for low-income parents, given their 70 percent baseline, essentially represents a more powerful effect than the 17 percent impact for parents generally, given their 55 percent baseline. I would have expected the impact here to be still larger than it is, given the differential in the last section's analysis between low-income parents and parents who are better off. But statistical results will vary from data set to data set, and these are certainly in the reasonable range.

Chapter 6

1. See, for example, Anthony Downs, *An Economic Theory of Democracy* (Harper, 1957); and Samuel L. Popkin, *The Reasoning Voter: Communication and Persuasion in Presidential Campaigns* (University of Chicago Press, 1991).

2. For assessments of the American public's low level of political information, knowledge, and interest, see Philip E. Converse, "The Nature of Belief Systems in Mass Publics," in *Ideology and Discontent,* edited by David E. Apter, pp. 206–61 (Free Press, 1964); Eric R.A.N. Smith, *The Unchanging American Voter* (University of California Press, 1989); Paul M. Sniderman, "The New Look in Public Opinion Research," in *Political Science: The State of the Discipline II,* edited by Ada W. Finifter, pp. 219–45 (Washington: American Political Science Association, 1993); and Michael X. Delli Carpini and Scott Keeter, *What Americans Know about Politics and Why It Matters* (Yale University Press, 1996).

3. Stanley Elam and Lowell C. Rose, "The Twenty-seventh Annual Phi Delta Kappa/Gallup Poll of the Public's Attitudes Toward the Public Schools," *Phi Delta Kappan,* vol. 77 (September 1995), pp. 41–56 (p. 44).

4. Information on this poll was obtained through the Roper Center at the University of Connecticut. The poll itself was carried out by Chilton Research Services for the *Washington Post,* the Kaiser Foundation, and Harvard University.

5. Public Agenda, *On Thin Ice: How Advocates and Opponents Could Misread the Public's Views on Vouchers and Charter Schools* (New York, 1999), p. 10.

6. See, for example, Donald R. Kinder, "Opinion and Action in the Realm of Politics," in *The Handbook of Social Psychology,* 4th ed., edited by Daniel T. Gilbert, Susan T. Fiske, and Gardner Lindzey, vol. 2, pp. 778–867 (McGraw-Hill, 1998).

7. See, for example, Vincent Price and John Zaller, "Who Gets the News? Alternative Measures of News Reception and Their Implications for Research," *Public Opinion Quarterly,* vol. 57 (Summer 1993), pp. 133–64.

8. See Converse, "The Nature of Belief Systems"; Kinder, "Opinion and Action"; Shanto Iyengar, "Shortcuts to Political Knowledge: The Role of Selective Attention and Accessibility," in *Information and Democratic Processes,* edited by John A. Ferejohn and James H. Kuklinski, pp. 160–85 (University of Illinois Press, 1990); David J. Elkins, *Manipulation and Consent: How Voters and Leaders Manage Complexity* (University of British Columbia Press, 1993).

9. In the recent battle over the Michigan voucher initiative, for example, voucher advocates went to court—unsuccessfully—to stop opponents from using public money ($1 million worth, advocates claimed) to distribute anti-voucher materials to parents through the public schools. See Malcolm Johnson, "Voucher Group Charges Misuse of Taxpayer Money," Associated Press, State and Local Wire, October 10, 2000.

10. Diversity can be argued either way. People *opposed* to diversity may be opposed to the integrationist efforts of the public schools, find private schools and vouchers attractive, and seek out information. On the other hand, people may also seek out information because they *support* diversity, find the segregation of the current system unacceptable, and see private schools and vouchers as more effective means of pursuing the same ends.

11. Actually, additional tests were carried out to explore these matters a bit further. The main test involved reconstructing some of the attitudinal variables, as well as performance, in such a way that people initially at the opposite extremes (either very high or very low) were given high scores, and people in the middle given low scores, to reflect their intensity and potential incentives. Results were disappointing and gave no indication that anything systematic is going on. But this, again, could largely be due to limitations of the data. More research is needed.

Chapter 7

1. Notable among the classic studies are Paul F. Lazersfeld, Bernard Berelson, and Hazel Gaudet, *The People's Choice: How the Voter Makes Up His Mind in a Presidential Campaign* (Duell, Sloan, & Pierce, 1944); and Bernard Berelson, Paul F. Lazersfeld, and William N. McPhee, *Voting: A Study of Opinion Formation in a Presidential Campaign* (University of Chicago Press, 1954).

2. Philip E. Converse, "The Nature of Belief Systems in Mass Publics," in *Ideology and Discontent* [International Yearbook of Political Behavior Research 5], edited by David E. Apter, pp. 205–61 (Free Press, 1964), p. 245.

3. See Converse, "The Nature of Belief Systems"; and Converse, "Public Opinion and Voting Behavior," in *Handbook of Political Science*, 4: *Nongovernmental Politics*, edited by Fred I. Greenstein and Nelson W. Polsby, pp. 75–169 (Addison-Wesley, 1975).

4. The quotation is from Converse, "Public Opinion and Voting Behavior," p. 78. For a somewhat more optimistic (but still sobering) portrayal of Americans' knowledge about politics, see Michael X. Delli Carpini and Scott Keeter, *What Americans Know about Politics and Why It Matters* (Yale University Press, 1996).

5. See, for example, Samuel L. Popkin, *The Reasoning Voter: Communication and Persuasion in Presidential Campaigns* (University of Chicago Press, 1991); Paul M. Sniderman, Richard A. Brody, and Philip E. Tetlock, *Reasoning and Choice: Explorations in Political Psychology* (Cambridge University Press, 1991); John A. Ferejohn and James H. Kuklinski, *Information and Democratic Processes* (University of Illinois Press, 1990).

6. John Zaller, *The Nature and Origins of Mass Opinion* (Cambridge University Press, 1992); and John Zaller and Stanley Feldman, "A Simple Theory of the Survey Response: Answering Questions versus Revealing Preferences," *American Journal of Political Science*, vol. 36 (August 1992), pp. 579–616.

7. It is well known that survey responses are sensitive to the way questions are worded and the ordering in which they appear. See, for example, Howard Schuman and Stanley Presser, *Questions and Answers in Attitude Surveys: Experiments on Question Form, Wording, and Context* (Academic Press, 1981); and Seymour Sudman and Norman M. Bradburn, *Asking Questions* (Jossey-Bass, 1982).

8. See James Fishkin, *Democracy and Deliberation: New Directions for Democratic Reform* (Yale University Press, 1991); and Fishkin, *The Voice of the People* (Yale University Press, 1995).

9. For a general overview of the PDK education surveys (now a bit dated), see Stanley M. Elam, *How America Views Its Schools: The PDK/Gallup Polls, 1969–1994* (Bloomington, Ind.: Phi Delta Kappa Educational Foundation, 1995).

10. Stanley M. Elam, Lowell C. Rose, and Alec M. Gallup, "The Twenty-third Annual Gallup Poll of the Public's Attitudes Toward the Public Schools," *Phi Delta Kappan,* vol. 70 (September 1991), pp. 41–56.

11. Elam, *How America Views Its Schools.*

12. Stanley M. Elam, Lowell C. Rose, and Alec M. Gallup, "The Twenty-fifth Annual Phi Delta Kappa/Gallup Poll of the Public's Attitudes Toward the Public Schools," *Phi Delta Kappan,* vol. 75 (September 1993), pp. 137–52.

13. Carnegie Foundation for the Advancement of Teaching, *School Choice: A Special Report* (Princeton, N.J., 1992).

14. National Catholic Educational Association, *The People's Poll on Schools and School Choice: A New Gallup Survey* (Washington, 1992).

15. Information on these and other polls is available from the Roper Center at the University of Connecticut, Public Opinion Online (www.ropercenter.uconn.edu [February 2001]).

16. Information on these Gallup Polls, one carried out in April of 1996 and the other in September of 1996, is available from the Roper Center at the University of Connecticut, Public Opinion Online.

17. Stanley M. Elam, Lowell C. Rose, and Alec M. Gallup, "The Twenty-eighth Annual Phi Delta Kappa/Gallup Poll of the Public's Attitudes Toward the Public Schools," *Phi Delta Kappan,* vol. 78 (September 1996), pp. 41–59.

18. Lowell C. Rose and Alec M. Gallup, "The Thirty-second Annual Phi Delta Kappa/Gallup Poll of the Public's Attitudes toward the Public Schools," *Phi Delta Kappan,* vol. 82 (September 2000), pp. 41–67 (p. 45).

19. That the survey instruments are quite different is not apparent from PDK's published reports, which do not discuss the survey items in the same order they were asked of respondents. To ascertain the actual order of items, I requested and received the (unpublished) survey instruments for 1999 and 2000 directly from PDK.

20. This survey can currently be found on the Internet at www.npr.org/programs/specials/poll/ education/education.results.html (February 2001).

21. In general, public opinion studies have shown that large portions of the public often change their minds when presented with good reasons on the other side of the issue. On racial issues, for example, see Paul M. Sniderman and Thomas Piazza, *The Scar of Race* (Harvard University Press, 1993).

22. Note that the support item begins with the phrase "According to reformers. . . ." This was done so respondents would be clear that the voucher proposal was not endorsed by the interviewer. It also provided a measure of continuity, because the previous items were about other types of education reforms. In retrospect, if I were able to design the survey over again, I think I would drop the "According to reformers" phrase in order to ensure that respondents are not biased by it (presumably by seeing vouchers in a more positive light). I say this simply out of caution. There is, however, little evidence to suggest it is a problem here. The follow-up voucher support item on this survey, as we will soon see, does not contain the "According to reformers" lead-in and actually produces more positive responses. Moreover, as Paul Sniderman observes in summarizing the research literature on this sort of survey problem, "attribution of a position to a range of *diffusely* prestigious sources (e.g., 'thoughtful people' or 'concerned

citizens') . . . makes no difference to the positions citizens take on a range of issues." "The New Look in Public Opinion Research," in *Political Science: The State of the Discipline II*, edited by Ada W. Finifter, pp. 219–45 (Washington: American Political Science Association, 1993), p. 237.

23. This kind of attempt to gain information about respondents by noting how they learn, change, and adapt during the interview is an important part of what Sniderman calls the "new look in public opinion research." As he puts it, "a signature feature of the new look in public opinion research is . . . the treatment of variation within the interview, not as methodological noise to be suppressed or isolated, but rather as substantive variance to be analyzed and explained." "The New Look in Public Opinion Research," p. 236.

24. The proper technique for this kind of estimation is ordered probit (or logit), but I have chosen to stick with regression because it is likely to be more familiar to readers, and because it provides measures of explained variance (R^2) that are useful for the assessments we'll be doing later on. As far as the impacts of variables and their significance levels are concerned, the results of ordered probit and regression turn out to be virtually identical in this case.

25. All of this section's analyses include a background control for whether respondents are informed about vouchers, although the results for this variable (as for many other control variables) are not reported in the tables. The proper— if horribly cumbersome—way to take information and sophistication into account is not simply through a dummy variable (as it is done here) but, as the next section explains, by recognizing that information and sophistication may affect the way all the *other* variables come into play in people's thinking. Political party, for instance, may have a big impact on support for vouchers among people who are in the well-informed stratum of society, but hardly any impact for other people. Because this is so, simply throwing a dummy into the equation, without modeling and estimating these other effects, may give misleading estimates of the influence that information and sophistication are actually having. These comprehensive models will be estimated in the next section.

26. The argument I gave earlier about performance—that the connection between vouchers and better schools is difficult for many people to understand, diluting the role of performance in their thinking—is not incompatible with the significance of the markets variable. The latter indicates that, when people already believe that competition and market incentives would help improve schools, they tend to support vouchers. Many people whose schools are performing poorly, however, may not even realize (or believe) that vouchers will create competition, and may have no notion of how vouchers could promote the cause of school improvement

27. Despite these limitations, it is worth noting that the estimated regression coefficients for income, education, and district context are about the same as those for parents generally. (The impact coefficient for income appears low by comparison to that for other parents, but this is presumably because income can only take on two categorical values rather than eight within the inner-city sample.)

28. See the prior note for clarifying comments on the income effect.

29. See John F. Witte, *The Market Approach to Education* (Princeton University Press, 2000); and Jay P. Greene, William G. Howell, and Paul E. Peterson, "Lessons from the Cleveland Scholarship Program," in *Learning from School Choice*, edited by Paul E. Peterson and Bryan C. Hassel, pp. 357–92 (Brookings, 1998).

30. See the estimate for the constant term, which in this table indicates whether there is a shift in average support for vouchers as a result of a person being informed, controlling for the effects of all other variables.

31. In each case, these results are taken from the performance model. Thus all relevant variables (background, context, attitude, performance) are taken into account, except for parental interest in going private, which was omitted to make the parent and nonparent results comparable.

32. These figures are based only on respondents who answered both the first and second support items.

33. See, for example, Philip E. Converse and Gregory B. Markus, "*Plus ça change . . .* : The New CPS Election Study Panel," *American Political Science Review*, vol. 73 (March 1979), pp. 32–49; and Gregory B. Markus, "Political Attitudes during an Election Year: A Report of the 1980 NES Panel Study," *American Political Science Review*, vol. 76 (September 1982), pp. 538–60.

Chapter 8

1. In this chapter, and throughout the rest of the data analysis, we will not pursue the kind of detailed comparison of informed and uninformed respondents carried out in chapter 7. This would be interesting, but there is simply too much other ground to cover, and adding an informational dimension would make the analysis overly long and complicated. Chapter 7 showed that the uninformed are quite similar to the informed, except that they are less able to make strong connections to their underlying values, beliefs, and interests. The same is true for the topics we cover in the analysis to follow. A more detailed analysis would not point to important conclusions that are at odds with the ones we will arrive at by taking a simpler path.

2. Public Agenda, *On Thin Ice: How Advocates and Opponents Could Misread the Public's Views on Vouchers and Charter Schools* (New York, 1999).

3. One way, for instance, is to have roughly equal numbers of agree-disagree items that are positively (pro-voucher) and negatively (anti-voucher) worded and to intersperse them so that people do not fall into a routine response-set. This approach was adopted in the design of our own survey.

4. Two other survey items are also relevant here. These are the agree-disagree items, asked early in the survey and discussed in chapter 2, that we have been using to measure the "markets" variable in the attitude model. One asserts that competition and choice make business more effective and cost-conscious and would do the same for schools. This item attracts very high levels of public support (69 percent). The other is based on a much more concrete (but substantively rather different) assertion: that to give the schools incentives to improve, we need a system that rewards good schools and punishes bad ones. This one leads to

somewhat lower levels of support (45 percent). Both measures of market support may be somewhat inflated, given their positive wording.

5. Public Agenda, *On Thin Ice*, p. 14.

6. Lowell C. Rose, Alec M. Gallup, and Stanley M. Elam, "The Twenty-ninth Annual Phi Delta Kappa/Gallup Poll of the Public's Attitudes toward the Public Schools," *Phi Delta Kappan*, vol. 79 (September 1997), pp. 41–56.

7. See Myron Lieberman, *Public Education: An Autopsy* (Harvard University Press, 1993); and Wilbur Rich, *Black Mayors and School Politics: The Failure of Reform in Detroit, Gary, and Newark* (Garland, 1996), for discussions of the role of jobs and patronage in education politics.

8. It is possible that this overstates the situation a bit, for a survey about education may tend to attract respondents (those willing to stay on the telephone for thirty minutes) who are particularly interested in education, as public school employees presumably are. I have seen other polls, however, that are presumably less subject to such bias (because they are shorter), and the figures on public school employment remain in the 30 to 40 percent range.

9. Two methodological issues are worthy of note here. (1) There may be some degree of mutual causality at work in the relationships we are investigating. We have good reason to believe that the support people express (or don't) for vouchers is shaped by their sense of the social consequences that vouchers would entail. But a causal connection could also operate in the reverse: people may associate positive or negative consequences with vouchers depending on whether they already support or oppose them. More generally, both sets of views—on social consequences and on voucher support—could be determined by the same set of underlying factors (background, context, and attitudes). To the extent that social concerns are indeed endogenous in these respects, modeling them as exogenous influences on voucher support could yield biased (in this case, inflated) estimates of their true causal impacts. Within our data set, however, there is no good way to correct for this, as it would require additional variables (either for instruments or to identify additional models) that we don't have; it would be a mistake, moreover, to move toward more "advanced" models when the proper data are unavailable—for while this might appear sophisticated on the surface, it would probably create more problems than it would solve. Throughout, then, we will simply model the relationship as though social concerns are causes of where people stand on the voucher issue and keep in mind that the estimates are just tentative indications of the true effects and may be subject to an upward bias. Future research can, I hope, clarify things further. (2) As noted in the text, some of the agree-disagree items are biased upward or downward, which means that some of the independent variables in our analysis are measured with systematic error. This is not as troublesome as it might seem. A shift in the mean response to an item is largely irrelevant, because it is the variance about the mean that we are concerned with in estimating its impact on other variables. Still, the bias is probably worse for some population groups (the uninformed, most obviously) than for others, which means that these items are not able to give us entirely valid estimates of the effects we are looking for. Some amount of this is inevitable on almost any survey, and there is nothing we can do about it here. (Corrections for response bias are sometimes possible, but not with a small number of items, especially when it

appears that the nature of the bias may be different for different items.) We simply have to be cautious about holding too firmly to the results, and, again, hope that future research can sort things out.

10. This variable is measured on a four-point scale, from strongly disagree to strongly agree. The proper method here would be to use ordered probit, but, as in past situations of this type, I have chosen to stick with regression because it is more easily interpreted. Were ordered probit used in this case, the results would be virtually the same.

11. The estimates for the personal interest variable are not included in the table, as the focus here is on the social concerns. An explicit comparison of social and personal considerations will be carried out in a later section, and estimates will be presented at that point.

12. Carnegie Foundation for the Advancement of Teaching, *School Choice: A Special Report* (Princeton, N.J., 1992); and, among the PDK studies of this issue, Rose, Gallup, and Elam, "Twenty-ninth [1997] Annual Phi Delta Kappa/ Gallup Poll."

13. It is measured on a four-point scale, which varies from definitely not to definitely yes in indicating how interested parents are in using a voucher. As in other situations of this type, I will use regression rather than ordered probit for ease of interpretation. The results are unaffected in all essential respects.

14. The same caveats apply here as in the previous section's analysis (see the earlier methodological note), except that there is much less reason to think that mutual causality might be a problem. Parents are likely to express support for vouchers because they think it will give them more control over their children's educations, and not vice versa.

15. Donald R. Kinder and D. Roderick Kiewiet, "Sociotropic Politics: The American Case," *British Journal of Political Science,* vol. 11 (April 1981), pp. 129–61.

16. Donald R. Kinder, "Opinion and Action in the Realm of Politics," in *The Handbook of Social Psychology,* 4th ed., edited by Daniel T. Gilbert, Susan T. Fiske, and Gardner Lindzey, vol. 2, pp. 778–867 (McGraw-Hill, 1998), p. 801.

17. David O. Sears and Jack Citrin, *Tax Revolt: Something for Nothing in California* (Harvard University Press, 1982).

18. Note that this simple model is constructed on the assumption that both the social and personal considerations are underlying causes of support for vouchers, and that causality does not flow in the other direction. This is unlikely to pose a problem for the personal dimension, but, as I discussed earlier (note 9), it may be something of a problem for the social dimension, as people may (to some extent) fashion their answers to the social items on the basis of their sympathy for vouchers. To the extent this is so, the estimates for the social dimension will tend to be somewhat inflated, giving it an unwarranted advantage in competition with the personal dimension. We cannot do anything about this, given our data, but we need to be aware of the possibility.

19. The only wrinkle is that public school ideology is included as an additional control. It is a component of the desire to go private that seems both personal and social, and factoring out its influence should help us get cleaner estimates of the other two variables' impacts.

20. These conclusions are justified even if the coefficient for the social dimension is inflated somewhat as a result of mutual causality. I doubt any bias is so substantial that, in its absence, the impact of the social dimension would be drastically reduced or eliminated. Indeed, compared to the effects of self-interest, the social effect is actually *smaller* than mainstream work would lead us to expect. This is another reason for thinking the bias probably is not too severe (if it exists).

21. It is possible, of course, that these patterns could be caused by other factors that shape the relative roles of the personal and the social in parents' thinking. One might argue, for instance, that the better-informed (or educated) parents are more likely to weigh the social consequences of vouchers, see their relevance, and translate them into positions of support or opposition—and that the less-informed (or educated) parents are likely to see the issue less conceptually, in terms of their own personal stakes. Another possibility is that, for reasons of socialization and culture, lower-class citizens should tend to be more "private-regarding," and citizens higher in social class more "public-regarding" (on this notion, see Edward Banfield and James Q. Wilson, *City Politics* (Harvard University Press, 1963), and that this too might explain the systematic changes in the relative roles of self-interest and social concerns. A more detailed analysis suggests, however, that these arguments don't hold up. When the effects of social concerns and self-interest are allowed to be a function of district context, performance, income, education, and information—and all these factors, as a result, are forced to compete with one another for explanatory power—education and information wash out. The evidence suggests quite strongly that personal need is what drives people to think in terms of their own self-interest.

Chapter 9

1. Milton Friedman, *Capitalism and Freedom* (University of Chicago Press, 1962); Milton Friedman and Rose Friedman, *Free to Choose: A Personal Statement* (Harcourt Brace Jovanovich, 1980).

2. Christopher Jencks, *Education Vouchers: A Report on Financing Education by Payments to Parents* (Cambridge, Mass.: Center for the Study of Public Policy, 1978); Jencks, "Giving Parents Money to Pay for Schooling: Education Vouchers," *New Republic,* July 4, 1992, pp. 19–21; John E. Coons and Stephen D. Sugarman, *Education by Choice: The Case for Family Control* (University of California Press, 1978); Coons and Sugarman, *Scholarships for Children* (Institute for Governmental Studies Press, 1992).

3. See, for example, Peter W. Cookson Jr., "Redesigning the Financing of American Education to Raise Productivity: The Case for a Just Voucher," chapter 7 of *Privatizing Education and Educational Choice: Concepts, Plans, and Experiences*, edited by Simon Hakim, Paul Seidenstat, and Gary W. Bowman (Praeger, 1994).

4. See, for example, Joseph P. Viteritti, *Choosing Equality: School Choice, the Constitution, and Civil Society* (Brookings, 1999); Coons and Sugarman, *Education by Choice*; Coons and Sugarman, *Scholarships for Children*; and John E. Chubb and Terry M. Moe, *Politics, Markets, and America's Schools* (Brookings, 1990). For a legal analysis of the separation of church and state issue, see Jesse H.

Choper, "Federal Constitutional Issues," in *School Choice and Social Controversy: Politics, Policy, and the Law,* edited by Stephen D. Sugarman and Frank R. Kemerer, pp. 235–65 (Brookings, 1999).

5. See, for example, the extended discussion of the religion issue in Amy Stuart Wells, *Time to Choose: America at the Crossroads of School Choice Policy* (Hill & Wang, 1993), who devotes a chapter to its politics and legal background and identifies the positions of specific opponents. See also the discussion in Jeffrey Henig, *Rethinking School Choice: Limits of the Market Metaphor* (Princeton University Press, 1994). For an explicit argument that vouchers are unconstitutional on religious grounds, see Peter W. Cookson Jr., "There Is No Escape Clause in the Social Contract: The Case against School Vouchers," part 2 of Jerome J. Hanus and Peter W. Cookson Jr., *Choosing Schools: Vouchers and American Education* (American University Press, 1996).

6. See Public Agenda, *On Thin Ice: How Advocates and Opponents Could Misread the Public's Views on Vouchers and Charter Schools* (New York, 1999).

7. Again, the classic argument is Friedman's. See *Capitalism and Freedom,* and *Free to Choose.*

8. Lowell C. Rose and Alec M. Gallup, "The Thirty-second Annual Phi Delta Kappa/Gallup Poll of the Public's Attitudes toward the Public Schools," *Phi Delta Kappan,* vol. 82 (September 2000), pp. 41–58.

9. Peter W. Cookson Jr., *School Choice: The Struggle for the Soul of American Education* (Yale University Press, 1994); Cookson, "Redesigning the Financing of American Education"; Wells, *Time to Choose;* and Bruce Fuller and Richard F. Elmore, eds., *Who Chooses? Who Loses? Culture, Institutions, and the Unequal Effects of School Choice* (Teachers College Press, 1996).

10. Again, see Jencks, *Education Vouchers,* and "Giving Parents Money"; Coons and Sugarman, *Education by Choice*; Coons and Sugarman, *Scholarships for Children;* and Coons and Sugarman, "Use U.S. Education Vouchers to Give Poor Families a Choice," in *A Choice for Our Children,* edited by Alan Bonsteel and Carlos A. Bonilla, pp. 217–19 (Institute for Contemporary Studies Press, 1997). See also Diane Ravitch, "Somebody's Children," in *New Schools for a New Century: The Redesign of Urban Education,* edited by Diane Ravitch and Joseph Viteritti, pp. 251–73 (Yale University Press, 1996); Clint Bolick, *Transformation: The Promise and Politics of Empowerment* (Institute for Contemporary Studies Press, 1998); as well as Daniel McGroarty's account of the coalition that fought for the Milwaukee voucher program in his *Break These Chains: The Battle for School Choice* (Forum, 1996).

11. See Coons and Sugarman, *Scholarships for Children.*

12. See Donald R. Kinder "Opinion and Action in the Realm of Politics," in *The Handbook of Social Psychology,* 4th ed., edited by Daniel T. Gilbert, Susan T. Fiske, and Gardner Lindzey, vol. 2, pp. 778–867 (McGraw-Hill, 1998), for an overview of the relevant research.

13. A complementary way to explore self-interest is by exploring the impact of the personal stakes variable (the desire to use a voucher), and how its magnitude and direction vary depending on personal income. The results, in the text below table 9-4, indicate that an increase in personal stakes causes low-income parents to become more supportive of regulation—and that, as income rises, an increase

in personal stakes becomes associated with opposition to regulation. This is what we ought to expect. A look at the actual magnitudes of these impacts might seem to imply that low-income people are not responding as strongly to regulation as higher-income people are, but this is somewhat misleading. The vast majority of people who are not low-income are bunched in the middle categories, and because this is so, the average impact for the higher income group as a whole is -.16. Note that the impact for the low-income group is .16, which suggests that there is actually a certain symmetry to the way the different income groups associate their self-interest with equity-promoting regulation.

14. See the discussion of these public and private voucher programs in chapter 1, pp. 37–39.

15. See Milton Friedman, "Programs for the Poor Are Poor Programs," in Bonsteel and Bonilla, *A Choice for Our Children*, pp. 191–93.

16. See, for example, the discussion in John F. Witte, *The Market Approach to Education* (Princeton University Press, 2000).

17. Public Agenda, *On Thin Ice*, p. 18.

18. Note that some 20 percent of those who say they prefer an immediate shift to universalism also say, about forty items later, that they have a basic preference for the low-income approach over universalism—which seems inconsistent. Some of this may simply be due to confusion on the part of certain respondents, which is inevitable. But for many respondents the reason may well be that they have been able to rethink their views over the course of the survey. The earlier question was based on little knowledge of vouchers and the considerations surrounding them, while the later item is based on much more information.

19. This ignores the 25 percent of voucher opponents who refused to answer the short-term item, a disproportionate number of whom may prefer targeting.

20. I should qualify this a bit. Some low-income parents might fear that their interests would get short shrift in a universal system and that a system catering solely to them would guarantee them greater benefits. To the extent this perception is prevalent, there could be incentives among low-income parents to favor targeting over universalism. But these incentives are likely to be weaker, in the aggregate, than the incentives of higher-income parents to favor universalism, because the latter know with certainty that they will be excluded from targeted systems.

21. Note that I have used the usual income variable for nonparents, but a low-income dummy (with low income = 1) for parents. For parents, what counts is whether they qualify for vouchers: low-income parents do, other parents don't. There should be a positive connection between the low-income dummy and support for targeting. Nonparents are not directly affected by the dichotomous nature of the programs and are presumably responding on social grounds; for them, we should expect a more or less continuous (and negative) connection between income and support for targeting.

22. Note that the estimated impact becomes slightly negative, rather than 0, among respondents who are definitely not interested in using a voucher; but this makes little sense and is probably due to statistical fluctuation. The important finding is that the impact is large and positive for parents who have a stake in the issue.

23. This is addressed in the descriptive material at the bottom of the table, which, in addition to showing how the impacts of income vary depending on whether the parent has a personal stake in the issue (findings used in the paragraph above), also show how the impacts of having a personal stake depend on the parent's income level (the findings used in this paragraph).

24. Recall from chapter 8's analysis, however, that higher-income parents are far more motivated by social concerns than low-income parents are, and self-interest has less to do with their decision to support vouchers overall.

25. See Chester E. Finn Jr., Bruno V. Manno, and Gregg Vanourek, *Charter Schools in Action: Renewing Public Education* (Princeton University Press, 2000), pp. 174–78; Mark Schneider, Paul Teske, and Melissa Marschall, *Choosing Schools* (Princeton University Press, 2000); Henig, *Rethinking School Choice;* Wells, *Time to Choose;* Bryan Hassel, *The Charter School Challenge* (Brookings, 1999); and Hubert Morken and Jo Renée Formicola, *The Politics of School Choice* (Rowman & Littlefield, 1999).

26. Here, as in certain other analyses we've carried out, ordered probit would be more appropriate than regression. But regression is used because it more easily allows for comparability across analyses, and because its results are virtually the same.

Chapter 10

1. See, for example, Robert A. Dahl, *Who Governs? Democracy and Power in an American City* (Yale University Press, 1961), and *Democracy and Its Critics* (Yale University Press, 1989).

2. For discussions of how citizens can use heuristics and cues—which may come from elites but may come from other sources as well—to compensate for their lack of information about politics, see Samuel L. Popkin, *The Reasoning Voter: Communication and Persuasion in Presidential Campaigns* (University of Chicago Press, 1991); Richard A. Brody, *Assessing the President* (Stanford University Press, 1991); Paul M. Sniderman, Richard A. Brody, and Philip E. Tetlock, *Reasoning and Choice: Explorations in Political Psychology* (Cambridge University Press, 1991); and Donald R. Kinder, "Opinion and Action in the Realm of Politics," in *The Handbook of Social Psychology,* 4th ed., edited by Daniel T. Gilbert, Susan T. Fiske, and Gardner Lindzey, vol. 2, pp. 778–867 (McGraw-Hill, 1998).

3. This two-way relationship between citizens and elites has long been a topic of study and debate among political scientists. See, for example, David J. Elkins, *Manipulation and Consent: How Voters and Leaders Manage Complexity* (University of British Columbia Press, 1993); V. O. Key Jr., *Public Opinion and American Democracy* (Alfred A. Knopf, 1961); Benjamin Ginsberg, *The Captive Public: How Mass Opinion Promotes State Power* (Basic Books, 1986); Robert Goodin, *Manipulatory Politics* (Yale University Press, 1980); Benjamin I. Page and Robert Y. Shapiro, "Effects of Public Opinion on Policy," *American Political Science Review,* vol. 77 (March 1983), pp. 175–90, and *The Rational Public* (University of Chicago Press, 1992); and James Stimson, Michael Mackuen, and Robert Erikson, "Dynamic Representation," *American Political Science Review,* vol. 89

(September 1995), pp. 543–65. See also the portion of the literature that is more explicitly concerned with elite framing, for example, Shanto Iyengar and Donald Kinder, *News that Matters: Television and American Opinion* (University of Chicago Press, 1987); Samuel L. Popkin, *The Reasoning Voter: Communication and Persuasion in Presidential Campaigns* (University of Chicago Press, 1991); and Paul M. Sniderman and Thomas Piazza, *The Scar of Race* (Harvard University Press, 1993).

4. This is not to say that they don't try. The American Federation of Teachers, for instance, has tried to influence opinion on vouchers through a nationwide campaign of radio ads. And pro-choice groups have recently begun running television spots that tout the value of parental choice and vouchers, with special attention to the needs of disadvantaged families. It is possible that these sorts of campaigns, especially if they are continued over a long period of time, could gradually make the voucher issue more familiar—in a positive or negative way—to the American public, or some segment of it, and gradually bring about changes in public opinion. At any given point in time, however, these elites (and others) would have to base their political strategies on public opinion as it exists and could not count on manipulating it.

5. David O. Sears and Richard E. Whitney, *Political Persuasion* (General Learning Press, 1973), p. 7.

6. The following account is based on Alan Bonsteel, "The Proposition 174 Story," and John E. Coons, "Free Market, Fair Market," in *A Choice for Our Children: Curing the Crisis in America's Schools,* edited by Alan Bonsteel and Carlos A. Bonilla, pp. 161–75 and 177–90, respectively (Institute for Contemporary Studies Press, 1997); and Myron Lieberman, *Public Education: An Autopsy* (Harvard University Press, 1993); as well as my own experiences as a participant in its politics.

7. As I pointed out in the previous chapter, internal polls conducted by the organizers of the Proposition 174 campaign convinced them (they've told me and others) that Californians were heavily in favor of universalism and would not vote in favor of programs targeted at the poor. As they describe it, they went for the libertarian ideal—a full-blown universal system—because they were convinced it was likely to gain more public support than a targeted plan. This does not account, of course, for why the plan they proposed contained no regulations for accountability or equity, and no protections for the public schools.

8. The actual wording of the initiative is reproduced in Lieberman, *Public Education,* pp. 327–32.

9. Editorial, "Proposition 174: Look Before You Leap," *Los Angeles Times,* October 7, 1993.

10. Editorial, "Fixing Public Schools," *Long Beach Press Telegram,* October 24, 1993.

11. See David S. Broder, "Shameful Silence on Vouchers," *Washington Post,* October 27, 1993.

12. For an overview of the most recent research, as well as a number of new studies on the topic, see the contributions collected in Shaun Bowler, Todd Donovan, and Caroline J. Tolbert, *Citizens as Legislators: Direct Democracy in the United States* (Ohio State University Press, 1998). See also David S. Broder, *Democracy*

Derailed: Initiative Campaigns and the Power of Money (Harcourt, 2000); Thomas E. Cronin, *Direct Democracy: The Politics of Initiative, Referendum, and Recall* (Harvard University Press, 1989); David B. Magleby, *Direct Legislation: Voting on Ballot Propositions in the United States* (Johns Hopkins University Press, 1984); David Butler and Austin Ranney, eds. *Referendums: A Comparative Study of Practice and Theory* (American Enterprise Institute, 1979).

13. Magleby, *Direct Legislation,* p. 151.

14. See, for example, Susan A. Banducci, "Direct Legislation: When Is It Used and When Does It Pass?" in Bowler, Donovan, and Tolbert, *Citizens as Legislators,* pp. 109–31.

15. A statement by Ken Masterton, quoted in Broder, *Democracy Derailed,* p. 86.

16. For the California and Michigan results from Election 2000, see Mark Walsh, "Voucher Initiatives Defeated in Calif, Mich," *Education Week,* November 15, 2000. For the Washington initiative, see Linda Jacobson, "Washington Choice Proposals Go Down to Defeat," *Education Week,* November 13, 1996. For all the others, see Nina Shokraii Rees, *School Choice 2000: What's Happening in the States* (Heritage Foundation, 2000).

17. For details on the California initiative and accounts of the campaign, see Walsh, "Voucher Initiatives Defeated; Jessica L. Sandham, "Vouchers Facing Two Major Tests," *Education Week,* September 27, 2000, and "Calif. Voucher Opponents Organizing to Fight Initiatives," *Education Week,* July 12, 2000; Nanette Asimov, "State's Reborn Voucher Plan Captures Nation's Attention," *San Francisco Chronicle,* October 7, 2000; Martha Groves, "Voters Ready to Give Vouchers a Drubbing," *Los Angeles Times,* October 26, 2000, and "Propositions: Vouchers Lose; School Bond Vote Leading," *Los Angeles Times,* November 8, 2000.

18. Spending figures are reported by the California Secretary of State and can be found on the Internet at www.ss.ca.gov (February 2001).

19. For details on the Michigan initiative and its campaign, see Walsh, "Voucher Initiatives Defeated"; Sandham, "Vouchers Facing Two Major Tests"; Mark Hornbeck, "Voucher Campaign Is Costliest," *Detroit News,* November 1, 2000, and "Voucher Win in Michigan Could Have U.S. Impact," *Detroit News,* October 26, 2000; Mark Honbeck and Tim Kiska, "School Vouchers Denied," *Detroit News,* November 8, 2000.

20. The spending figures are from Hornbeck, "Voucher Campaign Is Costliest."

21. National Education Association press release, November 7, 2000.

22. See Thomas E. Cronin and Michael A. Genovese, *The Paradoxes of the American Presidency* (Oxford University Press, 1998).

23. In the short term, however, opponents can still resort to the courts to try to overturn the new programs. Until the courts make up their minds on the separation of church and state issue—which is likely to happen soon, when the Supreme Court finally takes it up—even the existing voucher programs will really not have all the advantages of being part of the status quo. (More on this later.)

24. See Christopher Jencks, *Education Vouchers: A Report on Financing Education by Payments to Parents* (Cambridge, Mass.: Center for the Study of Public Policy, 1970), and "Giving Parents Money to Pay for Schooling: Education Vouchers," *New Republic,* July 4, 1970, pp. 19–21; and John E. Coons and Stephen D.

Sugarman, "Use U.S. Education Vouchers to Give Poor Families and Choice," in Bonsteel and Bonilla, *A Choice for Our Children*, pp. 217–19.

25. See, for example, John F. Witte, *The Market Approach to Education* (Princeton University Press, 2000); Jay P. Greene, William G. Howell, and Paul E. Peterson, "Lessons from the Cleveland Scholarship Program," in *Learning from School Choice*, edited by Paul E. Peterson and Bryan C. Hassel, pp. 357–92 (Brookings, 1998); and the studies contained in Terry Moe, ed., *Private Vouchers* (Hoover Institution Press, 1995).

26. See Frederick M. Hess, "Hints of the Pick-Axe: The Impact of Competition on Public Schooling in Milwaukee," paper presented at the annual meeting of the American Political Science Association, Washington, D.C., August 31–September 3, 2000.

27. See Gordon S. Black, "Wisconsin Citizen Survey," *Wisconsin Policy Research Institute Report*, vol. 13, no. 4 (July 2000).

28. Again, see Hess, "Hints of the Pick-Axe."

29. These figures were obtained directly from CEO America, Bentonville, Arkansas.

30. See William G. Howell and others, "Test-Score Effects of School Vouchers in Dayton, Ohio, New York City, and Washington, D.C.: Evidence from Randomized Field Trials," paper presented at the annual meeting of the American Political Science Association, Washington, D.C., August 31–September 3, 2000; Jay P. Greene, Paul E. Peterson, and Jiangtao Du, "School Choice in Milwaukee: A Randomized Experiment," in Peterson and Hassel, *Learning from School Choice*, pp. 335–56; Witte, *Market Approach to Education*; Greene, Howell, and Peterson, "Lessons from the Cleveland Scholarship Program"; and Kim K. Metcalf and others, "A Comparative Evaluation of the Cleveland Scholarship and Tutoring Grant Program: Year One: 1996–97," School of Education, Smith Research Center, Indiana University (March 1998).

31. See the studies cited in note 25.

32. See, for example, Witte, *Market Approach to Education*.

33. Milton Friedman, "Programs for the Poor Are Poor Programs," in Bonsteel and Bonilla, *A Choice for Our Children*, pp. 191–93.

34. For a presentation of his ideas about using markets and public policy to help the disadvantaged, see Clint Bolick, *Transformation: The Promise and Politics of Empowerment* (Institute for Contemporary Studies Press, 1998).

35. On charter schools and their politics, see Chester E. Finn, Bruno V. Manno, and Gregg Vanourek, *Charter Schools in Action* (Princeton University Press, 2000); Byran Hassel, *The Charter School Challenge* (Brookings, 1999); Hubert Morken and Jo Renée Formicola, *The Politics of School Choice* (Rowan & Littlefield, 1999); and Louann A. Bierlein, "The Charter School Movement," in *New Schools for a New Century: The Redesign of Urban Education*, edited by Diane Ravitch and Joseph P. Viteritti, pp. 37–60 (Yale University Press, 1997).

36. See, for example, Finn, Manno, and Vanourek, *Charter Schools in Action*.

37. On the NAACP's involvement in the voucher issue, see, for example, Daniel McGroarty, "School Choice Slandered," *Public Interest*, no. 117 (Fall 1994), pp. 94–111; Witte, *Market Approach to Education*, pp. 40, 177, 184; Jeff Archer, "Black Parents at Heart of Tug of War," *Education Week*, June 24, 1998.

38. Evan Thomas and Lynette Clemetson, "A New War Over Vouchers," *Newsweek,* November 22, 1999.

39. One example of disaffection within the ranks: Willie Breazell, who was forced to resign his position as head of the local NAACP in Colorado Springs because he spoke out publicly in favor of vouchers. He continues to be an active voucher proponent and a thorn in the NAACP's side on this issue. John Fund, "Breazell's Heresy," *Wall Street Journal,* October 20, 1999. On the more general topic of the attraction of younger, politically active blacks to school choice, see Jodi Wilgoren, "Young Blacks Turn to School Vouchers as Civil Rights Issue," *New York Times,* October 9, 2000.

40. See Samuel G. Freedman, "The Education Divide," *Salon,* September 30, 1997 (www.salon.com [February 2001]); Thomas and Clemetson, "New War Over Vouchers."

41. On the political and economic value of the public school system to middle-class minorities, see Wilbur Rich, *Black Mayors and School Politics: The Failure of Reform in Detroit, Gary, and Newark* (Garland, 1996).

42. For information on the Black Alliance for Educational Options, see Wilgoren, "Young Blacks Turn to School Vouchers"; Jay Mathews, "Group Pushes for Vouchers," *Washington Post,* December 19, 2000; and the Alliance's website, www.baeoonline.org (February 2001).

43. For statements of their positions, see Editorial: "Easy Choice, *New Republic,* September 11, 2000; Editorial: "Voucher Wars," *Washington Post,* November 1, 2000; Robert B. Reich, "The Case for Progressive Vouchers," *Wall Street Journal,* September 6, 2000; Bill Cotterell, "Andrew Young Tells Local NAACP that Vouchers Are Good for Schools," *Tallahassee Democrat,* September 10, 1999 (on Andrew Young); Robert Holland, "School Vouchers Are Gathering Bipartisan Support," *Friedman Report,* issue 9 (2000) (on Joseph Califano) (www. friedmanfoundation.org/9_01.pdf [February 2001]).

44. Editorial: "Easy Choice," *New Republic,* September 11, 2000, p. 11.

45. Editorial: "Teachers Against Reform," *Washington Post,* July 7, 2000, p. A26.

46. Probably the most detailed account of the dependence of Democrats on the teachers unions is set out in Myron Lieberman, *The Teacher Unions* (Free Press, 1997).

47. See, for example, Witte, *Market Approach to Education.*

48. For discussions of the constitutional issues involved, see Jesse H. Choper, "Federal Constitutional Issues," in *School Choice and Social Controversy: Politics, Policy, and the Law,* edited by Stephen D. Sugarman and Frank R. Kemerer, pp. 235–65 (Brookings, 1999); Joseph P. Viteritti, *Choosing Equality: School Choice, the Constitution, and Civil Society* (Brookings, 1999); and Kenneth Godwin and Frank Kemerer, *School Choice Tradeoffs* (forthcoming, University of Texas Press). On constitutional issues at the state level, see Frank R. Kemerer, "State Constitutions and School Vouchers," *West's Education Law Reporter,* vol. 120, October 7, 1997, pp. 1–42.

49. See, for example, Jeffrey A. Segal and Harold J. Spaeth, *The Supreme Court and the Attitudinal Model* (Cambridge University Press, 1993); Lee Epstein and Jack Knight, *The Choices Justices Make* (Congressional Quarterly Press, 1998).

50. See U.S. Department of Education, *Private Schools in the United States: A Statistical Profile, 1993–94* (National Center for Education Statistics, 1997).

51. The current preponderance of religious schools in the private sector is essentially a short-term phenomenon. Because the education system does not offer vouchers, and because the public schools are at once nonreligious and free of charge, nonreligious private schools are seriously disadvantaged. They must charge tuition to survive—but they must also compete with public schools that offer a nonreligious education for free. This keeps their numbers down. Religious private schools, on the other hand, have a comparative advantage. They are offering something that the public schools cannot provide. While they are offering it at a price, it is something that many parents value highly and are willing to pay for—especially with the help of church subsidies that keep the tuitions rather modest. Without vouchers, then, the mere existence of a free, nonreligious public school system virtually guarantees a private school system that is heavily religious. Were a voucher system actually adopted and families able to choose nonreligious private schools for the same cost (zero) that they are able to choose public schools, the number of nonreligious private schools would surely grow, and the relative "market share" of religious schools would decline.

Index

Abraham, Spencer, 367
Accountability, 69; voucher system regulation for, 297–300, 341–42, 355
Admissions policies: fairness concerns, 302; low-income set aside, 307–08; in religious schools, 303
Advantaged and disadvantaged school districts: definition, 74; demand for private school access in, 86, 125; determinants of voucher opinion in, 288–89; distribution, 74; methodology for analyzing school satisfaction data, 103; satisfaction with schools in, 74–76, 91–96, 109, 114–15, 346; stability of public opinion in, 248–49
Age demographics: and knowledge of voucher issues, 175, 176, 180; and voucher support, 220–21
American Civil Liberties Union, 2, 27
American Federation of Teachers, 41. See also Teacher unions

Black Alliance for Educational Options, 385–86

Bolick, Clint, 378
Boyer, Ernest, 200
Bureaucracy, 31–32
Bush, George W., 36, 394
Bush, Jeb, 38
Bush administration (George H. W.), 36
Busing, 61, 62–63

Califano, Joseph, 386
California, 22–23, 40, 366; Proposition 174 initiative, 359–65
Carnegie Foundation for the Advancement of Teaching, 200–01, 281
CEOAmerica, 38
Charter schools, 40; political prospects, 381–82
Chase, Robert, 368–69
Chubb, John E., 31
Church and state separation, 39, 295, 391, 392, 393; beliefs of voucher opponents, 28, 30; historical practice, 65
Civil rights movement, 20, 383–86, 388, 389
Cleveland, Ohio, 3, 37–38, 316